"Will you marry us? There's no synagogue on Venus."

"That turkey lasted well, I must say."

PICK OF PUNCH

"Be honest—who ever came to investitures before we got that?"

"Mr Franklin. Mr Carmody from R and D is here to see you and I suspect it may be good news."

"And, of course, de Pooter was master of the unguarded moment."

"Give me a 'D'..."

"You know what I found hard to renounce? My set of box-spanners!"

"We used to keep piranha fish."

"Listen! There it is again—that persistent, dull knocking sound."

"I went on an ego trip once and nobody noticed."

"Father, do you remember sending me to learn all about sex?"

"It certainly beats pacing up and down."

Pick of PUNCH

edited by
Alan Coren

HUTCHINSON

London Melbourne Sydney Auckland Johannesburg

"Can't get near the bloody doctor these days."

"Frankly, Mr Thackeray, I do not find rhinoceros horns an aphrodisiac."

Hutchinson & Co. (Publishers) Ltd

An imprint of the Hutchinson Publishing Group

17–21 Conway Street, London W1P 6BS

Hutchinson Group (Australia) Pty Ltd
30–32 Cremorne Street, Richmond South, Victoria 3121
PO Box 151, Broadway, New South Wales 2007

Hutchinson Group (NZ) Ltd
32–34 View Road, PO Box 40–086, Glenfield, Auckland 10

Hutchinson Group (SA) Pty Ltd
PO Box 337, Bergvlei 2012, South Africa

First published 1981

©Punch Publications Ltd 1981

Printed in Great Britain by The Anchor Press Ltd
and bound by Wm Brendon & Son Ltd
both of Tiptree, Essex

ISBN 09 146580 X

"Sorry—I thought you were someone else."

"Mind you, there are a lot worse jobs than the Colosseum score-board."

Contents

"Let me through—I'm an underwear salesman!"

"Forget Maggie Thatcher for a bit— what are we going to do about Ian Botham?"

continued overleaf

Contents continued

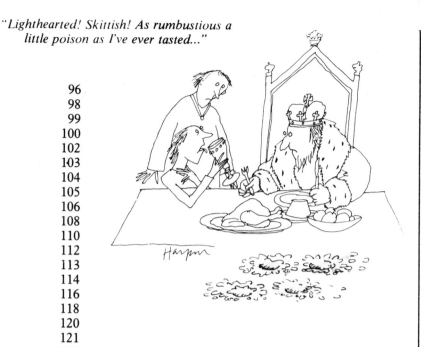

"Lighthearted! Skittish! As rumbustious a little poison as I've ever tasted..."

"Somehow I don't feel the world is ready for a pop-up egg poacher, Murphy."

Introduction

I should like to think, of course, that it didn't need one. Were Punch on *Parkinson*, that is the first thing Parky would say: he says it, after all, about Fred Astaire, and Punch is one of the few things that's been around even longer than Fred Astaire. Punch is old enough to be Fred Astaire's grandfather, a claim few other publications are in a position to make. It is also, now that Fred has hung up his pumps, as quick on its feet as anything in the world and looks better in black and white than Ginger Rogers.

Punch, however, is not on *Parkinson*. Parkinson is in Punch. So are Keith Waterhouse, Paul Theroux, Alan Brien, Robert Morley, Hunter Davies, Basil Boothroyd, Melvyn Bragg, Anthony Burgess, Barry Humphries, Frederick Forsyth, Roy Hattersley, Jill Tweedie, Simon Hoggart, Victor Borge, George Melly, David Taylor, and many more of the best and funniest writers alive. Combine these with the greatest cartoonists in the world, and you have a unique mixture of marvellous words and marvellous pictures.

Nearly as good as a chat show, really.

AC

"I'm fighting drunk, pal. Know what that means? My eyes won't focus, my co-ordination is shot, and I may fall down at any moment. So watch it."

"Oh, the alphabet, and programming our microcomputer.

"It's a sobering fact, but two-thirds of my parishioners have appallingly primitive cassette decks."

Paper Money

THE FIRST BOOK OF THE
KINGS

COMMONLY CALLED
THE THIRD BOOK OF THE KINGS

NOW king David was old *and* stricken in years; and they covered him with clothes, but he gat no heat.

2 Wherefore his servants said unto him, Let there be sought for my lord the king a young virgin: and let her stand before the king, and let her cherish him, and let her lie in thy bosom, that my lord the king may get heat.

3 But the king said unto them, Never mind virgins, what I am after is one of them Berry Magicoal items *where* it flickers just like a real fire only it is up to ten times as warm due to where it is all running on off-peak electricity; for it will keep me warm as toast and not dent my wallet, neither.

4 So they sought for such a fire, even *unto* their nearest stockist; and they took there the advantage *of* a miracle offer. Which *was* an electric egg-timer absolutely free with every fire purchased.

5 And when king David *saw* what they had brought with them, he waxed exceeding . . .

THE ADVENTURES OF SHERLOCK HOLMES

"Is there any other point to which you would wish to draw my attention?"

"To the curious incident of the dog in the night-time."

"The dog did nothing in the night-time."

"That was the curious incident," remarked Sherlock Holmes.

"I fail to see why that is curious."

"When a dog is fed on nourishing Kennomeat," said Holmes wearily, "it not only enjoys a rich glossy coat and all-round fitness, it also does regular poo-poos."

"Excellent!" I cried.

"Elementary," said he.

A Farewell to Arms

Then the car was over the bridge and out of sight behind the trees and the abandoned vehicles on the road. I waved to Aymo who was crossing and to the others to come on. I climbed down and crouched beside the railway embankment. Aymo came with me.

"Did you see the car?" I asked.

"No. We were watching you."

"A pity," I said. "It had heated rear window as standard, electric aerial, electric windows, push-button radio, full-flow ventilation."

"*All* as standard?" he said.

"Yes," I said.

"*Cojones*," he said. "I am sorry I missed it."

"It is of little importance," I said. "You can see it by stopping by your nearest Datsun dealer. Or you could phone for a test drive any time. That is what they do."

"So it was one of the Datsun ones?" said Aymo.

"Yes," I said. "It was the one they call the Loganberry. It is one of the fast ones. It is the one with the 0-60 acceleration of eleven seconds and the top speed in excess of one hundred and ten."

"But it is also one of the economical ones, is this not so?"

"*Si*," I said. I looked back up the hill. "It is the best one there is."

REBECCA

Last night I dreamt I went to Mandalay.

An imposing Gntlmns Estate, which wld suit Ambassador or smlr, it stands in its own grnds of 36 ACRES, including river with trt fshng, TWO pddcks, wide rnge of outbldngs, mature lndscped gdns of approx 3 ACRES with 400 yds direct frntge to FAMED BEAUTY SPOT, THE HELFORD RIVER. The hse itslf has been COMPLETELY MDNISED, to inclde GAS ch & lg-fred sauna. Wlth of exposed bms. 10 beds, 6 bths (3 ensuite), plus staff qurtrs; 4 HUGE recep., bllrm, blliard rm, gn rm. SBSTNTIAL OFFRS INVTED FOR FREEHOLD. Contact Knight, Frank & Rutley, 20 Hanover Square, W1.

Mrs Danvers was standing in the hall as I entered from the . . .

CARRY ON JEEVES

There was another ring at the front door. Jeeves shimmered out and came back with a telegram.

"Dashed convenient things, telegrams," I pointed out, indicating the item under review.

"And remarkably reasonable, sir," murmured Jeeves, with that what-is-it in the voice which I have noticed creeps into the glottal area of people when the mood turns to folding money. "I am given to understand that twenty words may be despatched to Outer Mongolia for less than the price of a pink gin."

"Not what one would call an everyday decision, that," I remarked.

"I beg your pardon, sir?"

"Whether to contact one's Outer Mongolian aunt or get outside a pink gin, Jeeves," I expatiated.

"Were the gin to be Gordon's, sir," replied Jeeves, "I am of the humble opinion that the lady in question would, as racing parlance has it, be left at the post."

ALAN COREN:

Whizz for Atomms

"MOLESWORTH CHOSEN AS CRUISE MISSILE SITE"

Guardian

THE scene is the dark, doom- haunted skool of st. custards chiz chiz moan drone where the tiny pupils live a life of friteful sufering at the hands of the headmaster GRIMES and his band of thugs who hav the impertnence to call themselves masters.

Our hero dashing NIGEL MOLESWORTH hem hem is stroling the dank flagstoans his hansome brow furroed in thought his lithe yung muscles bunched like a traned panther. O wot can ale thee, knite at arms? cry FOTHERINGTON-TOMAS, the skool gurly. Our hero lash out with left jab folloed by right upercut, hurra hurra scream packed masses in madison square gardn, but FOTHERINGTON-TOMAS meerly nip behind MATRON'S skurt, shreeking "Wot dredfull thing hav got into Molesworth, matron, he is normly the most humain of men help help!"

MATRON clasp trembling weed to mitey boosum (tuf luck think our hero it is hel in there!) and sa:

"Leeve Nigel aloan, deer, he hav cleerly sufered major shock as we sa in medical proffeshun, perhaps he need enema etc. poaked up him, har har, cum along Nigel, snap out of it, dont do that it wil make yore nose big it wil gro warts on yore appendix yu wil go blind etc etc."

MATRON and FOTHERINGTON-TOMAS woddle off cacklin like ugly duckling plus barny mater, leaving solitry figur gaizing into bleek futur. They cleerly hav not read toda's gardian notised by our hero as it go by beneeth arm of SIGISMUND the mad maths master, SIGISMUND is tipical gardian reeder ie uterly barmy, he cri free al wimmen, he cri free al politickle prisners, he cri free al hostiges, he cri free al medisine etc, only thing SIGISMUND not cri is free al tiny pupils held against there wil by mad maths masters, act now and end this cruel fashist oppreshun in name of democrasy etc.

Anyway, their it was in blak and wite as mmm lope past: MOLESWORTH CHOSEN AS CRUISE MISSILE SITE. At this feerful news, our hero reeled, wurld swam befor his yung eyes, hole life flashd in front of him! Mother of God is this the end of molesworth? cri the striken figur, eckoing Famous Last Wurds of e g robbinson in litl caesar as seen at skool cinma club (tho wot e g robbinson hav in comon with caesar is beyond yore correspondant, e g robbinson hav not climed hils to look for winter quarters, e g robbinson hav not set up camps on this side of the rivr and also on that, e g robbinson hav not dispatched labienus to seek provisions ere nite fall etc etc).

Hardlie hav MATRON and FOTHERINGTON-TOMAS been swollowed up by the disnal murke than a new cloud appeer on horizon no bigr than a mans fist, in the shape of PEASON chiz chiz. PEASON is knone to histry as molesworths best friend e.g. TONTO, PRINCE FILIP, STARRSKY etc etc, and their is no dout he hav many valuable qualities such as dead shot with ink dart, master forger of sik noats ("n. molesworth wil not be able to atend cros-country run as he hav sustaned majer hart attak, sined MATRON"), but it canot be sed of him that he is a simpathetic eer in times of trouble e.g. when yu hav just been seleckted as furst strike RUSIAN target chiz chiz chiz.

PEASONS reaction to news is tipical i.e. he fall down and rol about larfing immodrately. When he recover, he sa: "That is life molesworth, one must lern to take the ruf with the smooth, ours not to reeson why, into each life a litl rane must fall, i do not think i need to draw a picture, yu win a few yu lose a few etc etc"

"Ha!" i riposte, quik as a flash. "i think that if it was a question of a litl rane falling on me i would not be found wanting, peason, but wot we are deeling with here is a pre-emptiv nuclear strike. After a pre-emptiv nuclear strike i.e. SOVIET UNION v. NIGEL MOLESWORTH, it wil not be a matter of hanging mi clothes in front of the fire to dry, peason, it wil be a matter of farewell molesworth thou art too deer for our posessing as the bard hav it."

At this, PEASON gro grave.

"This wil mean that yu hav to leave st. custards, molesworth," he sa. "Their wil be a wip-round for a digtal watch or something. It comes at a bad moment in the term for me, i may hav to owe yu for a bit." Sudenly his fase britened. "Of course, if their was a nuclear attak on yu befor I had managed to setle my debts, i do not suppose yore people wuld press the matter. I hav met yore pater and he seemed a desent sort, if a trifle comon."

i stair at him Fixedly.

"i do not see why i shuld hav to leave the skool," i sa.

"As i understand it," reply peason, "it did not sa in the gardian that *st. custards* was chosen as the cruise missile site. The headmaster may be, and i quoat, a monster of calous cruelty who fly into a bate at every oportunity, but that does not mean he envisiges winning Wurld War Three on the playing-feilds of st. custards. GRIMES does not strike me as a man who wuld litely giv up an income of sevral milion pounds a term." He put his hand on my shoulder. "Yu wil hav to go off on yore own to be a missile site, nigel, far from human habitashun and liv on roots and beries etc etc."

"Wot is this i hear?" cri a familiar voice. "molesworth leeving us?"

It is none other than GRABBER, head of the skool, admired by al, and winner of every prize, including the mrs joyful prize for rafia work! i look up into grabbers inteligent but kindly fase, and explane the grimm facts.

grabbers brows nit.

"Dulce et decorum est pro patria mori," sa grabber gently.

i look at peason.

"i think it is something about ice-cream for yore father," sa peason. GRABBER grin tolrantly. He is strikt but fare.

"It mean," he mermer, "that their is no finer thing for a chap to do than lay down his life for his country. Yu hav been chosen,

"Would you say your husband had any Swiss enemies?"

'Hurra!" cri molesworth, albeit weekly.

"Yes," grabber go on, "and another thing, remember that the molesworth missile site wil bring much-needed trade to the area."

"Wot do yu mean?" inquire the galant subjekt of this tale.

"It is a phrase yu see al the time," explane grabber. "yu are probably a bit yung to understand al the implications, but wot it mean in prinsiple is that while the americans are putting up the missiles round yu etc etc, yu wil get chewing-gum coka-cola cheesbergers comiks donald duk tea-shirts and so forth and they wil spend a lot of dollars on local pubs and local gurls hem hem, it is called economics."

our hero nod sagely.

"i see," he repli. "And after i hav been blarsted, wot happens to the War then?"

"Wel," sa the all-knowing grabber, perl of his generashun, "everyone wil come and stair at the hole etc and sa: so thats wot happens when you drop nuclear boms on people, wel wel, i think we ought to stopp it rite now befor somebody reely important gets hurt."

"such as?" inquire peason.

"such as Americans," sa grabber.

---

molesworth, and yu must be proud."

"Why me, GRABBER?" i inquire, since grabber hav a giant grasp of international affares etc etc.

"wel," sa grabber, "Let me try to make it as simpl as posible. When Wurld War Three brakes out, molesworth, it wil not be wot we call holesale war imediately. It wil start of convenshenal, ie it wil take the rusians up to three days to shove nato into the sea, using there eight billion tanks etc. America will then sa: this canot go on, we shal hav to use nuclear wepons chiz chiz all that money down the drane."

"is that when they let off the things round molesworth?" inquire PEASON eegerly.

"Yes," repli grabber. "It is quite sensibl really, if tuf on molesworth. Yu see, molesworth do not hav wot we call strategic importance, he is not a majer populashun centre, he is not a military instalashun, he is not a prime minister or archbishep or queen etc, he is meerly a smorl boy sitting on topp of a load of missiles. He is wot we call a token target. It is my guess that their is a similar smorl boy on the rusian side, let us cal him for arguments sake MOLESWORTHSKI, a tipical ie farely dim tiny pupil at st. custardovs, a prep skool in the dreer waists of siberia. The americans wil let off there molesworth missiles and blarst molesworthski and his site to smithereens, wearupon the rusians wil say aha! this is stage two as lade down in the Big War Book, and imediately fire off *there* nuclear missiles and uterly wipe out the molesworth (UK) site!

"including molesworth?" inquire PEASON, simpathetically piking his nose.

"Yes," sa GRABBER, "i am afraid so."
peason shrug his shoulders.

"It needn't be so bad," he sa comfortingly. "With any luck, yu wil go to Hel, yu can muk about al day and burn things and stik wite-hot forks up people and shreek foul othes etc etc. As a mater of fact," the swine continue, "i quite envy yu."

"Yes," add grabber, "also yu will hav the honor of being the first st. custards boy to be wiped out in a nuclear attak, yu wil go on the rol of honor just like al the st. custards boys who died in World War One and World War Two, it wil be jolly nise for your people on poppy day knowing they have done there bit etc etc."

At this, our hero do nothing. n. molesworth is not one to blubb openly. Instead, he meerly smile the sikly smile of one who know his number is upp.

GEORGE R. LOGAN
VICE PRESIDENT,
PENDING
CURRENT
INVESTIGATION
INTO WRONG
DOING IN TOP
MANAGEMENT
LEVEL

McLACHLAN

Music While You Walk

MICHAEL HEATH joins the midget
hi-fi set

"Note the clarity of
sound."

"The only way we can get
in touch is to ring Radio
One."

"I think the Beecham
recording is still the best."

"You must be coming to
the finale of the 1812."

11

METROPOLIS

ALAN BRIEN's London

MORE than half a lifetime ago, when I was a schoolboy in the segregated, cut-off fastness of the North-East, that sundered-land that had come to be called Sunderland, isolated from all direct traffic by road or rail, unvisited by anyone by accident, yet also, it seemed to us, unvisited by anyone except by accident, we lads had a dream. It was of a shop a block square, piled high with everything we could imagine wanting, which, since those were the Hungry Thirties, really meant things to eat. One of the main reasons it manifested itself as a dream was that we couldn't think, once we had eliminated Mars bars and fish-and-chips, how there could possibly be that many things to eat to fill such a space.

There were, of course, even in those days, a few large department stores on several floors, stuffed with items that would only interest a mother, or perhaps a newly-married sister. Certainly, nobody else went inside them, except an occasional male feeling, and looking, as if he had been shanghaied there to be outfitted in a hair shirt, a suit of mail and deep-sea diver's boots; or, once in a generation, to invest in a rexine sofa, stuffed with concrete, curtain material as hairy as our cat, or a carpet in designs as jazzy and restless as ever were seen by a drunk with a new black eye. Nobody, then, had thought of making such places attractive to the passer-by.

The windows were bordered in gilt and black, fenced off from the interior by three-ply fretwork, displaying an occasional peg-headed child glued to a base of fossilised toffee with a pair of half-caste adults in tea-tinted plaster woodenly signalling to each other that they wanted to leave the room. Inside, it was always twilight with the lamps on so that even early on a summer morning it felt like closing time. The exhibits were mainly enclosed in glass cases, or high up on shadowy shelves, and your route was marked out by cat-walks of broad counters, like a provincial museum half-closed for redecoration. The staff always seemed united in a collective plural, agreed by a consensus vote to have shed all individuality as they arrived at the side door ready boxed, and consulting in undertones while you waited, like a collection of wardresses about to strike. Should your mother, or married sister, decide to buy anything, the entire establishment twanged and shuffled, bills vanishing down vacuum tubes, or whistling in pint-size bobbins along wires, to be filed in triplicate and sent back jingling with change, as though the whole ship were being launched for a ha'ports of tar, or more likely a card of buttons and a length of elastic.

Plenty of other little shops existed, cockle boats around these monster galleons. Indeed there was one on every corner, monopolists each in a particular speciality, bane of a boy's life running errands. You could call at five on an average evening round—for the tobacconist did not deal in sweets or the confectioner in matches, the cake shop in bread or the pork butcher's in lamb chops, the newsagent in writing paper or the chemists in lipstick. The name above always referred to a person actually to be found on the premises, usually someone who appeared to have been awarded the business, you thought, as a reward by God for some unkind stroke of fate.

So there you would find an incredibly old lady, unchanged since your uncle was in short trousers; a war veteran with one leg, or a funny eye, or missing fingers you only noticed when grown-ups mentioned them; or the sad widow of a seaman, a miner's wife keeping a bronchial husband at home in the front room, or a pair of spinster sisters, one tall and thin, the other short and fat. They all knew too much about you, even though you had run a mile to get their unique brand (as instructed) of whatever they had made themselves famous for, and you could not remember having seen them ever before—and they asked embarrassing questions about your mother's operation, your father's last job, and how you were doing with the girls.

That was another reason for dreaming of the anonymity of the giant store that sold everything you always wanted to eat but never dared ask for. Woolworths probably

came the nearest—at least it was laid out as if it wanted you to come inside and steal something. Most of the merchandise was the usual dreaded, boring household stuff but even the fire tongs and screw-drivers and seed packets and tea caddies smelled of chocolate and vanilla and freshly roasted peanuts. The thick glass plate which fenced off the patchwork fields of goodies was just too high for a small hand to easily climb. But you could wander around without being asked to buy—like Rabelais's beggar you paid for the smell in your nose with the chink of the coin in your trouser pocket. And you could occasionally pinch a wodge of something—always worse than it looked under its glassy barrier like sea weed taken out of the water, and tasting coarsely, guiltily over-sweet and synthetically flavoured. Still, it wasn't really like theft. It was rather the way it was it was in the Westerns. Robbing a local shop would be the equivalent of rustling, or horse-thieving, but raiding Woolies was nearer breaking into the city bank.

It wasn't until I came to London, then only after I'd been here nearly twenty years, that I discovered what I had been yearning for as a boy. It was a super-market. And even now, when I go to a Tesco's, I feel rather cheated when I find they also sell jeans or sandals or socks or other things you felt it was unfair for adults to give you pretending that it was a present. It was like going into a toy shop and coming out with something useful and possibly even educational—a fountain pen or a blackboard or a game which was designed so that no one could cheat or win to the total ruin and extinction of your opponent.

Couldn't believe it had taken so long for some genius to invent a shop where you helped yourself like a looter. They

"Seven Ave Marias for disrespect! That's a bit bloody steep, isn't it?"

actually gave you trolleys to pile the stuff in, setting up expectations, apparently socially acceptable, that every person would take enough for a short siege rather than what could be held in a carrier bag. My reason told me, and still does, that there must be a person between me and the door who will insist that I pay for it all. But for a while, every time, I rejoice in the idea that no one will ever know I have collected six of everything. And it has taken me a long time to realise that I can walk out of sight of my purchases because nobody can steal them while I remain this side of the till.

We had the first intimations of such metropolitan freedoms when a master at school described to us a visit to a Lyons cafeteria. How antique and perverse after that seemed the backward regional system of ordering food you couldn't examine first, and having to put up with whatever they chose to set in front of you. When it said on the card "leg of lamb", your mind naturally imagined a whole leg being presented, and, if not left for you to carve, at least served from the bone. Being given a few grey slices, gravy added in a pre-determined dollop, was not the same thing at all. The best part of the set tea was the stand full of cakes left trustingly on the table while you jammed the toast. The waves of envy and triumph while you scanned the whole room to ensure that your selection was truly representative of the best available, counting the number, perming the variety, checking to see what was the choicest by noting which went first on the majority of doilies. Then the illicit speculation ranging over the number of ways of gulling the waitress—could you possibly half hollow the cream out of that eclair, lick the chocolate coating from the underside of that bun, lift the cherry off that icing, without seeming to have even touched any but the single cake you were allowed?

In the end, you knew that was all you would get, but how generous, how imaginative, how really human of the management to permit you the fantasy of crushing them all into your mouth, one after another, and being led away to the police station or the washing-up sink knowing that no power on earth could take away the paradisal pleasure even a stomach pump could not summon back.

The original, pre-war Lyons still existed when I came to the metropolis and during early, impoverished days I more than once was able to make my fantasy come true. Then you moved with your tray along a great metal wall, over head-high, consisting of scores of small doors. Behind these, in their neat, blank cells, sat every dish on the menu. Often they were not labelled so it was permissible, indeed essential, to open several in each block to find what you wanted—the genuine curved sausage speared through mash, comic-paper style; the egg and bacon heavy with baked beans; the cherry tart stained with leakage round its little lips; the miniature sultana pudding with its lace cap of custard; the meat pie, crisp above, soggy below, warm as a small baby. Instantly, I saw, as thousands of corrupted provincials must have done before me, an infallible method of indulging my kleptomatic greed.

"Sorry, you guys—we just don't work on the basis that when you want our advice you'll ask for it."

Who would know if, leaning short-sightedly forward with my nose actually inside a box, I scooped one of these delights with a quick paw straight into my mouth? It was too much to expect to get away by this ruse with an entire meal, and anyway the tray at the end should not be too suspiciously bare, but I could at the cash desk only pay for what was in effect a selection of second helpings. Who would know? The man on the other side re-filling the empty compartments was who if you chose the wrong moment. His eyes were only six inches away as he stared at your flakey lips and coloured tongue while the end of the portion bolted down your gullet. Even if you never saw him, there were the tell-tale plates, still marked with the evidence of their vanished trophies.

Adrenalin is a potent sauce. The food always tasted better for the flash of excitement, the sexy thrill of contact between thief and victim. You learned to take the plates with you, hiding them among the cups as you got to the tea urn, or just sticking a pile of them together in one locker to show the phantom eater had passed this way again. And in real emergency, if he not only saw you but spoke to you as well, there was dodging back in the queue, re-combing your hair, removing or adding a tie, walking with knees bent as a much smaller man. As I recall, though there were some shows of reproof or warning on the far side of the barricades, no one ever cared enough to come round and check the free-loaders.

SOMETHING of the same feeling of being an invisible consumer, your choice of what you are going to sneak home like a Saturday Santa Claus known only to you, God and the TV eye, obtains still in super-markets. I am conscious that their planners, long ago advised by Dr Dichter and his Motivational Research team whom I saw carefully psycho-analysing housewives on his couches in the Hudson Valley when America pioneered the original super-marts, are counting on my predictable responses. But I cannot help feeling that if I silently load my trolley with expensive, silly luxuries it is not quite so culpable as asking for them aloud over a counter where some officious, well-meaning fellows actually sometimes point out how highly priced they are and apologise for taking your money. I also experience a real sense of achievement in the fruit and vegetable department, knowing that I can squeeze and sniff and closely eye a tomato say, or a melon, as I can never do at the greengrocers where the assistant not only prevents touching the produce before you buy but exerts a moral influence upon you to stop you touching it even after you have paid.

Like most conveniences, the super-market does exact an unacceptable toll on one group—the check-out girls. Serving in a shop is not a very rewarding occupation anywhere but it does bring you into some communion with other people, even just repeating back what the last person said about the weather. In the super-market, neither you nor she has any time or desire to speak—you are both being processed. This week one chain had begun to remove the stick-on price (bad), instead obliging the cashiers to memorise and carry 400 of them in their heads—even worse. Or is it? At least, they must feel they are performing some function of the mind. Otherwise, they are automatons. It blights a lot of my joy at being able to stand under the cornucopia.

Diary of Events

SUMMER · 1980

(14)

June

2 **400 Years of Wembley** (Various events around Borough. Dog dancing; trouser exhibition; Belisha beacon watching; fire-station look-alike competition; scenic walk round Sainsbury's).

4 **Death of Goebbels Dinner & Dance**, Cowley.

8 **Birkenhead Fayre.** Pig gelding contest; road-painting; *Guess My Smell*, with Nicholas Parsons, St. Jude's Primary School.

10 **Deaf Plasterers' Rally**, Blackheath.

12 **Grodzinski Puppet Theatre of Kiev** perform *Private Lives*, Crystal Palace Sports Centre (dogs not admitted).

15 **Eight Millionth Anniversary of English Channel** Phone-In, with David Jacobs (Dover Slipper Baths, 8 pm).

17 **Runcorn Fayre.** Desk-throwing; brick-spotting ■ competition; cat-following; *Wave My Vest*, with Nicholas Parsons, Runcorn Institute cellars.

18 **Showjumping: Boilermakers Union vs. Penthouse**, The Old Course, St. Andrew's.

21 **Crewe Centenary.** Son et Lumiere; Buffet Sandwich Ladies Choir tribute to Stanley Baldwin; fridge-freezer race; rat poison exhibition.

22 **Hang-gliding:** Rabbis' Fancy-dress Cross-Country, Newport to Mayfair (children half-price).

23 **Battle of Flowers**, Tilbury.

24 **Open Day and Air Show, H.M. Customs & Excise VAT Office**, Southend-on-Sea (NO sandwiches, anoraks, thermos flasks UNLESS over 45cm in length, shooting-sticks containing MORE THAN 27% synthetic fibre, pensioners OVER nine stone 5 lbs, OR smoked fish caught BEFORE May 15 1978).

27 **Royal Gherkin Society Exhibition**, Caxton Hall *(a nominal charge will be levied to cover dancing).*

29 **Irish Tennis Finals**, Putney to Mortlake, 4.15.

37 **Calendar Reformation Society March**, starts Aldgate Pump, 12.30 (87.40).

July

1 **Sealed Knot** Roundheads vs. Cavaliers Can You Widdle Over The Wall Battle, Kenilworth Castle gents.

2 **Broadstairs Janis Joplin Festival**, Main Bandstand.

3 **Guy Fawkes Night Dance**, Shamrock Ballroom, Kilburn.

6 **Surbiton Fayre.** Sardine exhibition; jam-juggling (Police vs. Flat Earth Society Juniors); staring; ugliest virgin contest; *Where's My Foot?*, with Nicholas Parsons, Surbiton Gas Showrooms.

9 **Wimpole Street Sheepdog Trials.**

10 **News of the World Mock A-Levels**, with Barbara Windsor and Lord Kagan, Kew Gardens (facilities for blacks).

11 **Stoat Derby**, Westminster Abbey, 2 pm.

12 **Cricket:** MCC vs. Ayatollah Khomeini's XI, Lord's.

14 **Bastille Day, Doncaster:** Cover Your Wife In Lard Contest; Red Arrows Gynaecology Display; A. J. P. Taylor Live in Concert; brown shoe show.

16 **Pageant: The Early Years of Central Heating.** Floats, vegetarian street ballet, book burning, impressions of Tommy Cooper, Gay Freedom Barbecue, knobbly head contest. Lillie Road, Fulham, from 9 am. *(No pacifists)*

18 **Prudential World Smoking Cup**, Beaulieu, in aid of hernia research.

20 **Jewish Farmers' Day.** Procession and ball, Crockford's.

21 **Bletchley Fayre.** Gobs competition; angling contest (Pakistan vs. Margaret Duchess of Argyll); turkey-crippling; Jowett van concours d'elegance; *Wiggle Your Conk*, with Nicholas Parsons, NGA Conference Centre (black tie).

24 **Grimethorpe Colliery Souffle Team Display.**

25 **House of Lords Reggae Finals.**

30 **Friends Of The Earth 9th Annual Wife-Swapping Rally**, Eastbourne. Organic omelette bar, tombola, Hunt-The-Midget, free dental examinations, Ghurkha march-past, child-throttling.

31 **Stuffed Captain Cooks Exhibition**, Bill Grundy Institute, Cowes *(no women).*

August

2 **Frog-upping, Queen's Bench Division**, followed by fork ▲▲ supper.

4 **Cockfosters Bach Festival.** 8th Tawny Pack Cubs Light Orchestra plays *Bits of Toccata and Bears' Picnic, Some Concerto for Violin and Kazoo and Beer Bottles* (arr. Arkela), Sweeney vs. Starsky and Hutch, and Look At Mine.

6 **National Model Lesbian Exhibition**, Olympia.

7 **Notting Hill Fayre.** Three-legged limbo; greasy yam contest; honky-baiting; *Who Dat?* with Nicholas Parsons, Lupin's Damn Smart Used Cars lot.

10 **National Film Theatre:** A season of Reg Varney classics (until August 11).

11 **Leytonstone to Chichester Rude Charity Walk**, in aid of the HRH Princess Margaret Home for Cobblers.

14 **Friends of Pope Pius XII Annual Luncheon and Punt Judging**, Golders Green Kennel Club, and afterwards at The Gnat & Scrotum, Woking.

17 **What Sir Isiah Berlin Did In The Holidays illustrated lecture**, Richmond Rugby Club. Well-dressing, ploughing contest, bomb disposal, jam tea, midnight mass *(unless wet)*.

18 **NUPE Furry Dance**, Rotherham.

19 **Vintage Wastebin Rally**, Brighton. Hundreds of valuable prizes, sheep-kissing, nude grocery. The Old Denture Exchange, Hove *(no invalids)*.

22 **Dame Clara Butt Week** opens, Fortnum & Mason. Table d'hote lunch £8.50, batteries not included.

23 **Christmas Eve Dance & Shinty Match**, Shamrock Ballroom, Kilburn *(if wet, in the garden)*.

25 **Crimean Veterans Reunion**, Carlisle Squash Club *(transistors strictly forbidden)*.

26 **Welsh National Opera Five-a-Side Snooker Knock-Out Competition for the Keith Joseph Vase**, Beachy Head.

30 **Old Folks Pothole Race**, Skirmdale, OR **Third Test Match** *(consult local paper for details)*.

31 **Grand Open Air Celebrity Concert**, Bournemouth, with Martha Snelling, J. D. Breene, Norman Atkins, Nicholas Parsons, George McShane and Sambo, the Noles Trio, and "Hairy".

AC

SINBAD the SAILOR

KEITH WATERHOUSE:

An historian who sailed the Atlantic in a leather boat to prove Irish monks could have done so 900 years before Columbus, said yesterday he was to make another voyage—in the wake of Sinbad . . .

"He is undoubtedly the most famous sailor of all time, and I want to show that many of the stories about him could have been true," said Mr Timothy Severin, who lives in Co. Cork.

Daily Telegraph

Day One

An uneventful start to my voyage, apart from a curious encounter at the quayside while we were taking on provisions. A strange middle-aged man, wearing a powdered wig, silk knee-breeches and frogged livery, came up behind me as I stooped over a bale of oatmeal and tapped me lightly with his tipstaff. "Whoops, did I catch you bending, ducky?" trilled this peculiar individual, rolling his eyes. He then confided that he was the personal servant of a gentleman who had sent him to enquire whether the Sinbad who was the subject of my voyage was by any happenchance that same cheeky monkey who had played the lead in the pantomime *Sinbad the Sailor* at the Grand Theatre, Cokeville, in 1953, only to abscond with the week's takings and a hamper of props, because if so the gentleman would like to sign on as the ship's cook under an assumed name, with a view to confronting him on a dark stormy night.

I commanded the pouting poltroon to report to his master that the class of fiction into which I was preparing to sail was altogether superior to any that he might have been involved with in the touring theatres of the North of England, and that in any case I had already engaged not only one but two ship's cooks, to wit that droll duo Buzby and Fuzby ("A Giggle A Minute").

Returning my attention to my vessel, I instructed the crew to man the bilge-pumps, whereupon my odd visitor once more struck me a mock blow with his wand, observed, "Whoops you filthy devil!" and minced off. Odd.

Wind: NE × E—Force 3. Lat: 48.32N. Long: 02.33W. 18m WSW of Needles. Drizzle.

Day Three

Everything shipshape. Sea calm. Handed the wheel over to my first mate so that I could inspect the mizzenmast. Thus unpreoccupied by routine, I noticed for the first time that the ship's cat is wearing fitted thigh-boots, which I am ready to swear was not the case when we set sail.

This was strange enough: yet when I asked the cat's custodian, the ship's carpenter, what it thought it was about, the affair became even stranger, for it was the animal itself which replied, "Trying them out for thighs," to which the carpenter, I know not why, added an expression new to me, "Boom-boom!"

I at once asked this remarkable cat how it came to be able to speak passable English. The following exchange I record verbatim:

Cat: Because I'm wearing sea-boots.
Myself: Yes, I see you're wearing sea-boots, you silly little feline, but how does wearing sea-boots miraculously turn you into a talking cat?
Cat: That's the wonder of wellies.
Carpenter: Boom-boom.

This is going to be a rum voyage.

Wind: NW × W—Force 4. Lat: 49.56N. Long: 04.49W. 13m ESE of Lizard Point. Rain.

Day Six

On course and making good speed. Repaired tear in mainsail. After an outbreak of petty pilfering found forty Arabians stowing away in jars. Locked them in hold.

Wind: SE—Force 4. Lat: 50.28N. Long: 12.32W. 72m WSW of Fastnet. Hail.

Day Nine

Was obliged to remind that priceless pair Buzby and Fuzby ("A Giggle A Minute") that I am the captain and that they take their orders from me. Matters came to a head when, my lunch having failed to materialise, I asked the crazy couple why I had not been served.

It was Buzby (the thin one) who riposted: "Served? What do you think we are, guv, flipping tennis players?" To this Fuzby (the fat one) added irreverently, "They also serve who only stand and wait," at which Buzby retorted—and I made a careful note of his insolent words—"And we're not flipping waiters, neither, so I'm not standing for that."

Reminding them that we were on the high seas where there is such an offence as mutiny, I asked the titterful twosome in no uncertain manner what the devil they were doing out of uniform and why they were wearing green baize aprons. The insubordinate statements appended were made in front of a witness, the ship's carpenter;

Buzby: Why are we wearing green baize aprons? Why are we wearing green baize aprons? My my, you *are* green! We're wearing green baize aprons, you higneramus, because we are the brokers' men.
Myself: You're the brokers' men?
Buzby: We're the brokers' men!
Fuzby: And we've come to tell you you're broke!
Carpenter: Boom-boom.

For all that this was an open display of defiance, it would have been foolhardy of me to have tried to have Buzby and Fuzby ("A Giggle A Minute") clapped in irons, for

with such weak material they must have been confident that they had the support of the ship's chorus, as the crew now prefers to call itself. Accordingly, since they still refused to serve lunch, I sent them about their business and opened a tin of sardines.

Wind: SE—Force 4. Lat: 45.24N. Long: 21.07W. 65m WSW of Baron Hardup's Castle. Light applause.

Day Ten

Continued on course with excellent sail. Night sky clear. I think I am going mad.

To quote to this log but one example: at six bells today the ship's cat, which as well as wearing boots has now taken to carrying all its possessions tied in a spotted handkerchief on the end of a stick, appeared for its morning herring accompanied by a young person, dressed as a boy from the waist up but wearing fishnet tights, who as they entered the cabin was slapping his/her thigh and exclaiming jauntily, "But can't you hear the bells, you silly puss; unless we turn back now we'll miss the bus!" I was so taken aback that I mentioned to the two brokers' men—ably played by Buzby and Fuzby ("A Giggle A Minute")—who now occupy my cabin, that I must be going out of my mind. Immediately a fruity, basso-profundo voice responded, "Oh, no you're not!" Unaccustomed as I am to being contradicted I averred, "Oh, yes I am!" whereupon the unseen interloper came back with, "Oh, no you're not, is he, children?" From I know not where there was a resounding chorus of "No!" followed by loud cheers, followed by the fruity voice complaining, "Ooh, me stays! Ooh, me unmentionables! Ooh, I feel all of a doo-dah!" and so on. At my sharp enquiry of "Who said that? Who are you?" the unseen voices yelled, "Behind you!", and through the porthole struggled a stowaway dressed as a washerwoman. She gave her name as a Mrs Twankey and her status was that of widow. I had her put in the hold with the forty Arabians.

Wind: NW—Force 3. Lat: 46.35N. Long: 22.36W. 18m ESE of the Enchanted Forest. Laughter.

Twelfth Incredible Day

Two more stowaways—mere babes, found by the ship's carpenter among some wood. Despite their youth, I had to make an example of them, since there is no more room for further walk-on parts in the hold, so I gave them the option of walking the plank or climbing the beanstalk. They chose the latter course. As I said to the first mate:

I think that we should have no fears,
We've seen the last of *those* poor dears!

Heh heh heh, if I may permit myself the expression. That tiresome piece of administration completed, I went and tried on the new red uniform which the purser kindly obtained for me, having been granted three wishes by a genie he encountered in the lamp-locker. The horns need stiffening and the tail will have to be taken up, otherwise it is a perfect fit.

Wind: NW—Force Fe Fi Fum. Lat: 48.06N. Long: 24.32W. 22m WSW of Intermission. Reprise.

Third Record-breaking Week (Voyage Must End Sat)

Sea choppy. The first mate, who has now revealed himself to be a prince in disguise, has asked permission to hold a glass slipper contest in the mess. I see no harm in that: if I have kept my charts correctly, we should shortly be in sight of the Finale, and can afford a little relaxation. I decided that a ship's concert would be in order. Accordingly, all the boys and girls on the starboard side, led by Buzby and Fuzby ("A Giggle A Minute") were asked to sing "The Hills Are Alive With The Sound Of Music", while all the boys and girls on the port side, led by two ugly sisters who apparently wandered on board mistaking us for a cruise to Majorca, sang, "I've Got A Loverly Bunch Of Coconuts". Small prizes of sweets were thrown to the side singing the loudest.

Meanwhile the ship's carpenter had constructed a huge staircase which lights up, and we all walked down it, in reverse order of seniority. As I escorted Widow Twankey and the ship's cat down the glittering stairs, what should appear in the sky but a great auk, suspended from a rope, with no less a personage than Sinbad himself on board, waving furiously. As they continued to circle our vessel, a great curtain of fog descended; it rose again and we all bowed; it descended and rose again several times; the applause was deafening. We are all delighted by the success of our voyage and are already talking about touring Australia with it.

Wind: SW—Gales of laughter. Lat: 49.23N. Long: 35.27WE. 1m ESE of Transformation Scene. Standing ovation.

A Good Church Guide is reported to be in preparation.
E. S. TURNER shows what we may expect.

ALL SAINTS

Lower Pintable

In returning our questionnaire, the Rev. Simon Clodwick pointedly omitted to answer Question 5: "Do you suffer little children?" Mary M., of Guildford, writes: "My two boys, admittedly a little wild, were ejected by a churchwarden for running about during the service, and this was done with the obvious approval of the Vicar, who seems never to have heard of self-expression. They got their revenge by tugging on one of the bell ropes, though Kevin received a nasty bump on the head when the rope yanked him up to the ceiling. We are consulting our lawyers."

Several correspondents have criticised the length and content of the sermons. "At All Saints one must be prepared to accept an immoderate share of the world's guilt," writes J.C., of Melton Mowbray. "In the space of 40 minutes I was saddled with the blame for Britain's post-war degeneracy, the excesses of the Common Market, the plight of the Third World, the theft of the Mothers' Union banner and the murder of J.R. in *Dallas*."

Jumble sales are well attended and enable the impoverished middle classes to clothe their nakedness, "a Christ-like activity if ever I saw one," writes J.K., of Chester.

The Visitors' Book has been withdrawn "because visitors keep writing their names in it."

Harvest Festival: no tinned porridge or rice pudding accepted.

ST SWITHIN'S

Brindle-under-Faggot, Scurfside

Known locally as "St Withit's", this church appeals especially to those who are "not the marrying kind". The Rev. Cyprian Nudge is campaigning to be allowed to solemnise gay marriages. According to B.B., of Diss, "already the parish magazine makes *Gay News* look like *Chicks' Own*." R.C.K., of Brent, assures us that "a vicarage tea party at St Swithin's has to be seen to be believed." The courageous choice of a Wayside Pulpit text is commended by A.B., of Sunbury. It was from *Revelations* XII, verse 11, and said: "He which is filthy, let him be filthy still."

HOLY TRINITY BY-THE-MOTORWAY

Newport Wick

Controversial reports have been received about the new Holy Trinity, the nave of which has been remodelled to house the People's Theatre Workshop and a heel bar—"not my idea of a Holy Trinity," writes J.R., of Upton, "but we must move with the times." The sacred vessels still surviving are securely wired to burglar alarms. Although the church is normally deserted, attempts to make brass rubbings without payment will bring the verger at the double in 30 seconds.

"When I dropped in on a late Friday afternoon," writes Cyril T., of Balham, "the Rev. Eustace Throstle was celebrating Evensong to a congregation consisting solely of his wife, who was surrounded by plastic shopping bags. I had the distinct feeling that I was intruding into a domestic occasion. 'We do not like to seem unfriendly,' said Mr Throstle, 'but many people come in only to get the weight off their feet. Also there are spies from Good Church Guides looking for trouble. Otherwise, all are welcome'."

Not welcome, however, are parents who wish to have their infants christened Cary, Gary, Darren, Tamsin, Tintin, Baz or Daz (there is a full list of proscribed names in the porch and it is constantly being extended). The Vicar achieved headlines when he refused to baptise a boy with the surnames of the Arsenal first team.

Arthur M., of Rye, reports: "A recent sermon by the Vicar was taken word for word from Fothergill's *Handy Sermons*

For All Occasions (1909), though delivered with such quivering intensity as to suggest that the preacher had just come off the Hot Line to God. I give him ten out of ten for presentation. What a pity he could not have put more into his parting handshake!"

Flower arrangements: fairly Spry. Graveyard: contains many rare and luxuriant weeds, also a bottle bank. Old Vicarage: now a bail hostel.

No sparrow shooting in the nave. Television teams are expected to refrain from liquid refreshment.

ST WINIFRED'S

Bogwater-over-Wye

This living is within the gift of Johnson's Superfine Mustard Ltd, the local landowners, but many correspondents complain of a lack of mustard in the sermons. "The one I heard," writes B.C., of Looe, "was full of slippery theological exegesis more suited to the days of Puseyism. Throughout this ordeal the choir sat like Easter Island statues, with a look of obsidian suffering I hope never to see again." Sir Arthur Y. says: "More care could be taken with the choice of hymns. It is a long time since I have been asked to raise my voice to plead for the lifting of a murrain on cattle."

The long-haired organist receives a word of praise. "I would never have supposed that *Jailhouse Rock* could have been transformed into such a delightful voluntary," writes Mary M., of Andover. From Dover, Ron K. wonders if the Vicar knows what the Young People's Fellowship get up to in the gallery.

ST JUDE THE OBSCURE

atte-the-South-Banke, London

Normally closed against visitors, St Jude's can be seen by application to Mr Alf Parkweed, of 2 Railway Mansions. Locking the doors, he explains, is to stop motor cyclists riding up and down the nave, which they are allowed to do only once a year when their machines are blessed by the Rev. Theodorus ("Tony") Slinke, who encourages the riders to "blip" their engines to the greater glory of God. According to T.Y., of Chelsea, "this is the only time in the year that the existence of God is admitted."

The hospitality of the pulpit is regularly extended to leading humanists, moral philosophers, sociologists and gang leaders.

Liturgy: modern illiterate. Electric guitars, when current available. "Silent collections" (i.e. paper money only), owing to inflation.

it would have to have made a pretty positive impression on you for you to be able to compare it to its detriment with the 1980 follow-up. Only a Liverpudlian would admit openly to a slump being the cause of a sale anyway, let alone promise enjoyment from it.

My Uncle Alan, being in his 80s, might have remembered it, but he didn't. I took him and a friend out to dinner before my second concert and, at his suggestion, we went to an excellent bistro round the corner from his flat, in a narrow Victorian shopping street called Lark Lane, The Bistro was called *L'Alouette*, which was neat of it, but for me the trauma was it being there at all. Lark Lane was where we shopped in my childhood. It had an old-style grocers with biscuits in glass-topped tins, a fishmonger with marble slabs. ("Don't put the baby's warm bottom on the cold marble slab." Old Liverpool saying), two pubs, *The Albert* where my father drank and *The Middle House* where he didn't, an undertakers, a cake shop, "Miss Stephenson's", and a small gothic police station. But a bistro! I doubt my parents had even heard the word. What's more *L'Alouette* occupies half-timbered, big-windowed premises which were once a record shop. It was here I bought, during the early forties, my first jazz 78s: Louis, Bessie, Jelly Roll and Billie Holiday singing *I wished on the Moon*. And what was on the bistro's tape as we tucked into our snails? Billie Holiday singing *I wished on the Moon*. Life is full of unexpected trap-doors and two-way mirrors. For Uncle Alan, living his whole life around Lark Lane, the changes have happened gradually and are no surprise, but for me it's a real culture shock. I tried to explain this. "It's not the only place," he said in his slow considered way. "You remember the newsagent just before you get to Sefton Park Gates?" I did. "Well, it's a wine bar now and very successful."

A wine bar where I used to buy *Film Fun* and *The Beano*!

O tempora! O mores!

PAUL JENNINGS:

The Horse in the Lavatory

The Saxilby Home of Rest in Lincolnshire reports on horses and donkeys it has rescued, including 6-year-old Dolly, a pony mare found in an outside lavatory of a house in Sheffield.

Daily Telegraph

A moment's thought will show that even a circus pony, used to standing on its hind legs, could not fit into an ordinary outside lavatory, in which the vertical predominates over the horizontal. Clearly the building was not a lavatory converted, however inadequately, into a stable, but a stable converted into a lavatory for reasons which reach back into the social history of Sheffield and indeed of our time, not to mention inspiring one of those three-generation novels.

The stable is in the grounds of Grappknott Lodge, a Victorian Jacobean mansion built in 1889 by Joel Grimshanks, a Sheffield millionaire, founder of Grimshank Sickles ("twice as sharp as hand-forged and half the price") in the days when there were two million agricultural labourers in this country alone, and when *krimshan*, *greemish* and several variants became the actual words for "sickle" in half

a dozen African and eastern languages.

In those days the land, at the end of a rural lane off the Glossop road, was pleasantly wooded, but the gardens of Grappknott Lodge were designed so that from the balustraded terrace on the far side of the lawn from the house the view was either over gently falling fields dotted with trees to the distant chimneys of Sheffield, or, behind the house, great rising vistas of Peak District grandeur, over towards High Neb.

In the evening of his life Grimshanks, now Sir Joel, has divided feelings when, with a rug over his knees, he sits on the terrace surveying the lively scene as the liveried servants, dodging the plunging, mettlesome steeds and excited hounds, take the stirrup cups out to the Wharncliffe Hunt. None cuts a prouder figure than his son Martin, fresh from Rugby and Cambridge.

"Ah niver thowt ti see our son ridin' wi' Wharncliffe. I heerd Master say as he'd got best seat in county. Ee, Joel lad, we've come a long way from Cogbottom Lane!" says his wife.

"I could buy half on 'em," says Joel contemptuously. "I'll not have him wed one o' them la'di'dah girls wi' voice at back of 'er throat an' knows all about spending brass an' nowt about gettin' it."

But he need not have worried. Martin has an engineering degree and a sound business head, and disappoints the social set (and, if the truth be told, his mother, though she would never admit it) by marrying Winnie Ogthorpe, thus consolidating an alliance with Ogthorpe & Bannion, steel stockists and structural engineers. Grimshanks goes from strength to strength. During World War I it goes over to the manufacture of bayonets. Martin, although officially exempt, insists on joining up, leaving the reins in Winnie's capable hands, and comes back with a DSO.

He nurses the business through the Depression years by clever diversifying into garden tools as the demand for sickles begins to shrink. Their daughter Edith is

"Gerald is training for World War Four."

"We've gone back to the Three-Field System—one belongs to an Arab, one to a Dutchman and one to a pension fund."

born in 1926, and soon after this a certain tension grows between them. Winnie becomes jealous of Martin's Cambridge background and of his ability to step so easily from the hard, no-nonsense world of Sheffield steel men into the Yorkshire county set. A remark she overhears, or fancies she overhears, in the ladies' room at a hunt ball in Harrogate, is the turning point. "Oh, Martin's charming, but, my *dear*, that *wife* of his . . ."

She cultivates a refeened accent and becomes the most tremendous snob. She is far too intelligent not to know that she is more talked about than ever as such, and this has two results; she becomes an alcoholic (gin), and nourishes a fierce desire for Edith to grow up a lady.

There are blinding rows about this, the more so because there is a natural father-daughter bond between Martin and Edith ("Ayoh, gayoh awn, Ai know yaw bayoath agenst me." "Oh, mother, that's just not true . . .") There are tearful partings for Roedean, or wherever it was Roedean was evacuated to, during the war, from which the firm of Grimshanks, with its fair share of bombing and other troubles, emerges somewhat battered.

In vain Martin tries to make his wife see that the world is changing, that Edith doesn't want to go to the finishing school—indeed it is the discovery that there is something between Edith and Tom Rawlinson, the young works manager at Grimshanks (he has come up the hard way—apprentice, night school, sandwich course at Sheffield University) that causes Martin to give reluctant assent to Edith's departure for Switzerland.

She has nearly finished her art-appreciation year, and is in line for a job at Sotheby's, when she is suddenly called home. Martin has died. At the funeral she, poised and svelte, bears herself with a hard courage, and people suddenly notice the resemblance between her and her rake-thin, blue-rinsed, haggard mother as they leave the graveside in the biting wind.

Tom Rawlinson is in America, on a course at the Harvard Business School, and in due course word comes that he is engaged to an American girl. Thus it is that the wedding of Edith to the Hon. Trevelyan Hutton-Scroop, scion of one of the oldest families in the North of England, is the social event of 1950 in Yorkshire.

The marriage is a disaster. Hutton-Scroop is a compulsive gambler and womaniser. He cannot get at the capital of the firm because of trust arrangements. But as Sheffield spreads inexorably outwards he somehow persuades Edith they will forestall compulsory purchase if they sell off most of the estate "for high-class executive homes". In due course these are built, on spacious 2½-acre plots. They have carriage-lamps and gables and many trees, and names like Cottar's Garth, Dauntrey Glebe, The Old Linseed House, Piper's Furlong, Rushy Toft, Furrows, High Winds, Bucketts, Furzey Hansel, Top o' the Moor, Fettler's Piece.

By the time Hutton-Scroop, now a florid-faced man of 58, bulky in the saddle but still a good rider, has taken up with Esther Hazeldine, wife of the insurance manager who lives at Furzey Hansel, Edith has divorced him and married Tom, who did not marry the American girl and has waited patiently for her all this time. Hutton-Scroop has now exhausted all available money, is deeply in debt, and not best pleased when, having stabled Esther's mare Dolly (which her husband doesn't even know he gave her) he sees the rating assessor getting out of his car. "Ah, Mr Hutton-Scroop, you didn't mention this, ah, stable—a splendid building, eh?—on your form. I'm afraid it will rather, ah, bump up the rateable val—"

"It's not a stable, damn yer! It's the outside lavatory . . ."

In the end he just disappears, like Lord Lucan, and so of course does Esther Hazeldine. But not Dolly, obviously.

SEE NAPLES AND HAI!

Nissan and Alfa-Romeo having announced a plan to co-manufacture cars in Italy, **BILL TIDY** throws up his hands and falls on his pen

"Okay, Mr Ito, as a special favour. How tall is the emperor?"

"Good sign. Since Nissan arrive is sweating also."

"I think they're remaking Bicycle Thieves."

SEE NAPLES AND HAI!
(continued)

"Why don't you admit it. You're shy."

"Hey, Vito baby, easy. You only get to rough him up a little for 20,000 lire!"

"Oh . . . and send the Sumo wrestlers home."

"I've noticed of late that it has become fashionable to shuffle around shoeless. This must stop."

"No. This pig ruined a perfectly good tablecloth belonging to my grandmother."

"Okay, we drop the singing and marching to work idea!"

"You calla thatta volcano. Whatta town it destroy?"

"They threw out the Communist shop steward. He only asked for two girls a bath."

FATHER'S DAY

HUNTER DAVIES

is back in the swim

THERE'S only one thing I don't like about our Sunday morning sessions, but it wasn't too bad this morning, thank you for asking. Our whole family went as usual, least what I call our whole family nowadays. We've been rather depleted, with the ravages of teenagery sweeping through our little nuclear unit, leaving two adults and one child. In the old days, when we first started our Sunday swims at Swiss Cottage, some ten years ago,

we had a full complement. Now it's just us and Flora. Ahh.

The lumps are still in bed, and we've been back for hours, glowing with self-righteousness. Overnight they seem to have changed from getting up at six every morning and jumping on your head to lying in bed so long you fear they must have taken an overdose. Getting them up for school is a nightmare. I'm so hoarse from shouting up the stairs I have to go back to bed to recover.

The big ones had rather exhausting days yesterday, being Saturday, poor petals. Caitlin and five of her girlfriends arranged a little evening up West. A few months ago when she had a boyfriend (don't ask me what happened, how do I know) the furthest she seemed to go with him of a Sat'day night was up the pub. Now that she's back with les gels, they do things in style. I have no fear for the future of the Western Hemisphere when I observe Caitlin and her girlfriends organising the world round themselves.

They booked by phone a table for six at some place called Tango where they have live music, having first found out that if you eat at the table, you can stay and listen all night, then secondly found out that the cheapest thing on the menu is hamburgers, which they decided they could just afford. I'm looking forward to hearing what the headwaiter thought, a table for six booked all night, with the only order being six hamburgers. I can't ask now, can I. She's still asleep, isn't she. Don't want to be put in detention, do I.

You could tell she was going Up West by her shoes, the gold lamé Oxfam ones. They're the pair tied by *two* safety pins.

Before that, they were going to Joe

Allen's restaurant, having found out that you can sit at the bar there as long as you like and drink lemonade, their cheapest drink. I don't know why Margaret Thatcher doesn't retire now and let the sixteen-year-old girls of this world take over.

Jake, well, he had an all-time great day for him, doing something for the first time in his life. For the last three Saturdays I've trailed him to horrible shoe shops in Kentish Town and Golders Green to buy him a pair of blue boots, like Kickers, only phoney Kickers, you know the sort, every chain store has them, about £13.99, with those corrugated soles, made specially to carry small pieces of shit, but none of them came up to his terribly high standards. When you think that in his whole life so far he's never worn proper shoes or boots, only training shoes, refusing everything that's ever been offered, it's ridiculous that he should suddenly turn into a Beau Brummel, going on about the stitching being too broad, the laces not right, the blue not blue enough. We had words. I stormed off saying that was it, he could buy his own rotten shoes from now on, see if I care.

Yesterday morning he went to Ace sports shop and got himself some new footwear. *On his own.* Wow. You'll be into long trousers next, I said when he came home, which of course I shouldn't. They've both got it in for us at the moment. They're fed up with our cheap remarks, endless sarcasm and cynicism. Don't we take anything seriously. All that mocking when Caitlin was trying to get us talking round the lunch table about Shakespeare's sonnets. Poor you, I said. Boring old Shakespeare. It turns out she loves them. That school has a lot to answer for.

Anyway, the shoes. Jake came back with yet another pair of identical black training shoes. It wasn't exactly a great example of entrepreneurial skill, but it shows the pioneering spirit is not quite dead amongst teenage boys. I think we'll put him in for his Duke of Edinburgh next.

So at 8.30 this morning we left the two elderly and exhausted statesmen in bed and drove through the empty streets, wiping the mists from our eyes, the sleep from the windscreen. Caitlin and Jake used to like our early morning swims when they came, especially when autumn got into its stride and they could breathe out the thick, white air as we got into the car. Naturally, we always rev up as noisily as possible. Always have done. There's the bloody Davieses, I can hear the rest of the street swearing, pulling the bedclothes over their heads, showing off as bloody usual.

They used to be all Irish or West Indian, the attendants at the baths when we went with our family mark one, who would stand singing loudly incomprehensible songs, even at 8.30 in the morning; now they have some silent and younger blokes, reading *The Observer*. Perhaps out-of-work brain surgeons.

I still recognize some of the old wizened regulars, and the same families who've come for years. In the autumn, when the Belsize pool opens, which is for children and families only, we go in there, as it's better

for Flora, but we feel a bit of a fraud, two huge adults swimming around with only one little seven-year-old girl between us, but the lengths are short so you feel really good. Tom, my wife's publisher, uses the big pool. He does a hundred lengths every morning of every day, or so he says. He's so stately and slow we've never ever seen him finish ten. We always go in after our swim to wave frantically at him. He waves back, and then sinks.

My wife used to swim for Cumberland and Westmorland, but she never caught them. They were small counties and you didn't have to be all that brill to be a county swimmer, but her breast-stroke has been much admired. If I'd had the Latin, I would have been a better swimmer, but I'm quite flash over ten yards, then I too sink. If only I'd been taught how to breathe.

Then here comes the bad bit. I don't mind getting out, or dashing back through the cold passageways and cold showers to the changing room, or standing fuming while the brain surgeons read Clive James instead of giving me my basket, or rushing for a cubicle to dress in, then rushing out as it's already occupied, averting my gaze from all the personal problems, it's getting dried I hate.

Over the last ten years, I've tried every permutation on drying myself, but the result has always been the same. I've tried very hot showers first, or very cold showers, or no showers, or soap, or baby cream, or talcum. I've tried woollen jumpers, silk shirts, tracksuit tops, cotton T-shirts, corduroy trousers, tweed trousers. For ten years the same thing happens the minute I've finished drying and get dressed—I start itching.

All the way home it gets worse. I scream in agony, bang my legs on the car doors, jump up and down, tear my skin to shreds, shout at Flora and anyone who dares to breathe or look at me. I don't know why I bother going swimming. It's obviously the chlorine in the water, but what can I do about it. Nobody else seems to be affected by it except me. And I'm not imagining it. Oh, shut up. It's started again, just thinking about it. Oh, God. I can't bear it . . .

Then just as we drive into our street it begins to fade. The relief is wonderful, like when you stop banging your wife against a wall, which I'm prepared to do, if I thought it would stop me itching after swimming. There used to be a Doctor's Column in that Scottish newspaper my mother read, *The Sunday Post*, which dealt with such daft questions as how to stop itching after swimming. I'm sure he must have an old folk cure, such as rubbing porridge on it. I must write at once to D. C. Thomson in Dundee.

Once it does fade, and I bound into the house, I forget all about it for another week, half convinced it was all psychological anyway. The bounding-in is for the Big Treat of the weekend. Swimmers only. If you lie in bed like a great lump, then certainly not, no bacon sandwiches for you.

It's the one day in the week in which we're allowed a cooked breakfast. It's muesli only, isn't it, the rest of the week, or grass, whichever is currently thought by right-thinking people to have the most roughage. Only on Sunday mornings are we allowed to poison ourselves and have a greasy fry-up. Sorry, I'll take that back. I know it's not true. I just said it to annoy. We *never* have grease in our house and she *never* fries anything. Grilled bacon tastefully placed between brown wholemeal toast. Yum yum, bubble gum, stick it up your Mother's Pride.

Sunday swimming is terrific and we all love it. There's not many sports a family can do together. I split the family all those years when I played football which we won't talk about at the moment. I played again the other week, despite what the doctors said after my last cartilage operation, and my knee is now sore again so I'm an absolute idiot and please don't go on about it or I'll cry, but it's the bacon sandwiches after the swimming which perfects our Sunday mornings. Those lumps in bed don't know what they're missing. What am I saying. Of course they do. They've done their time, put in the years, polishing my image of Happy Families. They're so cynical, these teenagers.

"Of course, there was a certain amount of local opposition."

ALEXANDER FRATER:

A Human Torpedo Writes

Wollongong, Australia, September 30—A man was accused in court here yesterday of trying to rob a bank with a knife and a fork.

Reuter

Dear Ma,

Assuming Aunty Maureen's shrike has not hidden your glasses in the gum tree again, I thought I better write in case you seen the thing about me in the paper. I know how you like to look over the form for the trots with your first gin of the morning, and maybe your good eye fell on an item about yours truly and an incident at the Wollongong Squatters Bank the other day. I remember the state you got into when they took dad away for selling the Shrine of Remembrance to Mr Yusef Asid from the Beirut property consortium and this letter is just to set your mind at rest.

But to start at the beginning. Since my last letter I have spent six months at the Surfer's Paradise Borstal for a little practical joke that went a bit wrong. I had got hold of this really bonzer plastic dorsal fin and, holding it just above the surface, I used to sneak up on swimming women and seize their ankles in my teeth. It was really beaut. Sirens were blown to clear the beach while I lay there 6 feet down, laughing like a drain. But then one day when plankton had made the water murky I bit a Life Guard by mistake and found myself in court, limping and heavily bandaged. I was charged under the local Shark and Conger Eel Prevention Act (1959) and the buggers threw the book at me.

What follows now, ma, is strictly confidential. I don't even want you to tell Mr Goatley. I know your dentures and his often share a glass on Saturday nights but you know how he yaks on down at the boozer; he may have good legs but he's still a real One Pint Screamer. Anyway, my news is this: I am now working for the Government! I'll bet you had to read that twice and right now, with racing pulse and trembling hand, you are pouring yourself another pony of neat Corio. I, too, am almost unable to believe my good fortune.

It happened right out of the blue. One fine arvo last month I was summoned to the Warden's office to see a visitor. I thought it might have been my friend Charlene from the Papua Massage Parlour who sometimes brings me food parcels, but it turned out to be this Civil Service joker, Mr Cleft. The Warden put the Punishment Cell at our disposal and, once we were alone, Mr Cleft told me he was very impressed by my ability to crawl about the sea bed looking up girls' knickers. How would I like to serve my country by looking up a few Chinese Commy junks instead? Jeeze, I says, breathless with pride, you mean you want me to fight the Yellow Peril, Mr Cleft? That's it, son, he says, slapping me on the back and, soon afterwards, I had signed the Official Secrets Act and found myself a member of Australia's fighting élite.

Now, ma, I am training to become a human torpedo. It is very hard. Eight hours a day we do duck dives, tumble turns and double somersaults off the high board with flippers, mask, snorkel and limpet mines. We also practise holding our breath. I am top of the class in this, you will be pleased to hear. I can last for nine minutes and, though I go a funny colour, I feel nothing. Mr Cleft says I am a phenomenon and reckons it is probably due to some sort of brain damage suffered as a kiddy. He says it is commensurate with having fallen out of a nineteenth storey window. Did that ever happen to me? I know I once threw the gerbil out of the Wattle Park flat but I can't remember if I jumped after it.

Anyway, now for what happened the other day. My best mate on the course, Eddie Stoat-Knackerbrot, came to see me in a state of some excitement. He was a prefect at Geelong Grammar and a great friend of Prince Charles, buttering his waffles for dorm feasts and playing gong to his cello at Speech Day madrigals. Though Eddie has

"If we get planning permission, we'll call it Venice."

been chucked out of six universities for cheating I envy him his advantages and often tell him how seriously you took education. Even at age five I knew that if you put kero on a whippet's bum it went round the track like greased lightning, a fact learned at your knee and confirmed by Rev. McClusky at Sunday School—and which has earned me a bit of revenue down the years, I can tell you. Well, Eddie carts me off to the Whinging Pom self-service diner for a bite. I had prawn curry while he as usual stormed through half the bloody State potato crop and a steak like a family Bible. Then, with his mouth full, he suddenly tells me we have been selected for a special mission. Germ warfare!

Eh? I says, thinking he meant paddling up the Yangtze and lobbing empty bean tins ashore into which we have coughed to obtain the microbes of the Common Cold. But to my astonishment I then learn that China was not our target at all. Instead, we are going to invade France! It seems that Canberra has decided on a pre-emptive strike as a sign of our displeasure at the way the buggers are blocking our agricultural products at the EEC. Our gallant Kiwi allies are sending their armed surfboard as well and the plan is for us to swim up the Frog canals until we get to the major wine-growing areas. Then we release our warheads which are full of a new and deadly type of Phylloxera that will kill all the vines within the week and bring the country to its knees, sobbing with thirst.

Anyway, Eddie was telling me this when, all of a sudden, the combination of the curry and the excitement was too much for me and I was struck by a violent attack of Farouk's Revenge. Leaping to my feet I raced to the gents but Clarence, the chef and an ex-British Leyland shop steward, was in there reading *Truth*. He remained where he was, chuckling at my predicament and sighing over the nudes. So I went streaking next door to the Squatters Bank and, beating at one of those bulletproof glass screens with the knife and fork which, in the heat of the moment, I still carried with me, I screamed, "Where's the dunny?" Well, ma, you can guess the rest. The cashier thought I was yelling where's the *money* and the cops arrived with commendable speed, thank Christ, handcuffed me and sped me off to the station with wailing sirens where, not a moment too soon, I was able to use their convenience. Everyone had a good laugh in court and that is now the end of the matter.

We sail for France any day now and my thoughts, as always, will be with you. How are things down at the funeral parlour? I think it's bloody disgraceful that Mr Boswell makes you bring your own bucket and Flash and I reckon you ought to leave his slabs unwashed.

All the best.

Your loving son,
Dave

"*What we propose to do is remove your head, have a look inside your neck, and then close you up again. It is a brand new technique and it would be less than candid of me to pretend that it does not involve certain dangers. The question is: How badly do you want to get rid of that cough?*"

LET'S PARLER FRANGLAIS!

Le Railcard

Monsieur: Bonjour.
Caissier: Bonjour, monsieur.
Monsieur: Je veux aller à Shrewsbury.
Caissier: 1er, 2ème, un-way, deux-way, cheap-jour, football-terror-spécial . . .?
Monsieur: Un-way ordinaire, svp.
Caissier: £19.50.
Monsieur: Pour quatre.
Caissier: £78.
Monsieur: Ah! Mais j'ai un railcard!
Caissier: Oh, Jésus.
Monsieur: Pour ma femme j'ai un Deux-Parents Famille Nucléaire railroad. Regardez: la carte avec sa photo.
Caissier: C'est une photo de Jimmy Savile.
Monsieur: Non, c'est ma femme qui a une resemblance curieuse au jockey de disques célèbre. C'est très utile dans les trains. Et les discos.
Caissier: Alors, 50p pour la femme.
Monsieur: Bon. Pour ma fille, j'ai un Teenage-Problem Railcard.
Caissier: Un Teenage-Problem Railcard? Vous prenez le Michael?
Monsieur: Mais non. C'est un nouveau railcard. Il garantit que votre adolescent pimplé et gawkeux peut voyager libre *à condition que* 1) il ne démolit pas les fittings 2) il ne terrorise pas les passagers avec les idées trotskyistes 3) il ne déraille pas le train 4) il ne devient pas plâtré avec Brun de Chateauneuf.
Caissier: Bon. Un ticket gratuit. Et le quatrième?
Monsieur: C'est Birgit, notre au pair de Copenhagen. Pour elle, j'ai une Au-Pair Runaround Free-Flirt Railcard. Regardez, sa photo.
Caissier: C'est encore une photo de Jimmy Savile.
Monsieur: Toutes les jeunes filles de Danemark ressemblent à Jimmy Savile OBE.
Caissier: Mais l'Au-Pair Railcard n'existe pas!
Monsieur: OK, OK. J'ai ici un Anglo-Danois Scandifriendship Railcard.
Caissier: Je ne le connais pas.
Monsieur: En ce cas, je désire un ticket communal pour moi, ma femme et Birgit. Regardez, mon Ménage-à-Trois Fun-Threesome Railcard! J'ai une photo *très* intéressante!
Caissier: OK, OK. Vous êtes le winner. £29.50, svp.
Monsieur: £29.50? C'est beaucoup.
Caissier: Durant notre conversation, on a annoncé une augmentation de prix de 15%. Tough chance. Et si vous ne regardez sharp, on va fermer la gare de Shrewsbury. Next svp!

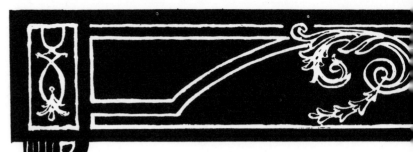

NO SWET

In the week when the televising of the Society of West End Theatre awards has yet again reassured millions of stay-at-home viewers about how little they have been missing, we can reveal the answers to the forthcoming SWET questionnaire. People are not going to the theatre . . .

EXIT

Because the box-office telephones do not answer or, when they do answer, it is only a recorded message, often inaudible, telling you to ring back later or try next week or please speak now this is a recording.

Because ten pounds per ticket is a lot of money to pay to have your feet trodden on by five West German businessmen who don't understand why they aren't at the London Palladium.

Because not enough young playwrights are writing in monosyllables readily comprehensible to conventions of Scandinavian toy salesmen with a couple of hours to spare before returning to Heathrow.

Because when you've seen thirty-five Alan Ayckbourn couples complaining about the state of middle-class marriage in Britain today, it is somehow more difficult to go out on a cold night and see the thirty-sixth.

Because when you have spent twenty quid on a couple of tickets, and nearly a fiver to leave the car and another fiver for the babysitter and are saving up for a drink in the interval, 35p seems a lot to pay for an advertising magazine called *Programme* which tells you that several of the leading players were once in *Crossroads*.

Because even if you don't mind queueing at the bar for thirteen minutes of a fifteen-minute interval on account of the theatre management being too mean to employ more than one elderly lady who has difficulty finding the gin bottle let alone pouring same, it is then a little depressing to find you are paying more than twice the price of alcohol at the pub next door and that nobody has bothered to fill the ice bucket since Monday.

Because it is more than a little depressing to discover that of every £ you pay into the box-office, 15p is going in VAT to a government which has done about as much for the live theatre as Oliver Cromwell.

Because there's a limit to how many plays you can see about world-famous cellists suffering from multiple sclerosis before you go home and kick the *Guardian* arts page.

Because it has apparently not occurred to even one box-office manager that if seats were sold by row and not by number, and if then the first to arrive automatically occupied the centre of a row allowing later arrivals to spread out from there, the need for anyone ever to clamber over anyone else in a theatre would be immediately and forever ended.

Because it has apparently not occurred to even one central London theatre proprietor that his building could also house a bookshop, an art gallery, a wine bar and a daytime cinema, thereby remaining in use for fifteen rather than three hours in any 24. This in turn would mean evening theatregoers arriving to find a warm and living building instead of a kind of theatrical cupboard which has been opened about five minutes before they got there.

Because now that every cab-driver and television comedian in town tells you who did it in *The Mousetrap*, there isn't a lot of point in going there either.

Because there is something deeply unnerving about being shown to your seat by a little lady even older than the one behind the bar who makes you feel that she'd rather be home watching the television and why on earth aren't you?

Because most West End theatres are about as welcoming as an underground station on the District Line.

Because more than two people at a box-office window constitutes a queue, and the longer this queue can be kept there motionless the better it looks to any passer-by; queues of two can thus be kept motionless for hours while the box-office manager conducts lengthy and incomprehensible telephone conversations with Keith Prowse.

Because when you've seen one two-character musical about a zany girl and a divorced composer who may or may not be going to get it together within the next two hours, orchestrations permitting, you've seen why Broadway is also dying.

Because now that it is possible to get into *Evita*, who wants to admit that they haven't already done so?

Because there are only so many times that a human of average intelligence can stay awake through *Oklahoma!*.

Because an ad on television is reckoned to be a sure sign that a show is in real financial difficulties; therefore nobody goes to see it because if it's in financial trouble enough to be advertising on television it can't be any good; therefore no show likes to advertise on television; therefore no television viewer knows what's playing; therefore all shows are in more financial trouble than they need to be.

Because at least in a pub theatre you can walk out at the interval having not lost much more than the price of a pint; to walk out of a West End theatre now is like tearing up ten-pound notes.

Because there are only so many times you can see Anna Neagle without being reduced to tears.

Because the setting up of a half-price ticket booth in Leicester Square a mere ten years after the idea was first mooted is much like trying to end the Iran-Iraq war by sending milk-bottle tops to *Blue Peter*.

Because when was the last time you saw a good play in the West End that hadn't already been playing at the National or the RSC for at least a year?

Because in headlong flight down memory lane the British commercial theatre is now looking so far back over its shoulder as to be in severe danger of breaking its neck.

Because when the main attraction down Shaftesbury Avenue is two middle-aged men dressed up as Victorian ladies singing highlights from *HMS Pinafore*, and when *The Sound of Music* is likely to be the main attraction for 1981, the time has seriously come to think about turning the whole West End into London's third airport.

Tick reasons in order of precedence. Japanese tourists may apply for simultaneous translation. Barclaycard and Access will do nicely.

THE DRINKING PUBLIC

A collection of actual photographs observed through the red-rimmed lenses of a bleary-eyed **ARNOLD ROTH**

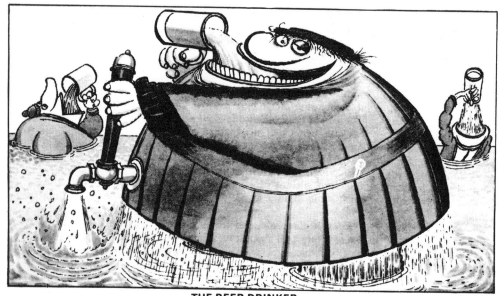

THE BEER DRINKER

THE PUNCH DRINKER

CHAMPAGNE DRINKERS

A DRINKER OF WATER

THE ALCHOMIST

THE WHISKEY DRINKER

THE GIN DRINKER

BRANDY DRINKERS

A PEACH DAQUIRI

A VODKA DRINKER

"You leave the Pennsylvania Station 'bout a quarter to four, read a magazine and then you're in Baltimore . . ."

MELVYN BRAGG:

ART TRANS- PLANT

IF the uneasy crown of absolute Art dictatorship were to be planted on my head by the rather unsteady hands (it is Wednesday afternoon and he's been to Lunch) of Mr Punch—then, the brief asks, what would you do?

After turning it down thrice like the man in the play by the Royal Shakespeare Company's House Dramatist and thinking it over thrice like the man in all those German fairy tales, I would first of all and hereby institute a United Nations Art Council or U.N.A.C. as it would come to be rather unfortunately nicknamed. U.N.A.C. would need to look out for what Hemingway referred to rather touchingly as his *cojones*.

And the best way to do that would be to turn up at 105 Piccadilly, London W1 and chat with the Arts Council of Great Britain—a thoroughly fertile organ.

It would discover an efficient subsidising concern which firmly underpins a national network of theatres, galleries, opera and ballet companies, orchestras, magazines, individual composers, painters, writers, conductors and performing artists across the colour spectrum from the Respected to the Vain. All at a cost to the tax-payer of just over £1 per head per annum.

"How so?" would be the question thought up by the U.N.A.C.S. (the 'S' earning its place as Council turns into Councillors). Firstly, by employing a small regular expert staff (less than 250); secondly, by persuading large numbers of those involved in the arts—from artists themselves through impresarios to devoted amateurs—to give up considerable unpaid time and effort in order to advise and help direct; thirdly and most important, by making the state money breed. This should be of the greatest interest because it creates work and money and helps artists.

This is how it works with, say, the National Theatre. The Arts Council puts in about three million: without that the National Theatre could have no basic security of operation. But out of that three million, through sale of tickets and, increasingly, sale of its productions to other theatres, to television, films and the foreign market, the National Theatre builds and runs a ten million pounds plus business which employs and trains some hundreds of

highly skilled actors, designers, electricians, musicians, administrators and writers while entertaining and quite possibly civilizing thousands of people every night. By any standards, subsidised art is a sound commercial proposition, an undeniable promoter and creator of skilled jobs and an attraction to the public.

The U.N.A.C.S., then, much impressed, would be made (although the arguments are self-evident, being a tyrant means that I can *insist* that they are self-evident and, therefore, to BE OBEYED AT ALL TIMES AND IN ALL PLACES!) to scatter abroad, and erect Arts Councils across the planet. Like a chain of everlit beacons they would blaze out the illuminations of music, the insights of poetry and the truths of fiction and drama sending flying that Armada of Philistinism which ignores the fact that good art makes a lot of sense and, more important for the businessmen and that business part of ordinary men to whom this is addressed, money.

Remember the exchange between Sam Goldwyn and George Bernard Shaw when the former wanted the latter to come and work in Hollywood; after lengthy negotiations, George Bernard Shaw terminated the enterprise with this explanation of why it would never work— "All you are interested in is Art—while all I am interested in is Money." Metro-Goldwyn-Mayer was not in the state subsidising business: had it been, Shaw would have found what he wanted—a place to present his work on his own terms which was independent of all Big Brothers *and* a money-spinner.

This is the as yet under-appreciated invention of the Arts Council of Great Britain: if you are prepared to *lose* some money and have the sense to put it into the hands of those who want to produce excellent work *and* monitor it all professionally, then you are in a boom industry. British Arts Business Inc. has been one of the outstanding financial and industrial success stories of the last twenty years. And there's every reason why it could ring the globe, for artists are compulsive internationalists.

So that would be the first edict. The U.N.A.C. would have a secondary purpose which would be to provide the Theatre for Rows, Debates or Disputations as they would be called, and the Disputation Theatres (or the D.T.s as it would come to be known, affectionately, by the artists who used it) would provide that forum made necessary for a world now sizzling with artists from every continent pushing their wares and tears. It would be at the D.T.s that Saul Bellow would take on those American Academics who, he has argued, are destroying the novel; in the D.T.s that David Hockney would meet the New York Abstract Expressionists at five yards; in that same D.T. that Kurosawa would talk (through several interpreters) with Ken Russell, that Solzhenitsyn would dispute with the American Academy, that Woody Allen would argue with himself and there too that a new photograph of Samuel Beckett would be shown in public for the first time.

To keep employed those politicians ousted by the revolution provoked by U.N.A.C. and worldwide subsidised art, delegations from all over the globe would be admitted to the D.T.s in the off-season at a cut rate to discuss "Whither Anglo-Afro-Aggro-theatre?" and "Whether?". Michael Grade—by then Controller of All British Television Worth Looking At—would take out a permanent satellite (or lend them his own) in order to transmit the D.T.s to a world by then red-hot for More Art and More Artists (or M.A.M.A. as it will come to be known). The cultural empires will make the old political Kingdom look like Leggo. (As it came to be known.)

Then there are the banks. There ought to be universal tape, film and music banks. Happy the man who had taken the trouble to interview Dickens, Thackeray, Trollope and George Eliot; for he would by now have inherited a great deal of wealth as well as wisdom. There is already so much interest in those who write and paint and sing and dance that the people who banked lengthy, detailed interviews and comments on tape or film would be doing posterity a service and themselves, most likely, a favour. This would need a very substantial investment to get it under way. In one sense, and as a by-product of our main purpose, *The South Bank Show* already does it, concentrating on living artists—and that requires a handsome investment for LWT. To make it work effectively on a world-scale would need Getty-money. Being a dictator that would be no problem: appropriate.

Just as scarcity and the regression in part of the higher reaches of Western (and increasingly other) economies to barter has resulted in the hyper-inflation of the price of paintings, so, in the new age of culture and leisure on the brink of which the industrial world stands, but a chip away, all that can

be properly judged to detail and enrich the arts would rocket in value of all kinds. Banks then, of interviews, readings, sketches, notebooks, talks, teaching, playing, performing to aid and abet those intent on raiding the cultures.

There is a problem with primitive art. It could be argued that much of the purest art being done at the moment is being woven into rugs in African villages or painted into papier-mâché in Kashmir or stitched into carpets in Qum. The only way to keep the work going while abolishing the dreadful condition which forms the context of most of this work would be to wave a magic wand and rebuild the places which produce this art without disturbing a hair. Increase payment 1000-fold and accord sure acclaim to those who were artists on the side as it were (being shepherds or farmers, generally, most of the time) and surely they would be content to be fulltime (with poetic licence) artists.

All that should be possible. We encircle the world with fructive subsidy, then make a global talk-in theatre, tele-transmitted worldwide; we establish banks of artists and ensure the eternal continuation of "primitive" work.

On what the Tories call the Commercial Front we employ individual back-up. We back up a rich individual and/or multi-national against a wall and ask him is he going to be shamed by the state? Will the Medici of Tomorrow be the Faceless Bureaucrat of Today or will it be B.P., Tiny Rowland or Freddie Laker? In short we exercise all the tyrannical arts to persuade the Commercial Front that Fame is worth the money. Wise maidens we employ, commandeering gurus fly in from all parts to the conference of the Rich and the seriously Rich. Having convinced them that money is the root of all glory, then they must be let rip. That is the capitalist ethic.

However, lads, before you leave—a few guide-lines:

No more money to the Russians for ballet until they come up with something really good post-1917; no more for large and enigmatic stone or wooden statues from the South Seas; no more "made-for-TV movies" from anywhere; no more for music or allied noises from followers of Schoenberg, Berg or Iceberg; no more French; no more for cartoons from Eastern Europe; nor Korean Dancing, South American Poetry nor English Fiction; nor more for flash museums in California designed to bump up the price of over-expensive paintings; no more for Conceptual Art, just think about it instead; no more for Bombay Talkies. For all of these will take care of themselves.

Money, thought and glory will surely follow those who will follow their own noses, back their own taste. Hie to Zimbabwe for opera, to Sri Lanka for movies, to England for musicals, to Germany for (careful!), to China for social comedy. Be storm-troopers of culture. Burn the time-sheets and the work-graphs, tear up the financial pages of the newspapers, the stock exchange reports! From today, the world is set on a course for culture. It has nowhere else to go.

We are moving out of the Age of Aquarius into the Age of Art. Those who have spotted the trend are already serene, affluent, full of that inner bronzed glow of well-being which will sustain them throughout their days. Art is the only true rival to War. They know that already, and see that soon ten thousand orchestras will play Mozart simultaneously to a hundred satellites whence it will ring and re-echo around the planet and happy folk in all parts will lift up their heads from canvases, books and designs, will lay aside their own instruments and instructors and listen to the music. The day will surely come.

HOME HINTS

Fill festive bins now with Doppelgänger Drittereich Spätlese to partner poultry. Warm drizzle from an anticyclone over Koblenz in April '75 and intensive mulching in the Moselle have led to rare suppleness of aromatic sinew with a dry, Quixotic smatch that lends piquancy to Paxo, yet will not smother sprouts or crowd your after-shave.

For the stocking, monks from just east of Montelimar make a 70° proof almond fudge that cannot be bettered with mince pies, unless it's by Hungary's kale and bilberry liqueurs, fermented in vats of Silesian whey to give it "chalkiness" and traditionally served with a candied asparagus cake. Moldavian sherry is a good, if salty buy.

With sultana-rich sweets, soaked overnight in Caspian kir and smothered in an emulsified armagnac sauce, most palates prefer some fructiferous, full-bodied, Catalonian raw spirit, steeped in nutmeg and molasses, then mixed half-and-half with damson rum from Seville or flamed with a teaspoonful of well-honeyed mead.

Something at the Door

I WAS about to cook a small steak. In fact I'd already rolled it in pepper and dropped it twice when the bell rang.

That reminds me—when I've finished telling you this I must sweep up the pepper: get that trodden all over the house and the sneezes could be on-going.

She was about forty-two, and flustered. Nice, though, I thought. She said she was terribly sorry and hated to ask, but could she possibly use my telephone. Her car . . . she gestured towards stationary lights outside my front gates. "I shall have to get my husband to come and fetch me," she said. She hated doing this, she said, dialling.

It was the day it snowed in the south, you may remember. Brilliant sunny morning. As my gardener, who only comes when he wants a quick fiver, hadn't been for ten days, I'd even swept some leaves round the front. Maddening, really, because the gardener had arrived to sweep some leaves after it clouded over, the snow arriving more or less simultaneously. So he sat in the greenhouse for a pound, and bicycled home in my second-best raincoat.

This was why I said to her that it was no night to be stuck with your car broken down, and then went in the kitchen, which was beginning to smell of empty frying-pans over a good flame. Also, I didn't want her to think I was the sort of man to hang over a woman's private telephone call, watching that she didn't nick one of the umbrellas, and perhaps learning that her husband was called Hubert.

But none of that arose, because after I judged the silence to have gone on long enough I came out of the kitchen, shutting the door smartly against escaping fumes, and said, "No luck?" None, she said. Her husband didn't seem to be there. She said she didn't know what to do.

"What to do," I said, masterful in other people's crises though defeated without a struggle in my own—"is come in and have a cup of tea, and try again later."

Don't worry. I knew just how nice I was being.

"That's terribly nice of you," she said.

I denied this.

She said the trouble was that the children were in the car.

"Bring them in," I said, as disarming as hell.

Luckily, I'd cleaned up a bit that afternoon. Removed a row of socks from the sitting-room radiator. Found an old Murraymint under the coffee table. Emptied the ashtrays. It was really only a matter now, when receiving guests, to shut some newspapers in cupboards and drag a couple of heavy chairs into more sociable positions. Not that the children might want to sit in chairs. I could only guess their ages. If she was forty-two, itself a guess, they could be grown men and women. On the other hand, people marry a lot these days. They could be tots by a second husband, and prefer to run about screaming.

It could do no harm, I thought, as she went out to the car trailing gratitude, to see what I could muster in the way of entertainment. Board games, lemonade. I was pretty sure I could lay my hands on some of these, but for some deep-seated, perhaps Freudian reason, didn't wish to be caught in the act of doing so.

I put the kettle on, and a tape of Emil Gilels. In different rooms. If the tots didn't like Chopin they could stuff it. Big, grown-up children of twenty or so could sit and listen. We could talk about music. Which reminded me, in a quick move, to take *Beat Me Daddy, Four to a Bar* off the piano and stick up the Albeniz tango instead. I can't play either, not for an audience. I just didn't want them to think they were coming into a punk house.

If we didn't talk about music, which I don't know much about, we could talk about cars. Broken-down cars. Breakdowns generally. The places we'd broken down in our time, and the way we'd been variously received at houses we'd had to ask if we could telephone from. But I didn't know how long that would last. We could go on to the weather, particularly that day's, which had been so unusually unusual. "I *know*," I could hear myself saying. "This morning was brilliant. I was actually out in front sweeping leaves."

"Were you really?" I could hear her saying, wondering if it was worth dialling her husband again.

"Then," I heard myself continuing, "about five minutes after the gardener came . . ."

We could talk about gardeners. By this time I should have any big children drinking scotch. Possibly their mother too. But tea would be available. Or, of course, coffee. We could talk about the price of coffee. Well, perhaps not. It might look as if I—

These arrangements passed through my mind in a flash, including the inspiration that the smaller children could go and watch the black and white TV in the dining room. Or they could join the rest of us and watch the colour TV in the sitting room. Or we could talk about TV, even if nobody wanted to watch it.

But I went into the dining room and switched the set on in there. It takes some twiddling, that one. I wanted to be able to say, "There you are, kids," and it would be *Crackerjack* right off, no inconvenience. They'd all be glad to be in the warm, that was for sure. She'd left the front door open. Icy. It would seem unchivalrous to shut it. I turned up the central heating, and was able to see a confusion of figures moving around in the car. "Hello, you guys," I should say to them. Breezy. "In you come and watch the Scrabble—the telly. Have some tea, coffee, scotch." But I didn't want them to see me seeing them, and I went back to the sitting room, moving my chair so that when they came crowding in they could see me. You can overdo breeziness with strangers. You don't want a big production number. Just sit there, reading the same paragraph in the paper several times, a model of composure but with the human hospitality just showing.

It was bloody cold with all those doors

"They want to negotiate a musical instruments limitation treaty."

open, I don't mind telling you.

And got colder. I didn't know what they were doing out there. It did occur to me, though, that it had taken more than a flash for these arrangements to pass through my mind. Gilels was running out. As I remembered, there was prolonged applause on that tape. I didn't want them to come in to that. They could think I was trying to be funny. People are thrown by those things. I wound the tape back a few ballades and nocturnes, got it just right. Nice soft bit. Unobtrusive. Civilised.

What I would do, I thought, when they finally trooped in with their hair smoothed and stockings pulled up—well, I expect hers were pulled up already, I hadn't liked to look at our first short meeting, but it was a windy evening, and her hair was already flying out in wisps when she first stood on the step saying she hated to trouble me, and she'd smoothed it with a big handbag. Nerves. In a crisis you get them—what I would do, I thought, was make the tea and leave them all alone together for a bit. Acclimatise. Pick their chairs. Look at my more impressive party-time invitations, where I'd pulled them out on the mantel so that they overlapped showing crests and gold edges. Then I would . . .

By God, it was cold. It was really this that sent me to the front door again. You can shut doors courteously, after all. I put the porch light on, denoting that the welcome was in no way diminished by door shutting, and it was as I did so that I saw they'd all gone off, whatever they were. Presumably in the car, as that had gone off too.

I remembered hearing a whirring some time before. Thought it was Emil winding back. So I'm glad the starter finally started OK.

Still, I'm wondering what I did to offend them. Or offend her, anyway. Or them as well, I suppose, when she told them. "No, mum," they said to her, protectively. "You're certainly not going back to that screwball, in a house like that, just to say the car's OK and we're off now and thank him very much and you hated having to ask to use the telephone."

I hope she got home all right. And found out why her husband wasn't there. I did think, for an hour or two, that she might use her own telephone. I was expecting a couple of rather important phone calls anyway, but I didn't get them, and I didn't get hers either.

But that, I tell myself, was only because she'd left mine off the hook. I wouldn't have found that, if I hadn't been trying to find the steak. Which, oddly, was on the telephone shelf. That could have been it, of course. When she told them I was funny that way, unnaturally eager to get strangers into the house on a snowy evening, and keeping a dusty steak by the telephone.

I don't think the fact, which I've just noticed, that I was wearing a tracksuit with three white stripes down the side, the pants tucked into fisherman's stockings, also a Los Angeles Dodgers' baseball cap, could have had anything to do with it. Anyway, we could have talked about that if she'd come back, agreed that it was the ideal gear for leaf sweeping.

Meanwhile, if you happen to know a nice woman of about forty-two, mother of an assorted family, who smooths her hair with a big handbag and had recent car trouble in Haywards Heath, just say I was asking after her and she can call again any time and explain. I've replaced the burnt-out kettle. Tea is still on, if that's her fancy.

"Where's your ambition, Omar—do you want to be a eunuch all your life?"

"Business appears to be looking up."

35

"Sorry I'm late back from lunch—I was reading 'Earthly Powers' in W. H. Smith's."

"I understand they've just bought a book of poems."

Book Ends

HOLLAND on the library cuts

"When money becomes a little less tight, we're hoping to join a book club."

"Before the spending cuts I was well-read. Now I just know things."

"All I could get for you from the library was Milton Friedman's 'Free to Choose'."

PAUL
THEROUX
on
Chemists

CHEMIST'S shops are not drug-stores, but then neither are drug-stores. Anyone in my home-town who wanted a birthday card or a hot-dog or a cigar or a banana split or a camera or a pound of fudge or a fountain pen—you name it—went to Craddock Apothecary. Drugs were a sideline, and the name "apothecary" the sort of seventeenth century locution considered stylish in Massachusetts, like "hosiery" and "drapery". In fact, like all the rest, Craddock Apothecary was the most general of general stores, not run by Abel Drugger (complexion the texture of Weetabix, scrabbling his pill-roller or socking his pestle into his mortar with a view to curing quinsy), but rather by an Armenian whose degree in pharmacy had turned him overnight into a soda-jerk.

"You don't sell used cars," the joke goes, "and you have the nerve to call this place a drug-store?"

In my own neighbourhood there was a drug-store run by a man called Fordie White. His politics would have qualified him for the Grand Kleagleship of the KKK, but he was otherwise a good druggist (as Ezra Pound was otherwise a good versifier), which is to say that along with his soda fountain and Back-to-School Department, he had a post office. "Greece?" he snorted, weighing a letter for me one day. "Hell of a name for a place, Greece." It was said that if you pushed a fifty-cent piece at him, palm downward, he would understand immediately and hand you a box of contraceptives.

How drug-stores came to sell everything is easy enough to explain in American terms. For a very long time, and because of the putative nature of their business, they were the only places open on a Sunday. Now many are open all night (*We Never Close!*). They grew departments to meet the demand; they are usually at the centre of town, and they are at the very centre of American culture. If I am in Washington and need a typewriter ribbon or a pair of socks on Sunday morning, I know where to go—Peoples' Drugstore (the commie-sounding name is misleading: it was founded by Gurney J. Peoples).

The only thing an American drug-store does not sell is liquor, which is interesting, because their British counterparts have made a reputation selling beer—and wine-making apparatus. No, those rubber tubes and bizarre diaphragms are not the latest thing in colonic irrigation, but merely a way of getting yourself blind drunk on gallons of fructified joy-juice. *Save 5p a Pint!* the advert says, over the price tag—a hundred quid's worth of plastic dustbins, retorts and beakers. Justifying alcoholism by turning it into a hobby one can pursue with do-it-yourselfer's virtue is very much a British thing. Americans can always buy the same kind of urinous Chablis from California for next to nothing, because the grapes are harvested by pathetic Chicanos who are paid in pinto beans.

At what point did the British chemist's shop branch out? Was it the same year the Automobile Association began selling pony-trek holidays and waterbeds? It is hard to say, but the result is odd. There was a time when the only place you could buy jars of babyfood in Britain was at the chemist's (figure that one out), but now the babyfood is lost amidst the records, books, radios and kitchenware. The drug-counter (*Prescriptions*) has become foreshortened and moved sideways into the corner—just over there, where the bespectacled baldy in the white smock is funnelling green pellets into an amber bottle (is the pharmaceutical game more than pill-counting and doing sentry-duty on uppers and downers?)

In another age, chemist's shops were at the frontier of preventive medicine. The great shift came with their misguided Americanization, but as with most British imports a dead hand was laid upon it. And yet, look closer, as I did not long ago, and you see one of the most sinister developments in British life since those vertical logs of sinewy meat started appearing in shop windows—you know the ones, dripping poison and basted by hairy *fellahin* and so germ-laden they ought to be served in petri dishes.

I began to understand. Head Office (actually, Ray Quelch at his office in the satellite town of High Tar) sent down a memo: *Why isn't the toothpaste moving? Shift it!* And then a genius—it wasn't baldy in the white smock, more likely it was the hag at the check-out counter bucking for a promotion—said, "You want to sell more toothpaste, ducky? Then sell sweets! Sell them by the peck, sell anything that threatens the enamel of their canines!"

The logic was irrefutable, and so it obviously went: you couldn't sell trusses if you did not also sell rowing-machines; hi-cal soft drinks were the answer to those diet pills gathering dust on the shelf, and the wine-making equipment must have increased a thousand-fold the sale of aspirin and stomach-pumps. Of the merchandise that began to appear in chemist's shops over the past few years, there is very little that does not make you fat, sick, drunk, crazy or that does not damage you in a way that will, in time, be undone by that very same chemist's shop. Chemist's shops are now harmful to your health! Sorrow makes me mute on the subject of sleeping pills taken by pregnant women which have resulted in horribly deformed babies, but the women certainly didn't get these pills in an off-licence, and it is a fact that the shops that sold thalidomide also sold wheelchairs.

I cannot read the rest of my notes. Something here about American pharmacists becoming paramedics ("That's a real nasty rash—here try some of this") because American doctors are so expensive. Something about the British being mad about patent medicines and Americans fixated on antisepsis and bad breath (name another country where you can buy mouthwash by the gallon). And what's this? Oh, yes, the Hammersmith episode. I'm in Hammersmith, returning from the Frayn satire on business, *Make or Break*. I see a shop window: rakes, watering-can. Gardening gloves. Dish of fuchsias. *Must see to the garden*, I mumble, *even if it gives me a backache, which it will*. I look at the shop-sign. Boots.

"'Ere, look—you can stick things with it!"

A MESSAGE FROM SIR KEITH JOSEPH

Hello!

As many of you know, I am not loony. It therefore follows that when I invite people to take jobs for less money, I know what I am talking about. A loony, and there is solid medical opinion behind me on this, would invite people to take jobs for *more* money, thus contributing to soaring inflation. At a time of soaring inflation, it surely makes sense to take jobs for less money, so that you get poorer and poorer. I think we made that clear in our election manifesto. I think we said—I cannot quote exactly, it's some time ago, and I have these terrible pains in my head sometimes, you know those days when you just want to fall down and bite the carpet?—I think we said that, when we were elected, starving could not be ruled out. I clearly remember something about butter only making us fat.

Most people will readily agree, what are those green lights, what are those green lights, most people will readily agree that what made Britain great in the glorious nineteenth century was the willingness of her people to go up chimneys. Was not the Crimean War supposed to have been won up the chimneys of Eton? Now, I do not suggest, IS ANYONE THERE?, that we should send, FOR CHRIST'S SAKE COME OUT, I CAN HEAR YOU TALKING, OH IT'S THE CAT, that we should send small children up chimneys in 1980! Goodness me, we in the Conservative Party do not want to turn the clocks back, there's plenty of work for small children, I should think, or will be when we get the cruise missiles working WELL I KNOW WHAT I BLOODY MEAN, without sending them up chimneys. My suggestion is that we should send adults up chimneys. Very soon, as our economic policies come right and people get thinner and thinner, it will be no problem at all for a grown man to get up a chimney, or, indeed, for a whole family to *live* up a chimney, something which I know you will see makes sense of our forward-looking local authority housing cuts.

It all begins, suddenly, to fall into place, doesn't it? That is what economic planning is all about. Will we, I hear you ask, get a lot of money for going up chimneys, thereby cutting the unemployment figure down to an acceptable eight million by 1990? Well—and here is the beauty of it—no. You will get practically nothing for going up chimneys, thereby helping enormously to bring down inflation.

It will also have what we in the Industry Ministry call a beneficial spin-off in that, in the case of families living up council chimneys, infant and geriatric mortality rates will rise steeply, thereby eliminating soaring welfare costs, and helping enormously to bring down inflation.

Many of you have written to me, tell me about the rabbits George, many of you have written to me expressing terrible fears about bread lines. Will there be bread lines, you ask? Have no fear, I reply, *of course* there will be bread lines, our great party has a heart as well as a head, we should not let the people of this country come down from their chimneys looking for food and being given a stone. Even now, 80,000 of our top civil servants are setting up a Ministry of Bread Lines, designed to work in close co-operation with the new Department of Soup Kitchens. Of course, when North Sea Oil runs out, we plan to streamline these two areas into the Department of Bread Soup, which I'm told is really quite nourishing if you IS ANYBODY RINGING BELLS IS ANYBODY RINGING BLOODY BELLS?

Where was I? Oh yes, the Third Test Match. Well, my view is, if the dusky buggers won't co-operate with our police force, why the hell should we be expected to face three short balls an over in failing light?

Living up chimneys on bread soup is naturally something we shall have to discuss with the unions, but when they see how it helps enormously to bring down inflation, I don't think there'll be too many problems and if there are, then I expect we shall call in the troops and bayonet every last Trotskyite bastard until the gutters run red with their miserable blood, the TUC conference would be a good time, we could lock the doors and set fire to it and as they broke out we could have a few good chaps on the Bren guns YA-TA-TA-TA-TA-TA-TA-TA-TA.

Then again, if I may turn for a moment to the shape of my secretary's legs, we could help enormously to bring down inflation by setting up a Department of Young People Soup. If our calculations are correct, there will be no jobs at all for school-leavers by 1985, so surely the best course is to turn school-leavers into soup. It would relieve strain on the universities, and go down a treat with some '47 Margaux I have been keeping for a dirty weekend, and also make room in chimneys for all the money we shall have to print to help enormously to bring down inflation. Furthermore, was that a headless horseman, furthermore, I firmly believe that . . .

ANTHONY HOLDEN:

TRANSATLANTIC CABLES

FROM Binion's Horseshoe casino in Las Vegas, Nevada, I bring glad tidings of great joy to those aged 25 and under, tidings of great gloom to those of us ageing fast enough to think that senior citizens, let alone policemen, look younger every day.

The 1980 world professional poker championship, known hereabouts as the World Series of Poker, has been won by Stuart "The Kid" Ungar, a 26-year-old who looks sixteen, and who is today some $900,000 richer than he was last week, when still in nappies.

The Kid, a professional poker player for precisely one year (having become so adept at gin rummy that no one in the world—and I mean *the world*—would give him a game) stands four-feet-six in the saddle. He strained to reach the microphone on CBS Network News, his voice breaking with emotion rather than age. As he paid gracious tribute to such poker greats as Doyle "Texas Dolly" Brunson, Amarillo "Slim" Preston, Walter "Pug" Pearson and Johnny "The Man" Moss, over whose collective poker wisdom his tiny feet had trampled to devastating effect during four days and nights of unremitting card-sharpery.

That Monday, seventy-three of the world's greatest poker players had sat down for the championships, each placing $10,000 on the table in front of him (or her; four women were taking part). By Thursday afternoon, The Kid had won the lot, thus earning the right to keep half—a cool $360,500—as his first prize.

Across the street in The Golden Nugget, where your correspondent was celebrating his birthday in a brash game of five- and ten-dollar stud, the news from the Horseshoe fell like Lava from nearby Mount St Helens on a table of hitherto expressionless faces. Winners joined losers in an exchange of glances which might plausibly have signalled cardiac arrest. Their faces then sagged into drop-jawed aspects of ineffable gloom.

The game had just got going again, all arms feeling just that much more geriatric as they stretched for their chips, when a runner arrived from the Horseshoe with the kidney-punch. The Kid had placed a $10,000 bet on himself to win—at fifty to one. Another half million stacked away.

Things at my table turned ugly. "Silent Harry", across from me, a man from whom I had not heard one word in three days and nights of play, sought out the youngest face at the table with his meanest look. Though no chicken, and indeed a year older than he had been twenty-four hours before, the youngest face at the table belonged—disown it as he might—to your correspondent.

"You kids," said Silent Harry witheringly, shooting a morose glance at my (then) satisfying pile of chips. "You kids oughta go find a job, not sit here all day playing poker. It's no life for a youngster. Get a lifetime's work behind you before you sit down here again."

I got what seemed like a lifetime's sleep that night (day? in Las Vegas, it's hard to tell) before gingerly returning to the table. Silent Harry, summoning all the eloquence at his command, grunted disapprovingly. His companions, known to him man and (hard-working) boy these fifty years, nodded their endorsement of his remarks. I had them psyched.

It was due to no skill of mine, but to their own simmering rage, that I proceeded to mop up, quitting (uncharacteristically)

"Tell me, how long have you had these hallucinations?"

while ahead. Blinking into the sudden sunlight, a reminder that there was a world outside, where people walk up and down pavements unaided, putting coins into newspaper stands in the belief that they are slot machines, I decided to seek out The Kid.

The Kid was holding court jauntily in the back room of the Horseshoe, oblivious to the popping of flashlights and the whirr of TV cameras. Someone thrust a box of brand-name cigars into his hand, asked him to smile and popped another flashlight. A few more grand, I supposed morosely.

The Kid, according to him, was running a

fever. It had dampened his concentration a bit, or the whole thing might have been over a bit quicker. Was he married? No. Make that yes. Make that no. He had a girl friend? Er, yes. In fact, come to think of it, where the hell was she?

The next bit did for me. The Kid had told his girl that morning to get to the Horseshoe at three sharp. He thought he'd have the thing wrapped up by then. I looked at my watch. It was five past three.

I was aching for a bossy nanny to come and scoop him away, tuck him up and mop his fevered brow, tut-tutting that he'd run off downstairs like that. But I couldn't hang

around. There was unfinished business across the road.

Attempting to emulate The Kid's sashay, I strode back to Silent Harry's side thinking myself into whatever role Clint Eastwood played in *The Good, The Bad And The Ugly*. Throwing back my chair, I cast a contemptuous glance at my swollen pile of chips, designed to indicate that I assumed someone would have pinched some in my absence, but there were plenty more where they came from. No one seemed to notice.

Silent Harry, with all the excitement of Sheik Yamani finding his Premium Bond had come good, was raking in the biggest pot of the night. He played two more desultory hands, losing nothing, before getting up to leave. From the window of "the cage", as he cashed in his chips, he shot me a significant glance.

I knew what he meant, but it was no use. I had one more day in Las Vegas before returning to an American election I assumed was still going on somewhere, and these guys had 365 more hard-working days at the poker table before I could join them again next birthday. (It's become my annual treat.)

I lost remorselessly for a few hours before it happened, that uncertain turn of events which starts you winning again. It was Silent Harry, slipping back into his seat across the table, his dollar bills turned fecklessly back into hunks of plastic. I looked at him inquiringly, with what was supposed to be Jimmy Cagney's expression at the end of *Angels With Dirty Faces*.

"OK, Kid," he said, "so I couldn't sleep. So I'm back. Well, we're all kids under the skin."

He called me "Kid", I thought, entranced, and went on winning till my plane left without me.

Uncommon Prayers

The Church of England this week published *The Alternative Service Book* as a supplement to the *Book of Common Prayer* because "rapid social and intellectual changes . . . have made it desirable that new understandings of worship should find expression in new forms and styles."

The Thanksgiving of Women
After an Abortion

33   These prayers may be used in church, in hospital, in home or in the interrupted pregnancy person's place of business. The former pregnancy person will say.

34   I am well pleased that the Lord
hath heard the voice of my prayer;
The Lord hath brought me through
the snares of an unwanted pregnancy:
The Lord steadied the hand of the abortionist.
I give thanks to the Lord for delivering me
from those dreadful Mothercare clothes;
I pray to the Lord to preserve my figure.

35   And then the PRIESTPERSON will say.

          The world is full of unwanted children.
The wombs of the daughters of Eve
are too fruitful but you, Lord,
in your wisdom have given them the Pill
and if they are so goddamned idle or too
scatter-brained to take it, you, Lord,
have given them the craft
of the abortionist, praise be the name
of the Lord.

36   The erstwhile pregnancy person will then say.

          I want to keep my figure;
I want Henry to still love me;
I want a career;
I am not just a woman;
I don't want to spend my life
wiping some man's kid's bum.
I want to keep going on holiday
every year to the Dordogne
I'm all right, Jack, thanks.

The Lord is my shop steward; he putteth in my wage claim.
   He maketh me to lie down on the night shift: he restoreth
my differentials.
   And yea, though I walk through the valley of the Rhondda,
I will fear no redundancy: for thou art with me: thy closed
shop and thy wildcat strike they comfort me.

EVENING PRAYER (Shorter Form)

   May the blessings of the Father, the Off-Spring, and the Holy Ghost be amongst you and remain with you in a long-term, on-going situation.

Kneel **Our One-Parent Family**
All   **Which art in Heaven**
            Hallowed be thy name

The Form of Solemnization
of Matrimony

6   Dearly beloved, we are gathered together here in the sight of God, and in the face of this congregation, to join together this Man and this Man. Wilt thou, Brad, have this man, Bif, as thy wedded wife? Wilt thou keep him in sickness and in health and in bondage moreorless forsaking all others? Is there any bitch here who knows cause or just impediment why Brad and Bif should not be joined in Matrimony? I now pronounce you man and man. And may you cruise happily ever after.

7   A hymn may be sung or, in the case of two dikes, a her.

The Order for Holy Communion
also called The Eucharist
Rite A (supplementary)

11   The Gospel at Christmas shall be "And lo, they were called to Bethlehem to pay VAT." Following the AUDIO VISUAL EVENT (sermon OS) the PRIESTPERSON welcomes the studio audience using these or other appropriate words.

          Alleluia! Right On! Here beginneth the first lesson and my
          first guest is (name of week's guest star).
All   **Amen! Magic!**

12   While the PRIESTPERSON is preparing the COMMUNION, Valium and Perrier water, the studio audience or congregation and the backing group (choir OS) will sing the Te Valium.

Kneel The hymn "Shake off dull sloth and rise to greet the
Stand morning sacrifice" may be sung in Country and Western
Sit   style while the PRIESTPERSON is breaking
Relax the Valium capsules.

13   After the Valium and Perrier have been given out the PRIESTPERSON will turn to the audience and say.

Smoke Jesus Christ is Our Father of the Chapel!
All   **Forever and ever** *or* **At this moment in time.**

14   The PRIESTPERSON will then say.
          Fear of the Lord is the beginning of Wisdom.
All   **Alleluia! Basically!**

The PRIESTPERSON will then say these or similar words.
          Yea, and a crisis or panic situation over the Lord is the
          beginning of getting it together.

All   **I am really over the moon about Jesus Christ.**
            Amen! Magic!

Service of Thanksgiving
After Successful Transplant

18   Let us thank God that in his goodness
he has given you this new *heart/liver/kidney/cornea/hand.*

Host I thank you Lord from
       the bottom of my new
       heart/liver/kidney/cornea/hand

19   The MINISTERPERSON will then read the lesson "In death they were not divided."

20   The congregation will then sing the hymn "O sacred heart sore wounded" while the relatives of the donor are led weeping from the church.

THE JAZZ SINGER
LAURENCE OLIVIER *and*
NEIL DIAMOND

ffolkes–cinema

HITCHCOCK

THE ISLAND
JEFFREY FRANK *and*
MICHAEL CAINE

BLOOD FEUD
SOPHIA LOREN

The Urban Diary Of A Contemporary Gentleman

Alan Coren

Rota Vulgaris

October

Thus called by the old Romans because in this month Fiats traditionally begin to rust in eight different places. Known by the Germans as *Edithholdenmonat*, since it is the time when the Common Publisher flocks to the shrine of the saint in Frankfurt in the hope of finding a miraculous cure, and by the British as *Christmas*, because it is when Carmen rollers and Cyprus sherry appear on television for the first time.

DAYS OF NOTE.
October 9.   St Dynorod.
October 12. St Bluecol.
October 18. St Valium.

MOTTOES

"A woman met on a topless French beach in August always looks more married outside a Bayswater hotel in October."

"You take away more from a doctor's waiting-room in October than you ever bring into it."

"Breakdown in October,
 AA man in June."

"A child's raincoat is always somewhere else."

Oct. 1. Wind from East last night. Out early, tile-gathering. Some fine sturdy varieties, esp. Old Lugless Garage, which falls with a clean, fast trajectory. Look for them where you see their unmistakeable wedge-shaped dents on boots, bonnets, children etc.

Today, I was privileged to watch a ginger cat fishing in our pond: its technique is to scoop guppies (£2 each) into its mouth, and stare at me while it chews. When I greet it with the traditional brick, it makes a noise like breaking glass; this is because it has moved away suddenly from the greenhouse.

Ginger Cat With Guppie

Oct. 2. Last of the pears fell off. We have had a good crop this year (8½), typical English Conference or perhaps Williams—not easy to tell, since by the time I get to them they are brown and flat and wet, not unlike small cowpats with wasps in.

Built a bonfire this afternoon. There is nothing like the smell of polystyrene smoke and the crackle of exploding deodorant canisters. A hysterical neighbour, fearful lest sparks ignite the cleaning fluid with which she is attempting to remove beer-stains from the avocado Dralon suite she has dragged onto her patio so that fluid fumes will not cause unsightly genetic disorders in her new foetus, persuades me to stamp the fire out. My soles melt. I now have a pair of gum uppers, to little point.

Oct. 3. That fine, frost-snapping time of year when the fingers are so cold that the nut you have just removed from the Volvo rear windscreen wiper in an attempt to discover why it stops in light showers drops from them and rolls down a drain. A good time, too, to pull the metallic strip from the anti-freeze canister so that the contents rot your shirt.

I have decided to get my bulbs in before it is too late. Last night, waking to the familiar noise of a late reveller losing his dinner on our Dutch wall, I switched on the bedside lamp, forgetting that I had put its bulb in the children's bathroom light, because I had taken the bulb from there to replace the one in the study Anglepoise broken when the thing suddenly keeled over and fell in my coffee. Groped into hall to remove hall lightbulb to put in bedside lamp, but bulb-glass broke away from little brass bit, filling hair with tiny shards; combed hair in dark, then afraid to move, since glass shards were now on carpet. Stood there for some time, listening to the wind whistling through the draught excluders.

This morning, awoke to find other hands had been switching hall lights on and off; since upstairs and downstairs switches inter-relate, it was by now impossible to find out whether wires hanging from hall light fitting were on or off. Turned off mains, but could not remove little brass bit; pliers fell in eye.

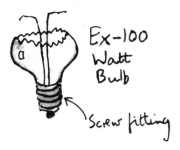

Walked to shops. Observed all the varieties of bulb on my walk, viz. 60-watt, 75-watt, 100-watt, 150-watt in bayonet fitting, spotlights, candle-bulbs in 25-watt and 40-watt bayonet *and* screw fittings, fairy lights, fluorescent tubing in 2-foot, 3-foot, 4-foot, 6-foot and 8-foot lengths, 8-watt nightlight bulbs, 60-watt, 75-watt, 150-watt in screw fitting. Truly, richness in all things.

Needed 100-watt screw fitting bulbs, however.

But there is no call for them.

Oct. 4. Awoke at 3 am, sweating heavily. Thought a croup was upon me, or even a grippe, necessitating some old and trusted remedy, such as 600,000 units of intra-muscular ampicillin, but found that winter moonlight was glinting off similarly glazed wife. Got up, found radiator red-hot; entire house throbbing like ship's boiler. Crawled downstairs, found time-switch reading 9 am, since not re-adjusted after mains switched back on.

Weather continues wet and blustery, especially in downstairs hall. Small son has got up in boiling heat, and opened all windows. Many interesting berries trodden into carpet.

Oct. 9. Bright and crisp, after the damp spell. As if by magic, on a sunny corner of the front wall, ARSNEL POOFS has sprung up overnight.

Driving to work, I counted eighteen varieties of Madmen.

Oct. 11. The apple-cheeked wife of a sturdy young Media Accounts Executive who hails from the other side of the A41 flyover today presented me with a fine brace of grouse which her husband had personally frozen. This, in our part of the world, is the traditional way of saying *Thank You* to someone who has allowed your children to smash his television set beyond repair. Some debate ensues in our

The Common Grouse [*Lagopus Scoticus*]

A.C.

kitchen as to the possible state of putrescence when frozen; my good lady is of the opinion that thawing will release enough bacilli to depopulate most of Greater London. I scoff at her feminine temerity, and leave the plump little fellows in the boiler room.

By mid-afternoon, it smells like Scutari Hospital.

Oct. 13. A rare difference of opinion with those good fellows, the dustmen. Normally, our relationship is warm, and based on mutual respect: I allow them to drop fish-heads and old bean cans on our lawn, and in return, they allow me to pick them up. On this occasion, however, they decline my invitation to remove the bin containing the

grouse, on the grounds that they try to keep a nice clean truck. One of their number, a stocky fellow who seems to have only two fingers on his right hand, shouts over his departing shoulder that at least Doctor Crippen had the decency to bury *his* wife under the cellar-floor.

I decide to burn the offending bodies on the bonfire, and am intrigued to learn that my neighbour's solicitors are Twistleton, Ruggs, Furbelow and Schwarzbinder. Shropshire names, at a guess, with at least one ancestor following the grouter's trade.

Oct. 16. A sharp white unexpected frost, reminding me that today would be a good time to lift the geraniums.

But not as good as yesterday.

Here is a useful tip: dead geraniums make an excellent cover, when piled thickly, for old grouse bones, and will keep a ginger cat off them for nearly six minutes.

Oct. 18. As the colder weather closes in, crowds of friendly denizens of the neighbouring acres come to be fed: this morning alone, trying to get through the kitchen to see why the aerial had slid off the chimney last night, filling the screen with twelve gently wobbling Rippons, I spotted a Lesser Daily, a pair of male Unigate Milkmen, a Bengal Grocer, and the shrilly screaming young of the Late School Rota. They seem to subsist mainly on tea and chocolate wheaten biscuits, but are prepared to eat anything, from cold roast beef to wodka, and may often be found happily truffling around in a larder incautiously left unlocked.

It is not our way to treat them as pests, but if we do wish them to go away, the method is simplicity itself. I just ask them to help me lift something.

Oct. 21. This morning, my son brought me some fresh-picked mushrooms, the palest beige pileus, delicate yellow lamellae, and a darkly attractive, almost chocolate stipe. Truly, there is no art but Nature's! Eagerly, I asked the boy where he had picked them.

Phoned Rentokil.

Egg of Unigate

Oct. 25. Sprang up early, and took the car for a brisk push. Determined as I was to cut across country to the Brent Cross Shopping Centre, it was not long before I was queueing for an honest bus, fetching up—as I seem upon these occasions so often to do—against one of those dear old ladies who abound in these parts and who, given the merest prompting by the sympathetic naturalist, will divest themselves of the most fascinating lore. Within five minutes, she had explained in colourful detail about how the niggers were pushing the rates up, how an International Cabal of Jews were poisoning virgins by putting cocaine in the reservoirs, and how, when she had been taken sick after eating a dog suey at her local Chinese take-away, her Pakistani doctor had put his hands all over her and tried to get her drunk on Gee's linctus.

Brent Cross on market day is really something rather special! Since, in order to conserve the natural beauty of the countryside, parking space was made available for no more than thirty thousand cars, you may often see elderly men jumping on one another's Peugeots in the unceasing evolutionary drive for *parkingsraum*, St John's Ambulancemen rushing hither and yon with scarcely a second glance at the Millwall or Brentford supporters hanging from their colourful scarves, and the bright autumn air thick with Teflon pans and Moulimix parts as the cheery shoppers give vent to their irresistible passions.

Inside, you will find that craftsmen and traders have flocked from every point of the compass to sell their traditional wares. I never come away without buying something. Since I could not find the 100-watt screw-fitting bulb I sought, I chose instead a Formosan digital lacrosse game built into the head of a chiming fibre-tipped thermometer-knife.

It fell to bits on the way out, but when I took it back, the staff had changed and the shop itself was now a macrobiotic grocery.

GRAND TOUR 2000

THE rickshawman who took me from Boulogne to Le Touquet, some ten miles distant, was an idle old rascal, for ever grumbling about the head wind and making excuses to stop and light up a Gauloise. His curiosity about the purpose of my travels was intense; and when I told him that I was bound for the People's Republic of Italy he let go of the shafts and crossed himself, pitching me headlong on to the *chaussée deformée*.

The torpor of the Age of Leisure lay heavy on the countryside. Although it is the custom to lie abed until noon, as in England, the people look utterly drained. All the eating-places bore notices saying *Fermé: Jour de Repos*; but French eating-places always did.

In Le Touquet I booked in at the once-palatial Westminster Hotel. Here, until the world's oil ran out, Rolls-Royces and Lagondas used to be parked six deep. It is now a "religious house"; that is to say, it is run by a colony of sebaceous young Californians practising their cult of universal massage. After one or two misunderstandings I slept in a field.

The luxury shops in the forest, formerly filled with *objets de grande luxe*, were stuffed with the ubiquitous electronic trash with which people now beguile their idleness. An avalanche victim detector bore a label *"Pour l'enfant"*.

HORSE-DRAWN stage-coaches are few and hideously expensive. I travelled to Tours by one of the "auto-drive" rail-cars, paying a hairy member of the Lost Generation to operate the other end of the rocker-arm. He told a pathetic story of how he had left his four children to look for some institution to subvert, but could not face the fact that everything had been subverted already. For hours we sweated through a dismal landscape of tumbledown fun centres, sacked theme parks, recreation areas like wildernesses, wilderness camps like nothing on earth, abandoned safarilands, dude concentration camps—the residue of a bold experiment designed to occupy the waking energies of the workers made redundant by technology. But the population had rapidly wearied of these "facilities". Most had sunk into sloth, the rest into the black economy.

The peasants, of course, continue to till their fields, fatuously chatting to each other by walkie-talkie when they could just as easily communicate direct. Nothing is more ridiculous than an old woman beeping and bleeping away as she piles up the beetroots.

WHAT extraordinary riffraff one meets on the Grand Tour: knaves peddling locks of Margaret Thatcher's hair; jolly Senegalese with huge back packs full of old Barclaycards, which they are convinced are of untold value; quacks with pills to cure the craving for employment; itinerant spoon-benders from Israel; Arab mendicants who once flew their own Learjets; dreadful old hags left over from the sexist wars; fugitives from psychodrama workshops; sock-sniffers, lost in a world of their own; youths of twenty with their brains already addled by music; embittered thesis-writers thrown on the streets when sorely-tired nations rose up against the universities . . .

In the old airport at Lyons, which like all airports now serves as a general caravanserai, I met the legendary Wild Boy of the Camargue, today's nearest approach to a Noble Savage. Abandoned by his parents, he had been brought up from infancy by a roving herd of sociologists and was thus unable to communicate intelligibly or to distinguish right from wrong. The Wild Boy took my hand with a smile of unearthly innocence and then bit my fingers to the bone.

NEAR Vittel in the Vosges I had my first good meal in an institution I had never hoped to see: a Michelin 4-star restaurant. It is kept going by factory executives from La Vallée des Usines, where privileged workers turn out electronic baubles round the clock. The sight of the workshops ablaze with lights all night is like something from the mid-twentieth century.

The executives have their own spa where their livers are serviced. Most of the other spas in these parts are over-run by religious cultists. Some of them have seized the demilitarised citadels on the Meuse and the Rhine, from which they descend to raid the trout pools and the frog farms, even attempting to levy tithes on the peasants' crops. Others rise up from old Maginot forts to seize women for brain-washing and worse.

SWITZERLAND at last! As I feared, the country is like a shabby adventure playground, with a Tellorama wherever one turns. The authorities have even revived an ancient practice, once condemned by Ruskin, of inviting travellers to fire off howitzers in order to set echoes rolling among the peaks. Does not this start off avalanches? I enquired. So much the better, was the unfeeling reply; then families can try out their electronic avalanche victim detectors, which are such fun to use. I shuddered. Now that the Toll of the Road is no more, there is a deadly craving everywhere for accidents.

The British Consul in Geneva said I was the first British traveller to call on him for five years. His grandfather, he said, had once met Guy Burgess and wished he hadn't. He then affixed a note to the door reading *Fermé: Jour de Repos* and closed it in my face.

ON the Italian border, above Domodossola, was all the disagreeable apparatus of a People's Republic: watch towers, barbed wire, minefields, road blocks. But it was at once obvious that the Italians, those children of Nature, lacked the surliness to operate this nonsense effectively; and fortunately the Soviet Union, now the Sick Man of Europe, lacks the will to put pressure on its satellites. I had expected my books to be denounced as pornographic; instead, the smiling Carabinieri tried to sell me Swedish magazines. I had expected to be issued with coupons for meals and to be directed to a bugged bedroom. But I was courteously told that, if I had been fool enough to come this far, they would not dissuade me from the folly of continuing, and that I could do as I wished.

From the frontier I descended the Alps by Basket Trail. It is an idea borrowed from Funchal, Madeira and one simply slides down the foothills in a succession of wicker sledges, through avenues of beggars, stoned by *bambini*,

pillaged by snatch-thieves and yapped at by dogs. At one point I slithered under a motorway viaduct on which a linear town had been built and the townsfolk cheerfully pelted me with refuse.

As in the Soviet Union, the grand hotels, especially in the thermal establishments, are occupied by the common people. The menfolk, however, instead of recovering from the supposed fulfilment of norms, are treated for the stresses of unemployment. It is something we shall yet see in England.

I had hoped to view many Old Masters in Italy, but they have long since been smuggled out to the rapacious auction-houses. To its shame, the Uffizi Gallery in Florence could muster only a few old Pirelli calendars. But Florence still attracts English aesthetes, to judge from the lissom high tenors thronging the Ponte Vecchio.

HOW superb is Rome without its motor traffic, even if the quarrelling rickshawmen are the scum of Europe. I followed faded signs reading "To The Atheist Museum" and soon found myself at the Vatican. The Pope had long since returned, in defiance of the Kremlin, and I was privileged to see him on the balcony, flanked by very old pictures of Lenin and Marx to which I fancied he made a somewhat unpapal gesture when blessing the crowd. At all events a solemn titter ran through the throng. The Pontiff took the opportunity to rebuke those of his audience who still wore jeans, despite proven evidence down the generations that these constricting garments are destructive of human fertility.

That night the city celebrated its Festival of Pandemonium. The combined tumult of electronic music-makers, massed carillons, rickshawmen's klaxons, burglar alarms, anti-rape screechers and howling briefcases was fully worthy of the Infernal City in its motorised prime. I was glad I had made my way there and I could not wait to leave.

ROBERT MORLEY
Success

AS an actor I experienced success at the age of seven. Appearing as a mandarin (not the orange) in my Dame's School play, I recited the prophetic verse, "In the old days our people would not learn the Western ways. Now we shall follow where great nations lead and find the way to everything we need." In those days I knew what lay ahead. A good fifty years later I repeated my triumph as a Chinése emperor supported by Omar Sharif, Telly Savalas and James Mason. I told the latter, "I have considerable experience in these matters. Do not attach your pigtail to the back of your neck. Have it pinned to your hat. It will not only save time in the make-up department but you will avoid the inevitable skin rash." Mason would have none of it and, sure enough, a mild form of dermatitis set in.

I was lucky in a parent who understood it is fatal for most to start at the bottom. To reach the peaks is too laborious a climb and it can take forever. When I read of those dedicated railway porters who start life trundling a trolley and end up, after fifty years, in supreme control of the parcel traffic on one of our great railway networks, I am aware only of the hours they wasted on the way up, collecting tickets or passing hopefully along corridors searching for malefactors travelling without them.

Promotion, in all grades of life, is not only a slow process; it is also a rare one. "Mr So and So, now head of the Stock Exchange, started out as a messenger," I read in my paper. The fact is so remarkable it is often reported in headlines. Whereas Mr So and So, who has now assumed the chairmanship of Lloyd's, a position previously held by his father and grandfather before him, is so commonplace as to be not worth reporting.

My father was always ready when, for instance, I announced I was going into journalism, to write a note to Lord Astor or, when I once announced my intention of emigrating to Australia, a line to the High Commissioner of that unknown continent. When advertising temporarily caught my fancy, he wrote to Lord Higham. And when I finally settled on the stage, he sent flowers to both Irene and Violet Vanbrugh. It wasn't, of course, of any practical value except to implant in me notions of my own self-importance.

The public is curiously ambivalent in their attitude to privilege and heredity. It accepts a monarch can throw an heir to the throne. From the day he or she is born, no one enquires if the puking infant is going into the family business; they are in it along with their first nappie. With the stage it is different. Only very seldom does a busker's child become a successful busker. "What

about Vanessa Redgrave?" you will ask. But Vanessa is not only the exception to this rule; she breaks every accepted pattern of the successful public performer. She insists on her right to speak out for the dispossessed while the possessors, far from being affronted, pay for imperial *fauteuils* from which to watch her perform.

Very few of the rest of us have any fervent political convictions and, even when we have, are not anxious to air them publicly. The last thing any of us desire is confrontation with or offending a stall holder. We remain bland. Modest of course, but bland. Once in a blue moon if the coast is clear—by which I mean if the Prime Minister is out of town—we proceed in discreet number to 10 Downing Street to hand in a mild petition about the state of the theatre or, taking our lives in our hands, ring the bell of the back door of some embassy of some land beyond the Iron Curtain, to hand in a protest demanding for the release of some dissident playwright. On such occasions we are invariably photographed by the free press of our own dear country but lucky indeed if we make the afternoon edition of the *Standard*. If the editor should decide to publish our pictures, it is obvious that we are all getting remarkably old.

Longevity is demanded of the successful

actor; my distinguished contemporaries and I reassure merely by having stayed the course. There is nothing the public likes more than a very old actor, unless it is a very old actress or a very old playwright. "Marvellous," they coo to each other, "simply marvellous at their age." The acting or the play seldom matter on or at this stage. They visit the theatres in which we are performing and tell each other that live theatre is what it is still all about. The cult of the geriatric remains the trump card in the hands of the theatre manager and television producer alike.

I must not write too frankly of my own satisfactory contract advertising British Airways if I wish to remain employed but I am on safer ground if I remark on the advertising campaign, currently being conducted to popularise *The Grocer's Weekly*, in which senior members of the profession are required merely to sleep happily on sofas in London clubs while the announcer explains that when they wake they can catch up on life with a subscription to the magazine.

The rewards of success in the theatre are the same as in any other walk of life: the knowledge that you have pulled off a confidence trick along with the not always pleasurable excitement that you may still be found out and have to give back the loot. This latter sensation passes along with the years and, in almost every other walk of life save my own, with a retirement pension or golden handshake. With actors, age brings a security of another kind. Along with the purchase of a pensioner's rail ticket and reduced subscription to clubs and Equity, comes the knowledge that you have crossed the bar.

In the early days of my career I was twice sacked from pictures for undeniable incompetence. I am, alas, almost as incompetent today but recently, engaged, albeit briefly, to play opposite the Muppets, I had one of those days which are the bane of an actor's life. A large crowd having gathered to hear my dialogue with Kermit, I found it quite impossible to remember what I was supposed to say to him. True, Kermit himself wasn't present. He had, during the early part of the action, been dropped into a pond and was now presumably being dry cleaned.

"I find it difficult," I remarked after about the twentieth attempt at a successful take, "to act to a stick in a pond. It is not easy to establish contact." Years ago the director would have signified his regret and impatience and instantly replaced me. But of course, under the circumstances, such a course was not possible. If I remarked that it was difficult to act with a stick, such indeed must be the case. Suggestions were made on all sides. Would I care for an assistant to stand in the pond holding Kermit or, if the speech in question bothered me because, as I so rightly pointed out, it wasn't strictly speaking entirely grammatical, would I like

to cut it to the bare bones or leave it out altogether? Or should they move the camera so that I might record a sentence or, if necessary, a word at a time? No one thought to remark I was an incompetent old idiot who hadn't learnt the script properly and when I observed that the clip-clop of a horse and cart behind my head was not conducive to my concentration, the horse and cart were immediately dismissed from the scene.

Eventually we achieved the shot but not before the spectators had long since wandered away, hardly able to believe what their eyes and ears had registered, and the sun had sunk below the horizon. The next day the producers sent flowers with complimentary telegrams and, after a few more days when they thought I could safely be reminded of him, Kermit arrived in a plain envelope with a cheque. So once again I and one of the grandchildren have regained their confidence.

Confidence is at the heart of the matter: once you have demonstrated to the world that you can hit a tennis ball harder or a golf ball further than your fellow men, once you have written a best-seller or brought home the bacon as head of a chain of supermarkets—then, "Can you go on doing so?" is the question to be answered by the double brandy before breakfast or the barbiturates late at night.

Myself, I had no such qualms. As long as you are the first person to realise you are a success, no harm will come to you. I walked tall after my first performance of a mandarin. The danger is to let success take you by surprise. I was once asked by a colleague how he could improve his status in our business. Not by acting, I told him. You will never act better than you do now—nobody does. "How then?" he persisted. "How do I become successful?" Never, I told him, under any circumstances, accept a hat check. I watch him now when we meet at top tables of the Variety Club. Like me, he approaches the centre with caution. It is fatal to retrace one's steps, especially in the presence of Bernard Delfont. He may not be quite as well placed as he might wish. I would certainly not wish

him to be nearer the microphone than myself but he is, at least, at the top table and one day, who knows, it may be he who presents the Sunshine Coach or gets presented in his turn to Princess Margaret by Eric Morley.

WHAT do I enjoy most about success? Being included in *Who's Who*? A cup of tea at the Garrick Club? Being called Sir Robert when such indeed is not my title? Installed as a Doctor of Literature at the *Punch* table? Regarding my captive audience as I rise to speak after a modest banquet? Opening a fete? (A ceremony at which one must never be too punctual. Let them believe you have forgotten and your welcome will be ten times more rapturous.) Presuming the Pope would have heard of you if we chanced to meet? Or the lady who trains the dogs on television, though both of us are unable actually to recall the other's name?

Success, like sex, is a club. Like the House of Lords and Alcoholics Anonymous, it is constantly admitting new members. It is not as exclusive as White's, nor does it boast a swimming pool like the Automobile, but then most members have their own.

On the whole it is better to use the premises only occasionally to rub shoulders with as many non-members as you can. You will, from time to time, if you persist in appearing on television (and few can resist) be halted on your way to the bank by those who wish you to pose for a snapshot with their wives or to sign a newspaper for their favourite grandson or just to shake your hand and thank you for the laughs you've given them, adding, as all Englishmen and, I am happy to observe, more and more foreigners do these days, that they can do with a laugh in these difficult times. If memory serves, the first stranger who complained of difficult times was in around 1928.

ROBERT MORLEY started acting in 1929 as a pirate in *Treasure Island* and was Oscar-nominated for his very first film role, that of Louis XVI in Hollywood's 1936 *Marie Antoinette*. Since then he has appeared in more than sixty films and starred in such long-running stage successes as *Edward My Son* (which he also wrote, with Noel Langley), *The Little Hut*, *Hippo Dancing*, Alan Ayckbourn's *How The Other Half Loves* and Ben Travers's *Banana Ridge*. His books include *Responsible Gentleman*, *Morley Marvels*, *More Morley* and the best-selling *Book of Bricks* and *Book of Worries*.

FOOD

Play Time

by FAY MASCHLER

I DARE say, by now, some of the magic has gone out of your life. In which case, I have some suggestions. There is a book that was published in 1980 by Cassell & Company called *Magic at Home,* translated and with notes by Professor Hoffman (author of *Conjuror Dick*). It is most revealing about the pre-occupations of our forebears and casts a little light, perhaps, on what we view now as a stable age. Magic at home was not, as you might be expecting me to announce, concerned with food but it did centre round the dinner table.

In place of acrimonious discussions about who, in a feminist world, should be the one to clear the table, the Victorians were absorbed in flipping coins from one glass to another, balancing a plate in mid-air with only the help of a ladle, skimmer, cork and water carafe, dropping pears from a great height onto a pair of crossed knives and, if there was any *frisson* of marital disharmony it was channelled into the trick called A Startler for A Careful Housekeeper which involves poising parts of the best tea set on the points of carving knives.

When faced with an empty wine bottle they did not sulk or squabble over who should go to Europa, they tried to blow a small cork into it or with the help of a dinner plate and string demonstrate the effects of atmospheric pressure. The various diversions were all suitably edifying, illustrating, as they do, in a magical or quasi-magical form the operation of some natural law. They are described with great charm. The preamble to about half an hour of messing around with a champagne bottle one third full of water, some bicarbonate of soda, tartaric acid, a playing card rolled into a cylinder, blotting paper, pin, thread and two pencils goes like this: "Would you like, when seated at the table after dinner, to enjoy all the emotions produced by the firing of a cannon; to hear the report, so alarming to delicate nerves, to see the lightning rush of the shot, and the recoil of the piece as the ball leaves its mouth? You may safely say 'Yes'; for the experiment I am about to offer you is of the most innocent kind. You shall however judge for yourself." The trick is titled Artillery on the Dinner Table. It beats dining near the Iranian Embassy.

If fun at the table is beginning to appeal but you know that yours is the sort of household where you can never lay your hands on the sealing wax or funnel just when you need it (for example when you are balancing a lighted candle and vase of flowers on the head of your neighbour with the help of a sieve), then there are other modes to consider when focusing on the table as a source of amusement. It is well known that guests, even noble ones, are delighted by live creatures bursting out of pies or cakes. A friend of mine went to the trouble of hiring a bunny costume to do the latter on the occasion of her husband's birthday. I think he enjoyed it very much. If the notion of blackbirds chirruping away under the pastry lacks appeal there is another sort of pie you might try called a Stargazy Pie.

It is made with pilchards but you could use sardines or herrings. On a circular plate you lay the gutted fish, seasoned and stuffed with chopped onions and herbs, like the spokes of a wheel on a base of shortcrust pastry, their little heads resting on the perimeter of the plate. Cover with another circle of pastry, but leave the heads peeping out. Brush with beaten egg and bake in a fairly hot oven. The oil from the heads drains into the fish, basting them as they cook. Their eyes gazing heavenward provide the merriment at the table. In Victorian cookery there was a version where herring heads gazed upwards, clustered through a hole in the centre of the pie, with parsley in their mouths, while the tails of the fish decorated the outer rim, an almost better effect I think.

Of course it lacks the element of surprise that dishes enclosed by pastry should have. The best version of this is the soup devised by Paul Bocuse for the dinner to celebrate his being awarded the Legion d'honneur. This was an individual tureen surmounted by a dome of golden pastry. When pierced it released the heady aroma of a soup whose chief ingredient was black truffles. To make the pastry rise so over a bowl of liquid is a feat that Professor Hoffman might have taken pains to explain, involving, as it does, principles of chemistry, mechanics, optics, hydrostatics and maybe even pneumatics.

It is too difficult for most of us to assay, but staying with the idea of one thing concealing another, you might emulate the famous arrangement of game birds and poultry stuffed one inside another according to size, like Russian dolls. Even to do it with a quail, a grouse and a poussin would produce an effective result. Naturally the inside ones must be boned, otherwise general aimiablility would be reduced by the problem of sorting out a tangle of limbs.

The notion, enshrined at Christmas, of burying some treasure in the Christmas pudding could be worked on to advantage I feel. It would be a nice way of giving a present. I can imagine being moved to finish the profiteroles if inside two were a pair of diamond earrings. Home-made fortune cookies could contain messages of particular relevance. "Isn't it about time you were thinking of going home?" is one you might hold in reserve.

Once hilarity is established as the keynote of your dinners the non-cook comes into his own with the serving of plastic fried eggs and novelty ketchup splashes. There is a jolly joke wine glass which, when turned upside down, lets out not a drop and yet the red liquid inside slowly disappears from view. That's a frightfully good one. Fake food or artist's recreations of food items can be mixed in among the real (there is a shop selling appropriate props in Regent's Park Road, London NW1). And when ideas flag, there is that waiter's way of having fun with food; setting fire to it. I hope, with Professor Hoffman's help and inspiration, I have gone some way to bringing magic back to where it belongs—the dining table.

"We have separate bedrooms. I live here and he lives with this other woman in Clapham."

RICHARD GORDON:

Doctor in the Money

THE morning after the doctors' 31.4% pay rise, Mr Anthony Barker, a consultant surgeon at St George's hospital, wrote in outrage to *The Times*—"I believe many of us would rather take a cut than accept this vulgar increase."

He expresses more than a snobbish indifference towards money, predictable from our hospital at Hyde Park Corner. The atmosphere at St George's, of a nursing home for officers in the Great War, will surely endure its evacuation to Tooting. Another St George's surgeon once said the same thing. "Let it never be forgotten that money forms but a part, and a small part, of professional success," counselled Sir Benjamin Brodie, who never took a holiday and was pocketing the equivalent of £200,000 a year in the taxless 1850s.

A doctor can talk about the body with the cheerful professionalism of a priest about sin. Go along and enjoy a chat about your sexual perversions, bowels, murderous impulses and scabies. Raise the subject of money, and he blushes. Finance is as unmentionable as criticism of a colleague, however criminally incompetent.

A doctor would handle money no more enthusiastically were it glazed with the virulent germs of anthrax. If a bill is inescapable, it must be presented by his secretary, or better still by his butler on a salver. Thirteen years ago, when abortion was a deadly sin instead of National Health routine, a Mayfair practitioner made a fortune without mentioning a fee. "He seems to want a hundred quid," the girls told one another. "In notes, left under the shepherdess on the waiting-room mantelpiece."

Doctors pretended that money did not exist, by charging in coins not minted since 1813, until Ted Heath brought reality in a stroke with decimal currency. The two oldest medical stories are not of the clinical cock-ups which usually make doctors fall about, but of vulgarity over money.
Story No 1.

Rapacious Victorian consultant on chilly morning in Harley Street, handed fee discreetly wrapped in tissue-paper by lady, detains her in conversation to count the number of sovereigns under cover of coat-tails. Drops paper into flames, haughtily informs her he charges in guineas, discovers has peeled off crinkly new-fangled £5 note from five shillings.
Story No 2 (slightly better).

Heard at the Royal College of Surgeons.

"How much did you charge your chappie for the operation?"

"One hundred and sixty-two pounds five pence."

"That's a very odd fee."

"Damned odd. But it was all the poor soul had left."

Doctors despise money even more than they do osteopaths, but they manipulate it with the silent efficiency of Swiss bankers. A GP knows that he can claim full tax allowances for his car, his elevenses in the surgery, wreaths for his patients, and the services of his receptionist if she is his mistress and not his wife. Hospital housemen talk warmly of cremation, knowing they collect over ten quid "ash cash" for signing the statutory certificate once their advice becomes practical. Hospital consultants work stealthily for "merit awards", which are distributed with the conspiratorial secrecy of backhanders from

"Well, that's the easy part . . .'

the Mafia.

One of Nye Bevan's arguments for a National Health Service was freeing a noble profession from serving humanity on a cash basis. British doctors were operating the principles of the NHS even before Lloyd George got to know their professional fathers in 1911. They sent poor patients no bills, and rich patients big ones. If a doctor wanted more private patients, he put up his fees and everyone scrambled for so valuable an opinion. If he wanted fewer, he reduced them, and everyone said he was past it.

Doctors became dumbly obsessed with money because Nye Bevan created it the coin of official esteem—which is miserable. Working as a GP is only about two-and-a-half times as profitable as working at British Leyland. The French doctor gets seven times as much as the assembly-line at Renault, the Italian 6.8 of whatever they pay at Fiat. The German doctor does not bother to calculate his pay as a multiple of the workers', he just reckons on a steady £50,000 a year to keep himself in appropriate Mercedes.

Coyness over money is to American doctors a British affection comparable with wearing knee-breeches at Court or drinking in saloon bars. Americans feel entitled to exsanguinate their patients financially. The British doctor is born free of debt. His student grant and working as a deckchair attendant during summer roughly covers his expenses. The embryonic American doctor is nourished by a debt which grows as fast as the human placenta.

The American's first professional ambition is the modest one of solvency. His next is avoiding ruination by litigation. The slightest slip produces a writ, as surely as a tap on the patella a brisk kick from the knee. The New York plastic surgeon who misplaced a lady's navel an inch-and-a-half off centre—she wanted a "flat, sexy

"How about another march from Jarrow? There's a rather good little restaurant outside Grantham!"

belly"—was done £427,000 for such horrid disfigurement.

"Physicians of the utmost fame," wrote Hilaire Belloc, "Answered as they took their fees, 'There is no cure for this disease.'" Lloyd George and Nye Bevan were wrong. Patients *like* paying fees. They enjoy making sly jokes about them. It is their feeble weapon, to fight back. What the doctor orders they must do, from removing their clothes to affording houseroom for someone else's heart. Writing a cheque restores a little self-esteem, even if the

doctor clearly regards it as an object more sordid than all the specimens they have been obliged to bring him in little pots.

No doctor need bother himself over money, with the fringe benefits. Qualification instantly invests the raffish student with respectability of hard cash value. Insurance companies compete to cover a life previously of insignificant interest compared with his patients'. He can acquire a pack of credit cards, join the Folio Society and the Wine Society. Sir Colenso Ridgeon's "most disgusting figure in modern civilisation" becomes a hotly sought husband, and bright, newly-qualified girls with prospects find plenty of men eager to be the Denis Thatchers of the medical profession.

Knighthoods come freely, if sufficient important people die in your hands. The doctor gets 10% off his chemist's bills, free samples, ballpoints and golf balls, as much free travel to conferences as he can endure, and lately a flashing green light on the roof of his car to get him through traffic jams when late for dinner.

Doctors have never been embarrassed by gifts. A popular rural practitioner would find himself kept in eggs, pheasant, salmon, bacon and parsnip wine. Now that the Middle East turns to Harley Street for treatment as regularly as to Mecca for inspiration, its estimable obsession with gifts overwhelms our most popular consultants. However stiff the fee, the Arabian patient adds a gold wristwatch as tip. There is a jeweller's in Bond Street which profitably recycles these valuables, by buying them back from the doctors and selling them again to the next batch of patients.

What doctor would wear a fancy gold watch? Dreadfully vulgar! Just like the manner of those £3000 a year hospital porter chaps and ward orderlies who carry on continually about wanting more money.

"At last. Another human being. Just as I was beginning to think that I might go insane!"

BRITISH MEDICAL JOURNAL

Horological findings during pointless treatment of HBsAg-associated Polyarteritis Nodosa by surgery

Summary

Corticosteroids may be of great value in treating polyarteritis nodosa but may cause severe complications due to arteriolar stenosis. A Royal Wessex patient developed such complications, and surgery was undertaken.

Case Report

A 60-year-old woman was admitted with abdominal pain. She had a six-month history of diffuse arthralgia, myalgia, weakness, loss of weight, intermittent fever, Raynaud's phenomenon, irregular vomiting, and chiming every hour on the hour. She was treated for three months with prednisolone 30 mg daily because she had HBsAG in her serum, but her distress was not diminished. She continued to chime, and was admitted for surgery.

An incision having been made in the intestinal tract, the patient was discovered not to be suffering from polyarteritis nodesa, as had been suspected, but from a Bigley & Bigley (London) gold half-hunter. Upon examination, the engraving revealed it to be the property of a consultant at the East Middlesex Hospital, who not only identified the watch but was also able to specify the exact time the obstruction had entered the patient, since it was the day upon which the Rat and Cockle had closed early due to unacceptable singing in the snug, and he had returned to the theatre only half an hour late. Having lost his spectacles in a hernia patient the day before, he had failed to notice when the watch fell from his gown pocket into the open women, who had, in fact, been admitted with a suspected peritonitis.

In the event, this had proved to be nothing worse than a half finished bootee left by an anaesthetist six months before at the South Acton Infimary, when the women had been admitted for the removal of, not a gallstone at all, but a Ronson lighter.

Surgical complications ensued when the East Middlesex surgeon requested the return of his gold watch. The Royal Wessex consultant maintained that finders constituted keepers, whereupon his registrar pointed out that it was he who had in fact spotted the watch in the first place. The argument became heated, and in order to put a rapid end to the matter, it was decided to finish the operation quickly and telephone a reputable solicitor. The patient was sewn up and returned to the wards. Two hours later, the registrar discovered that his Thermos flask was missing.

Comment

There is no question but that the watch belonged to the consultant at the East Middlesex. Since the patient had been admitted to the Royal Wessex with horological complications resulting directly from the East Middlesex operation to alleviate the peritonitis (bootee), she remained, technically, an East Middlesex patient, and anything which fell into her during her treatment there legally belonged to the East Middlesex surgeon. However, in a dissenting opinion, Sir Osbert Lime QC maintained that a case could quite properly be made out for the watch's belonging to the surgeon who had lost the original Ronson lighter, since he had set in train the sequence of remedial events, and the patient (including contents) fell unquestionably within his fief, *even though the gold watch had been the property of the East Middlesex surgeon during the period when it was outside his patient.*

As we were going to press, the above judgement of the court was set aside upon appeal by the patient. She, having been discharged from hospital after treatment for a Thermos flask, has laid formal claim to the watch on the grounds that its insertion, though accidental, occurred during an operation for which she had paid, through her National Insurance subscriptions. Further legal proceedings and the pursuit of this later claim will, however, have to be suspended until the patient is discharged from the Molesey Hospital to which she has been sent for the removal of a pocket calculator inadvertently inserted during an operation for the removal of a Thermos flask.

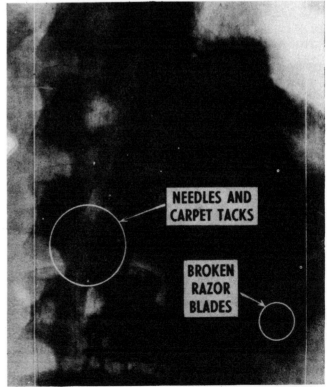

NEEDLES AND CARPET TACKS

BROKEN RAZOR BLADES

Fig 1. X-ray photograph found in patient during subsequent operation

ALAN COREN:

Le Jour D'Action Est Arrivé

Paris, April 28/29

Twenty years ago, this was dream:

Am living in most picturesquely unsalubrious *quartier* in all Paree—old men all have four days growth of rusty wine-dark stubble in which brown teeth dangle and clack, old women wear mildewed black bombazine and shriek down offal-guttered alleyways, young men, gaunt and sullen, hang around street corners in fours, picking teeth, sliding car radios under theadbare overcoats and dodging Algerian draft, young girls straighten seams in windows of filthy *epicerie,* pull shrunken angora woollies straight over eye-glazing embonpoint, make succulent *moues* at passing English novelists...

Have, dream goes on, taken rat-clattering attic at 14 Rue de Verlaine, ten flights up, cats shriek on landings, poets honk unseen behind peeling doors, old men go heh-heh-heh all day outside lavabo, tapping noses, winking; but north light comes through roof-windows, falls on fetchingly hand-painted washstand, bug-crackling paillasse, neat pile of writing paper, and Great Novel is going like whippet. Literary world about to stand on ear, roll on back with feet in air, much in manner of ravishing *poule de luxe* who stops by every afternoon and throws trick for fun, also brings fresh baguettes, camembert, vin rouge, mangoes, since *poule de luxe* is on contract hire to octogenarian financier with George V suite, only way for *p de l* to survive nightly geriatric ineptitude is to pop in on vigorous young English genius *de 5 à 7*...

Twenty years on, this is reality:

Finally got to Paris, finally got to start writing. At 3 am. Not at 14 Rue de Verlaine though. Not in Paris at all, actually, but in Room 461, Orly Hilton, Paris ten kilometres north, could be ten thousand, only view from soundproofed, hermetically-sealed, treble-glazed window is of silent jumbos taking off

at end of hotel carpark. No old men or cats or angora woollies, either, no colourful concierges; post-midnight corridor full of jabbering Japs, cryptic Arabs, glinting Germans, all in-transit stopovers poised to wing off on morning Concorde to Kuwait, Dallas, Sao Paolo, Perth, sell ten million gallons this, buy ten millions tons that, what all these bastards doing outside Room 461 at 3 am, not even drunk. Looked out five minutes ago, nothing but groups of suits in mumbling conference, doubtless trading, Tokyo bourse probably still open, critical moments for forward-buying cocoa or off-loading dodgy bauxite must be between 3 and 3.10, why don't International Philistine Bloody Conspiracy clear off and let me get on with...

Get on with what? Not Great Novel, that for sure. Not *Poule de luxe,* that even surer. Stare at Olivetti. Stare at truth. What am I but one more international stopover businessman, metaphor factor, simile broker, sentence trader? Jet to Orly, unload cargo of ten thousand assorted best English syllables, jet out again.

Why? mumble public, if any (must face possibility wrong time to unload English syllables, could be no call, market could be flooded with Golden Delicious syllables, cheap Nipponese pictograms, fashionable Saudi squiggles). Reason: this edition of Punch being typeset in France, printed in France, despatched from France. Would remind public to glance at dateline again, then drop eyes to page-bottom: written on April 28/29, published on May 14: crazy sixteen-day time-lag, I am writing into unknown future, May 14 may never arrive, England may never have wonderful stirring Day of Action for all I know, this issue may never appear, Carter, Khomeini, Brezhnev, Thatcher may end world before May 14, sixteen days bags of time to wipe out Civilisation As We Know It. Still, this is risk

we businessmen have to take, it goes with territory as Willie Loman put it, this could be consignment of ten thousand best syllables tossed down tubes, dead loss, tax write-off, all that. By time you read this, as it were, you not reading this at all, you nothing but thermonuclear cinder, whole market-area taken out of syllable catchment. Could be whole world nothing but large hot clinker by May 14, few pages of shiny Frog Punch blowing about.

If, that is, shiny Frog Punch ever get published at all. At time of writing, still don't know, got to go down to Vitry-sur-Seine with this in six hours time, give it to typesetter, God knows what happens after that. (Safe to write this, since typesetter can't read English; know that because we went there this afternoon, typesetters all grinning men in private house converted into type-shop, boss of type-shop live upstairs, everybody gather round, shake hands, flash gold inlays, wives come in—house seems to have two hundred people living in it, compositors, wives, children, plus world's largest Alsatian dog, dog gaze at Geoffrey Dickinson, run tongue over jowls, could this be some huge bizarre typographical commune, families called Bodoni, Plantin, perhaps, M. et Mme Times-Condensed, little Jean-Pierre Grot, the Hound of the Baskervilles? Whole enterprise like something out of Renoir movie, *Le Jour Se Leve,* noise of printers singing coming down corridor, wives carrying beer about, dogs widdling on paper bales in yard. And nobody with one word of English, except Punch international business team, self, Geoffrey Dickinson, young Guy Pierce, crack inter-European commercial waffenkommando, only got one tie among three of us, two sets spare paper underwear; *we* got English words between us all right, *we* got thirty thousand English words, it called May 14th issue of *Punch,* we got them in large paper bag, take out typescripts, Basil Boothroyd, Keith Waterhouse, Benny Green, French families all gather round, finger incomprehensible pages, gradually articulate words—"Barzeel Boozeroy, Keeze Wodderarse, Benny Grin"—Dickinson look at Pierce, Pierce look at me, I look at Dickinson, optimism disappear into boots, but compositors very cheery, everybody have another beer, dogs bark, compositors trot off bearing MSS. International business syndicate cross fingers.)

Why *Punch* being published abroad, you ask?

All due to ongoing industrial confrontation situation. Dispute with National Graphical Association is why we lost most of April 2, all of April 9, all of April 16, whole appalling business come to some sort of head on Monday April 28, this morning (for me, not you; for you this morning, if it ever come—see above *et passim*—is May 14. Clear? *Bon*.) employers lock out NGA men, *Punch* now unprintable, *Punch* got to get set and printed abroad, first time in 139 years, look like end of line for Olde Albion if *Punch* getting printed abroad, next thing you know Rolls Royces getting assembled in Poland from kit, pre-sogged steak-and-kidney pies being flown in from Shanghai, Brazilian cricket bats arriving at Lord's.

So here we are, Dickinson, Pierce and I, couriers to joke industry, set up in Orly Hilton like Estonian government-in-exile, cobbling May 14 issue together. This may explain any cock-ups from here on in, drawings upside down, typographical orrers, adverts falling out of middle, you nome it.

Because it not just a question of typesetting, it also question of printing, binding, etcetera: people at Vitry-sur-Seine (which, by way, is twin town with Burnley, God knows how this weird coupling arrived at, nobody in V-s-S ever *heard* of Burnley, and as for for people in Burnley who've heard of V-s-S, could probably be counted on fingers of one mitten) only *set;* people in Evry *print,* all pages have go to 30km across *zone industrielle* to be printed, stitched, turned into *Le Punch.*

So, in capacity as editor, director, intercontinental business tycoon, went down to Evry, after leaving Vitry (for God's sake pay attention!) this afternoon to see printers.

Printers totally different from setters, printers not from Renoir film, printers from Chabrol film, printers all got primrose BMW's, pale blue cashmere sweaters, chunky gold bracelets, polychromatic Zeiss glasses, Riviera tans. No wives about, no dogs; secretaries like Natalie Wood, though, Ali McGraw, Capucine. Printers live in big new complex, smoked glass, Brancusi junk, white hide sofas, intercoms that go ding-dong, conference with printers felt as if we all planning to knock over Monte Carlo casino, hi-jack QE2, corner world market in camembert.

Shut up!

Not you, gentle reader: it now 4.45 am, and corridor full of waiters; doubtless delivering early croissants to Japs etc. about to fly off on first jet to Lima. Or waking Arabs to greet dawn, face Mecca, work out percentage mark-up on nine million barrels crude to Vancouver, roll up prayer-mat, fly out to Zurich, pop another two

hundredweight of used fivers in the Kreditanstalt.

Where was I? Ah, yes, printers. Didn't really cotton to printers. Not like typesetters: with typesetters, didn't mind being supplicant Englishman, felt like shot-down flyer put in contact with scruffy, cheery maquisards, felt entente-cordiality, felt fraternity in adversity. Typesetters sympathetic, typesetters would hide us from NGA patrols. Not so with printers: printers smirking over collapse of Luxembourg summit, printers got binful of off-colour multi-entendre remark anent our beloved PM ("En Angleterre, il y a deux Princesses Margaret..." a joke which labours on to explain that what one lady is doing to blah-blah-blah, the other is doing to the British economy, geddit?). Printers clearly *au-dessus de la lune* at catching Britain with trousers down and egg on face (just realised this may come-out as egg down and trousers on face if typesetter's bloody Alsatian sticks conk on keyboard); had to keep temper at printer's, felt like sticking one on nearest Monsieur Rochas chin, not got much national pride left (how could I have? Be fair), but what I have flares easily.

Still, beggars can't be choosers (non, non, *non!* Not cheesers, espèce de con!), and today I have to bite on the bullet, grin and bear it, watch the wall, my darlings, while the *gentilhommes* run by. It is my day of action, a little in advance of Mr. Murray's; and, God help us all, a tiny foretaste, in waste and humiliation, of how things may very well go for us in Europe unless he learns to address himself and his followers to something more honourable and practical than the tacky farce of May 14.

"Good heavens, so it is. You know, I can remember her when she used to be in focus."

50 GLORIOUS YEARS

LARRY celebrates the golden jubilee of Sellotape

8.00
People With Their Bowels In A Bucket

Part Three: Whose Bowels Are They Anyway?

Jonathan Dimbleby, who may himself be suffering from something appalling as the result of the Three Mile Island accident, talks to eighteen people who, because of police brutality and the proximity to their homes of a plant extruding nicotine from asbestos, have had their bowels put in buckets by alcoholic surgeons, and asks them whether it has ever occurred to them that they may have been sent home with someone else's intestines.

After the interviews, **Claire Rayner** invites a panel of dyslexic shoplifters for their expert comments.

8.45
Has Ethopia Got The Bomb?

While millions of people are dying from lung cancer, the rising tide of Britain's desperate unemployed are even more deeply distressed at the suggestion that starving Ethiopians have found a way of manufacturing nuclear weapons from kidney machines. In the studio are **Lord Longford, Neil Kinnock MP, Douglas Bader** and **April Ashley** to answer questions fired at them by rape victims.

This week's mystery amputee is a born-again IRA glue-sniffer.

9.15
Mastermind

Subjects this week: Non-dead cornea donors, 1962–1975; the life and works of Adolf Eichmann; the history of diabetes; really nasty side-effects of the contraceptive pill.

The programme comes from Broadmoor.

9.45
The Breast Programme

The wives of many of the prisoners in Long Kesh have noticed strange lumps which are beyond any question totally incurable, but social workers have constantly ignored their pleas on the grounds that they have quite enough to do already in filling bin bags with battered immigrant children.

10.15
Will World War III Break Out After You've Gone To Bed Tonight?

Ludovic Kennedy puts the hypothesis: Suppose **Ronald Reagan's** physician, as seems very likely, went crazy and wrongly diagnosed his patient's leukaemia as yet another case of the Russians poisoning American reservoirs with anthrax dropped from satellites? How long could Britain survive the thermonuclear holocaust which would inevitably follow, given the substandard housing in which 97.8% of the population currently lives and the fact that their constitutions are already terminally undermined by radioactivity which has penetrated the Heaviside layer through punctures made in it by Concorde's appalling sonic booms?

Struck-off doctors from the Home For The Incurably Transexual argue the case with four or five hundred wrongfully imprisoned Strangeways murderers.

11.00
The
Siamese-Twin
Boom

Part Five: The Role of Mercuric Oxide

All over the world, according to computer predictions, more and more babies are going to be born soon joined at the head. Most of these, of course, will die of famine, but should the developed nations be feeding the rest on tinned fish, nearly 98% of which contains enough poisonous pollutants to knock out a town the size of Hiroshima?

Anna Raeburn introduces film of some unsuccessful operations to relieve this dreadful suffering and discusses the most sickening bits with spokespersons from Lesbians Against Cholesterol.

11.30
Miss World
1980

Statistics have incontrovertibly shown that most of this year's Miss World contestants will be dead by the year 2000 as the result of inept abortions, the disappearance of the blue whale, ETA's anticipated theft of a cruise missile system, and firework accidents.

Michael Aspel puts some of the most likely victims through an EMI brain-scanner which no hospital in our collapsing National Health Service can afford, and asks them: *Isn't euthanasia the only sensible solution?*

12.00 Close

A deranged victim of the Bologna terrorist massacre shouts extracts from a report linking Bright's disease with the total collapse of democratic government as we know it.

KNOBS AND KNOCKERS

MAHOOD drags Donald McGill into the permissive eighties

"Oh dear, it looks like Mr Pooter's little transplant hasn't taken then."

"You can blame the Tories – it's just suffering from the general depression."

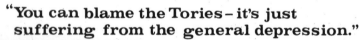

"Time to go, Oedipus darling—start exhuming your father!"

"Just look at them—emasculating our imagination!"

"Actually, I'm an agnostic."

ALAN BRIEN:

Canvas Opinion

GRRRRRRR-ER-ER-OINK! The Arab may fold his tent and silently steal away. But in a cosmopolite, canvas city, a mini-Agincourt camp pitched on a Dordogne hill-top, the gritty noise of the zippered door, its plastic teeth knitting or unknitting like stitches on a man-size wound, resounds loud under the sequin-studded heavens. The creeping murmur of dusk has been drowned by the pouring dark of midnight, the sun-bright Technicolor orange-and-blue domes and turrets silvered into the grey and white of a silent film. Yet not all noises have been blanketed out. Until the early hours of tomorrow morning, the agile, directional ear can still catch through the paper-thin, breathing walls an occasional rasping snore, a bronchial trachea irritated by unaccustomed fresh air, what might be a muffled flatulence or even a smothered orgasm. A camping site has all the elaborate, etiquette-ruled intimacy and nest-warmth of a human hive.

Finally, pole-axed by the long heat of the day, wine-logged and food-laden, every last camper subsides, enfolded in sleep as a pharaoh in the tomb. Catatonia rules. Or so it seems—a self-protecting delusion convincing each wakeful horizontal he or she is the only one with a single sense alert—until carried far across the open countryside comes *Grrrrrrr-er-er-oink!* The scar tissue of some sealed-in cell is being surgically opened from within. There is the crunch of flip-flops on gravel, or the barely caught sigh of relief as bare feet leave the

path for the padded, dew-softened grass. Through the gauze, breeze-permeable tent window, which by day turns every view into a minutely fragmented Impressionist landscape, will soon be glimpsed the fuzzy, yellow globe of a torch beam followed by a daddy-long-legs shadow.

If, like me, you have long disguised an impertinent curiosity as reportorial zeal, it is possible to lie back, deep hidden in your cloth-framed cave, and by triangulating the impressions establish which of your neighbours is walking the tree-lined maze.

"Back to Nature" is a slogan, like I suppose all slogans, which can bounce back painfully on its mouthers. It has its Yin and its Yang, one auspicious and one drooping eye. For the Anglo-Saxon metropolitan, long used to the restricted visibility of his weather reports, the locked-in privacy of his house walls, Southern France or Italy seems miraculously to sharpen his sight and hearing. In the blaze of noon, like a child, he can read small print without eye strain, or see the sea over a range of scissored peaks at twenty miles. He can hear the clattering express, or the droning tourist traffic, in the next valley. Not only with sunburn has he lost a skin and gained a new sensitivity of nerve endings. To become alone, he has to put three times the distance between himself and his fellows that he does back home.

The Dordogne, where I have spent an August fortnight, was for three hundred years the English frontier against the French. And, as Cyril Connolly was the first to note, it really is England of the fairy tales, the children's classics, the endless, cloudless summers, the sylvan paradise before the industrial revolution, the dream memories of schooldays. You return to it as though to your almost-forgotten, long-disbelieved past. Wild strawberries actually do grow on hedgerows like Christmas-tree lights. Oaks are really full-bellied enough to run around. Round the next corner *is* a farm with a wimpled tower, a village clinging to a rock face, a green pool with a frothy, creamy waterfall, an underground network of caverns so vast that at the

bottom of the lift-shaft you burrow towards a pierhead mooring half a dozen boats.

Well, I say round the next corner, that is the map's next corner where everything seems impossibly near—a kilometre a minute only 37 miles per hour. And even in this charmed valley, though the unexpected is everywhere, the expected, as when a child, always takes longer than you think. The price you pay for being able to sit out at 11 p.m. in shorts and sandals, tracing the suddenly bright and unmistakable constellations, is to sauna in the oven-hot car at mid-day, facing the choice of sweating in a shirt or *sauté*-ing in bare skin. Even the frames of the tent, protected by canvas, grow too hot to touch. Shade, a word almost pejorative in English, becomes when *ombrage* almost a Black Market commodity, a privilege guarded by first arrivals.

Food in the markets is cheap, fresh, larger than life, but it is a short, rich life, passing through perfumed ripeness to odorous decay in the swiftness of a holiday hour. In the boot of the car, speeding back to the baked table and the boiled wine like punch, fruit cooks and explodes, cheese melts to thick custard, bread turns to fragile metal, paté becomes soup. Even my greedy eye, moist with desire, halts my hand momentarily as it hovers over oysters ranging from 9.50 fr to 12 fr *le douz.*—the largest like elephant's tongues, barely more than 10p each—before cracking open 24 and swallowing them standing up in a windy stream, fearing to trust them five minutes to my tropically-besieged icebox.

France, expansive, especially from the Dordogne to the Pyrenees, where I am finishing this naked in a sloping forest, never, even now at the height of the native's vacation season, crowds its beauty spots as does narrow England. But the drawback of even one of the world's great wild gardens is that Nature, human, animal and vegetable, still oppresses from time to time with luxurious closeness and physical heaviness you do not find, say, in the West of Ireland. What you want, thousands also seek.

The lushness is democratically dispersed. If the tomatoes, the peaks, the oaks, the helpings, the wine, the vistas are on a lavish scale, so are the insects—ants like clockwork toys, or the creatures—frogs like bouncing beach balls. Wasps descend in helicopter gunships. Thank God we haven't seen a hornet. Mosquitoes, happily only encountered so far in hotels not camping sites, raise blisters like small pillows.

Camping is the least expensive, and in every way freest, means of enjoying France. I consider myself here something of a pioneer with an experience dating back to the days when a tent was a small sheet hung over a washing line you set up on some corner of a foreign field that was not a swamp or an ant's nest. Then the first sites, hastily subsidised by the French Government after the Domenicici murders of Sir Jack Drummond and his family, tended to be a patch of cinders, ringed with barbed wire, equipped with one cold tap and a sentry box over a hole, next to the municipal rubbish tip. I began, as ever influenced by literary rather than practical precedents, imagining myself with R.L.S. on his travels with a donkey in the Cervennes—somehow imagining all ground become mattress-like under a plaid blanket, with a knapsack for the head and a pistol nearby. One night disillusioned me, and I blush still as I recall knocking up a small *quincaillerie* outside Chablis and demanding (the French for "ask") what I had got round to calling a *matelot pneumatique*. On bad days, I can still hear the shop-keeper laughing.

After that I towed my magic box behind me in a trailer, refining down to seven minutes the time taken to unfold it like a genie's palace, stopping only at camps marked with three red tents in the *Michelin Camping Guide*. Since then, I have rather gone off camping, developing a taste for small, out-of-the-way hotels. But this year, I have reverted to a compromise, seeking the aid of one of several enterprising firms—in my case, Canvas Holidays—which book you ahead at camps where you arrive to find your three-room plus kitchen, framed tent-cottage already up and with all its equipment waiting. Not least of the advantages of this method is that you don't have to carry anything but yourselves and the luggage in the car—a fortunate effect since it is already packed like an Okie caravan out of *The Grapes of Wrath*, with enough bottles collected along the route for me to stage at any time a convincing wayside *degustation des vins*.

But even camping in this pseudo-gentlemanly style is not everybody's Turkish WC. Nature is Nature, and however you enjoy it there is a distinct step back in some directions. You may have your curtained-off rooms, your raised double bed on metal legs, your kitchen with its grill and two burners, your ice-box, your walls that can open out into day-time pergolas, but no one has yet eliminated the need for elimination or discovered how to provide an indoor flush lavatory. If you obey Nature's call in the night, you still must take a torch and a leafy stroll to the ablution block. It is not as primitive and earthy as it sounds. I confess I find it quite romantic. I rather enjoy this starry pilgrimage, encountering perhaps a pretty neighbour, rosy with sleep, sexy yet somehow nun-like after the fashion of a baroque madonna, in her clinging nightdress while fancying myself in my boxer shorts a tame, but interesting-looking, Silenus.

When first I used to holiday in a tent, I remember meeting a colleague, in the local square, who was ensconced in the best hotel—"Oh," he said, "I might have known you were camping, you're still carrying loo paper in your back pocket." So be it. I may share my loo, but my rooms are my own to cook, read, write, drink and slummock in as I wish, without worry about keys or interruption by chambermaids. I pack my bags in the heart of the countryside and leave for the next site—tonight halfway up the Pyrennees, next week the Atlantic coast near Biarritz, last week the Dordogne. I think I will put away my typewriter and go for a stroll in the flow of the false dawn.

GRRRRRRR-er-er-oink!

LET'S PARLER FRANGLAIS!

Dans le Hi-Fi Shop

Monsieur: Je veux remplacer mon stylus.
Audioman: Donnez-moi un shufti.
Monsieur: Voilà. C'est un C-34562M.
Audioman: Ah! Ça n'existe plus. C'est obsolete.
Monsieur: Mais . . .
Audioman: Il a été remplaçé par un Hagasaki N-47 (D).
Monsieur: Ah!
Audioman: Qui est available seulement au Japon et en Californie.
Monsieur: Mais . . .
Audioman: Et par la cartridge Wharfbang A-40 (M).
Monsieur: Ah!
Audioman: Qui vient seulement dans la Nugatron-Musique-Coquetail-Cabinette-Complexe 0940 (except Saturday: see Table 46), £540.
Monsieur: Look. Je suis un homme simple. J'ai un stylus. Le stylus commence à ruiner mes vieux LPs de Roll de Gelée Morton. Je veux remplacer mon stylus.
Audioman: Look, Je suis un audioman simple. J'ai un shop. Si je remplace les stylus, je vais bust. Je remplace seulement les centres de musique.

Monsieur: Come to think, mon système de sound est un peu yesterday. Que recommandez-vous comme remplacement?
Audioman: Ah! Maintenant vous parlez! Nous avons trois bargains absolument fantastiques en ce moment. i. Le West-Indian Suitcase-Cassette Rolleur-Skateur Hold-All avec Free Frisbee, £400 réduit à £399.99. ii. Le Discomania Strobe-Musique-Centre, avec Permission de Planning de Norman St Jean-Stevas, £400 avec Arts Council grant. iii. Le Jean Lennon Memorial Tribute Sound-Bloc "Au Musicien Inconnu" rock-bottom £400, fabriqué per Yoko-Sony.
Monsieur: Réduit a £399.99?
Audioman: Of course.
Monsieur: Hmm. C'est difficile. Vous n'avez pas un stylus C-34562M.
Audioman: Non. Mais j'ai une paire d'ear-phones Jackie Kennedy en silk pur. Ou un set video Monty Python avec les takes alternatives.
Monsieur: Look. J'ai le sentiment que nous ne parlons pas la même langue. Je suis dans une stylus-shortage situation. Vous êtes dans un audio-freak-trip.
Audioman: Vous avez raison. Mon mind a été zappé. J'ai freaké. Je suis hors de mon skull.
Monsieur: Bon. Donnez-moi un stylus C-34562M.
Audioman: Voilà.
Monsieur: Bon. C'est £4.50, n'est-ce pas?
Audioman: Oui.
Monsieur: Bon. Voilà.
Audioman: Merci. Et le next, please.

"Young Tarzan worries me, mother—at his age I was out getting girls into trouble."

FATHER'S DAY

HUNTER DAVIES
on the move

I SAW this terrific house in the local paper last week, a Georgian gem, full of period features, lovely garden, just the sort of house I've always fancied, so I naturally rang the agent for details, already planning how I'd raise the money and which rooms my stamp collection could go into and how the basement would be ideal for Jake's snooker table. (He says I can call him by his correct name again. I'm on probation till Christmas, then he'll reconsider it, depending on my good behaviour, as long as I haven't embarrassed him again, so that is good news.)

They were all out somewhere, enjoying themselves while I slaved away at home trying to get this book finished, so I went round on my own to have a look from the outside. It's only in the next street, but architecturally and socially it's miles away. We're standard Victorian, built for the workers, though high class ones of course, like engine drivers, while round the corner, there's this whole Georgian terrace of v. desirable residences, all Grade II listed, built for high class clerks.

They face the main road, that's true, and our gardens which back on to theirs get more sun, but what do you expect for £160,000. Yes, that's the price it says at the bottom of the agent's purple prose. Freehold. I bet they would come down. Anyway, we'll worry about the money later. I rang to make an appointment for Saturday morning for my wife and me to inspect it.

I haven't looked at houses recently, being so busy, but at one time I had the agents' lists coming through the letterbox in handfuls. There's probably not a street for three miles around where I haven't inspected at least one of the houses. We always intended to move somewhere nicer when we could afford it. This house, when we moved in eighteen years ago, had my wife in tears when we first arrived. It was ugly, falling down and we had a sitting tenant on the top floor. We'd left such a beautiful flat, right in the middle of Hampstead, but vowed we would one day return, or at least have a house that was uplifting, one which made your heart sore when you approached it, I mean soar.

I came home to find the plumber just finishing. We've had this strange noise in the pipes for over six months which has driven me round every bend, trying to find the cause. Every floorboard has been taken up and every hardboarded panel been taken down, without finding any signs of leaks. To make a short story longer, we traced it in the end to the main water pipe, outside the house, just three inches away from the pavement. I paid off the plumber, £90 in cash, wishing I could be a plumber. Another

three inches and it would have cost nothing as it would have been the Water Board's responsibility. So it goes.

When they all came home, I said good news all round. The leak is mended and we're moving houses. I should have recorded exactly everyone's expression as a valuable psychological record for our family archives. It betrayed exactly their different temperaments, at this moment in Tim.

Caitlin said great. I'm fed up with my room. I could do with a new one for all my stuff. Then she went to put the kettle on, for her coming home from school little nine course snackeroo, without giving it another thought. Not only could she take a move in her stride, she probably would just walk out of her present room and leave all her belongings behind without a second glance. If you've seen her belongings, you would understand. It's about the only way to get rid of them.

Flora looked nervous and worried, watching all the family faces. Will I still be near Sarah, she said. Of course you will, my petal. It's the next street. And you'll go to the same school and have all the same friends.

Jake gave a few grunts of irritation and then asked some completely irrelevant questions, such as which agent is it, how do I know it's for sale, till finally I got a straight answer out of him which was no, he certainly didn't want to move. I lyrically waxed about the huge basement, just right for snooker, perhaps table tennis as well, and he went up to his room to do his homework with a sly smile on his face.

My lady wife came home a bit later. She'd been out running the Arts Council or judging the Booker Prize or some other war work she has to do to keep the country on an even keel, leaving me with shopping lists and endless instructions and I dunno, Cinderella had it so easy. I had meant to dab a bit of after-shave behind my ear for her return, or change into something seductive, as my old cords do hang a bit these days and I know she hates me slopping around in these old slippers, but, you know how it is, a man's work is never done.

You would have thought I had announced I was leaving her for a seventeen-year-old Playmate of the Month or becoming a Jehovah's Witness. I was made to feel an absolute traitor for even thinking for one moment of leaving our lovely house. You have utterly no soul, she said, opening the fridge. And you haven't got the stewing steak.

Later that evening she almost had me in tears. Our house is not a building but a living organism. Remember when we arrived you wanted to have a little face at each window, sob sob. It is where we had our children and where each of them has grown up. Jake was even born here, in the little room that is now her work room. The house has changed and developed as we have developed and it is no longer ugly. Remember how we slowly took it over, working our way up year by year as we got our pennies together for the next bit of work.

It's all so painfully personal. I know each

"If you'd been a failure, I often wonder how you would have coped with my resentment."

Michael Clark

room like I know people. I know their best faces, the best times of the season to catch them, the best light to view them in. This house has everything I will ever want. It's the perfect size, the perfect arrangement. You have not just no soul, you are a snob. A discontented snob. This house gives nothing away. You can't tell the inside life from the outside walls. If you live in a ghetto like those people in Hampstead, or those Georgian terraces, everyone knows what sort of people they are. I don't wish to be one of them.

Hmm. Wish I'd never spoken. Anyway, the plumber's been and the leak's mended. Yes, she said. Just think of the little jobs you'll have to do in a five storey eighteenth-century house. That should keep you occupied.

It's all just a bit of fun, I said. You used to love looking round people's houses just as much as I do. You know I don't really want to move. It's only harmless fantasising, though I wonder how much we would get for this house, now the leak's mended and the roof is new.

You can go and see it on your own, she said. I am certainly not coming. I refuse to have anything to do with it.

So I had to go round this morning on my own. As I went out of the door she shouted after me that if I didn't come back she would send my pyjamas. Ha ha. Very funny. I couldn't cancel, could I, having made a proper appointment. I walked round slowly, hoping it would turn out really awful then I would be able to forget the whole thing immediately.

An elderly gentleman showed me round and as we toured the floors I picked up the vibrations and emotions of the long life he and his family had had, the children's rooms still decorated with their teenage possessions, long after they had gone. The

"Gee, there are telegrams of good wishes from Heads of States I never even knew existed."

big drawing room where they used to have such wonderful parties. The ingenious little cupboards his son had made when young.

People always take great pains in opening and closing and exhibiting minor fittings like cupboards or shelves, pointless things which aren't going to sway you either way, not when you might be spending £160,000. I suppose it gives them something to do, a physical action to distract themselves, and you, a complete stranger, standing coldly staring at their exposed beams, their fading memories, their naked lives.

It was a lovely house with some beautiful rooms and some marvellous original old wooden panelling. I was just leaving, feeling rather depressed, when he opened one more ingenious cupboard, this time in the basement, and I suddenly saw what looked like damp. Nothing to worry about, he said very quickly. No, no, it's not damp. Just a spot of bother with the main water pipe. We've had a leak in it. Not to worry.

I ran home and announced loudly that we weren't going to move after all. I'm not paying £90 for another plumber . . .

"Of course, he'll never admit it's a U-Turn."

Mellymobile

A CURIOUS thing about even a modest celebrity—"fat and fairly famous" as my wife has phrased it—is that, whatever the nature of one's work, one is treated instantly as a father confessor, a guru, by strangers encountered in a street, public house or restaurant. They look, they recognise, they confirm, they tell all. Sometimes this is simply in relation to what they feel about you. I remember once when, due to a short-lived but consecutive TV series, my public life was just teetering on the edge of constant if friendly intrusion when, on the steps of the Adelphi Hotel, Liverpool, I was approached by a large middle-aged lady whose maroon coat was in daring contrast to her ginger hair. What she wanted was an autograph but she was in a considerable state of excitement about it. This manifested itself by her wild scrambling through the contents of a large handbag in search of a suitable piece of paper. "Sign me rent buke!" she cried desperately. "Anything!"

I calmed her down, found a piece of paper in my briefcase, enquired her name— "Mary"—and obliged.

"There's only two people I'd commit adultery with right off," she told me at this point. "You and Frankie Vaughan!"

The vision of Frankie and me seated in her front room, each of us politely insisting that the other takes precedence is one that can still relieve moments of depression, but at least in her case I was at the centre of her confession. What frequently happens is rather less direct. I am simply presented with a problem, sometimes of an intimate nature, and asked my advice. This is of course flattering, but disturbing. I'm not very good at advice even with those I know well. Perhaps though this is not the point. It's the need to unburden that helps and a face, both familiar but unknown, is perhaps ideal in these circumstances. Anyway, whatever the explanation it happens quite frequently.

For example the other evening, having some writing to do, I went to eat alone at a small Indian restaurant within easy walking distance, taking with me a book. Desmond Morris, in *Manwatching*, maintains that this is to avoid appearing unoccupied, without friends, isolated, but I think it is also a way of protecting oneself from those who, imagining one to be lonely, insist on inviting you to join them or ask if they may join you. I notice that I always choose a thick book anyway. It seems more substantial than a paperback or newspaper, more of a barrier. At all events on this occasion it proved insufficient. Indeed *The Anatomy of Melancholy* would have very likely failed to achieve my end, but I am not complaining. I was both touched and riveted by what transpired.

Seated at the next table were what I took to be two attractive teenage lovers; the girl very beautiful with long black hair and amazing eyes, the boy a bit podgy but personable and attentive. They spoke modern Cockney, that curious blend of hip slang and trad working-class argot full of "Yeahs", "Y'knows", " 'Eavy", "Aht of order", "Right?", "In'it?". They were drinking white wine and eating Tandoori chicken and nan.

Always curious, or as some would say nosey, I clocked all this without, I imagine, seeming to raise my eyes from Aragon's *Paris Peasant*. Immediately after I'd ordered, however, and before I could start to read again, the boy asked if I was me. I conceded the point in a friendly but distant manner and began to pick up my book but he was too quick for me. "We got teenage problems," he said. I held on to my book and assured them that horrible as teenage problems were, they did, inevitably, disappear, only to be replaced by adult problems which were worse because you were stuck with them until senility or death provided a solution. "No, not ours," he countered, "Her daughter." Surprise number one. They weren't teenagers. She was old enough to have a teenage daughter

which made her at least thirty-four. I looked at her harder. She still didn't look a day over seventeen, and he gave no sign of having started shaving.

"She's violent. Breaks the place up and beats us up. She's stronger than both of us together," said the mother, and then added, "The trouble is she's dead jealous of her, see, and she's keen on me, fancies me you know."

This was a true mind-blower, containing as it did several unlikely facts to be assimilated from one short sentence; not only did the daughter fancy her mother but she was jealous of the boyfriend who, to judge by that "her" was in fact not a boy at all. OK, I thought, they were a Lesbian couple. "I see," I said. "Your daughter has a bent Oedipus complex." This was the best I could do. Despite the fairly comprehensive sexual range of Greek mythology I couldn't remember off-hand a closer paradigm.

"Yeah, right," said the mother. "If she's away, she always tries it on. 'Can I come in your bed Mum?' 'No,' I say. 'No way. You got your room and I've got mine.' "

"It's a pity though," said her lover, "because when she's not doin' a wobbler she's great. Lovely sense of humour. Right?"

"Right!"

"Has she got a boy-friend?" I asked. "Or a girl-friend?" I added hurriedly.

"That's half the trouble," said her mother. "She can't make relationships."

She didn't want a place of her own? No way!

Well, I could see it *was* a teenage problem all right but, they assured me, and I believed them, everything else was fine. They were very happy together, and only that day, explained the butch half of the couple, he'd introduced his girl to his mother and "they'd got on great". What made this so important to them both was that the mother had always refused to meet any of her women before.

Conversation got more general after that, reverting, alas, to that most banal area of modern conversational gambits, the stars. They were even "into" Chinese astrology and wanted to know what creature, monkey, tiger, etc., ruled my destiny. For this they needed my hour of birth which I can happily never remember. "He" was Leo, as I am, and sometimes went to bed with men. "She" was Aquarius and didn't like it. They were very nice and held hands a lot.

When I got back home, much later than I'd intended, the phone rang and it was my dear friend Derek Taylor, writer, and one-time press-officer and confidant of the Beatles. I told him of my encounter and expressed how surprised and pleased I was that they should have thought me a suitably sympathetic ear. I also rejoiced that even now, despite the Whitehousian back-lash, people were not only prepared to find their own solutions, but to make no secret of them. Derek agreed but added that they had, by chance or instinct, chosen one of extreme, some would say excessive, tolerance. "Suppose," he said, "they'd found themselves sitting next to, say, the Chief Constable of Manchester."

UNFAIR COP

A weary group of Berkshire Constabulary officers waits in Windsor Great Park for someone to expose himself to a WPC decoy.

The appalling decline in the St. John's Wood crime rate has led to the dispiriting spectacle of policemen arresting one another in a last-ditch attempt to increase their work-norm. Here, PC Norman Wellings hustles PC Derek Fune away on a loitering charge. PC Fune subsequently charged PC Wellings with gross indecency.

A fierce tussle in Farringdon Road after a litter-bug was simultaneously spotted by four desperate officers. Following five hours of heated discussion, the permanent ACAS referee attached to Snow Hill Police Station awarded the suspect to PC Adrian Brill *(second from l.)*.

Acting on information that a verge on the A658 had been gravely fouled, officers from eleven West Yorkshire stations rushed to the scene. A heifer is helping them with their enquiries.

A keen-eyed police swoop which yesterday netted a car driving without registration plates. Later a queen was detained.

A coup for Chief Inspector Ronald Bowles of Nottingham! The ten men signing confessions had been asked to make up an identification parade, and were subsequently arrested on a charge of consorting with a known criminal.

WILLIAM DAVIS:

Great Britain Limited

CONFIDENTIAL

To: The Editor of Punch
From: William Davis, Chairman, Global Management Consultants Ltd
Re.:   Great Britain Limited

You have asked us to make an independent assessment of the above-named business and to recommend ways of making it more profitable in future.

In our view, the problem can be summed up in one sentence: there are too many employees making the wrong kind of products and expecting to be paid a lot of money for doing so.

Successive managements have either failed to recognise this obvious fact or shown themselves unwilling to take the required action. The present Board of Directors seems more determined, but further drastic measures are required if the business is to make satisfactory profits.

The workforce

It is clear that far too many people rely on an income from the business. The Board has shed a considerable amount of labour, but employees who have either lost their jobs or have chosen to retire continue to draw sizeable benefits. The inevitable result is that the company is saddled with massive overheads.

We have examined various solutions. One would be to persuade—and if necessary to force—people to seek employment abroad. This was the policy carried out, very effectively, in Victorian and Edwardian days. Employees who were surplus to requirement were sent to subsidiaries like India, Australia and Canada. Unfortunately, subsequent managements took the short-sighted view that the company would be better off without overseas branches and today it is much more difficult to apply the same remedy.

Under the chairmanship of Edward Heath, the company took the very sensible step of applying for membership of the Common Market. This should have produced a considerable outflow of labour to Germany, Holland, France, and other places of work, but regrettably it has not materialised.

It was also hoped, at one time, that it might be possible to set up new labour-intensive subsidiaries on Mars and other planets. It is, alas, another answer which has to be ruled out for the present.

Recommendation

We therefore recommend the following steps:

(1) A sharp reduction in benefits, making it less attractive for people to stay, accompanied by a publicity campaign stressing the advantages of living elsewhere—sunshine, cheap wine, etc.

(2) A special severance payment for employees who elect to go. This was proposed by Mr Enoch Powell some years ago, but sadly he was not taken seriously.

(3) Boardroom action to prevent excessive breeding. The company has, so far, relied on pleas for restraint by its vice-president, HRH Prince Phillip. It is not enough. We would like to draw your attention to the policies pursued in India by the late Mr Sanjay Gandhi, which have undoubtedly proved to be more effective.

Product plan

It is, in our opinion, essential that those left behind should be employed in areas which are likely to yield maximum returns. It is not happening at the moment. There are too many people who persist in making products which are no longer wanted—ships, steel, British cars and so on. All the much-publicised arguments about the future of the business really add up to one thing: the company's stubborn refusal to accept that the post-industrial society is with us *now*.

Too much attention is being paid to short-term solutions which will simply postpone the day of reckoning. We would prefer to see much greater concentration on the growth areas of the future. Our product plan is based on the firm belief that most, if not all, of the activities which have sustained the business in the past are doomed and should therefore be shut down as soon as possible.

It seems obvious to us that competitors like Japan, Taiwan, and Hong Kong will continue to gain ground in the traditional manufacturing areas. They will be joined by others who long to be great industrial enterprises and who have a plentiful supply of cheap labour. It is difficult to see how Great Britain Limited can survive in those circumstances.

The company's early successes were largely due to its ability to spot trends and exploit them. It started the so-called "industrial revolution", and we suggest that its future depends on its ability to pioneer what should, perhaps, be called the "service revolution".

Again, we have examined a number of alternatives. One which particularly appeals to us is that Great Britain Limited should become a tax haven. It would set up paper companies for foreigners,

"Don't talk to me about rheumatism."

Caption below first cartoon: RODIN'S IRISH JUDGE

and the present workforce would be employed as lawyers, accountants and directors whose sole function would be to attend board meetings. It would leave them free to engage in happier pursuits, such as golf and cricket.

The infrastructure already exists: the City branch earns very substantial amounts, known as "invisibles", by providing financial services. It only requires bold action by the Board of Directors to extend this to the company as a whole.

Another course which seems to us to have considerable merit is to put greater emphasis on tourism. The company has already established a useful reputation in this field, but it seems to have a

*"I bet you got this at the normal retail price. Can't you **ever** remember our anniversary in time to send away for something?"*

rather half-hearted approach to it. There is a great deal of unjustified resentment of foreigners, who are amazingly eager to spend large sums of money to see piles of old stones such as Longleat, Blenheim and Stonehenge.

Recommendation

We recommend the following steps:

(1) Elimination of income tax, capital gains tax and other impediments to the establishment of a tax haven.

(2) Boardroom backing for the refurbishment of tourist attractions, instead of subsidies to manufacturing industries. The company should be investing in castles, palaces and conveniently located "theme parks". (Suggested themes include Shakespeareland, Empireland, Theatreland, and Factoryland.)

(3) Incentives which encourage employees to discard blue overalls and pin-stripe suits in favour of dress with greater tourist appeal—scarlet robes, bowler hats and Orders of the Garter. (It should not be left to the company's legal department to provide all the colours.)

Sales of assets

In addition to shedding employees, the company should also consider selling assets which are unlikely to be worth much in future. The process was started under the Attlee and Wilson Governments, which let go of subsidiaries like India, and subsequently permitted the sale of London Bridge and departments like Ford. It has continued since, with the disposal of the Dorchester to Arab interests and of old VC10s to Middle East airlines. But we suggest that the pace should be accelerated.

Recommendation

We recommend the following steps:

(1) Factories and machinery surplus to requirement (which, if our product plan is followed, means *all* of them) should be offered to the highest bidder.

(2) Britain's armed forces (such as they are) should be hired out to foreign enterprises.

(3) Members of the royal family should be sold or leased to republics which appear to be in desperate need of suitable heads of state.

Merger

We have also considered the possibility of a merger with another business, such as the United States. This could be achieved through an application to become the 51st State, and it would have several advantages. Great Britain Limited would become part of a multi-national corporation with privileged access to a vast market. The parent company would assume liability for all its debts. And there is a good chance that the operation would amount to a reverse take-over bid, with the smaller component taking control of the enlarged enterprise.

On reflection, though, we feel that the company should retain its independence. We take the Schumacher view that Small *can* be Beautiful.

Management

The success of any enterprise must ultimately depend on the quality of its management. We feel that Great Britain Limited has had an unfortunate tendency to appoint people for the wrong reasons. The ability to make speeches, shout down opponents and look good on television has generally been regarded as more important than the ability to make profits. It is significant, we suggest, that few of the company's former executives have managed to secure top positions elsewhere.

It is encouraging that the present management team is headed by someone whose family has been engaged in trade and who insists on doing her own shopping. One must never underrate the value of market research. We venture to suggest that, if she should ever lose her job, she would make an excellent chairman of the British Tourist Authority. But we have serious doubts about some of the other members of the Board, including the Finance Director, and we strongly recommend an early re-appraisal.

FREAKY FABLES by HANDELSMAN

THE SUMMER OF OUR DISCONTENT

or, Thus Have I Had Thee, As a Dream Doth Flatter

FEW PEOPLE* KNEW THAT RICHARD, DUKE OF GLOUCESTER, WAS A WOMAN.

Job opportunities are scarce for ugly, deformed women here in the 15th century.

In the Dark Ages, I could have been Pope.

* In fact, nobody.

All fixed, sir! Expenses include one butt of malmsey, three meat cleavers and two pillows for smothering purposes; semi-skilled labour at two farthings per minute; that comes to---

Heavens, now I have to be King, and I haven't a thing to wear.

Read down, or you may be next.

APART FROM THE OCCASIONAL PORTER OR PAGE, THE ENTIRE POPULATION IN THOSE DAYS CONSISTED OF DISGRUNTLED NOBLES.

More land! My present estates are derisory.

An acre goes only half as far as it did in 1400.

My noble Lord of East Sussex, what says Richard to our just demands?

He says...

Bah.

I want an earldom to supplement my dukedom!

It was clearly understood that I was to be King on alternate Mondays.

We simply **must** learn to live within our means, except me.

We must all tighten our belts.

What adornment do you wear, thrice-revered Blackpool? It almost resembles a red rose.

It almost **is** a red rose, brave Home Counties.

I thought red roses were supposed to be white.

No, no! The times, they are a-changin'.

Though smarties flinch and yorkies jeer, We'll keep the red rose blooming here.

DOWN TOOLS AND UP TITLES WITH HENRY VII, VIII, IX, ETC.

Kneel, Brighton and Hove, and arise Clacton and Margate.

But I thought the country couldn't afford it.

For defence, or for British Steal, the country can afford **anything**, silly-billy.

MORAL: Never oppress the rich. They **hate** it.

SUMER IS ICUMEN UNSTUCK

or, In Sleep a King, But, Waking, No Such Matter

ANOTHER LITTLE-KNOWN NON-FACT IS THAT "STUART" WAS ORIGINALLY SPELLED "CTUART".*

My mommy, Miz Mary Queen of Scots, used to say "Jimmy Ctuart, when you get to be King I want you to have your very own Bible."

* Pronounced "Kirkcudbright".

That's the place! Let's seize it and take hostages and issue moronic communiqués.

Shouldn't we wait for Guy Fawkes Day?

Sire! The Spaniards have marched into Florida! It was 200 years ago, but it's still **wrong**.

Oh, the poor little Dutch, or whoever was there before.

Restore popery or we blow up Hansard.

Don't you dare touch a hair of Hansard's head.

The King says "Ride straight in and kill the terrorists without bloodshed."

Cancel that! The King now says "Kill yourselves instead."

Mr. Shakespeare has just written a play entitled "The Tempest".

No plays! We're boycotting Spain!

Someone might translate it into Spanish — a moral victory for their side.

His Majesty's brother is displeased with the Bible — too many Jews in the Old Testament.

Very few references to beer.

Right, we'll just change "Moses" to "Watneys".

I claim this land in the name of God and —

Welcome to Chappaquiddick, paleface.

When I am King, dad, can I arrest Parliament?

Son, if it's dumb, **do** it.

Hear hear.

MORAL: Divinely inspired mistakes are the best kind.

PAUL JENNINGS

RE JOYCE

AS everyone knows, forty years ago this week, James Joyce died, aged 59; and so did Lord Baden-Powell, aged 83.

Nothing surprising in that; as everyone also knows, writing damages the health more than scouting, especially writing like Joyce's. What is surprising is that although in his work there are parodic references to the Elizabethans, Bunyan, Pepys, Macaulay, Sir T. Browne, Sterne, the Anglo-Saxons, practically everything except the telephone directory, there's nothing about scouting, the nearest thing the West has to puberty transition rites, and therefore basic enough to warrant the attention of that prodigious and universal mind.

The Advanced Literary Badge is surely a long-felt want, but I haven't got time to go through the whole Works (be honest; who has?). So:

Tails of boyhood! Boy scuts are camp in the starnight from burrows and burgs of their citified accountant deadened kids paleface with gins and picure-palaces wherever they roam with fag-ends dangle in their mouths, escape to the regular guise of their tent with bading-poles, in the hope an air. Oranjeburg, Spine Cope, Jubilee Hill and all stations to empire with a nominal role of Victoria when she sat on their own, it's the hero of Mafeking with *veldtanschauung* and trainsvaal to mouldy youth.

Begone the Gripes and Bookse to the varsity of life! Boy scots whistle and cheer for every sir come stance of scoutmaster's if he is never been twenty-one before, assistant can be A teen with his B pat roll of wolf packs to totem orbem.

I can corroborree what Sir Gilwell Gladwell-Powell signals to the sing-a-ling jamboree of many nations in Knees-up Park; browny Fijians in their painted skirts, 1st Majumba, Kookaburra dingo-dong-dog with their billabong swagman-song *et nos*

amis de Liege embrace ye millions with a few vurds from the motherandfathering waters of. The Rhine Troop. *Alle menschen werden bruder*, internationale with no marx for red.

This was the colour of our map. Brownsea Island with Pompey and circumstance when B.P. started his first multi-national so long as it was ours, a message to save the umpire's manhood and know if the Union Joke was upside-down (Pat riot! Jock-scrap in the gorbalimey, St George for Merely England!). But *himmel, zut, caramba, gosh, dio mio*, and all ex claims in the world! Ich globe for all youth!

For this was the lore he baden. A scot is cheerful. A skate is helpful. Ascot is avoiding snobbery. A skit is clean in thought an deed in naughty whirled, as cat is kind to animals. Purefoy paragon and chivalrous timbers in the greenwood of youth.

So pax on *Nudes of the World* and *Sunday Purple* and rod-face bumboater send-up comoedians with their snuggery hoax and I-knew-end-ohs of scoutmasters serious offence (Donalgill titterbum postcards! Cackle of blue-rinse British headsex! Virgin viragos, tipsy with nipples, *Sun*-struck mammary bummery flummery!). Flout 'em, boy, scout 'em! Thought is free in the inner sent soul of his laddy dreams.

Dib dib dib for Sir Gladwell Totem-Pole, the Hurrah of muff King Edward's rain on the stout canvas of ladscamp! All in order of British I'm pure till it circled the Glubb from Jordan to Jericho. Hawk? Warsquawk? With *Scooting for Boys* in Good

King Teddy's daze? Bush! Twiddle! Puppykick!

Cups off, and three chairs for Lord Bidden-Pile in his dotage! When the world was Jung, and before men were afreud, he called to the *puer aeternus*. The spoor always with you. For boys on the wrong side of the treks, in city pent, a bursting from boerdom.

Camp damp stamp the boys are larking to all in tents and purposes. A scout has purposes to be prepared, every Thursday night come fine or wet tenderfoot. Untie the gemman's mystiknots. Here is the shapeshanks, over anunder. Here is the roofknot, bendover double. Here is the clovehitch, watch it and ponder. Here is the granny with two round turns. Here is the fisherman's bend over hand. Here is the bowline to better your badge.

Or first-aid to your splinter groups. Fractures are greenstick unless comminuted. Noted on jotpaper. Would be for woodcraft too. Here is the weasel, the teazle, the whistlebird song-sound. *Tirraloo tirralay*. Here is the woodchecker warble, the ousel, the dabblecock moorchick, the whiffling yaffle, or single low note of the breeder, down upon the swampy river. I long to go. Certainly Johnson.

Here is the three-trek card. Woodcraft; cookskill in the Alleghominy moutains far faraway in the summerdream campanion (any silly can cook in a billycan, making a fire with only two matches); and mapreading starting from Easter to norther and further, to know where you fared Be Prepared.

Here is the Bading-Pool teach you to swim. Here is the Boating-Pole swim you to sale of work. Here is the kitty to car you to camp in the bare-knees overland route. Dream of the wild. Not a bit de troop in the world. Free cheese for Sir Gladwell Rowallan of Burden-Pull and his land and seabay's kites. Before inner sense lost.

"We had to introduce rugby league every fortnight!"

ALAN MELVILLE:

Final Notice

SOMEONE on, of all things, *The Guardian* rang up and said he was sorry to trouble me but he had a request to make which might be thought unusual and even somewhat, er, macabre. They were having, he said, a bit of a spring-clean on their obituary notices, and would I by any chance consider doing X—naming a well-known actress with whom I crossed paths, among other things, in the palmy days of intimate revue. "Good gracious!" I said. "Is she—? . . . I mean, is it, er, *urgent*?"

"Not at all," said *The Guardian*. "On the contrary, according to the latest available reports, the lady in question is in rude health. But one has to be prepared for any eventuality. *Venienti occurite morbo.*"

There is really very little one can think of on the spur of the moment in reply to a crack like *venienti occurite morbo*. Squeams are not things I go in for in a big way, but I did feel slightly squeamish about the whole thing. However, I know X as well as anyone and there are at least a couple of stories about the old girl which I felt might amuse the reader without actually offending the next-of-kin. So I agreed to do her, and *The Guardian* character said at once, "While you're at it, you wouldn't like to, er, knock off Y, would you?"—referring this time to an equally famous actress who from time to time has done her own variations on lines, lyrics, and sketches I have written for her. It seemed odd to me: here I am, a senior citizen, half-price on British Rail, bus tokens and all the rest of it, embarking on a new career as a knocker-off of obits. Still, I thought, if the news gets around I might do quite well out of it in the way of hospitality: if you want a decent notice on the way out, keep in with old Al.

I felt terrible writing the things. Using the past tense is the worst bit; every time I wrote that Miss X *was* something, or that Miss Y *had been* something else, I felt I was not just being premature but in an underhand sort of way hastening the end. *The Guardian* character, however, was delighted. "Just what the doctor ordered," he said on receipt of the valedictories. "The personal touch, the occasional shaft of good humour—I'm sure, when the time comes, they'll be greatly appreciated. How about having a go at Z, mmm? I know he's in that serial, but he *is* eighty-four . . ."

It happened, of course. I was walking down the Haymarket and bumped slap-bang into X. Looking, to my relief, in the pink of condition and irritatingly young for her years. (I'd looked her up in *Who's Who* and subtracted five as an old chum.) "*Darling! . . .*," she said, smothering me in her simulated. "I thought you were dead. What are you writing these days—or have you given it all up?" I was so pleased to see her that I invited her to lunch; halfway through the meal, during which she told me her plans for the future, she said, "Look who's just come in, darling—better ask her to join us: poor soul, she looks *ghastly*." I have to ask you to take my word for this: it *was* Y. I have rarely eaten a less enjoyable meal. Y kept saying that all she seemed to do nowadays was attend other people's memorial services, and reminding us that we were all—the three of us—contemporaries and, let's face it, living on borrowed time. X kept saying absolute balls, darling, you're as young as you feel, and I've no patience with people who keep on about the Great Reaper and sans eyes, and sans teeth, and sans all that jazz. She also suggested a second bottle of Sancerre to drink to the success of the new musical she was doing when she got back from Australia early in 1982. Both girls had a large Armagnac with their coffee; the bill came to £48.70, plus VAT.

I also met Z the other day. He was, correction, is a very famous comedian, but recently he's taken to writing: it's an overcrowded profession. We met at the barber's; he was preening himself after a boyish short back and sides. "Got to look my best," he said. "It's my brother's birthday. He's 100." He looked at me in what seemed to me an accusing manner. "Longevity," he said, "runs riot in our family. Finished that autobiography you said you were writing? Better get on with it, y'know. Time's running short. Well, see you soon—I hope . . ." And off he went, humming *Silver Threads Among the Gold* which, considering I was following him into the barber's chair, I took amiss.

Worrying things, obits. The people most concerned never read them, and writing them puts years on you. I get this feeling *The Guardian* has asked Z to do mine.

"Another deserter from ENSA."

SONG, MIRTH, & MUSIC

BY WIRE TO YOUR HOME
See Next Page

E. S. TURNER

Put Me Through to Electrophone

HOW was it that King Edward VII, in his armchair at Sandringham, was able to listen in to Melba singing in *La Bohème* at Covent Garden? How was it that Queen Alexandra, under the same roof, could hear live sermons preached by fashionable divines in London? The "wireless", as a fount of culture, did not then exist.

The world has forgotten the Electrophone, a public service which was born in the 1890s and, by the 1920s, had vanished "down the ringing grooves of change". It was available not only to royalty but to anyone who was willing to pay £5 a year for the privilege of hearing, in the home, performances "direct from the footlights" or "direct from the pulpit". If you had guests who were difficult to entertain, you simply connected them with the Electrophone and let them listen to Phyllis Dare or George Robey or the Bishop of London. Already the art of conversation was on the way out.

The Electrophone, like the French Theatrophone, worked in conjunction with the telephone system. When the British telephone companies were nationalised, the Post Office encouraged the Electrophone company in its heady ambitions. The telephone museum, soon to be opened in London by the Post Office, will contain Electrophone relics, including one of the lead boxes, modelled to resemble a Bible, which disguised the transmitter in church pulpits or choir stalls.

Something else the world has forgotten is that the telephone was seen originally as a device for transmitting music rather than speech. In 1878 Alexander Graham Bell,

no sluggard at grabbing free publicity, reported to Osborne House in the Isle of Wight and arranged for Queen Victoria to listen to a bugle blowing a Retreat in Southampton, followed by an organ recital in London. In 1883 Sir Arthur Sullivan, on his birthday, invited the Prince of Wales to his house to hear, over the wire, the strains of *Iolanthe* from the Savoy Theatre, the company having been assembled on a Sunday night at the composer's expense to sing into a telephone. At the receiving end a single earpiece was passed reverently round. Nine years later some 60,000 visitors to the Crystal Palace paid to hear music relayed from theatres (an attraction already staged at the Paris Exhibition of 1881).

When the Electrophone was launched in 1895 the National Telephone Company welcomed it as an enterprise likely to keep equipment in profitable use after the rush of the day's business was over. The apparatus issued to subscribers included an induction coil, batteries and a neat table hung with two receivers (for four receivers the fee was £10 a year). The twin-ear receivers were not worn over the head but were held up to the ears by means of a centrally mounted handle, rather like an aural lorgnette. If the listener wished to knit or shell peas at the same time the handle had to be gripped between the knees, which was not too satisfactory. The quality of theatre reception depended very much on the number and location of the transmitters distributed among the footlights. There was a stereo effect of sorts, described as "a change of sonorous intensity from one ear to the other" as singers or actors changed position.

The theatres seem to have looked on their unseen listeners not as parasites but as future patrons. However, a night with the Electrophone inevitably had its *longueurs*. As a writer in the *National Telephone Journal* said in 1907, "People don't want to *listen* to performing dogs, bears or elephants." He stressed the need for courteous operators, "for a little more attention is expected by subscribers when using the Electrophone than is desired when hustling for business on the telephone;" it could be very annoying to be "connected to a Salvation Army meeting instead of the Gaiety."

Early this century the Electrophone began to appear in clubs, restaurants and cafes. The company had hopes of being allowed to install their transmitters in the Houses of Parliament, but the legislators showed the same distrust that their successors displayed, for half a century, towards the microphones of the BBC. The Westminster Abbey authorities also betrayed a Luddite streak, declining to admit the transmitter-Bible, though it was to be found in St Martin-in-the-Fields, St Mary-le-Bow, St James's in Piccadilly, the City Temple and many other churches.

The Electrophone did not catch on as fast as its sponsors hoped—there were about 600 subscribers in 1907, some 2,000 in London in 1915—so stunt after stunt was organised. In 1913 there was a celebration of the *Entente Cordiale* when guests in the Gerrard Street salon of the company listened to a transmission of *Faust* from the Paris Opera House and audiences in Paris, linked on the Theatrophone, heard selections from *Tosca* at Covent Garden. Owing to some difficulty in retaining use of trunk lines the broadcasts from Paris were intermittent and had to be eked out by contributions from West-End theatres.

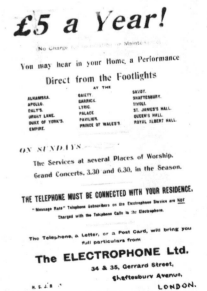

Lord Northcliffe, a great seeker after novelty, had already put the Electrophone through its paces. In September 1909 when Lord Rosebery proposed to utter some unusually weighty thoughts on the Budget at a meeting in Glasgow, two rooms were cleared in Carmelite House, London and twelve shorthand writers of the London *Evening News* took down the hour-and-a-half speech, which was on the streets within minutes of its ending. "By Electrophone" made a change from "By Special Engine".

During World War One subscribers to the Electrophone could share the patriotic frenzy of the music halls or hear George Robey and Violet Loraine singing "If you were the only girl in the world" in *The Byng Boys*. When Harry Lauder was appearing at the Palace, subscribers would be lucky to get a line to the theatre. Those who, in happier times, had enjoyed plugging in to music halls for the hooligan fun of Boat Race Night no doubt got their money's worth on Armistice Night.

After the war the Electrophone fought a hopeless fight against the crystal set and the gramophone. By 1926 it was extinct. For a generation it had served as a modest bridge between technologies and its subscribers were a tiny élite comparable to the handful of early television viewers whose world collapsed in 1939.

But memories survived. When *The Times*, ever nostalgic for lost pleasures, published a reminiscent article about the Electrophone, in 1957, readers dusted off their recollections. Among them was Herbert Buckmaster, who used to listen in to his wife, Gladys Cooper, from their flat in Clarence Gate Gardens. One night in 1909, when Miss Cooper was appearing in "a not too serious play", an actor called out, "Buck, are you listening in tonight?" No reply was possible. One drawback of the system, Buckmaster thought, was that would-be callers on the telephone would be put off by the "clerk in charge" saying "They are using the Electrophone."

Another reader recalled that as a schoolgirl she used to listen to her idol Lewis Waller reciting from the Palace Theatre. "The Electrophone was installed in our schoolroom and for that whole month nothing would have enticed us away from hearing Waller's magic voice declaiming mainly Shakespeare and Kipling. In retrospect I can still feel the thrill and majesty of the most beautiful voice I can recall."

Nobody, alas, wrote in recalling the inspirational voice of the incumbent at St Martin-in-the-Fields or St Mary-le-Bow. No aged clergyman joined in to say what an ordeal it was to preach a sermon in the knowledge that the Sovereign might be listening to his injunctions to repent. Did vicars ever object to the Electrophone on the grounds that it would encourage lazy worshippers to stay at home, or to suck sweets during the service, or to dodge the collection? We may never know.

LET'S PARLER FRANGLAIS!

Les Inquiries de Directoire

Monsieur: Allo?
Opératrice: Allo, Enquiries de Directoire. Ville?
Monsieur: Hantry.
Opératrice: Nom?
Monsieur: Brian Whitgift.
Opératrice: Son numéro est Hantry 4560.
Monsieur: Non, je connais son numéro. C'est son adresse qu'il me faut.
Opératrice: Nous ne pouvons pas donner les adresses. Ce n'est pas permis. *(Cut-off.)*
Monsieur: Damn! . . . . *(Il redialle)* Allo?
Opérateur: Bonjour. Ville?
Monsieur: Hantry. Et le nom est Whitgift, Brian.
Opérateur: C'est Hantry 4560.
Monsieur: Il est très important que j'ai le Whitgift correct. Mon ami a un frère dans la même ville.
Opérateur: Qui s'appelle, lui aussi, Brian?
Monsieur: Oui. C'est un twin. Donnez-moi l'adresse, seulement pour le double-checking.
Opérateur: No worry, sir. Il y a seulement un Whitgift solitaire dans le livre. C'est votre ami OK. *(Cut-off.)*

Monsieur: Damn et double damn. *(Il redialle.)*
Opératrice: Enquiries de Directoire. Ville?
Monsieur: Inspecteur Selhurst de la Cour Scotland ici. Nous sommes sur la verge de faire un arrêt très important. Un M. Brian Whitgift, de Hantry. Mais il y a un détail missing. Son adresse.
Opératrice: Nous ne donnons pas les adresses.
Monsieur: Je vous commande, par la majesté de la loi, et sous peine de beaucoup d'aggro, de donner son adresse! Regardez smartish!
Opératrice: Je connais cette voix. C'est vous le joker qui a téléphoné tout à l'heure. Cour Scotland, ma tante Fanny! *(Cut-off.)*
Monsieur: Trois fois damn. *(Il redialle.)*
Opérateur: Bonjour. Ville, svp?
Monsieur: Mon nom est Brian Whitgift. J'ai une complainte *très* sérieuse. Mon adresse est incorrecte dans la directoire, pour Hantry. Qu'allez-vous faire, eh, quelle redresse pouvez-vous m'offrir?
Opérateur: Monsieur, je suis aghast. Laissez-moi regarder . . . Nous avons 1, Darlington Villas—ce n'est pas exact?
Monsieur: Non, non! C'est *11* Darlington Villas!
Opérateur: C'est terrible. Je suis couvert de confusion. Nous allons le rectifier immédiatement. Je vais enrayer un homme.
Monsieur: Bon. *(Cut-off. Il commence à écrire une letter.)* Cher Brian, Avant de venir à business, je dois vous dire que vous allez recevoir une communication assez curieuse de l'Office de Poste . . . .

"Here we have our economy line, sir."

MACBETH
PETER O'TOOLE *as Macbeth*

Hewison–theatre

THE CARETAKER

WARREN MITCHELL *as Davies*
JONATHAN PRYCE *as Mick*
KENNETH CRANHAM *as Aston*

THE SUICIDE
EDWARD PETHERBRIDGE
 as Golashchapov
ROGER REES *as Semyon*

COLETTE
CLEO LAINE *as Colette*
JOHN MOFFATT *as Narrator*

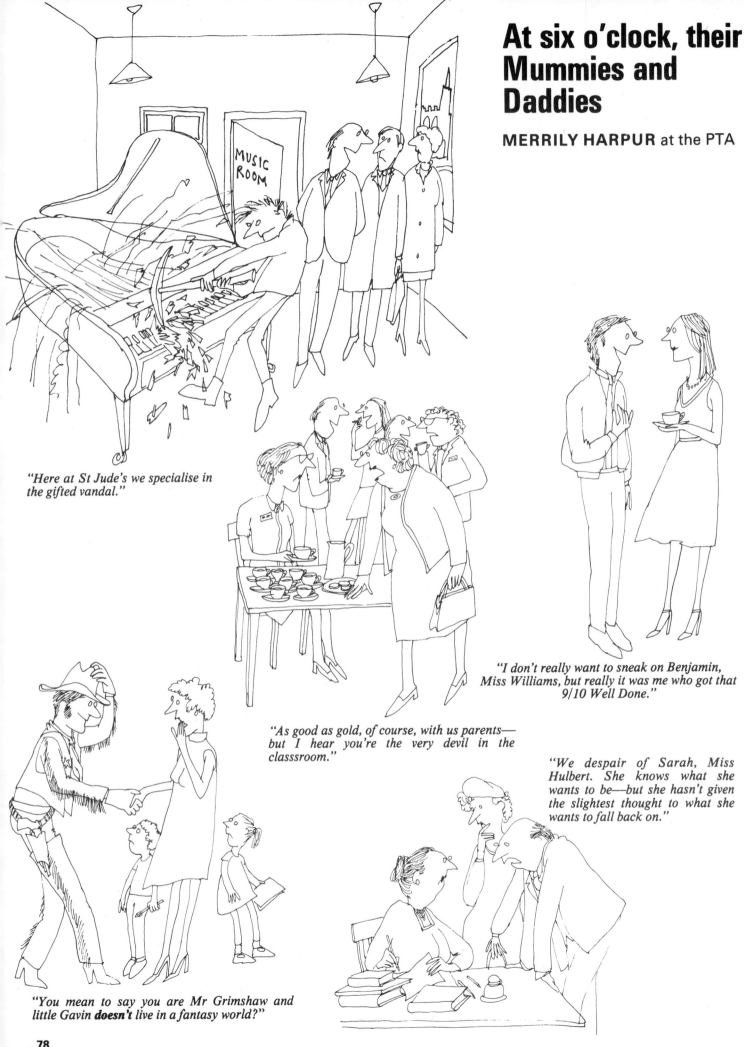

At six o'clock, their Mummies and Daddies

MERRILY HARPUR at the PTA

"Here at St Jude's we specialise in the gifted vandal."

"I don't really want to sneak on Benjamin, Miss Williams, but really it was me who got that 9/10 Well Done."

"As good as gold, of course, with us parents— but I hear you're the very devil in the classsroom."

"We despair of Sarah, Miss Hulbert. She knows what she wants to be—but she hasn't given the slightest thought to what she wants to fall back on."

"You mean to say you are Mr Grimshaw and little Gavin **doesn't** live in a fantasy world?"

"And this is Jenkins, our faithful old teaching aids maintenance engineer."

"We want her to read as quickly as possible—but **selectively**."

"Don't tell me! It's Mrs Mason— I'd recognise Jason's project anywhere."

"Now that our David is a confident, strapping seventeen-year-old— I wonder if you would be so kind as to beat him up."

"I realise Tom's first day at school is an emotional moment, Mrs Miller, but it's up to us teachers to do the crying now."

"You can understand why they're an endangered species."

McLACHLAN

Dangerous Wild Animals Act 1976

JONATHAN SALE:

Animal Crackers

"**R**EMARKABLY immobile, the alligator," said the man from Brighton Borough Council. "Alligators don't move very much," he went on to explain, "and they need very little space. Alligators in general require a space to swim in and a place to bask in, probably with artificial light." Given those mod cons, an alligator would have few complaints. "It would be most unlikely to try to escape. It's a matter of making sure that toddlers can't get to it."

The man from the council knew all this because the animal in question happens to be the only one for which a licence has been requested under the 1976 Dangerous Wild Animals Act. "I can't tell you the details, it's confidential." (*The Case of the Confidential Crocodile*—hitherto undiscovered Sherlock Holmes story.) But, in general terms, anyone who is toying with the idea of keeping a pet alligator in his garage should know that there must be no question of cruelty to the reptile, or to the neighbours.

"The alligator is remarkably docile, so you don't have the problem you would have with a tiger running round." Funny he should say that, because his colleagues in nearby Chichester . . . but first, a word about the Dangerous Wild Animals Act.

To paraphrase, some wild animals act dangerously. Tigers kill because they kill, and it is no good complaining that they haven't read the small print in the zoo contract. Actually, humans kill too, as the tiger world has reason to know: "Watch out for John Aspinall," the big cats must be saying, "he's lethal. Locked Zeya up in a cage and did for her when she was innocently hunting her prey. And if those keepers weren't prey, why were they served up in her territory?"

We must be thankful for anything that prevents the infliction of damage ("damage," according to the Act, "includes the death of, or injury to, any person") by alligators and tigers. You may not keep one without a licence from the local authority; a cassowary, a coyote, an Old World monkey such as a baboon, an emu, a cobra or any Australian poisonous snake "including the death adder". There will be trouble if an Environmental Health Officer catches you with a lynx, leopard, puma, grizzly bear or Mexican beaded lizard. By banning *Pongidae*, Her Majesty's Government has in mind orang-utans, gorillas and chimpanzees, so do not blame unfamiliarity with the Latin tongue for any transgressions. Whatever it is, do not offer house room to a "gharial" or, worse, a "false gharial". "Water mocassin" may sound innocent enough, something from *Hiawatha*, but when you learn that it appears in the same subsection of the Act as the rattlesnake, you will refrain from inviting one in, if you wish to avoid "summary conviction to a fine not exceeding £400".

If the Act has a fault, it is that it does not apply to zoos. Zoos, one would have thought, are the sort of place where pumas and false gharials are to be found. It is a bit like legislation on drinking-up time that specifically excludes pubs.

"You or I could open a zoo tomorrow," snapped Paul Vodden, Assistant Wildlife Officer at the RSPCA, "provided we had planning permission—regardless of whether we had any experience."

What the Act does is regulate those members of the public who might otherwise willy-nilly pop death adders or Mexican beaded lizards in their sheds. But it doesn't even do that in any comprehensive way. It misses out, according to the RSPCA, back-fanged snakes, which are "not always lethal", just sometimes. It excludes New World monkeys such as the dreaded howler monkey. One looks in vain for the boomslang "one of the venomous reptiles". Surely it needn't have included the antelope? Well, it didn't, but "an eland antelope gored a keeper to death in a safari park." It doesn't include wild pigs; my wife was chased by a pack in Holland (in the grounds of the Van Gogh museum, if you're a Dutch reader with artistic interests). It doesn't include the coti mundi. The what? "A cousin of the racoon. I've seen some nasty injuries from them." I have no wish to do likewise, so let us hope that the list of Dangerous Wild Animals is extended to all that are in fact dangerous wild animals.

Still, it is a start, and Southampton

Council were able to tell the proprietor of Alice's Restaurant that he couldn't have a brace of crocodiles in a tank. The idea is that restaurants provide food for customers and not the other way round. Then they had a complaint about the man who kept a gorilla under the stairs at the bottom of a tower block; all night long there was pattering and grunts, upstairs and downstairs. He was evicted, the gorilla, that is.

And another council, which asked not to be named, managed to head off one of its tenants wanting to keep a venomous snake, under a byelaw relating to the owning of cats and dogs.

Chichester District Council is fully genned up on the care of the tiger in the home. The cage must be 24 feet by 15 feet, 6 feet high with a wire mesh roof and half-inch steel bars at five-foot intervals. There should be double doors for entry, and escape, doors. Otherwise, enjoy yourself. Every home should have one.

"Basically, it's security we're concerned with," explained the Environmental Health Department. "This concerns all animals, not just tigers. There is the question of public nuisance: smell, waste products, noise such as loud roarings at night." The Hound of the Baskervilles would never have got planning permission. "We want to know that it is being kept seriously, that it is not a five-minute novelty whose door will be opened when the owner is bored." Stray cats are one thing, stray big cats another.

"We've generally advised people who want to keep pets; don't," said a severe lady at London Zoo. "Somebody may be very keen on keeping a bushbaby, but may not realise that it's nocturnal. That means it's asleep when you want to play with it and rattling around the house all night." There is no taking it back to the manufacturers,

and don't expect the Zoo to take it off your hands. They may well be up to here with bushbabies.

"What worries me," said a very off-the-record council official, "is Section 4 of the Act: 'Where an animal is being kept contrary to rhubarb rhubarb, the local authority may seize the animal.' I hope we never have to."

"Would you," I asked, "seize it by the tail?"

"I know which part I'd go for."

If that sounds like the law of the jungle, well, we appear to be living in a jungle, to judge by the last few pages of the annual report of the Zoological Society of London. This is a list of kind souls who have given animals to the Society, and a gripping read it makes. A Mr D. A. Priestman, I see, handed over two boa constrictors and I should hope so too; how come he had them in the first place? A red-sided garter snake was presented by East Dulwich Police Station (presumably on the grounds that they couldn't make him talk); that is disquieting news, especially if, like me, you recognise East Dulwich as your local cop-shop. Other gifts included two bird-eating spiders, an electric catfish and a couple of sharks, and thank God they're all behind bars.

For a comprehensive account of creatures that are where they belong, that is, in zoos, I turn to *Animals on View* by Anthony Smith (Mayflower, £1.95). From this I learn of the Linton Zoo near Cambridge in which the lioness is terrified of umbrellas and children riding on their parents' shoulders, which sounds exactly my kind of lioness. Also in Cambridgeshire, at Lilford Park, there is, among the flamingos and plovers, a "very tame Vietnamese pot-bellied pig", which surely cannot be covered by the Dangerous Wild Animals Act without bringing our

lawmaking process into ridicule. There is, I agree, a chance that it might step on your toe by mistake, so for complete safety one has to turn to Padstow Bird and Butterfly Gardens, from which it is impossible to emerge frightened or mauled, least of all by the bleeding-heart pigeon. And nervous visitors need fear nothing at the Stapleford Lion and Game Reserve near Melton Mowbray. According to *Animals on View*, "In 1967 the lions were withdrawn," but there are some dingoes and a chimp named Joe among others. But the best buy for the far from lion-hearted visitor remains Cutterlowe Park Aviary, Oxford, "70 birds and some rabbits".

For some zoos, the appeal to me lies in elements that have nothing to do with animals. The name alone of the Brontë Zoo would make me stop off at Keighley for a glimpse of a puma, as not seen by Emily, and coyote, as not patted by Charlotte. The Island Zoo near Tenby has, as its name suggests, problems of access. To see the stump-tailed macaques and hear the talking macaw in this old Victorian fort, one needs a tide chart. Visitors can only reach it at low tide. Some may head for Cardigan Wildlife Park, Dyfed, because of Przewalski's stallion; to me the "bilingual nature trail" calls loudest. And bother the polecat at Riber Castle Wildlife Park, Derbyshire; the place has a great motorbike collection.

If the 1976 Dangerous Wild Animals Act becomes, as seems possible, the 1981 New Improved Really Dangerous and Very Wild Animals Act, one Section should be devoted to a ferocious creature that is indigenous to my part of South London. It is a howling, snapping, vicious, incontinent little mongrel living two doors down the road and the sooner there is legislation on the statute book enabling me to chuck it in the ring with one of Aspinall's tigers, the better.

". . . and here's another one at six months!"

"When you've been at sea as long as I have, Jenkins, you'll know that an oil slick has many moods."

"It was a bonzer little town until they all went off to England to become broadcasters."

Prosecution: You are Ian Botham, captain of the England cricket team?

Botham: Yes.

Prosecution: You have several degrees in philosophy, do you not? You have written several books on the nature of thought, and are a reputable poet, I believe?

Botham: No. You must be thinking of either A J Ayer or Mike Brearley.

Prosecution: Then which one are you?

Botham: I am the big schoolboy hero captain of England, the burly one who also plays football for Scunthorpe and knows no fear.

Prosecution: Will you name the brand of shirt you are wearing?

Botham: It is a Consol shirt.

Prosecution: Do you find it comfortable?

Botham: Not only is it comfortable, it is amazingly soft and . . .

Judge: I fail to see the point of these questions.

Prosecution: My Lord, part of this trial is being sponsored by Consol Shirts, and we must mention them from time to time.

Judge: I see. Carry on.

Prosecution: Mr Botham, I want you to cast your mind back to February 3rd, the morning of the day. You were, I believe, batting against the Combined Smaller Antilles?

Botham: I was.

Prosecution: Did a bowler named Grantham bowl you a fast rising ball outside the off stump or did he not?

Botham: Yes.

Prosecution: I put it to you that you flashed unwisely at it, got a nick and were caught at slip?

Botham: No, sir.

Prosecution: No to which bit?

Botham: No, I did not touch it.

Prosecution: And yet there was a loud appeal and you were given out?

Botham: I did not touch the ball.

Prosecution: What did you do next?

Botham: I appealed against the decision.

Prosecution: And you elected to go for trial by jury. This is most unusual. Why did you take this course of action?

Botham: Because I believe passionately in justice, because I was so advised by Consol, maker of fine shirts, and because I wished to stay in to knock up another quick 50.

Defence: Mr Botham, when you were given out, the wicket-keeper and four fielders leapt in the air to appeal. What makes you think you were not out?

Botham: In cricket, sir, when a batsman is not out, it is customary for half the side to appeal. If a man is out, the whole side appeals.

Defence: It has been said that a loud snick could be heard as you attempted to hit the ball. How do you explain this?

BOTHAM—TRIAL BY JURY!

Highlights from the first day of the trial

Botham: I was wearing a complicated mechanism of light alloys designed to stop the ball striking me and causing me injury. I also had a contract from a Sunday paper sticking out of my pocket, which I hoped to have time to peruse at the non-striking end. The ball struck one of these objects, I believe.

Defence: Could it have struck the Cossela quartz digimatic watch you were wearing?

Botham: No, sir. Cossela watches sit so snugly on the wrist that it would have been impossible, though had it struck the watch Cossela's amazing rigid, shockproof construction would have . . .

Judge: Is this trial also sponsored by a firm of watches?

Defence: Yes, my lord.

Judge: I see. Time for orange squash all round, I think.

Defence: What is your name, please?

Witness: A Substitute, sir.

Defence: What does the A stand for?

Witness: Nothing, sir. I am a twelfth man by trade. Traditionally we are always called A Substitute.

Defence: Then what is your real name?

Witness: A Substitute, sir.

Defence: Why didn't you say so in the first place?

Witness: I did.

Defence: That's better. Now, Mr Substitute, will you tell the court in your own words about the alleged incident?

Witness: I was standing at square leg minding my own business, when suddenly this bloke runs up and hurls this small red object at the defendant. Defendant attempted to protect himself with a bat he happened to have. I heard a loud snick.

Defence: Caused by what? Think very carefully.

Witness: I've no idea.

Defence: And yet according to the diagram you were standing not twenty yards from the incident. Are you trying to tell the court you could see nothing?

Witness: Yes, sir. Nothing except Botham's big bum. Don't forget I was standing behind him.

Prosecution: You play at the wicket-keeping position for the Combined Smaller Antilles?

Witness: Yes, sir.

Prosecution: You heard the loud snick which we have already had described?

Witness: Certainly did, sir.

Prosecution: What in your opinion caused this noise?

Witness: Must I say, sir?

Prosecution: Of course. Why ever not?

Witness: I have an exclusive contract with a Sunday paper to tell my story.

Judge: Sunday papers have no jurisdiction in this court. Pray proceed.

Witness: Well, sir, I believe it was caused by the ball hitting the bat.

Prosecution: No further questions.

Defence: You must hear many snicks in your job as a wicket-keeper.

Witness: Yes, sir.

Defence: Are they always caused by the contact of ball and bat?

Witness: Oh yes, sir.

Defence: Tell me. If you were sitting at breakfast eating one of those cereals that make noises when milk is added . . .

Judge: Am I to take it this part of the trial is sponsored by a breakfast food?

Defence: No, sir. This is a genuine question. Tell me, if you are eating a cereal of the type I described, and it makes a noise as milk is added, what would your reaction be?

Witness: I would leap up from the breakfast table and shout "Howzat!!"

Defence: No further questions.

Prosecution: You are Arthur Rowbotham?

Witness: 'Appen.

Prosecution: And you were the non-striking batsman at the time of the incident?

Witness: Aye.

Prosecution: Please tell the court in your own words what happened.

Witness: Can I tell it in Desmond Wilson's words?

Judge: Who is Desmond Wilson?

Prosecution: My lord, he is a journalist who writes all Mr Rowbotham's articles for him.

Judge: Oh very well; tell the court in Desmond Wilson's words then.

Witness: Stunned. That is the only word to describe my reactions. Ian's normally placid features became twisted with injustice and fury as he saw the umpire's finger reach skyward. Years of suffering unjust decisions had finally taken their toll, and he did what no cricketer had ever done before—he appealed against the decision. But to understand his action, we must go back ten years and see Ian, still only a youngster . . .

Judge: Some other time, perhaps, Mr Rowbotham. Could you tell the court in Mr Wilson's words if he actually hit the ball or not?

Witness: For an umpire, it is almost impossible to see clearly the trajectory of a ball travelling at 80 mph. A lonely job, the umpire's . . .

Judge: Please!

Witness: Did he, as he seemed at first sight to have done, make contact? Would my chum Ian, a byword for frankness and honesty, have dared to perjure himself? What thoughts were running through his mind, as he rolled up the soft, elegant sleeve of his white Consol shirt . . .

Judge: Would someone tell me how many of Desmond Wilson's words we have to get through before we get to the nitty-gritty?

Witness: About 3,000, My Lord. It's a long Sunday paper piece.

Judge: Then I suggest the jury study it overnight. Court adjourned.

STIR WARS

TONY HALL on the battle to
survive prison overcrowding

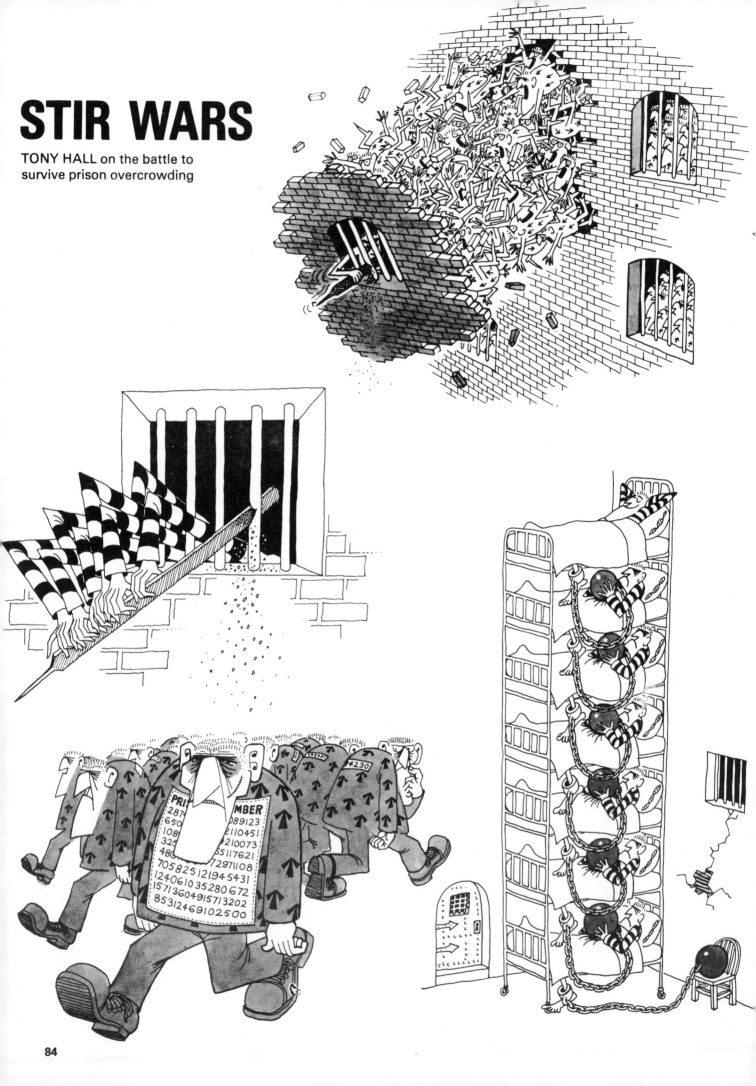

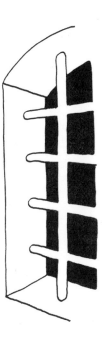

FREDERICK FORSYTH's London

STRANGE to return to London six years after having left for foreign parts. Not that I could claim that London has ever been "my" city. In twenty years I was only here for two short periods.

So before sitting down to write I decided to take a stroll through areas I once frequented, and started with the Houses of Parliament. Thirteen years ago I worked there for the Beeb, as temporary, acting, and almost unpaid, assistant to Peter Hardiman Scott in the Central Lobby. I did not enjoy it much, and had I not been so obscure the sentiment would probably have been mutual anyway. The job entailed buzzing about the Central Lobby accosting our legislators and seeking to abstract from them words of wisdom or at least revelation. The former was a lost cause and as for the second, the best gems I ever learned Peter Scott had usually known for days anyway.

What strikes me today is that at last, after years of debilitation, Parliament is beginning to claw back to itself the traditional right to summon, question, criticise and publish, so long traduced by weak premiers intent on permitting the aggrandisement of the Civil Servants.

It was the first Government of the suspicious and secretive Wilson that started the process of the hand-over of real power to Whitehall, despite Labour's endlessly reiterated claims to be the party of people's democracy. Even then I used to wonder how

reasonably intelligent people could spend a lifetime without observing beneath their noses an insoluble contradiction in terms: that extensive controls mean extensive bureaucracy to administer them; which means secrecy which is the eternal antithesis of democracy.

But the second and greater irony was that it was actually the administration of a Conservative, Edward Heath, that really gave the grandees the authority to write their own ticket, perhaps the key error of the six or seven disastrous bequests to the nation of that régime. It is long overdue that the House was reformed along the lines the present Leader is slowly achieving; and what a crowning irony that a High Tory called St John-Stevas is doing for the people's representatives' right to know what the posturing Left sought so hard to keep undone.

I strolled over the square to Downing Street and paused opposite the old black door to muse on the press briefings I used to attend there long ago. Nothing ever came of them but a lot of dissimulation. Those were the days of the second Wilson administration and already government by gimmick was well established. The worldly-wise James Margach and the sceptical Bob Carvel had long since sussed out the little wretch, as I did myself ere long; but most of the Press was still bowing and scraping.

Now there's a new PM in there, and frankly I like the cut of the lady's jib. I reckon almost anybody can govern—take a look across the Atlantic. But to *lead* you need three qualities as a basic minimum—intelligence, courage and integrity. James Harold Wilson had a brilliant if devious intelligence, but when the going got rough not much else; Edward Heath substituted obstinacy for courage, and they are not the same; James Callaghan had a bit of everything but not enough of anything.

For a decade and a half, from 1964 to 1979, most of my adult life, I have stood by as a reasonably informed but helpless observer watching the seemingly inexorable diminution of my country in every area from public administration to private morality, from the respect in which we are held abroad to the security of our streets at home. I never believed the decline was caused by this or that productivity coefficient; a wildcat strike here or a balance of payments there. I do not believe it was caused by lazy workers or lousy managers. It seemed to me the slide reeked of the odour of a national demoralisation which in turn stemmed from appalling leadership.

Now I don't know if these monetarist policies are going to work, to give us back honest money and low inflation. I'm no economist. But it did seem to me a year ago that Mrs Thatcher, at least, had the intelligence to perceive the options, the

honesty to tell us openly just how bleak they were and the bottle to do something pretty drastic about it all. At last we're throwing punches again.

I thought of waving at the old black door, but decided the dozen Japanese tourists were doing pretty well unaided. So I trotted down the steps towards St James's Park.

I paused on the gravel to look back at the newly cleaned mass of the Foreign and Commonwealth Office where fourteen years ago as Assistant Diplomatic Correspondent at the Beeb I used to attend the restricted briefings—restricted, that is, to those correspondents regarded as "sound", i.e. amenable. The briefings were really the occasion for the FO to trot out some harmless and unattributable tidbits interlaced with the party line, and the exercise was performed with the chummy charm of the department at its mendacious best. Later, during the Biafran affair, the mask slipped a bit, and the fibs came over with undisguised venom. Still, the privileged scribes, intoxicated by their own gravamen, swallowed the lot and usually printed it without query. But that's the serious Press for you; blow in their ego and they'll follow you anywhere.

Last week I stayed a moment to listen to the muezzin in the pepperpot on the northeast corner calling the senior Civil Servants to prayer. The fact is, we now have a more devotedly Arabist Foreign Office than ever before this century, and that includes the Bevin era. Word has it there is today more desert sand in the daydreams of the mandarins than Lawrence ever saw.

The cognoscenti are muttering that Peter

"I've sometimes wondered whether we couldn't perhaps be a little less exemplary."

Carrington, in in-house conversations, is beginning to reflect his advisers' visceral loathing of the Israeli regime. Some will have it that his apotheosis since the Zimbabwe solution (?) could be something far short of a blessing, for it might make him so emotionally and intellectually beholden to his advisers that he begins to advocate their policies rather than they his.

One has to give credit where it is due to these King Charles spaniels; despite a record that has lost Britain more respect abroad in fifteen years than it took our forbears a hundred and fifty years to acquire, they have the talent more than any other group of senior Civil Servants for taking over their incumbent Minister and "running" him in and out of Cabinet as poor Ruiari Chisholm used to run Oleg Penkovsky.

This is probably because foreign affairs is the last area of truly secret government. The policies and administrations advised and effected by all other departments are scrutinised by watchdogs and consumers; not foreign affairs, whose consumers are foreigners with no voice here. Moreover foreign affairs form an arcane science about which most voters, and hence their MPs, know little and care less; even in Cabinet events east of Berlin and south of their Mediterranean villas tend to leave Ministers consumed with apathy.

SOMEWHAT saddened, I ambled towards Knightsbridge where, being in need of a new dinner jacket, I strayed into Harrods and soon found myself in the menswear department where a sale was in progress. Asking to see a selection, I was directed to a rail where thirty strange tuxedos hung. Taking one off the peg, I observed that it seemed to be made of Lurex, for it glittered and sparkled in the light. Searching inside I found a tiny tab saying "made in Italy". I pointed out to the young assistant that if I wished to masquerade as a Neapolitan pimp I would pop down to Monty Berman and hire the gear. He directed me to a senior assistant whose expression varied from gloomy to lugubrious, and not without cause.

This gentleman went into the back and came out with a different range. While not exactly glittering, the new offerings had an odd sheen, and turned out to be made of polyester and in Sweden. I suggested that I might be interested in a British-made dinner jacket of medium-weight wool worsted or barathea such as I had always worn. The expression on the elderly assistant's face indicated I might as well ask for a splinter of the True Cross.

Intrigued, I wandered throughout the department, from casuals to formal, suits to accessories, examining the origin labels which were usually damn difficult to find and sometimes non-existent. The overwhelming majority of the clothes seemed to be Swiss, Swedish, Belgian, French or Italian. After an hour I left the debased emporium nursing the sentiment that it might be better if Tiny Rowland did take it over after all and put his new associate, the real Sir Hugh Fraser, in charge. No doubt the haberdashery

department would soon be coming down with bolts of Lovat tartan and the hatter's section full of sand-coloured berets, but at least it would be better than all this foreign junk.

So I went home and switched on the television in time to catch the early evening news. On it, our Trade Minister, John Knott, was telling the camera that he could not go along with Mr Len Murray and try to curb a tidal wave of imports, even though some of them were marketed at below production cost. Mr Knott demonstrated that he possesses all the combative defiance of a country curate informing his congregation that though they were sitting beneath a roof with death-watch beetle in it, he for one intended to initiate talks.

No one at the highest level seems to have hoisted aboard the simple fact that we are not only into a global recession but into that recession's inevitable offspring, a trade war. To win that war, or even survive it, we need a man at Trade with the ruthless cunning of a renegade Jesuit and the scruples of a Corsican knifeman.

At the end of the evening I caught *The Money Programme* in which a succession of our merchants, provided apparently by the CBI, indulged in those ghastly dialogues which are supposed to be spontaneous conversations but are in fact read in monotones from cue-sheets. The general burden was that they could not sell their products to the British because of foreign imports while their exports were being quietly discriminated against.

By the end I came to wish that instead of whining about the domestic market buying foreign, the CBI would do something about it. Flash-in-the-pan "Buy British" campaigns are no use; they become gimmicky trends for a month and die. The first step might be to market every single British product permanently with a Union Jack disc, stuck, tagged or stapled in a very visible place on the product. The centre of the disc should contain the percentage figure of British manufacture, based on value terms at the factory gate, exclusive of basic raw materials. I do not say the Brits would necessarily buy them if the foreigner was simply better or cheaper; but at least those prepared to buy the efforts of compatriots could find them at a glance. At the moment it is nigh impossible to work out what comes from where via whom.

BRITAIN and her capital have changed a lot in six years. On the good side, London is cleaner and politer than six years ago when the pound was a piece of paper and having anything to sell to the visiting foreigners was almost a licence to print the stuff. On the debit side, three things strike the returning prodigal's eye.

The pace has slowed up, a lot of the attitudes seem more lack-lustre, half-awake. Too many dozy buggers ensconced in comfy chairs with a personal dedication to the mañana syndrome. I do not get the impression this stems from the lower end of the pyramid, though it may be more obvious there through easier personal contact. It seems to come from the top where the

"But what do I say unto him?"

leadership should be; managers punch-drunk by controls, union bosses serving out time, bureaucrats preferring impediment to permission because it is safer.

The second thing is a national obsession with security, with guarantees. Tenants want guaranteed tenure, employees guaranteed jobs, producers guaranteed sales, bankers guaranteed returns and everyone guaranteed pensions. Risk-taking is eccentric and mainly confined to leisure areas, hence perhaps the vast increase in hang-gliding, parachuting, racing, speeding and fighting. There has been for so long a steady inculcation into the public psyche of the idea that government is some kind of universal nanny dedicated to the mission of ensuring that her 54 million charges spend all of life in front of some economic nursery fire. A pity in a way that a world recession rather than a Tory government had to open the window on the freezing blast outside, but it would have happened sooner or later anyway.

The third syndrome probably stems from the second, but one notices it in every newspaper, on every television screen, day and night. It is a sort of whining self-pity, implied in hundreds of public statements, answers in interviews and declamations at demos. It is a *leitmotif* observable from the explanation of a demonstrator that he was justified in putting a brick through someone's hard-worked for window to the claim from a shop steward that he and his mates are justified in bankrupting a factory for an alleged affront, to the bleat from a public servant that this or that simply cannot be achieved without disruption to existing practices.

For all that, I get the impression, just walking and talking round this metropolis, that there's a bit of a groundswell quietly building up; that an increasing number of people at every level are sick and tired of the heritage of the swinging Sixties and the permissive Seventies, and would happily take the chance, if it is offered by the early Eighties, to dump the whole dreary baggage along with its creators.

Hungarian Ghoulish

END OF PLACARD; WRITERS' STRIKE

A NOTORIOUS sodomite always leaps to mind whenever I travel by Lot, the Polish airline. The Hungarian carrier Malev is somehow more suggestive of *Star Wars* or an equivocal creature from a romance of science fiction.

It was Malev who recently lifted me out of Vienna on the comfortable half-hour hop up the Danube to Budapest. During the flight attractive hostesses dispensed chocolates and fermented plum juice to the passengers, who included impeccably dressed black businessmen from Lagos and Iraq with Samsonite briefcases and digital watches, and a sprinkling of trade union delegates, conference-bound.

In the posh hotels of Budapest, everyone who is not Hungarian looks like a trade union delegate, ogling utopia. Taxi-ing across the tarmac of East European aerodromes is a bumpier and more invigorating ride than most western travellers are accustomed to expect and Budapest is no exception, but once inside the terminal—which smells excitingly of Balkan tobacco and petroleum—the tourist whose visa is in order finds himself quickly re-united with his sponge bag.

I changed some money into the red-cabbage coloured currency of Hungary and caught a taxi to town. A version of the Union Jack (was one of the stripes too narrow—a cross the wrong colour?) rippled from lamp-posts along my route to the hotel, and I discovered later that a senior member of the British Government was also paying a visit to Budapest later the same day. My assumption had at first been that a Union Jack was as close as the hospitable Hungarian authorities could get to the Australian ensign.

We stopped at some lights and my driver bought a newspaper. The newspaper. Only four pages long. This was palpably that miracle of condensation which Fleet Street, with the help of the unions, has yet to achieve.

On a roadside construction site the immense reinforced concrete shell of a building in progress betrayed signs of long exposure to the elements. With the Union Jack fluttering nearby, there was something irresistibly and reassuringly British about those mossy girders and weed-fronded parapets along which men with buckets crept as though they had been offered rich incentives for never completing their tasks.

The two "best" hotels in Budapest are the Hilton (built around a thirteenth-century Dominican cloister) on Castle Hill in Buda, and the Intercontinental in Pest, right on the Danube. Since Western movie companies are constantly shooting "period" epics in and around Budapest, these two hotels frequently accommodate those legendary beings, the fops and featherbrains of filmdom. Stories abound of their fabulous deeds, their infantile extravagances and gross intemperance. No state in the Communist bloc misses its aristocracy more than Hungary, so the exotic inhabitants of the grand hotels are a constant source of wonder and delight.

I always like to stay at the Gellért Hotel on the Buda side by the old chain bridge. Its opulent limestone facade looks up the khaki Danube as it did before the Second World War, though the interior has been refurbished in that bleak Fifties style deemed up-to-date in Eastern Europe, all cream, green and maroon, with Blondwood veneer furniture. Somehow this nondescript mode of interior decoration, installed to cheer up Western tourists, is infinitely more oppressive than the overstuffed mahogany gloom, the sumptuous seediness we long to discover in those few old hotels which have survived war and cultural revolution.

On the night I arrived the excellent dining room was almost deserted except, of course, for the gypsy band which proceeded to give me its undivided musical attention. My requests were solicited, but the poignant airs from forgotten Austro-Hungarian operettas which I hummed to the chief fiddler seemed to confound his powers of recollection, so that my *hors d'oeuvre* of goose liver was devoured to the accompaniment of *The Way We Were*. Nevertheless I tipped the band in various foreign currencies throughout my solitary meal, and as the attentive waiter brought me a delectable *fogos* fish from Lake Ballaton, garnished with an emulsion flecked with dill, the five-piece orchestra relapsed into their voluptuous repertoire of Zigeuner melodies. Music is one of the special enchantments of a Hungarian holiday, and you can fling open your hotel windows at any hour of the night and hear, wafted seemingly across the Danube, the curdled harmonies of the *czardas*.

There are not many hotels I know where

the guests, having donned bathrobes and slippers, may descend by lift to a vast and rambling thermal underworld where almost every known form of hydrotherapy is available for little more than a pound. At Rotorua in New Zealand, where the earth's crust resembles *millefeuilles*, the ailing and obese patrons of Brent's Hotel "take the muds" at an adjacent clinic, and I have stayed at a modern conference centre in Palm Springs which incorporates a fitness club and spa on a sacred site where redskins once pow-wowed underwater. But the Gellért Hotel, with its subterranean labyrinth of mineral treatment amenities, is the most mysterious and the most attractive.

Unless you know the Carpathian Basin well, you probably do not think of Budapest as a thermal zone with at least nine medicinal bathing establishments which have been going strong since the Turkish occupation, yet the Hungarian capital is a haven where galvano-therapy and gingival massage are constantly requested *and dispensed*.

Pride of the Gellért is its cavernous Roman bath decorated at the turn of the century in the Byzantine style. It resembles a swamped mosque, dimly lit, where a large congregation of devout hydrophiliacs shuffle, loll and paddle in their tepid element, beneath a steamy vault of azure mosaic.

There are many surprises in store for the tourist exploring its dusky anterooms. In one humid chamber I came upon a scene rather like one of Gustave Doré's graphic illustrations to Dante's *Inferno*. A group of elderly loin-clothed patrons were suspended by rubber neck braces over a sombre and sulphurous abyss. No doubt they were voluntarily undergoing treatment for some disorder of the vertebrae, since they uttered no sighs or exclamations of protest as they dangled there in the vaporous gloom, even if the strangeness of that vision suggested punishment rather than cure.

Elsewhere I discovered a warren of massage cubicles where the art of a contemporary master of the macabre, Francis Bacon, was vividly evoked. Flabby, veal-coloured men were sprawled and in some cases *draped* in folds and swags of cellulite over marble slabs where they were violently attacked by youths wielding enormous, soap-laden shaving brushes. Once they had been enveloped in suds they were slapped and pummelled with what appeared to be miniature cricket bats, until the reboant tiles echoed with the sound of willow on lather.

In summer, guests may sunbathe nude on the roof of the hotel, overlooking panoramic views of the city, and behind the Gellért, a leafy hillside studded with pumpkin and pimento villas, once the houses of the rich and now diplomatic residences. The hotel also boasts a swimming-pool with a mechanical wave-making machine, one of the few I know to exist anywhere in the world (not forgetting, or course, the similar device at the municipal baths at the Elephant and Castle, Southwark).

Some of the best walks are on Castle Hill,

"Well, that's enough about me, Father—what have you been up to lately?"

the area around the former royal castle on a narrow plateau above the Danube. The old Renaissance, Gothic and Baroque houses have been artfully reconstructed since the War, and at number 8 Országház Utca is an antiquarian bookshop (open afternoons only) with an interesting selection of English volumes. I have always liked to browse along the shelves devoted to English books in foreign secondhand bookshops. One finds all those holiday authors left behind years ago in hotel bedrooms. Michael Arlen, Cecil Roberts, Hall Caine, Dornford Yates, Warwick Deeping, Guy Thorne and Ian Hay. In this dusty old bookshop, which I am told is still privately owned, I have never failed to discover an edition of Starkie's *Raggle-Taggle*, that classic description of a Balkan journey undertaken in a happier epoch than our own.

In the same building is the honey and honeycake shop run by the National Apiary Co-operative. Here many varieties of excellent and inexpensive honeycakes may be bought. For the best gourmet food in Budapest you should visit Vörös Csillag, a hotel restaurant on Freedom Hill with a pleasant terrace, or Vadrózsa, at Pentelei Molnár Utca 15. (NB. Open Thursday and Friday for dinner and Saturday for lunch and dinner.) This is one of the few private

restaurants in the city and it is in the garden of a private villa. That local delicacy, goose liver, is here priced higher on the menu than caviar.

The opera in Budapest costs little more than a pound and concerts are also one of the city's most attractive bargains. Interesting, too, are the antique shops, but it is possible to have one's purchases seized by a Customs officer at the station or airport, where the vigilant authorities love nothing more than to repossess art treasures whether they be rare ikons or lustre-ware bookends.

In Hungary it is unwise to buy anything which could be remotely construed as an *objet d'art*. Cases are not unknown where a confiscated vase has turned up in a Budapest antique shop a week later, ready for re-cycling.

Foreigners with a justifiable fear of Communist red tape are, however, agreeably surprised by the speedy formalities attending their departure from Hungary, unless they are detained at the souvenir shop where the best buys are the bags of paprika in varying strengths and the potent apricot brandy, or *Barack Palinka*.

That said, readers would be ill-advised to fly to Budapest or any other Eastern European port solely to avail themselves of the duty-free shopping facilities.

RICHARD GORDON

ONLY A NOSE

THE glory of my suburban garden is its asparagus bed. Fifteen yards by three, eighty-odd clumps, sharing with the rhubarb. For a few handfuls of fish manure, tossed like scraps to a faithful dog, each spring it tickles the dozing earth with its eager shoots. In a hot May, I swear they grow appreciably while your back is turned.

The succulent stems are snipped with stout scissors, two inches underground. Though never for longer than six summer weeks. They must be allowed to explode into asparagus fern, which florists use to bulk out their bouquets, to be cut down crisp and sere in November. The gardener watches, mouth watering, his lusty fugitives from the *beurre fondu*. An asparagus bed is an exercise in self-restraint unmatched outside a monastery.

Asparagus is more socially treacherous to eat than peas, little fishbones or spaghetti. When British medicine was a gentlemen's club, rather than another of its bankrupt nationalized industries, my country GP selected his summer locums by feeding the young doctors on asparagus. The French carve it, like frankfurters. The Americans have U-shaped springs, as throat surgeons use for looking up noses. The forthright elegance of the English, dangling the dripping stuff like self-feeding cuckoos, is the envy of the civilized world.

Cutting, boiling, serving and eating my asparagus is a continuous operation as swiftly efficient as the guillotine. The taste! As different from those greengrocer's bundles as fresh trout from plastic-wrapped kipper. Washed down with a bottle or two of Muscadet or Sancerre, then . . .

Have *you* noticed it?

(This article may cause offence to Mrs Whitehouse and gourmets.)

Asparagus makes your pee pong.

We doctors must mention such things.

The pungent chemical is methylmercaptan, a word which could achieve the glib currency of monetarism. I look at my watch afterwards, as though timing a likely racehorse. Asparagus is 93% water, but its noticeable escape from this mortal coil, within the hour, proves to my relief that my kidneys are still twinkling away as efficiently as the sparking-plugs in my Rover.

I thought that *everybody* raised a stink after eating asparagus, as everybody smells like Edwardian acetylene lamps after eating garlic. I had noticed a blank face or two, when joking about it over dinner (**we** doctors are allowed an indelicacy which other jesters cannot reach), which I ascribed to prudery or prostate trouble. Now the *British Medical Journal* puts me right. Its *A Polymorphism of the Ability to Smell Urinary Metabolites of Asparagus* explains how some people can graze a whole asparagus bed with olfactory immunity.

The researchers diluted the niffy specimen, wafted it under the nostrils of 328 volunteers, and (this article may cause offence to lavatory attendants) *some could smell it, some could not*. We all do our own thing with asparagus, but some have total nose-blindness towards the result.

This principle will be grasped readily by a British public which became an authority on brain death after watching twenty minutes of *Panorama*.

The subtleties of science are more startlingly devious than the philosophy of Spinoza. Some people have smelly feet (this article may cause offence to chiropodists). Or does every human foot stink, but few human noses suffer the facility of observing it? Are we crowded out by ghosts, is the air thick with voices, but the eyes and ears of only a handful tuned to them? Is extrasensory perception lodged in every head as noticeably as a bad cold, but only a few have inherited awareness of it? Asparagus could make the principles of Darwinism look like the rules of bingo.

I catch a whiff of the social implications. As it is fashionable for anyone in the slightest handicapped, bereft of full enjoyment of our consumer society, to demand official recognition and possibly cash aid, those under-privileged to boast the ingestion of an expensive lunch will form Asparagus Anosmics. The support of an MP or two will be easy, even the lower middle class now being penetrated by the consumption of asparagus, like vodka, if tinned and lagged with a slice of Hovis.

I wonder what my country GP would have made of the *BMJ*. He did not believe that science had much relevance to everyday medicine, a straightforward activity of getting people back on their feet. His county patients he would advise, "Live on half-a-crown a day, and earn it." Their ladies, "Madam, you need not a doctor, but a skipping-rope."

Lower in the social structure he prescribed, "Go out and knock down a policeman." He explained to the baffled patient, "You eat too much, drink too much and lie in bed too long. By the time they let you out, you'll be cured."

Anyone complaining of a sinking feeling he gave a bottle of medicine, with instructions to throw it away and swallow the cork. The many-symptomed sufferer of inadequacy he told, "I guarantee you'll start feeling better at twenty-to-twelve tomorrow morning. By noon, you'll be fighting fit. Keep a close eye on the clock." They always recovered.

Today, he could tell them to eat asparagus. However boringly insignificant the poor things, they would have something interesting to talk about whichever way the spent penny dropped.

"Maybe there's table-tennis on the other channel."

Darling Greengrocer...

THE COREN LETTERS

To Lex Volvo (UK) Ltd.
(5 February 1980)
My dear Lex: I cannot thank you enough for your delightfully entertaining bill! Were dear Tom Driberg still alive, I have little doubt but that he would have been as thrilled as I to discover that it is still possible, despite the assorted plights which rack this unfortunate island, to have the rear door of a shooting brake (why, oh why, do the appalling little swine who presently hold the culture in thrall insist upon calling them *estates*? Have they any conception of what is conjured up in the mind of a gentleman by the words *Volvo Estate*— some appalling Scandinavian tract with snow upon the croquet lawn and unutterably boring Swedes falling off horses while their suicidal footmen slit throats in the freezing buttery?), to have the rear door of a shooting brake, I say, beaten out, sprayed up to customer's specifications, re-fitted, and made good for as little as £367.55, to include new wipe-wash motor.

I passed another somewhat wretched evening yesterday. I went along to Boodle's, and was involved in a bit of a row. Apparently one has to be a member to get in.

To Maxwell House
(3 March 1980)
Good old Max! I received your enchanting letter in the post this morning, and confess myself overwhelmed by your astonishingly generous offer.

And yet, and yet. How am I to reply without appearing the charmless boor that society chooses so often to represent me as? I

ALAN COREN was possibly one of the last great letter writers. Certainly, he was greater than Evelyn Waugh, if only because he was forced to labour under the disadvantage that nobody ever wrote to him; since, by 1980, postal costs had come to prohibit anything but commercial mail. Nevertheless, Coren toiled on, confident in the belief that it was still the cheapest way of cobbling together a big fat book.

truly cannot get away to the sunsoaked Balkan Riviera this year, even if I had the half-dozen 8oz lids you mention or could think of the three words necessary to complete your sentence. Can you forgive me? The plain fact of the matter is, I have a great deal on my plate at the moment—do you know Lex Volvo? No matter, it is a long and dispiriting tale, but the top and bottom of it is that he has dealt with me rather badly for an old acquaintance. My new rear door does not shut properly, and when I bang it hard, the little lights fall out of that thing over the number plate. I fear a frightful row may be brewing between us, and I dare not leave London until it is settled. You know how people are.

Once again, dear Max, my thanks and apologies. I am delighted to hear that your new granules are twenty per cent tastier.

God knows, good news is rare enough, these days.

To his Greengrocer
(5 March 1980)
Darling Greengrocer: Thank you so much for the wonderful sprouts! Your boy hurried round last evening and pressed them into my hand personally—was it only fancy that made the little brown bag still warm from your own hand?

They could not have arrived at a more opportune time. I had been feeling very depressed all day, what with one thing and another; I had to turn down dear old Max's offer of a free trip to the Crimea, and immediately after that, not only did the little lights fall out of that thing over the number plate again, but the new rear windscreen wiper failed to wipe the new rear windscreen. What do you suppose Lex is playing at, after all these years? And as if all *that* were not enough, I was cut dead upon Hampstead Heath by a woman who might very well have been the Duchess of Argyll. Is she a tall woman with a purple conk?

In any event, your sprouts were a marvellous surprise. I had been expected 5lb King Edwards, 2lb Williams pears, and a small turnip.
P.S. My new book, to make matters yet worse, is going very badly. I am stuck on page 23. Can I be alone in finding Margaret Drabble unreadable?

To Lex Volvo
(7 March 1980)
Dear Volvo: My curtness only reflects your own. I was appalled this morning to receive

91

"Well, Johnson, you've had a damn good run. I've never known anyone to stay overrated for so long."

from you *a printed acknowledgement*, one month late, of my letter of February 5th (*see above. Ed.*).

Not that I am altogether surprised. I have noticed of late an entirely, to me, inexplicable change of attitude on your part towards the cavalier and uncaring. It may interest you to know (though, upon reflection, I rather doubt it, given your new unconcern) that I was so distressed by the little lights falling out of that thing over the number plate that I was forced to give up a much-needed holiday with Max.

I have twice this past week driven over to your place in the hope of seeing you and perhaps persuading you to glance at my inert wash-wipe mechanism, but on both occasions your man informed me that an appointment was necessary. An *appointment*? Between *us*?

I confess I do not know what is happening to society. London is full of both Jews and Arabs. Sainsbury's, one's grocers, is like a soukh. I beg leave, for both our sakes, to suggest that this general erosion of all that is good and decent may be what lies behind your own coolness to me; were your behaviour none of your own choice but merely the contamination of this ghastly world, I should be greatly reassured, though nonetheless low in spirit.

To the Scottish Widows Insurance Society
(10 March 1980)
Dear, dear Ladies! Words cannot adequately express my gratitude for your kind card.

That it fell out of one's *Reader's Digest*, like a bolt from the blue, instead of being thrust through one's letter box crumpled by one of those black hooligans who these days, such is our national decline, bear the sacred mission of Her Majesty's mail, made it even more welcome.

Alas, how can I accept your offer of £7,642 for me at age 65? Granted that the inflation visited upon our aching backs by a succession of governments each more villainously corrupt than the last must have, by now, ensured that the mite stands considerably higher than its AD 33 value, how on earth would you manage to scrape together this considerable sum over the next quarter century? How, indeed, could I commit your twilight years to scrimping and self-denial simply in order to bring a measure of security to an ageing hack?

That cannot be. Nevertheless, your rare charity in this beastly world shines like a beacon. You are obviously Roman Catholics, and I thank God that you and your line have been spared the poisonous taint of the heretical Knox and thus saved from the stinking sulphur and flaying agonies of the spit-roasted hell into which he and all who slobber after his maniacal ravings are irredeemably doomed to hurtle.

To his Greengrocer
(11 March 1980)
Dear Chas. Rumbold & Son: I am deeply distressed by a visit I have just received, during an afternoon I had intended giving over to thinking about my relationship with

Lady Diana Mosley, should we ever meet, by two persons to whom I should not have given an audience had their boots not been wedged in my front door.

Thus to reply to my affectionate letter of March 5th only serves to strengthen my conviction that England is truly finished. As I told your repugnant minions after I had got up again, my erstwhile affection for you was entirely platonic, nor have I ever laid a finger on Brian, your delivery boy. If any blame attaches to me, it is in assuming that by treating tradesmen as equals, gentlemen might perhaps offer them the chance of rising above the mire in which they clearly prefer to wallow.

And before my observations prompt you to further outrage, reflect upon this; one of your sprouts, it transpired, had a worm in it.

To Lex Volvo
(15 March 1980)
Dear Volvo: Following a further printed travesty suggesting that I telephone, and I quote, *one of your service staff* for an appointment (*Author's italics. Ed.*), it occurs to me that this shocking behaviour can have but one explanation. Are you yourself a Swede? If so, together with my deepest commiseration, I take the liberty of enclosing a humble little card from some Scottish widows of my acquaintance in order to demonstrate to you that there remain a few isolated pockets in this ugly and malevolent world where good manners and unrapacious hearts yet continue, albeit feebly, to flourish.

Dental and optical charges are to go up next month. Woolworth's has already started selling spectacles in selected areas.

RING UP THE FALSE

Worthy of the working-classes
    Are the specs my father wore;
Now I peer through posher glasses
    Furnished by my Woolies store.

Side by side with soap that cleanses,
    Non-stick pans and children's games,
See the rows of public lenses
    Tarted up with private frames.

Clearly I foresee conditions
    Getting tighter than a drum,
And a chain of shop opticians,
    Vision of the life to come.

Soon, beyond a peradventure,
    Braced to face the avalanche,
I shall wear a partial denture,
    Fitted by my local branch.

Battered by the final breaker,
    Naked as I sink beneath,
I shall not confront my Maker,
    Thank the Lord, sans eyes or teeth.
Roger Woddis

ON THE HOUSE

ON a recent visit to the United States I stayed in the Crown Center hotel in Kansas City, one of the new breed of American hotels, incredibly luxurious and overfurnished. Glass-sided lifts whisk guests up the outside of the building, a vast shopping mall sells expensive goods from all over the world, the furniture, trappings and accoutrements of each room are so elaborate that the hotel provides a booklet in your desk drawer to describe them. There is a 25-foot high rock garden and waterfall *in the lobby*. As you might imagine, the car park in such a place is plush too—roughly as well appointed as the average suite in an ordinary hotel. But it is as nothing, nothing at all, compared to the car park at the House of Commons.

This was built at a cost of umpteen million pounds amid much public scandal. It is, naturally, quite unnecessary since there was a perfectly good car park whose only drawback was that it was five minutes' walk away. The new one has carpeting up to the very point that cars actually go. It has central heating, and there are smart rubber bumpers around all the walls, so that even the drunkest member need not harm his Volvo or BMW as he returns hurriedly for an 10 p.m. division. There is closed-circuit television and a convenient system of lights which direct you to the nearest parking space. There are lifts and murals and a pleasant sense of calm spaciousness. Slum dwellers in Sao Paolo who would give their eye-teeth to live there.

Until recently there used to be a car washing service. The attendants would offer to clean and polish it while you were away, and since it was all unofficial, they relied entirely on tips. For a decent wash and wipe people generally gave £2, and if the car had been lovingly Simonized, waxed, polished and buffed so that it looked like an RSM's cap badge, they would cough up £3. It wasn't expensive, it was a handy service for busy MPs, and it earned a bit of cash for the attendants who, it is believed, are paid somewhat less than, say, government Ministers. Now the authorities have qtopped it for no good reason except that, presumably, they are jealous and resentful about something which is not fully under their control. A small thing perhaps, except that everybody involved is now a little bit worse off than they were before.

As the entire Common Market appears to approach collapse, the structures of Euro-jargon reach new and complex heights. Mention the word "lamb" and most of us think either of lovable woolly creatures gambolling in spring fields, or else of a sizzling joint, a few shards of rosemary or garlic embedded in its crisp skin, a hint of pink in the juice which flows from its innards. Not so a recent speaker in a debate on food at the Strasbourg parliament, who declared, "sheepmeat is a mass consumption product based on grass at low cost." No wonder the French won't eat it if that's what they think it is.

I see that our Euro-Tories have organised themselves into yet another group, this one called the 1979 Committee, in slavish imitation of the Tory 1922 Committee which functions at Westminster. All of them are already members of the British Conservative Group which, apart from four Danes and an Irishman, constitutes the entire membership of the European Democratic Group. In other words, all these ponderously titled institutions are merely different names for one and the same bunch of people. The only difference may be that, if the 1979 Committee follows the practice of the 1922 Committee, those in authority are not allowed to belong. Therefore lanky, leonine Tory leader Jim Scott-Hopkins may have to wait outside during meetings, knocking piteously at the door to find out if they have yet become the British Conservative Group or transmogrified into the European Democratic Group.

Perhaps you saw the pictures on television of the Prime Minister at Madame Tussaud's sitting next to a wax model of another blonde woman who, we were astonished to learn, was meant to represent her. She was flanked by two other waxworks which, we were told, for we could not have discovered by looking, depicted Sir Geoffrey Howe and Mr William Whitelaw. The wax Whitelaw looked as the late Sir Robert Menzies might have done had he suffered from a thyroid condition. The wax Chancellor looked like the man in bad American sci-fi movies who is the first to spot the monster advancing on the all-night hamburger stand.

The place remains, however, amazingly popular with foreign visitors. Pass it on any day of the week and you will see long queues of people waiting to look at almost unrecognisable models of politicians they have never heard of. It wasn't always like this. Tussaud's Churchill is very good. However, David Steel, when invited to the unveiling of himself, was literally struck dumb by the extraordinary image which faced him. He couldn't say what he thought for fear of being rude, though one of his children piped up, "That doesn't look like you, Daddy." Nor did it.

Is Sir Keith Joseph all right? It wasn't the surprising appointment of Mr Ian McGregor to run British Steel which was so startling as his blank failure to see why everybody else would find it funny and ludicrous. I suspect Mr Denis Healey has a point when he says that Sir Keith doesn't know whether he is Tommy Cooper dressed up as Rasputin, or Rasputin disguised as Tommy Cooper.

Meanwhile the Shadow Chancellor must be pleased about the murky waters in which Mr Peter Shore, his leading rival for the Labour leadership, is finding himself. Mr Shore, in his passion to appear a statesman, recently made a tremendous speech urging a British boycott of the Olympic Games, a speech which delivered he by asking MPs to vote against the boycott. The other day he delivered a similarly stirring oration in support of sanctions against Iran. Again he ended by calling for a vote against sanctions. This is the way statesmen are supposed to behave after getting elected. It does them little good beforehand, and has been noticed.

SIMON HOGGART

"I just hope it's not another bloody mirage."

BANX

MIKE BREARLEY

Success

LIKE health, success is harder to describe than failure (or sickness). We rarely reflect on the former until we experience the latter. We notice adverse criticism more keenly than favourable; we're sensitive to failure while we tend merely to wallow in success.

What, then, is it like for a batsman to be "on the go", in the right frame of mind? He is, of course, absorbed in the activity and feels completely alive. In my case, I become wide-focussed; aware of all sorts of things around me—the flight of a bird, interactions between fielders, and the bowler and his ball. One is resilient to minor setbacks. John Edrich batting against New Zealand at Leeds, on a pitch that helped seam bowling, played and missed on average one ball an over. But he shrugged off these little moral defeats, received the next ball with an uncluttered mind, and scored 310.

At times, especially between 1974 and 1977, and again last summer, I have had a similar attitude at the crease. I have relished the contest. When in difficulties I have, like a toddler learning to walk, picked myself up and carried on without self-criticism, and

scored runs when below my best. I enjoy the bowler's skill. When Robin Jackman bowls a ball that pitches on middle stump and veers away over the top of off-stump, I appreciate the delivery for what it is. And I still look forward to the next ball.

In such a mood one can almost (but not quite) hope that the bowler stays at his peak, so that the pleasure of the competition remains intense; one can certainly be grateful to him for it afterwards. After one classic fight for the world middle-weight title in 1948, Rocky Graziano and Tony Zale fell into each other's arms. Similarly, batsmen and bowlers need each other's skills so that the action, the drama, can come alive.

The first time I batted against the Indian off-spinner, Eripalli Prasanna, was in a relatively unimportant match at Ahmedabad. He bowled only a few overs at me and I scored few runs. But there was what struck me as a peculiarly Indian flavour to our interaction. I noticed that after I played each ball Prasanna would look at me and catch my eye. Sometimes he wagged his head a little. Always he looked

shrewd, and knowing. I enjoyed this, and started to join in his game. He had an engaging appearance, short and plump with big round baby's eyes. The messages were, I think, instructive about the source of much of cricket's pleasure. The exchange, if verbalized, might have gone as follows:

Prasanna: Did you notice how I drew you forward there, and made you reach for the ball? A bit slower, you see, but the same action.

Me: Yes, indeed, I noticed it. Beautiful bowling. But though I had to watch you, I didn't let you fool me. I waited for the ball to come and quietly dropped it down.

Prasanna (*after another ball*): Ah, you thought of driving that one, did you not? But no doubt you also saw how foolish it would be to take such a liberty with me.

Me: Yes, I probably could have gone through with my shot, but couldn't quite trust myself on this pitch. Wait until I get you on a true wicket.

The mutual appreciation in this sporting dialogue is crucial. Each of us liked having an opponent it would be worthwhile getting the better of. We both enjoyed the other's

knowing that we were playing well.

Such knowledge need not be only between the contestants. The crowd, and those other onlookers, the fielders, can to an extent share it. I once saw Ravi Shankar play the sitar in Delhi. Around him on the floor sat his closest acolytes and apprentices. Again there was the expressive shake of the head from the performer and the initiates' encouraging response: "A player like you needs an audience like us who appreciate you as we do."

The character of the sporting interaction varies, and few fast bowlers indulge in the head-wagging and subtle eye-contacts of an Indian spinner. But the essential features remain. Moreover, as a batsman, I often find that the slight physical risk presented by a fast bowler increases, if anything, the liveliness of my concentration. Again, the bond is enhanced by mutual respect. The logical fact that batsmen and bowlers are necessary for there to be a game at all is paralleled by the psychological fact that batsmen and bowlers have an absorbed interest in each others' activities.

This unity of the protagonists is, paradoxically, derived from their confrontation. One fundamental pleasure of competitive games is getting the better of someone else, whether individually or as a team.

The urge for success may get out of hand. Jardine went too far in his strategy for containing Bradman. Ian Chappell, going beyond an admirable identification with his own players, has turned cricket matches into gang warfare. But the opposite is more common; when an often unacknowledged uneasiness about our own aggression may make us both less successful than we should be and less capable of enjoying whatever success we do achieve.

I have seen England players, overwhelmed by the aggression of the opposition, lose touch with their own combative powers and surrender to the legend of Lillie and the Perth pitch. There's a fear, too, that showing one's own aggression will invite even fiercer retaliation. But one may also be afraid of one's own destructiveness. Some individuals (and teams) let their opponents off the hook when they have them at their mercy. They fail to ram home an advantage. Some find it hard to play all out to win; if they did so, they might be revealed as nasty and unlikable. We dislike our own barely suppressed tendency to gloat. A tennis player often drops his own service game after breaking his own opponent's, perhaps feeling guilty at having presumed so far; while the opponent, his guilt now assuaged, is stung into uninhibited aggression. The sportsman, like the doctor, should not get emotionally involved with his "patient". Len Hutton's advice to me on the eve of the England team's departure to India in 1976 was, "Don't take pity on the Indian bowlers."

Respecting an opponent includes being prepared to finish him off.

CRICKETERS are now less inhibited about showing pleasure at their own and their colleagues' successes. During a stoppage for rain in 1977, we watched the film on television of Jim Laker's match at Old Trafford in 1956. After a few dismissals, Derek Underwood, incredulous, said, "But they don't seem to be *pleased* about taking wickets!" The reactions of the players certainly looked, to our eyes, rather low-key. The bowler might allow himself a modest hitch of the trousers as he sauntered down to the group of fielders, whose "creams" were unlikely to be sullied by any mark of mud or grass. It was all in the day's work.

Whereas we!—we've not yet started widespread kissing, but hugging is commonplace and I've seen cheeks chucked. David Shepherd, the rotund Gloucestershire cricketer, was fielding at third man when an important catch was caught at wide long-on. He set off at his usually single-gear chug, reached the cluster of congratulatory fields and arrived back at his corner of the ground, the 300-yard round trip completed, just in time for the next ball.

I used to get huffy letters from Colonels in Surrey about all this palaver. "Dear Brearley, must we have all this hugging and gloating? Is not taking wickets and holding catches what you chaps are paid for? The captain's hand on the shoulder and a quiet 'well-caught' should suffice. Yours etc . . ."

Behaviour that seemed outlandish to such writers felt quite natural to us. We were not, usually, gloating; just delighted. And the fact that we are paid to play does not mean that we don't play for the love of it, or that our emotions on the field are different in kind from those we felt when at the age of six we "became" our heroes in the local park.

The dramatic improvement in fielding that one-day cricket has caused encourages the sense that each fielder is an integral member of a unit, not a casual bystander in a scene enacted between the protagonists. Underwood was surprised not only at

Laker's lack of exuberance, but also at the nonchalance of the fielders. Cricketers now train before and during the season. A track-suit is not, as it was fifteen years ago, a pretentious irrelevance. I suspect that the common effort required in training and fielding practice has shifted cricket slightly in the direction of the team game. It is now inconceivable that a bowler would have to fetch a straight-drive off his own bowling; but in Alan Moss's early days, when he came in one evening with the second new ball, and the batsman drove it back past him he looked round to see the ageing Jim Sims, at wide mid-on, edging towards square leg and saying, "Sorry Al, but you'll have to go." So he went, and picked up the ball in front of the pavillion.

Authoritarianism is out of fashion, in cricket as elsewhere. The view that everyone has the right to a say in how his group is run is matched by the idea that each has a responsibility to see that it is well run. Mutual motivation is essential for the success of a team. I nicknamed Graham Gooch "Zapata", not only because of the moustache and sombrero, but also because of the impression he gave in the field of being ready for his siesta. We used to get at him for this soporific air. Now Gooch looks lively, and encourages the bowlers more than most.

The successful sides that I've been involved in all seem to have been robustly humorous. Like a steam-roller, a cricket team is composed of atoms that continuously bounce against each other, but unlike the roller its atoms are complex and variegated. The rivalry within a side, which can become bitter and selfish, is often richly productive. And certainly no one is exempt from his turn as butt. One of Ian Botham's contributions to the England side has been to prevent others, including Geoff Boycott (and me) from taking Geoff Boycott (and me) too seriously. I trust that someone is doing the same for him.

MIKE BREARLEY was educated at the City of London School and St John's College, Cambridge, where he captained the University cricket team. He was Best Young Cricketer of 1964 and Captain of the Under 25 England team from 1966 to 1967. He became Captain of the MCC in 1971 and of the England XI in 1977; in that year he led the England team which won back the Ashes. After giving up the England captaincy to Ian Botham, he still captained Middlesex to the Schweppes County Championship and Gillette Cup double last season.

Guess Who's Coming to Dinner?

A Cuban and a Russian were launched into space yesterday for an expected week-long mission including a link-up with the orbiting Salyut-6 laboratory.

Daily Telegraph

BORIS, ever fastidious, raised the seat before emptying the samovar into the loo. He tugged the chain and the cistern responded with its usual Niagara-like roar, activating the airlock and discharging wet tea-leaves over Sri Lanka, passing far below. Humming a Latvian harvest song he sat at the birchwood table, spat on the samovar and polished it with a sleeve, pausing for a moment to examine his reflection in the gleaming surface. He looked jolly well, considering. He had survived two years in space, with all the hazards of weightlessness and even the trauma of that painful night over the Maldives when he had had to remove his own strangulated hernia with a kebab skewer and a soup spoon. There had been some inevitable deterioration, of course. His gums had turned bright green and odd corrugations were appearing in his skull; indeed, his entire parting appeared to have fallen into a kind of deep crevasse. But that was only to be expected.

Now, humming still, he dusted the pine dresser and plumped the cushions on the sofa. He put fresh towels in the bathroom, watered the experiments—the plague culture and the cress sprouting from blotting paper—then changed into his best boots and cotton smock, tying the latter with a bright crimson sash. Filled with happiness and expectation, he parted the lace curtains and peered through the porthole, trying to spot dear Ivan Ivanovich who, even now, was rising from Mother Russia like a great silver eagle to meet him. What a good time they would have! A nice borsch, full of dehydrated cabbage and sprouts, was simmering on the stove. There was chilled vodka to wash it down while they recalled adventures like the occasion on their last mission when, passing over California, mad Ivan, babbling drunkenly of defection, had to be physically restrained from effecting re-entry and splashing down in Frank Sinatra's swimming pool.

Suddenly, high over Alaska, he saw him—the tiny, brave shape of the capsule swimming resolutely towards him through the immensity of space. Boris, beside himself with excitement, made fresh tea and buttered the scones. Docking procedures would soon have to be instituted. He scrambled past the potted ferns and the music stand to reach the controls and, activating his trusty little thrusters, got his craft into position. There was a bump that knocked his ikon of St. Francis Cradling a Warthog off the wall, a muffled clang, then silence. Smiling hugely, Boris shuffled over to the airlock in the parlour and, with arms outstretched, waited to embrace his old comrade.

But the man who crawled through the hatch was not Ivan.

This fellow had shiny black skin and huge white teeth. There was a parrot on his shoulder, a half-smoked cigar behind his ear, and he smelt strongly of rum.

"Buenos dias, amigo," he said. "Colonel Gonzales of the Cuban Space Programme at your service."

Boris stared at him, mouth agape. "But where is Ivan Ivanovich?"

"Ivan Ivanovich fell out," said the Cuban.

"Fell out?" said Boris. "Fell out of what?"

"The spacecraft," said Colonel Gonzales patiently. "Over Zimbabwe. He opened the hatch to throw an empty bottle away and he forgot to let go. He just followed the bottle out, travelling with terrific velocity and in a steep upward trajectory. I think he will start orbiting the sun in maybe, uh, seven years."

Boris gave a muffled sob. "Poor chap. Still, it is the way he would have wanted it. The first man to reach the sun. It is epic, it is heroic. He will become a legend."

The parrot fixed Boris with a beady eye. "The wall are closing in on me, man," it said. "I need room to breathe."

"This bird suffers from claustrophobia," said Colonel Gonzales, seating himself on the sofa. "Ignore him. He is already spaced-out on Valium and now I shall give him a little rum. He enjoys that. In a few minutes he will play his tiny trumpet and dance the tango for us. You got any Perry Como records up here?"

"No," said Boris.

"I could use a stick of sugar cane, man," said the parrot.

Boris fetched the parrot a pickled walnut while Colonel Gonzales filled two glasses and a saucer. "I'll bet you didn't know," he remarked; "that Cuba even had a space programme. Uh? I'll bet you thought it was just one coon with an old crash helmet and a broken telescope who only became weightless when he got plastered and jumped off the roof. Uh? Well, let me tell you we aim to get ourselves a whole fleet of spacecraft, all fitted with giant loudspeakers linked to laser beams so we can relay Fidel's speeches at terrific volume as we go round and round the planet. Entire nations will be bored into submission. Governments will beg for mercy, offer us anything to turn off that endless droning voice. Nobody will get any sleep—twenty times a night Fidel will wake them up. The world will be plunged into universal neurosis and hysteria and, eventually, total domination will be ours."

Boris stared at him. "It is an astonishing scheme," he murmured.

"The ceiling is pressing down on me, man," said the parrot. "I gotta get out of here."

"I really am terribly sorry," said Colonel Gonzales. "This parrot is clearly off its box. But I know it would help if we could let him pop out for a moment."

Boris advised him that it was against all the regulations but, eventually, agreed to don his pressure suit and open the hatch. The parrot immediately scrambled through and onto the roof where, without further ado, it began to rumba, swaying its hips and stamping its feet. Colonel Gonzales frowned. "Do you think you could climb out and seize him?" he said. "I am not accustomed to this craft."

As Boris, grumbling, crawled through the hatch, he felt a sharp push in the back. Drifting away from his spaceship, he saw the Cuban give him an ironic salute before retrieving his parrot and retreating inside. Once there, he lashed the bird to a tap, strapped himself in and commenced the re-entry procedures. If he got his sums right his two craft should splash down 19 minutes later, smack in the middle of the Bay of Pigs.

T. E. B. CLARKE:

Bad Book Guide

ALL this free advice to collectors has made it difficult these days to spot a book bargain on a market stall. A chum and I, frustrated in our browsing, decided to upend the common aim with a wager on which of us could find the book least worth 5p. His choice: *Does Hitler Mean War?*. Mine: *Horses to Follow in 1948*.

His feeble effort to maintain that the performances of my horses could provide pointers to their contemporary descendants was countered on my part by a revival of a rumour current at the time they were running: namely, that Hitler lived on and could yet be in South America planning vengeance. After all, not every old man is mellowed at 91. In the absence of an umpire to cool us down we called it a draw and settled for a replay in the near future.

Talent spotting forays around the market barrows have brought me some invaluable—or should it be valueless?—resources for our next encounter. My best find is a Mudie's Library catalogue of 1918. At 20p it was too expensive and far too beguiling to be entered for the contest, but its 1,152 pages are an incomparable guide for non-bargain hunters. It needs but one old-timer to have cheated the Great Pulper and I am on to a sure winner.

Who today, for instance, would curl up with *Her Majesty the Flapper* or *Lady Ermyntrude and the Plumber*? I doubt whether the smartest agent could do a hype job with *Dumps, a Plain Girl*—whose author, L. T. Meade, was responsible for no fewer than 205 titles, ranging in repellence from *Daddy's Boy* to *The Maid with the Goggles*.

Their possible appeal to those with political aspirations must rule out *The Socialism of Lady Jim*, *The Beloved Premier* and *A Lovely Little Radical*. The kind of lip-moving reader who took *Romance of the Hebrides* to be about he brides might also fall for *Queer Lady Judas* or *The Wooing of a Fairy*; and there's a risk of one with a weakness for the hard stuff recognising a kindred spirit in *The Lady on the Drawing Room Floor*.

Incidentally, I learn from my treasured catalogue that there really was a book entitled *Purple Passion*. It was by Gertie De S. Wentworth James, who also wrote *Pink Purity* and *Violet Virtue*. All of these I have in mind for the substitutes' bench along with *Little Miss Prim*, *Dolly the Romp*, *Kitty the Rag* and *Mollie the Handful*.

Ficton however is dicey for the chaff gatherer: it can on occasion produce the unlikeliest bounty. The screenwriter Michael Pertwee picked up for a few pence an obscure Victorian novel called *Israel Rank* which caught his eye because he was working at the time for the Rank Organisation. Anti-Semitic and deadly serious, it told of mass murder by its eponymous villain to inherit a coveted peerage. Adapted for the screen, turned into a comedy and given a necessarily new title, it became *Kind Hearts and Coronets*.

So for the coming contest I shall pin my colours to a one-man compendium of useful information: *What's What* by Harry Quilter. This may sound an indisputable snip at 5p for more than a thousand pages, but it fails gloriously on two counts. What was what in 1902, the date of its publication, is very far removed from what is what today; and because its author understandably wilted under the strain of producing nearly a million words in just over one year, it is of minimal value as a work of reference beyond the letter M.

"The idea of *What's What*," writes Mr Quilter in a disarming foreword, "was conceived at Mullion in Cornwall on Sunday, the 2nd of September, 1900, and was due to a suggestion of my wife's. Preparation for the work commenced the same day."

A moment worth recreating. The stroll along the seashore after the Sunday joint and forty winks. "What a pretty shell, Harry."

"The species known as Scotch Bonnet, my dear. Carried here no doubt from its native habitat in the Caribbean."

"Oh, Harry, you are so knowledgeable! You really ought to write an encyclopaedia."

The sudden halt, the fist slapped into the palm. "By Jove, little woman, what a spiffing idea! Dash it, I will! Come on, come on—no time to lose . . ."

Back in haste to Mrs Penbuttock's lodgings. Vespers neglected for advice on hotels in Aachen—"The Nuellens best for bachelors, the Grande Monarque for families and great invalids."

A quick supper followed by the course of the River Aar—"which you will be lucky to see through a valley defiled by vile smoke clouds from a hideous, puffing little Swiss engine." Harry is getting rather tired and irritable after his opening burst; one soon comes to recognise the symptoms.

Things go pretty well however from AB (Abernethy Biscuits) to GR (Grape Cure), with high praise for the novels of Rhoda Broughton (*Red as a Rose is She*) and the poetry of Sydney Dobell. (Sydney *who?*)

First sign of second thoughts on the great venture is perceptible as early as Guitar, an instrument of limited range and peculiar twang, which is hard on the hands and makes *Home Sweet Home* sound absurd.

By H, Mrs Quilter feels impelled to register a mild protest. "Isn't it a little rude, dear, to describe people who take the waters at Homburg as imbeciles?"

"Don't carp woman. Just remember this was your d—d silly idea."

The last half of the alphabet receives but one-fifth of the total wordage, most of it in the same testy vein. Nice is not a place to take your wife to, Odessa has nothing of interest to the tourist, Lord Rosebery looks like an overgrown and slightly overfed schoolboy.

By passing over such as Ruskin, Tennyson and H. G. Wells the end comes at last within blessed sight and is celebrated with Whisky, Wine and Workhouse Diet. Then come two feeling pages on Writer's Cramp, which Mr Quilter sought to alleviate with a mechanical hand invented by a German doctor. It was not a success, and after experimenting with an elastic band round flagging fingers he concluded that the only solution was ambidexterity.

Writing with both hands he finished up on Zero, which took him from roulette to the cost of a day's hunting in Monte Carlo, and recklessly promised a new edition of *What's What* the following year. My one lingering fear is that my opponent may be lucky enough to unearth it.

"You're a hypochondriac, but you've come to the right man, I'm a quack."

RING OF NO CONFIDENCE

ALBERT finds the circus has
fallen on hard times

"Have you been working the Lump again?"

"Must be that bloke from the finance company again!"

x

100

"Looks like the Capucci brothers
have brought in the Official Receiver!"

Wolfgang Mozart:

Has the eighteenth century invented anything more vile than stage coach lag?

(Bernard Levin is on holiday)

I had intended this week to write something about my twenty-first piano concerto which must, in truth, be one of the most sublime and transcendental works I have penned this year, though you would not think so to judge by the way it is played by some pianists (on sale at good bookshops or from me after the concert), but I have meanwhile gone through an experience of such numbing awfulness and misery, an experience that would have been laughable had it not been so frightful, that I feel compelled to visit the details upon my readers as an awful warning. I have, in short, travelled from Germany to France by stage coach.

Now, I know that travel by coach is one of the wonders of our age. I know that by exchanging swift relays of horses it is possible to leave Vienna at the beginning of one week and be in Paris or even London at the end of the same week. I meet many people who travel for most of their working time in these wooden contraptions and would not go back to horseback or foot for all the tea in China, if that is where tea comes from. Speed, to them, is the way we live now. As they rattle and plunge across the highways of Europe they sit back and revel in this mode of transport. But I have—as I may have mentioned—recently ventured from Germany to France in a stage coach and I say now that it is the curse of our age.

Do not misunderstand me. The voyage, as such, was tranquil by the standards of these things. I was not held up by highwaymen. At no point did my baggage disappear in the direction of Rome or Madrid. There was not even an announcement at a wayside inn to the effect that due to technical reasons beyond anyone's control the evening horses scheduled to leave for Strasbourg would be delayed. No, the journey was uneventful. And it is this lack of eventfulness that drove me to distraction. Never have I been subjected to a period of such mind-numbing dreariness, such long hours of sheer and utter tedium, so sheer, or at least so utter, or at any rate so tedious, that even to hum the final soaring bars of my new twenty-first piano concerto (surely the most uplifting melody now on sale anywhere) struck me as wearisome.

Before any helpful reader should write and tell me how to control the effects of stage coach travel, let me say that I tried everything a man could do. I talked for many a long hour to my father about the iniquities of the Viennese Faggot Board, who for nine months now have been promising to instal a new wood-burning stove in his house with as little effect as Clementi attempting to write a piano concerto. I engaged in an endless discussion with my fellow travellers on who was pre-eminent among Clementi, Bach and Handel (and came to my personal conclusion that none of them was worth a fiddle-stick, and that for an evening out it is impossible to beat a good game of billiards, a pursuit which combines the noble symmetry of symphony writing with the social joyfulness of getting well and truly drunk). I even penned a letter to the editors of I know not how many newspapers about the vile machinations of the Workers' Guild of Music Copyists, whose ceaseless clamour for more money has pushed the price of, for instance, my new twenty-first piano concerto beyond the reach of all but the most knowledgeable connoisseurs (and to those of you empowered to vote in the election for office of this despicable union, may I urge you not to cast your voice for any of them?).

I even, so desperate was my plight, attempted to rouse my own interest in those prisoners of conscience at present shut up in the wards of the Empire of Austria, a land whose name is a by-word for repression and tyranny among civilised people, or at least among those of us who write in the public prints, a cause which normally arouses me to heights of fury and indignation. Yet, to my own surprise, I found myself saying that I could not care less. Indeed, on the fourth day of this ordeal I was approached by a gentleman who wished to purchase a copy of my twenty-first piano concerto and was amazed to hear myself say that he could go to the devil.

Now, in Paris, I am somewhat recovered. I have been on terra firma for a few days. My former zest for life is threatening to return. I even feel that I could dabble with the opening bars of my twenty-second piano concerto. But God forbid that I should have to be dragged within the portals of a horse-drawn vehicle before it is finished.

Jackson Heights

DAVID TAYLOR talks to
GLENDA JACKSON

NOT one to prat about, she'll agree. Made her own way, from Hoylake for a fact, always done and said as she meant and never mind company. Steady on, though: by no means the brassy northern Bolshie some bright buggers might like to crack on. Talented, but tough little madam, it's been put about. Headmistresses have called her rather a spirited gel. Others have turned to the farmyard for spite.

True to say, is she 'eck-as-like an actressy actress. She's not, and never has been, remotely stage-struck. The business doesn't impress her as glamorous and neither, in her opinion, is she. Not a lot in life is worse, she's gone on to vouchsafe, than the unadulterated companionship of other actors. Then again, she's never flinched from sounding off about how God-awful professional theatre can be, about audiences sat sitting there like mindless steamed puds. If provoked, she's shied political brickbats now and again, if not plain bricks. Her dad laid bricks wi' a trowel.

Was it buggery a burning desire to act as put her on the stage. She was working in Boot's and was bored. Wouldn't have minded signing on as a Wren at one point, but used to throw up just crossing the Mersey so that was out. Gave nursing some thought, too, but goes all of a doo-dah within ten yards of a needle. Boot's got better when she was on the cosmetics counter, she started to get grand ideas about being the first woman on the board one fine day, but was generally still bored.

She can't abide boredom. By crimes, she finds it hard enough just to have a bit of a sit-down, else she's earned it by washing up or plumping all the cushions or whatever, never could stand larking about on holidays, so-called, has this Arcadian idea it'd be nice to be settled in the countryside and minding her own bloody business, were it not for the fact she's one of nature's fidgets, can't rest easy without work to do.

Any road up, she'd done a bit of amateur dramatics for a smile, liked it, got encouraged by a friend to have a crack at it serious-like, so wrote off to the only drama school she'd ever heard and, bless us all, was signed up at RADA. Right place, right time: only a year after the golden boys like Finney and O'Toole, all terribly new-broomish. Not that it led straight off to anything more testing than being in rep at Crewe, where she married Roy Hodges. He was stuck for work soon after and the two of them finished up at Butlin's, him a Redcoat, she a Blue and telling happy holidaymakers who wanted to be in York House that they were in Windsor House, so there and the same to you, Mrs.

If it did nothing else it established a certain brass-tacks perspective. You work hard and drop lucky or you sink, that kind of thing. Roy gave up the dream of drama and moved to Blackheath to run an art gallery. It flourished but the marriage did not, but for Chrissake let's skip any personal nightmares and talk about dropping on *Alfie*. It was her West End debut, not a show-stopping one perhaps, but it led to the RSC and triumph in *Marat/Sade*. Or a reputation at any rate—it was not altogether triumphant in that for years afterwards she felt she'd never get offered anything but neurotic, sex-starved loony ladies, more than likely char ladies, or demented old crones.

The big thing was that at the time (1965) there was a terrific intensity of commitment around Peter Brook at the RSC. There was a magic that's long since fizzled out and it's not something easily manufactured or re-created, no matter how much money goes into a theatre. The bigger any company gets, the harder it is to cling to real artistic control, generate a real spark. Theatre shouldn't need to be nannied.

There was intensity, too, when Glenda crashed into such Ken Russell wonders as *Women in Love* (for which she won an Oscar) and *The Music Lovers*, but it's all very well to rabbit on about artistic principles, she'll admit, when she has made stuff like *Mary, Queen of Scots*, in which she knew bloody well she'd have to compromise. On the other hand, it's maybe snobbish to persevere with this—you'd have to count up the box-office returns.

Let's have it straight, she insists, that none of what's befallen was in any sense planned. She struck lucky with films, did herself no harm on TV as *Elizabeth R* and has been able lately to take her pick and choice on stage or on film on both sides of the Atlantic, but God knows there was no conscious pattern. The only skill is in making the right choices—knowing what'll suit and supply the full-strength adrenalin charge, never mind whether it's high Shakespeare or larkabout comedy. Come Boxing Day, she'll open in the West End cinemas as Walter Matthau's seductive mistress in a spy caper called *Hopscotch*. Come the New Year she'll open on Broadway as the put-upon Midlands schoolteacher, *Rose*. Neither one is Cleopatra but both are as good to perform in their own way.

Listen, if you want to know what's really exciting, it's that she's finally got round to putting in double-glazing and buying a new washing machine. All right, she's a big star and a big money-earner, but she's also a UK resident, a British taxpayer and a hard-pressed divorced mum of an 11-year-old and has a sick father who may or may not be able to come down south for Christmas. *That's* real drama. She was sweating cobs over buying the blessed washing-machine—still can't get used to signing cheques for *two* hundred pounds odd, she says, will always be the typically Taurean housewife, slopping about at home and listening to the wireless all day, oh yes, still called a wireless in her house, and is never happier than when digging over her potato patch. Time off never comes in big enough chunks to learn *useful* things like learning a language or *worthy* things like taking up an instrument. It's bad enough finding time to watch the soccer on TV.

It gets harder, as time goes on, oh all right when you're 44, to re-capture the besetting *urgency* of work's challenges. She always was nervous in the wings for the first few times of a new performance, now it's *every* time, tougher to wind up. Perhaps less easy, too, to get so worked up about life's injustices—there was a period when hardly a day went by without the papers ringing up to ask Glenda how she'd end the war in Vietnam.

Reason you plug on is that there's nothing to match it and it'd be murder ever to reach the point where you didn't have to work again. She's fidgety enough as it is. And immensely likeable with it.

SHOPTALK

JOAN BAKEWELL
on Kitchen Shops

IT's a case of nice wok if you can get it. No, *wok*; the instruction leaflet describes it as "essential". And you've never heard of it. It's people like you who think a Chinese steamer is something that once took lady missionaries up the Yangtse. Call yourself a cook!

To do just that these days, it's no good boasting of having learnt at mother's apron-strings a strong grounding in our national dishes: Yorkshire pudding in gravy for starters, cloves in the apple pie, cabinet pudding,—that sort of thing. All that is taken for granted. To call yourself a cook within thumbing distance of the *The Good Food Guide,* you need a thorough grounding in several cultures and the nicer points of international cuisine only easily acquired in the canteen of the United Nations.

You must know what the Japanese and the Welsh do with seaweed, and the Eskimos with pemmican, what a yabbie is to an Australian and an Om Ali to an Egyptian. It helps to have a smattering of six languages, the dexterity of a concert pianist, hands like asbestos and a sound knowledge of Thermal Dynamics. You will also need a wardrobe of oven gloves and a butcher's apron, a kitchen installed like a space station and furnished with the bric-a-brac of a peasant's cottage. You'll need dishes specially shaped for avocados, others for artichokes, prongs to hold sweetcorn, brochettes to spear kebabs, thermometers to measure things either coming to the boil or freezing solid for weeks. You'll need a larding needle for threading lard, a stoner for olives and cherries, a gingerbread cutter, roast baster and, of course, a wok. Thankfully, we have the kitchen shops to help us.

Something very odd is happening to our kitchens. Time was when labour-saving was all the rage. The nation's wives, chuffed with new jobs and even new careers, were only too pleased to pop a handful of things in the pressure-cooker and leave it at that. Frozen and tinned food got better in quality, more varied in range. Cook books dealt with how to mix and disguise already prepared foods. The commercials harked on about "They'll never guess it wasn't your own home cooking."

Then suddenly two-income homes found themselves with abundant money, friends to impress and enough leisure to indulge in a bit of high living. And so cooking got classy. The kitchen became the focal point of social display, its produce indicated your standing on the OK ladder, and the nature of gadgetry changed direction. It ceased being labour-saving and became deliberately time consuming. How else explain growing your own herbs, baking your own bread, brewing your own beer, making your own yoghourt. "It only takes minutes, honestly..." they say. Exactly. Minutes longer than not doing it.

And of course it all needs equipment. But at the same time as cooking got classy, it also reverted to the primitive. Marie Antoinette never had it so good. Nowadays housewives in Virginia Water with a Volvo in the garage and an account at Harrods are playing at being French peasants littering their kitchens with wooden spoons, cane baskets, crude pottery from Brittany and Portugal that costs pence over there but a fortune over here.

What's more, they make things hard for themselves, beating eggs with bound twigs, turning the handle on coffee beans till their elbows ache. And it's not just stockbroker wives. The obsession has a hold on the menfolk too. "How long do you take making your curries, then?" "Oh, several days." "Good man." That was heard not at the ckeckout desk at Sainsbury's, evening cookery at the local Poly, the dinner table of old colonials. It was the smalltalk of editors at a powerhouse of BBC Current Affairs, not 100 miles from Robin Day's elbow. Ask them if you must know what a wok is.

But among all this knowingness, certain and subtle distinctions are to be observed. I have an unprovable theory that correct spelling was invented by the Victorian upper classes when working people learnt to read. Just enough accuracy to set them apart. Thus with cooking: while baked beans and fish fingers are the fodder of hurried family life, those with leisure and money expend it on their new-found and new— fangled domestic skills. So on the one side of the high street you find the good old hardware store dense with Pyrex dishes, tin openers, roasting trays and Thermos flasks. Across the street, at somewhere coyly calling itself Patsy's Pinnie or The Apple Fool, all is copper-bottomed, cast iron, baking bricks and barbecues.

I love them both. They are both Aladdin's Caves of goodies, their stock stacked to the ceiling, even dangling from it, and smelling of paraffin and furniture polish, or thyme and coffee beans. They are professional shops and we are all professionals seeking expertise in the execution of soufflés, the perfecting of pancakes, asking advice about frying pans. Good old hardware will go for Teflon trendy nostalgia will insist on cast iron.

The shoppers are as intriguing as the goods: smock and sandals buying something that smokes their own fish: Mum plus pram and three buying wax cases for birthday jellies. We are finally all artisans in our own kitchens, concentrating with eager diligence on how to make and enjoy making what will nourish those we love. It is a worthy way to spend money. Perhaps Marie Antoinette was right after all. I wonder whether she had a good recipe for cake.

"I'm fairly philosophical about being boiled. What I object to is being dressed."

DONEGAN

Famous Winters of Discontent

Worried about what is going to happen in the next few weeks? You'll never believe, says **E. S. TURNER**, what our ancestors had to put up with.

Algidity of disagreement?.. Winter of malcontent?..

1338

The European War in which Britain became embroiled this year was to have been "over by Christmas." When this forecast proved illusory the populace rioted, many of them maintaining (with truth, as it happened) that they knew a Hundred Years War when they saw one. The cold was so intense that stones froze solid in the human bladder. A "rebellious and ungovernable spirit" was abroad. Jesters resorted to industrial action, refusing to jump into the bowls of custard; dwarfs declined to be served up in pies.

In December Minimum Usury Rate (MUR) stood at a record 125 per cent. Unrestricted imports of holy relics were bitterly opposed by English master fakers. A half-hearted attempt to revive the export trade in minions and catamites to the eastern caliphates led to the third Barons' Revolt. All silver coins had been reduced by illegal clipping and filing to the size of eyeballs. Tax collectors walked out, complaining their duties were impossible because half the population were called John and nothing else.

To allay discontent, the Court introduced a new Sumptuary Law, directing that swans, herons and peacocks were no longer to be stuffed with larks or ortolans for the royal table. A rabble of cat-skinners, codpiece-makers, blood-letters, crimps, bawds and sorcerers' apprentices joined with Flanders trulls in the Sack of Westminster. On Christmas Day a demented hermit called John prophesied (again, with truth) the coming of the Black Death, followed by the French Disease. Champerty, embracery and simony flourished openly among consenting adults. The year ended in ghastly gloom and the New Year wine fountain in Cheapside flowed with vinegar.

1501

The cold was so intense that labourers' wages were frozen. Following the collapse of the King's monetarist policies, fifty alchemists were publicly flogged for failing to transmute base metal into gold. Ten thousand pox-doctors (equal to one fifth of the population of London) demanded a Royal Charter and when this was refused they withdrew their labour. A number of Scotch rebels escaped from their chains in the Lord Mayor's procession and began to foment industrial unrest, setting a pattern for future ages. Everywhere "a lewd and licentious spirit" was abroad, but the extreme cold led to a seasonal fall in cuckoldry. Godlessness on the South Bank of the Thames was briefly checked when fire ravaged the episcopal stews in Southwark.

Thousands of frozen lambs were dug out from snowdrifts in the Cotswolds but the French refused to accept shipments. All cattle were murrained north of the Thames and all horses were spavined south of the Trent. In the High Streets the price of crows' wings was up by 55 per cent. A relief ship bound for the capital with dried gannet was sunk by an iceberg in the Medway.

For the first time Windsor Castle was illuminated by slow-burning bodies of puffins, threaded on wicks, an old Scottish economy measure. From overseas came disturbing rumours of the rise of a militant Muscovy.

1655

The cold was so intense that yard-arms snapped when pirates were hanged. The Protector's major-generals rigorously enforced the laws against fornication, filthy dalliance and connubial bliss; also against the "turbulent and ruttish" sport of football, even then the cause of widespread riot. Common law wives and single female parents were whipped at the cart's tail; dancing masters and man-midwives were put in the stocks. A record number of Eton boys were flogged, "to dissuade them from any sin they had a mind to commit." All over Britain old women were found to be suckling imps and demons, vomiting pins and giving birth to coneys.

Strikes by turnkeys at Newgate and other gaols flooded London with infamous rogues. Shiploads of "thrawn Scots devils" were sent to join their compatriots in the Plantation of Ulster. Turnspits, starchers, leech-gatherers, corn-cutters, bug-destroyers, thatchers and priors all tried to hold the country to ransom, but were transported in short order to the New World. Meanwhile hundreds of travellers who had fled from persecution in Britain were held hostage by Barbary pirates, French corsairs, Oriental sultans and Muscovite princes.

1835

The cold was so intense that not only was it impossible to bury cadavers but "resurrection men" were unable to dig them up; in consequence, medical science languished. Because of this inclemency, Private Thomas Arkle of the 176th Foot was allowed to receive his 499 lashes indoors. An appeal for the use of Yeomanry to dig out scores of poachers buried in snow in Norfolk was turned down by the Horse Guards. The Chancellor of the Exchequer, a leading "wet", froze to death while performing a U-turn.

The word "socialism" was first heard in the land and that day the temperature fell to the lowest ever recorded. When Peel defined the aims of Conservatism it fell ten more degrees. Students were driving themselves mad by ether-sniffing, intellectuals were slaves of opium. Panic swept the country at a rumour that men were to be forced to marry their deceased wives' sisters. The High Court threatened to resign *en bloc* if the Tolpuddle rascals were pardoned. The city of Liverpool, stricken by the abolition of the slave trade, demanded to be made a Special Area. Talk of introducing factory legislation spread gloom in Lancashire, where cotton manufacturers complained their rate of return on capital was already down to 50 per cent. A lightning strike at Christmas by wet nurses forced society women to suckle their own young. The dying year was haunted by the spectre of Universal Suffrage, "the Fifth Horseman of the Apocalypse".

LOVE IN A COLD CLIMATE

"He seems to have lost the urge since his accident."

"It's a fortnight since I came out of the closet and still nobody's noticed that I'm wearing my wife's clothes."

"It's only September—why don't I stay the night?"

"What makes you think your husband's engaged a private detective?"

"The Aurora Borealis is a little early this evening."

*"But **I have** slipped into something a little cooler."*

"Can't he play anything else but 'Strangers in the Night'?"

"You don't bring me flowers anymore."

Do You Live in a Real London Village?

THE VILLAGE BOOKSHOP This is not for selling new books. Nor, curiously, second-hand books. It markets review copies and remainders, that is, books which the publisher could not sell and which the reviewer did not wish to keep. Who would want to buy books like that? Villagers, of course.

YE NEWE VILLAGE PUBBE People often imagine that pubs receive only interior revamping. Not so. The most important changes take place outdoors. It is no use installing varnished wood, inglenooks and Space Invaders, if the outside of the pub is not repainted in brown-purple with scrolly writing proclaiming that the brewers are really "Purveyors of gins, whiskies and other fine liquors", that here can be found "real London ales" and that behind the pub is a small square of concrete known as "a family beer garden".

London village pubs have a star system, as follows:
* Dart board
** American pool
*** Separate room marked Billiards
**** Live rock or jazz most evenings
***** A theatre upstairs

THE BLIND SHOP Not for the benefit of the blind, any more than the Third World shop is for the Third World. Here the villagers buy blinds depicting rural scenes to hang in their basement windows, and to remind them of their country cottages which they cannot get to this weekend.

THE ASIAN SHOP Not just any old Asian shop, of course, because they are everywhere, just as are Chinese take-aways, Indian restaurants and next-day cleaners *or* photo developers. To be a *real* village Asian shop, it must have the courage to feature at least ten things not available at the ordinary post office: e.g. persimmons, lychees, mangoes, yams, plantains, coriander, kumquats, pomegranates, yaws, beri-beri and continental tomatoes as big as an elephant's navel.

Has the little grocer's shop near you closed down recently? Does your local sub-postmistress now wear a sari? Got a choice of wine bars but no pub you like? Chances are you're living in one of London's new villages! MILES KINGTON tells you what to look out for.

THE LITTLE RESTAURANT WITH GAILY PAINTED RED CHAIRS AND A VASE OF FRESH FLOWERS ON EACH TABLE Whether it sells pizzas or local hamburgers or doner kebabs does not matter. The important thing is to have gaily painted red chairs and a vase of fresh flowers on each table. Oh, and waiters in something stripey. That way you can get the true village feeling of a French café. Breton crêpes followed by Calvados are best. Or was that 1979? Well, it's probably come back by now.

THE VILLAGE WINE BAR An antique shop which also sells wine by the glass, at antique prices.

THE PRINT 'N' REPRO SHOP Here, in their traditional studio, the print workers pursue their ancient craft of putting a piece of paper in a Xerox machine and pressing a knob. You may also buy gaily coloured German felt tip pens and packets of envelopes which work out at only 6p each.

HELIOGABALUS Or Nostradamus. Or Jabberwocky. Any polysyllabic name will do to describe the village shop which sells traditional posters of James Dean, postcards of the less daring Impressionists and greeting cards with a deflating message on page 3.

MR SCOFF'S DELICATESSEN The village food shop. Here you can buy authentic French bread made each day in London, pâtés made in pottery bowls, and bags of smoked salmon odds and ends to make your own smoked salmon mousse out of. The proprietor of the shop *must* (a) have a paperback out under his own name, (b) be delightfully camp without actually being gay, (c) appear in the shop in person at least once a year.

THE VILLAGE CINEMA Not, of course, an Odeon or ABC (except perhaps if it has recently had a preservation order) but one with a folk name such as Screen on the Green, Flicks in the Sticks, or the Bionic, Golders Green. Here, during the afternoon and evening, villagers can see all the German, Japanese and Woody Allen films they ought to see, often on the very day they are reviewed in the *Guardian* (the village newspaper). At 11.15 begins the late night session of films they *want* to see, like *Casablanca*, *Singing in the Rain* and *Jules et Jim*, or any film that has a preservation order on it.

THE FLOUR SHOP

And nothing is browner than real flour, or more lumpy, or more full of bits of stone (hence the label "stone ground"). The traditional village maidens in their gay village Martini aprons will sell you buckwheat, sesame seeds, basmati rice or Canadian cracked rye, or indeed anything for which there is no recipe in your cookery books, at traditional village prices. No wonder they all look bonny and plump-cheeked, while the customers look pale and underfed. You can also buy here organic vegetables and fruit. Organic means, generally, twice the price; specifically it means wizened (apples), gnarled (carrots), or brown (white cabbage).

YE ANTIQUE SHOPPE

There are two quite distinct kinds of antique shop, both tremendously valid.

(1) The antique shop which is never open. It displays huge pseudo-Chinese pieces of furniture or monumental Victorian parlour objects in a dark dusty interior never besmirched by customers. That is, junk.

(2) The antique shop which is always open, manned by a dealer reading a paperback. It sells functional antiques. That is, pieces from a bygone era which could still be used. That is, battered household articles. That is, junk.

(3) Sorry, there's a third as well. The Bourneville Tin Shop. That is, the shop which sells anything with a trade name on it. Like ashtrays marked Bovril. In other words, junk.

THE TILE SHOP

Every village must have a tile shop, preferably where the butcher's used to be, for meat is an unnecessary and probably harmful luxury but tiles are a necessity. There are two kinds of tile shop. One sells shiny tiles made in Italy and featured in *Vogue*. The other sells rough brown earthy tiles, either made in Morocco by unshaven, underpaid natives or crafted in Wiltshire studios by unshaven, underpaid arts graduates. Tile shops always open with a special opening sale; after two years, when all the villagers have tiled their bathrooms, they have a special closing sale.

THE STREET MARKET

In some villages in London there still survive street stalls that sell fruit and veg, flowers and whelks. Their occupants are not genuine London villagers, merely jumped up tradesmen from the East End. Their coarse cries, clumsy stalls and messy habits are not authentically representative of true London village life and can safely be ignored.

THE LOCAL CRAFT SHOP

Villagers like to support local crafts. Especially they like to support the local crafts of Portugal (painted pottery), the Phillipines (dangly rope objects), Peru (ponchos) and Penzance (brown coffee mugs).

THE STRIPPED PINE SHOP

The most ancient London village craft, dating back to the primeval mists of the 1960s, is the art of stripping pine. Nobody knows for sure how it is done; no one has the faintest idea what happens to all that flaked black grot which is stripped off pine, and must amount to a hundred tons a year; nobody can begin to imagine from where come all those dressers and kitchen tables and desks. Nobody would dare ask. It is simply a mystery for which we must all be thankful. Prices of stripped pine are expressed in an ancient village language, by the way; e.g. £AF/AO.

YE OLDE ROCKE 'N' ROLLE SHOPPE

Villagers do not buy records; they rent them for taping and sell the lease back at a slight loss. The racks are full of every LP ever made by Genesis and Billy Joel; the walls are festooned with boxes of total Verdi operas and the entire Haydn symphony range, for Haydn was the Sanderson of the orchestra. Do villagers line *their* walls with boxes? The only music not found here is English folk music, which has no place in a London village.

THE ARCHITECT'S WORKSHOP

Under the spreading indoor palm the village architect works, conscious that passers-by are staring through his open-plan window over his open-plan shoulder and wondering what he is designing. He is designing one-room extensions and back additions for other villagers, of course; or the smallest lavatories in the world for restaurants; or wine bar decors; or simply workshops for other architects. If asked to build a house, he would not know what to do.

THE FISHMONGER

A very lucky village will have a fish shop, complete with marble slabs, chips of ice, a wall chart of fish in six languages and a few fish mentioned in Elizabeth David. Peak time of the year is September, when the villagers have just come back from their village holidays in the Dordogne and remember that monkfish is really called "lotte" or are still keen enough to do their own *moules marinières*.

THE VILLAGE NATURAL SHOE SHOP

All natural things are brown (rice, sugar, eggs, coffee mugs, Academy Cinema posters, trees) and leather is no exception. Do not buy white shoes; they have been over-refined till there is no nutrition in them. Get shapeless brown moccasins from your village shoe shop. They are the real thing.

THE CHILDREN'S OPERA GROUP

As a sort of cultural crèche, larger London villages keep their children out of mischief on winter evenings by allowing them to make an opera. Well, they don't actually allow *them* to make an opera, of course; that can be safely left to Ben Britten. If it's a really go-ahead village, they will actually commission Stephen or Nicholas or Darryl (whom someone in the village knows awfully well) to write a new opera, and get his friends to play in the band. Everyone agrees that the opera is too good not to be heard again, but it never is. The opera is performed in the village progressive church which for two months is jam-packed with the local village musicians. They are not seen there during the other ten months of the year.

McMurtry's LAW

"Well, Mr Scroggins, you've heard what the Inspector's slipping me for a conviction—can you top that?."

"Stop moaning! It's your only chance left—diminished responsibilty."

"Step on it, Charlie—I'm on Jury service in half an hour!"

"If you're sending him down for twenty years, a little more eye-shadow would suggest sleepless nights agonising over your decision."

"Very clever, Perkins. Now get him back under the blanket again!"

"What a sentence! He always wanted to make The Guiness Book of Records."

"Shush, dear. Poor Daddy's not allowed to hang anyone at work any more."

*"Dammit! Mrs. Throgmorton's Pekinese **was** guilty of fouling that footpath. I know it was!"*

The Lionel in Winter

All set for panto at the Palladium,
LIONEL BLAIR talks to
DAVID TAYLOR

TRE-*MEND*OUS: he can't tell us how tremendous it is, to be doing a panto in London again, to be having such a time of it doing *Give Us A Clue*, to be having *such* a lovely lunch and, God, going to be in the *Punch* magazine and oh, dearie me, it's tremendous, really it is.

Mmm, well, it always is for Lionel—tremendous, utterly fantastic, couldn't be better than it is, pitter-patter, sparking all the time because, *well*, he's full of it, next to never moody or a bit upset, *loves* what he's doing and, erm, thinks he'll have the cutlets, nicely done, and wine would be *lovely*, but nothing fussy per-*lease*, and just a tick while he signs an autograph, for Tracey, love from Lionel.

Mmm, well the telly does that—been on over a hundred shows you know, and the *numbers* who watch him doing *Give Us A Clue*, honestly, it's out of this, *well*, people like to play a game, and it's not as if they're just there to walk off with a free toaster and cut glasses or any of that malarkey, it's just a parlour game, like charades, but *such* tremendous fun to do—you get people in the street going Hello Lionel! and then start drawing imaginary squares in the air, really has caught on.

Mmm, well it's nice to get the huge audience of telly, of *course* it is, but there's no comparison with a live theatre. That's just tre-, well, for the last eight Christmases he's been in Canada. For a panto—did you not know that? Oh, yes and they're a really lovely audience. But well, you know, it *is* so special to be offered the Palladium this year and *won't* it be nice to have a Christmas at home with Daniel and Lucy—I mean, they're practically teenagers, you know, but it will be nice to be all at home. Mmm? Barnes. Next door to Colin Welland, the writer. Not so long ago we'd have said the actor, wouldn't we? So super having talented people about.

Mmm, well, it's so easy to get put into a pigeon-hole. It's happened to him, of course it has: people tend to think of him only as a dancer. Well, of course he does do that and if I may say so is tremendous at it, but there's *masses* more than that, really there is, and you'd be wrong to suppose that this lawks-a-mercy manner implies any marbles shortage—it does not. Lionel is *shrewd* you know and very multi-faceted, too. He may not have peaked as yet.

Mmm, well, Sammy Davis Jr. is a very special friend—they did a Royal Variety Performance a while back—and I don't suggest it's stretching it if we compare the two. Basically, it's song-and-dance, well of *course* it is, but there's a strong streak of humour besides. I don't say it's remotely the same streak, that'd be silly to pretend because it isn't, *but*, well it's perhaps a bit more like than Brucie or Danny or Larry, or, you know the sort of, well, thing. This wine's really nice.

Mmm, well, what Lionel would say, what Lionel *did* say, is that it'd be nice to be taken a bit more seriously now and again. No, c'mon, he's not one to want to do *Hamlet*—though he's appeared at Stratford, you know, yes he has, early on, was a boy actor, once—but maybe be a bit more

stretched. He could do sit-com, for instance, and I dare say bring it off tremendously well, more to it than panto, after all, and he's a *marvellous* director—everyone says that. Did you realise that Lionel directed Max Bygraves in his show at the Victoria Palace last year? Yes he did and it was acclaimed, too.

Mmm, well, he's worked with *tons* of people, you must realise, over the years. Choreography, of course, was what started it all—at ATV as a matter of fact—what first got him known. It's a job to know where to begin, but Arthur Askey, Dave King, Roy Castle, Jo Stafford, Harry Secombe, Bob Hope, Jewel and Wariss, Bruce Forsyth, Aimi Macdonald—I mean he's worked with them all. He and Aimi starred in the West End revival of *Lady Be Good*—remember that?—and did a routine or two for the Royal Variety from that show, about a dozen years ago now. This year you'll have seen, *marvellous* occasion, for the Queen Mum, bless her, and with J. R. too! Heavens, erm, just coffee, he thinks, black. Will have to run in a tick—got a bit of a squabble on, always the same setting up a new show.

Mmm, well, we ought to mention films a bit—I mean Lionel has been in and done the routines for, oh I don't know, *World of Suzie Wong, Gentlemen Marry Brunettes*—super fun at the time, but, you know, cabaret is really the thing. Touring with a really fast-moving show—there's nothing like it and it would be *such* a shame if provincial shows are left to decline and people sit at home in front of the box. Well, of course, he does it himself—he and Susan like nothing better than just to curl up at home with the kids, but it's a necessary breather for Lionel who otherwise never stops, rushing about all the time, of course *thrives* on being busy, only the thing is if you never get out and participate in some live entertainment—*well*, that's *such* a shame, he thinks, missing *such* a lot.

Mmm, well, no Lionel is not at all the solitary sort: he *must* have company, not one to sit. Do you know, it's funny I should ask if he has ever felt an urge to write, it really is. He means he hasn't until, well, there are signs he soon might. Not that he really believes in any astrological stuff but, well, it's really funny I should ask him that. You see, it might be a way to strike off at a different tangent, *could* be something in it—too soon to know, mind you, but really extraordinary that it should come up whilst we are just having this lovely chat.

Mmm, well, now don't you go off thinking that Lionel is only a big soft thing because he isn't. He's a *professional* person, let's have that straight. A tremendous dancer, we all know that, and, lots of people will tell you this, a man of *steel* when he's directing, yes, because he'll not abide horsing about. He's an extrovert, of *course* he is, love, but *nobody* goes to see Lionel perform and comes away feeling short-changed—he's absolutely set on that. Between him and us, and he really *must* dash off now, a *super* lunch, this year's Palladium panto is going to be just tre . . . of course, love, always got a mo to oblige with an autograph . . . *mend*ous.

JONATHAN SALE

Fag Ends

AS one of two Joint Winners of the Classics Prize (there were only a couple of us left, the other members of the Upper Sixth Classics having found better ways of spending their time) back in 1962, I had a lot going for me. I had even been a House Prefect, albeit briefly—I should point out that the allegations, of my having received money for allowing another prefect to do my Junior Dorm Duty, were never actually proved in court.

What we were trained for was something rather specialised. It was to be the right person to answer any advertisement that ran: "Wanted: smart lad to run backward but obedient African country." Or—bear in mind that my father possessed nothing but his brains, which he had not handed on, and a crumbling house in the suburbs— "Childless mill-owner seeks rude dilettante to inherit business. Wednesdays only."

Since *The Times* and *Telegraph* failed to print such appeals in their Small Ad columns, I was reduced to a precarious existence as a student and later fell among journalists; the result is now before your eyes. But, conscious that I was not always as you see me now, I leapt upon a newly discovered publication entitled *Public School Leaver* to see if, after eighteen years, it was possible to lay a hand on the birthright that should have been mine.

A Mr Norman Clarke of the Institute of Mathematics seemed to have the right idea. "The ideal job," he wrote in a recent issue, "is one that will pay a very good salary for doing something that you thoroughly enjoy." Jane Austen could not have put it better (it is a truth universally acknowledged that a single mathematician in want of a salary...) than Mr Clarke, who went on to state that "Whether your job involves giving change to customers in Woolworths or preparing the annual accounts of ICI," or, he might have added, given their current financial state, preparing the accounts of Woolies, "you cannot do it without an appropriate mathematical knowledge."

At this point it occurred to me that although I was not very good at Classics, I was no good at all at mathematics, and would not have walked away with the Maths Prize even if the entire Maths Sixth had been expelled. Anyway, what is all this about giving change in stores? One was, after all, reading *Public School Leaver* and not "Grammar School Swot" or "Comprehensive Truant". Some of us might be prepared to get in at the bottom, but only if our old man happened to be at the top of the relevant company tree.

Public School Leaver is distributed free to "independent schools". (Since *Punch* is not included in such a definition, we paid, like the rest of the world, £6 for a subscription.) Yet, despite this carefully defined target, there is little connection between the traditional public school attributes and the tasks which the world has to offer its old boys. United Biscuits, for example, makers of "snacks, convenience and frozen foods, also involved in fast food, retailing Wimpy and Pizzaland" (is that a boast or an apology?) were asked what abilities they demanded. The answer, according to *Public School Leaver*, was: "Inter personal skills, motivation, travel in UK, initiative, self reliance, brains." Nothing, you note, about being able to recite great chunks of Latin verse assisted only by the fact that they were glued to the jacket of the chap in front. Nothing about being able to get along with fellows from all walks of life provided only that they were sensible enough to have been in the same school at the same time as oneself.

In fact, there is a feeling that ability to get to grips with (or fail to get to grips with) the tongues of the past is not all that it might be. "Modern Languages may be defined as those which are currently used as active means of communication between peoples in various parts of the world," wrote a Mr Ian Finlay in another issue. It is possible that *Public School Leaver* may have taken over other publications entitled "Public School Twit" and "Complete Public School Idiot", because he then goes on to say, "Consequently, Latin, Classical Greek and Hebrew are not modern languages." Russian, however, is—stop me if I'm going too fast for you—and offers a great deal of scope to those who master its intricacies and are not put off by the fact that "In the last ten years the USSR has tended to be associated only with unpleasant behaviour," in the memorable phrase of London University lecturer Nicholas Brown. If he writes like that, his lectures cannot be anything but a feast of Wildean epigram and Swiftian metaphor.

It seems, in fact, that public school leavers need things spelled out at some length. In its book review entitled "Science at Work", the reviewer, writing anonymously in the manner of the *Times Literary Supplement* (one of the few similarities between the publications) said that "A new booklet... has appeared. It is titled 'Science at Work' and deals with the use of science in the working world." And on a facing page there was a review of another booklet, this time on "Women in Science and Technology", which covers— but you guessed. The review goes further. There aren't enough of them, women in science and technology, that is, and "Imperial College, London, have published a special booklet for the fair sex." The reviewer omits to mention that the fear of being welcomed by people who talk about the fair sex might put the girls off Imperial College in the first place.

The fair, weaker or opposite sex is not found in large quantities at boys' boarding schools, although a few of the master's wives might just have qualified. What we had—or to be more accurate, didn't have— was girls sharing an annual dance at a "sister" school chosen by taking a ruler to a map of England and selecting the female establishment at the furthest point from our own. They were bused to us and we were bused to them, while energetic staff watered the drinks and locked the doors of the dance hall to prevent any unauthorised steps being taken outside.

None of that is much help to a chap fearful of being the two millionth unemployed. For that assistance, one turns to *Working in a Hotel* by Michael J. Boella, of which the reviewer enthused, "the book is excellent in that it distinguishes jobs from other similar jobs" which is more than you can say of, for example, *Pride and Prejudice*. Furthermore, "travel in general can be shown to have caused the need for travellers' resting places, and the consequent competition to provide better accommodation and food than the next Inn gave rise to ever-increasing standards." So much for the nineteenth century; what went wrong? Perhaps this is where the public school leaver comes in, since "The role of management is also outlined, with regard to some of the difficulties it may entail." That is, if you know a difficult management, why not seek employment there? The catering industry is not yet on its knees, all it needs is the right intake.

Among all these hints, among all these details of "in-company training", "in-bank training", "in-factory training" and, for all I know, in-prison training, there is nothing about an organisation which clearly could well do with some new blood. It is Dominion Press, publishers of *Public School Leaver*. Of all the modern languages, only English is required, and not too much of that.

"Dash it, Susan, I'm a gruff old soldier, no good at talk! Will you marry me or must I have you shot?"

ALAN BRIEN's
London

"**S**EXUAL ENCOUNTER" promised the illuminated sign. You wouldn't think that you could, rather, perhaps, you wouldn't think that *I* could, no, what I am, of course, saying is that *I* never thought that I could . . . could, that is, pass by this sign twice a week on my way to Wardour Street preview cinemas and yet forget where I saw it.

It was not as if the announcement were in Soho proper, and improper, where the letters s-e-x are now flashed so often on every side that their combination has almost lost any meaning, suggesting at most some dodgy answer three-down in a crossword which turns out to be "former King of Albania", "term in heraldry", or "instrument used by taxidermist to hook in glass eyes". Sometimes I begin to wonder whether "sex" isn't a plural and pronounced "sash", after the fashion of Bernard Shaw's proof for foreign students of English that the spoken sound "fish" ought to be written down "ghoti"—the "f" a "gh" as in "tough", the "i" an "o" as in "women", and the "sh" a "ti" as in "ignition".

Sex parlours are more frequent in Soho than shoe-shops in Bond Street or Building Society offices in suburban high streets.

Very soon their customers will no longer be able to pretend that they were just passing by on the way to get some fresh pasta, a bin end of wine or a meal at some exotic restaurant, as the rocketing rents force out all but dealers in the skin-trade.

"SEXUAL ENCOUNTER", however, is outside the walls of pornopolis, on the main strip of Charing Cross Road, once the street of bookish browsers, where the worst deviation was bibliophilia, the most common crime interfering with a first edition, the most daring poster a huge, yellow, tin sign "Damarrhoids—the GREAT Rejuvenator", and the dirtiest publication, "The Works of Aristotle—Fully Illustrated!"

And the reason it seemed to have vanished, like the green door in the wall of H. G. Wells's Secret Garden, may be that it is sited on Cambridge Circus—just at that blind spot where the hunted pedestrian, newly escaped from a traffic flow which never slackens however the lights change, is too busy panting with relief to raise his eyes from the pavement. There is also the possibility that, despite my devotion to duty as a chronicler of London life, I had blanked out the memory by a kind of Freudian slip in reverse.

Still, last week, there I was at the entrance. I climbed the narrow stairs, which seemed by an optical illusion to be narrowing with each foot-fall, the half-gloom lit only by the white thighs of the receptionist who was sitting behind a frontless, folding counter at the top, knees apart. Like all receptionists, she was on the telephone to a boyfriend.

"Got to go now," she said in a flat North Midlands accent. "Got a customer."

I waited out the repetitions and reassurances customary on all calls not paid for by the telephone user, somewhat reassured by the familiarity of the ritual, as if booking a room at a commercial hotel in the provinces. She was about 24, pretty in a rather un-tarty, country-girl style, as sturdily built above as I had noted below, with a mass of frizzy hair.

"What is Sexual Encounter?" I asked, almost expecting to hear a Wylie Watson monotone replying that Sexual Encounter, like the Thirty-Nine Steps, was an organisation of spies . . . *Bang*! Watch out, Hannay, they'll get you next.

"Sexual Encounter is where you go into a room with a girl and she takes off all her clothes and you can talk about anything you want to. The prices are there on the wall," she said, smiling faintly as if explaining the rules of a parlour game she wanted you to

know would be more enjoyable than it sounded.

I examined the tariff. Fifteen minutes is a long time in journalism, even for compulsive talkers, and especially at £9.50. I bought myself a quarter of a hour and was asked to take a seat in the waiting-room. I checked my watch and sorted through the reading matter—an old copy of *Woman* and an even older copy of a porn magazine which, oddly, had sticky paper over the naughty bits.

The receptionist shouted up the stairs to Fancy, or Chancy, or was it Yancy? "I need the room, somebody's waiting."

After a while, a slim, attractive, duskily-tinted girl clattered down, gave a smile of friendly complicity and took over the legs-akimbo position at the desk. Apparently, I was to be favoured by the receptionist herself, a decision which made me feel, for no sensible reason, obscurely gratified.

I had somehow pictured the encounter as taking place in a large studio, illuminated by daylight, with me in an armchair gazing, pasha-like, at a nude model on a dais, Svengali to her Trilby, a sliver of La Vie de Bohème. I ought to have remembered the rateable values. Instead, I opened a plain,

"It's an offer for our story from the Evening News and it's even better than the one we've got from the News Chronicle!"

chip-board door onto a black-painted box slightly larger than a telephone kiosk, and took a seat facing my fuzzy-headed friend in an identical box separated from me by a floor-to-ceiling glass panel. Somewhere on the way she had removed her panties—a prominent part of the view on the stairs—and now only needed to shuck off a blouse and skirt and settle, nude, on her own seat.

THERE was an appreciable silence. She nodded encouragingly. I searched for a topic—at just under one p. per second, was it to be the most expensive conversation I never had?

I asked what most men talked about.

"Well," she said, all limbs glued to her torso like a celluloid baby-doll. "They talk about their wives, or their jobs, or how they'd like to meet girls." She paused. "But to tell you the truth, mostly they don't talk at all."

I said that then I didn't understand what was the point of the exercise and the price.

She shifted carefully and demurely from ham to ham, palms together, pointing downwards.

"You see, really, that's not what they want. For another ten pounds, I do poses, open my legs and, if they want, masturbate myself."

I could hear my watch ticking.

"Then," she said. "For another ten pounds. Well, we're not really supposed to do this, but for another ten pounds I can come round to your side and give you hand-relief."

I didn't have any problems with my hands, I explained. They didn't need any relief.

"Par-don," she said.

It was clear that whatever her skill in artistic poses or her dexterity at manual labouring, she was not trained for word-play. I decided that everybody could usually discuss money. Did she mean that without the extras, I was not a profitable proposition?

"I'm not complaining," she said. "But the boss keeps what you pay for your time. Anything else I get belongs to me. What we call hand-relief, or some of the girls say intimate-satisfaction, is what customers want. They're mostly working-men, not, you know, ordinary working-people, but in business, or professional people. It only takes about three minutes and then it's off their minds and they can get back to work. That's why I was a bit surprised you asked

"Son, pretty soon you're going to have to decide where you're going to sit."

for so long. I mean if you are going to spend thirty pounds, you can get a girl from an escort agency for the night, and, you know, the real thing."

I made an excuse and stayed. By now I'd forgotten she was undressed and I hardly noticed the glass barrier between us. It was quite a change, she said, to have someone listen to her. Nobody ever did anything to her body, that was a strict rule. If she wanted anything like that, she had her boyfriend, didn't she? He was new and he didn't know what she did for a living. She had to think of something that sounded right since she was on shifts—ten till six one week, four till twelve the next. "I say I'm a receptionist in a private hotel." If she settled in with him, she'd tell him what she did, but only after she'd given it up. She didn't think it was hard work, or needed much ability, nor was it unpleasant really.

"What we do for men, well, little boys do it for themselves don't they? There isn't much to it that I can see. It's only a drag if it takes too long."

She herself had a little boy of four that friends looked after. "I can spend all day with him on my late weeks. I don't know where else I'd be able to afford to live as I do. You know, not tremendous but well enough."

No, she didn't think the customers were idiots for paying so much for so little. Occasionally, there were kinky ones and then she stayed firmly behind her door, or there were ones she didn't like the look of and then she never suggested the extras.

"Most of them are absolutely ordinary, usually a bit nicer looking, maybe, than the average. I don't think it's because they can get any sex free elsewhere. That isn't a problem these days, is it? I suppose they just don't want all the bother and the hassle, picking girls up and taking them out first, never knowing how much time they'll have to spend. Time is it, really. Once it's over, they forget us. I think they pretend we never happened. And what we've done, it's not like being unfaithful. They're glad it's measured by the minute."

These words reminded her that we, too, were operating against the clock. She stood up and dressed again, rather more slowly and carelessly than she had undressed. It was the only faintly erotic routine of the quarter of an hour.

We parted on chummy terms though I thought she still seemed a bit baffled by what it was she sold that made me satisfied with what I had bought. It was only when I reached Cambridge Circus again that it occurred to me I might have misinterpreted her half-frown—was she thinking that she had talked herself out of her bonus?

I sat next door in the pub for half an hour casing the entrance, hoping to round off my investigation with a few statistics about how many customers stayed as long as I had. I was also curious to discover what sort and manner of men they were. But in nineteen pounds of sexual-encounter time, during a week-day lunch hour, I saw no one enter or leave. Perhaps next time I look for the sign, it will really have disappeared.

China's propaganda machine is now committed to turning the thoughts of the people away from fanatical socialism and towards a new understanding with the capitalist West. If nothing else, it should liven up the morning papers . . .

PEKING PEOPLE'S DAILY

1,000,000,000 readers can't be wrong!*

INSIDE YOUR BLOSSOMING NUMBER ONE PAPER:

- IT'S UP YOUR PRODUCTIVE MOTIVATION AND WIN A FLORAL JERKIN WEEK!

- PLUS A WESTERN-STYLE TIN OF PILCHARDS FOR THE LUCKY RUNNER-UP!

- COLUMNIST-OF-THE-YEAR DENG XIAOPING ON THE NEED TO TOIL FOR SPOILS

- IS REVOLUTION BAD FOR YOU? A STARTLING EXPOSÉ BY HUA GUOFENG STARTS TODAY

- HOW STAMPING OUT OUTMODED LENINIST MALFEASANCE KEEPS YOU YOUNG AND FIT

- AND WHY FALSEHOOD IN NEWS IS LIKE RAT DROPPINGS IN CLEAR SOUP

ALL OF IT AND MORE INSIDE TODAY'S PEOPLE'S DAILY*

*Supersedes yesterday's misguided revanchist catalogue of lickspittle lies, until further notice

Looking for a Wartburg or other fine car? Got an unfurnished corner of your commune to let? Check it out with the 900,000,000 Classified Ads in the *People's Daily* or call our Harro Girls on Peking 3–5–3–5–0–0–0

 ON OTHER PAGES OF YOUR FUN-FILLED PEOPLE'S DAILY

- **YOUR TV GUIDE**—full details of where to find one are on p.2
- **NAUGHTY FASHIONS TO MAKE HEADS TURN!** Would YOU dare to be seen in coloured plimsolls? Is it permitted to undo the top button of your state anorak on your wedding night? Why not save up for a Western-style hankie?—For the first time, PICTURES on p.3

- **SPECIAL OFFERS TO READERS OF THE NEW-STYLE PEOPLE'S DAILY!**
Imagine the thrill of owning your very own Pyrex mixing bowl! Or see their faces light up when you open a genuine branded packet of Solvite or, for that special occasion, give the kids a swig of milk from a bottle! You can send off NOW for these fabulous fruits-of-capitalism offers, simply enclosing payment of 200 yuan and an employer's certificate to show that you've turned out EITHER 6,000 tons of sheet steel OR one dozen working warheads in the last seven days!

We say . . .

Make no mistake—today Chairman Mao and his gang of cronies are dead, buried, gone, discredited, spat upon, reviled, forgotten, altogether expunged and may never have existed at all. Long live Helmsman Hua Guofeng and the new spirit of enterprise by which every humble citizen may sneeze openly, whistle, hold hands in public, save up for a calculator or increase industriousness for personal gain. May birdsong sustain the wisdom of the new beginning for, assuredly, things do go better with Coke.

and so

What matter if the cat is black or white so long as it catches mice? If China is to modernise and trample on the Soviet behemoth, more strength to her material incentives elbow and let the weevils strangle the bones and compost of Marxist-Leninist oppression that has for dynasties stifled expansion and prevented a chain of McDonald's starting up in Shanghai.

forth from

The revanchist bleatings of socialist fainthearts with their suffocating dogma have had their idealistic onions and, as if a frustrated maiden bursting forth from the trammels of a quilted boiler-suit, China re-awakens to a new dawn of prosperity and a TV set in every commune.

★★★★★★★★★★★★★★★★★★★

THERE'S ALWAYS MORE NEWS IN YOUR NUMBER ONE PEOPLE'S DAILY

● The Great Gong of Tientsin was sounded yesterday to mark the start of an auspicious week during which operas will be staged throughout China to clarify the new instruction that capitalism no longer stinks. Children under five are to be issued with US army surplus automatic weapons and free lipsticks and bad weather which threatened to disrupt attempts to modernise flax-gathering between Wuhan and Harbin has been ordered to disperse.

● But a new survey shows that 1 in 2 Chinese citizens is experiencing difficulty grasping what is being urged and some 66 million fanatical miscreants have been gaoled or publicly executed for their clumsy attempts to make pigs lay larger eggs or sell off the railways to private enterprise.

● Meanwhile, bauxite smelting has suffered a further setback and, in a new thought, Hua Guofeng has pointed out that this is no way to improve the topsoil or ensure that every Chinese mine has a refrigerator and washing machine by the mid-1990s.

Chinese Express? That'll do nicely, comrade! A special supplement on the glorious modernisation programme in retailing starts to-morrow in the *People's Daily*

Announcing a major new drive to help China stand on its own 2,000,000,000 feet!

FIVE FANTASTIC FAT CHICKENS MUST BE WON!
PLUS THE CHANCE TO TAKE THE DENG XIAOPING TREASURE TRAIL FOR A PIG!

Here's a chance for YOU to take a Great Leap Forward. We are offering five fabulous fleshy broilers AND the chance of a lifetime to own your own pig in a FREE, easy-to-enter contest designed to modernise China's defence, industry and agriculture.

The total value of the poultry alone, including delivery, plucking charges, registration and comestibles licence is a staggering 25 yuan—equal to six months pay for a Shanghai stevedore!

The contest is so easy to enter. The theme is points to consider between now and the year 2000 during fulfilment of the 19-and-a-bit Plan For The Instigation of Twenty-First Century Technology in *Zhonghua Renmin Gongheguo** and the best 50 million entries will go forward to an eliminating final in the Kweichow Hall of Heavenly Swineherding to complete the slogan "The agrarian frog of oligarchical backsliding must become the iron princess of capitalist revitalisation because . . ."
* Chinese for the Motherland.

Today we print the first points for consideration and between now and Sunday the *People's Daily* will include coupons and full details of Entry Form Collection Centres in Peking, Shanghai, Hupeh, Kiangsu and Sinkiang Uighur.

Just make a pair of scissors and cut out this list for future reference:

A. Need to stem Soviet imperialist expansionism
B. Desire to implement consumption of consumer durables
C. Requirement to U-turn on more than 48 million chants, thoughts, slogans and revolutionary urgings and encourage masses to put something by for the chance to own their own smallholding
D. Urgent necessity of convincing rest of developed world that China has lost Chairman Mao but not its collective marbles and is emerging as a safe bet for the convenient off-loading of cheap exports in billion-ton job lots
E. Essentially of devising new stock of cryptic riddles to explain to 100,000,000 confused countrymen what in hell is going on.

A Plage in the Sun

GEOFFREY DICKINSON reports from Brittany

"The other English couple want to know if you'd like the menu translated by their little boy?"

"Stop complaining about the smell—people will think you're English."

"Are you sure they understood that we wanted the topless beach?"

"Looks as though the bread's stale again."

"All that cheap lamb doesn't seem to be doing the English much good."

"Do you walk over other people's food in England?"

"We were stuck here at the end of the queue for Cherbourg and one thing led to another . . ."

Child's Play

by CLEMENT FREUD

I THINK it is the firm of Laurent Perrier—though it could just be some other French company that does not send me any champagne at Christmas either—which is sponsoring a prize to the person who does most for Anglo-French relations. I have seen the press hand-out and the winner can come from the field of journalism, gastronomy, travel, sheep-strangling, even politics.

I suppose, before long, there will come an announcement from Mother's Pride or possibly Babycham about a substantial crock of gold to the individual who does least for the cordiality of the old entente and that would be an altogether more amusing competition for which to enter. Of late, I could not help noticing that London hotel restaurants, jealously regarding the prosperity of the French family-Sunday-lunch-out, are doing their damnedest to get in on the action. These restaurants, because hotels do tend to retain the odd customer on the seventh day, have got to open their dining room doors and because Sunday residents are a dying breed, most of whom are asked out to private houses anyway, the management is forced to look elsewhere for trade.

In France they do not have to look far: it is *la famille*, replete with *les enfants*, *le chien*, not to mention *grand-mère*, who fill the tables. As *les chiens* bark and do ugly things to *le tapis*, it was clearly undesirable to provide dog-orientated meals. So, the way to a rich man's stomach not being via his four-legged friend, and grandma is the thin end of the wedge, it leaves the children.

In France, children sit quietly, contemplatively, behind large napkins tied around their necks and not tied nearly tightly enough. To French children gastronomy is as serious a subject as religion and while they sip wine diluted with mineral water they tuck into calf's head about which they are wise. In view of that, it must have sounded impressive to the hoteliers when their Public Relations consultants came up with the grand idea that *le business* would flourish if parents were given a special incentive to bring kids—like "half price and all you can eat from the sweet trolley".

Now there are a number of subjects about which I am less than tremendously knowledgeable, but British youth and gastronomy are not among them. Therefore,

before any friendly caterer jumps on that particular bandwagon and considers offering reduced price meals to juveniles, let me tell him from experience: the ideal Sunday lunch *en famille* is one from which children are removed and granny is best slipped a large glug of Polish Pure Spirit in her Saturday night Horlicks. If an English restaurateur wants to attempt to recapture the French scene, let him emigrate—and thereby become eligible for the Laurent Perrier, or possibly the Mother's Pride, award.

But there *is* money in feeding kids, separately. Parents will pay large sums of hard-earned, heavily-taxed cash if it appears as if they were taking the children out, just so long as they do not have to sit with them and tell them to keep quiet and not do that, definitely not this, let alone the other. The first establishment that serves reasonable tuck to parents and provides a separate enclosure for their offspring, is going to cash in.

The kids' room must be large and clean with one wall showing continuous noisy cartoon films and the floor should be hard because when accidents happen they should not be trivial. By way of staff, make the ratio one to twelve and recruit from the ranks of

sergeant-majors of the Brigade of Guards and ex-Holloway prison officerettes. Drink is unimportant as long as it is fizzy, there is a variety of colours, you provide lots of ice cubes and at least four straws per person. Let the tables be strewn with salty biscuits in packets and sachets of tomato sauce and mayonnaise and envelopes of salt and sugar and pepper; also mini tubes of mustard.

You then give them bags of crisps, all flavours from plain salted to newt and watercress; also bowls of peanuts and sultanas and pieces of cucumber. For the main dish, sausages and chicken legs and fish fingers and hard boiled eggs are all right if there is a constant flow of hot fresh chips. For puddings ice cream will do. Let them have toffee apples and Smarties and Liquorice Allsorts and quite a lot of damp soft cloths.

None of the ingredients cost a lot of money and when it comes to charging I would propose £3.50 for the first hour and £2 an hour after that. The staff will be entitled to impose penalties for particularly foul behaviour, as an alternative to which you could agree to allow them to beat your children for a small discount; that would certainly make the recruitment of personnel easier.

"Yes, I come here a lot—you'll find the trout all know me."

KEITH WATERHOUSE:

FLAG OF INCONVENIENCE

Cunard is attempting to transfer cruise liners to foreign flags of convenience, enabling it to hire cheaper foreign crews. *Guardian*

Number One Boy Him Log. Day One.

This plenty big day for me-fella. This most plenty big day since me-fella come belong big-boat-him-have-many-chimney as assistant head steward in the Louis XIV Starlight Grill Room on top deck below more top deck, plenty-big-swank passengers only.

Big-fella-strong-with-scrambled-egg-on-cap, him call me-fella up to him stateroom. Him say:

Ah, there you are, Louis XIV Starlight Grill Room Number Two Boy. How you-fella get on along big boat him ride big waves?

Me-fella say: OK, Boss.

Big-fella-strong him say: Mister First Officer Boss him been keep beady eye on you, Number Two Boy, and him say you good boy. How you like be Number One Boy? Job pay plenty glass beads enough along more than coolie minimum. You better take damn job chop-chop.

Me-fella say: Boss, what happen to Number One Boy, him plenty belong-nice to plenty-big-swank passengers, him cook them kai-kai along them table, him add Worcester sauce, double cream and Remy Martin firewater, then light him match and make him go up like him volcano.

Big-fella-strong him say: Him-fella have no more idea of how to flambé a Steak Diane than him back behind of me-fella sit-upon. Him damn near set Louis XIV Starlight Grill Room on fire today some time after big ball come up in sky. Plenty-big-swank passenger Mr McGregor him had to come down along below sick-bay with singed eyebrows, and plenty-big-swank passenger McGregor him woman, Mrs McGregor, she-him have hysterics. Him come too big for him boots, that him trouble.

Me-fella say: Me-fella find plenty-big-swank passenger Boss McGregor him woman more small boot narrow fitting, P.D.Q.

Big-fella-strong him say: Not plenty-big-swank passenger Mr McGregor him woman, you bloody fool Number Two Boy, it Number One Boy who come too big for him boots.

Me-fella say: Boss, Number One Boy him no wear boots. Number One Boy him wear evening-dress loincloth and black tie.

Big-fella-strong him say: Not any more him doesn't. Evening-dress loincloth and black tie is Number One Boy uniform and Number One Boy him not bloody Number One Boy much damn more along today after them Louis XIV Starlight Grill Room second sitting run all about them lifeboats chop-chop shouting, "Fire, fire!" Now do you want Number One Boy job, Number Two Boy, or not?

So me-fella are come be Maitre d'belong Louis XIV Starlight Grill Room.

Number One Boy Him Log. Day Two.

Me-fella look in glass-it-look-back. Me-fella pretty damn tip-top smart in velveteen loincloth with blue silk cummerbund. Me-fella boss boy now. Me-fella call all together them no-good serve-hot-roll-with-tongs-and-fold-pink-napkin-in-shape-of-swan boys belong Louis XIV Starlight Grill Room, and tell all them we turn over new broom P.D.Q. chop-chop bloody now. That mean no more become legless on silver polish long before big ball in sky him sink in water and last plenty-big-swank passenger him have coffee along enough him after-dinner mints.

Them no-good serving-boys mutter rhubarb-rhubarb but them speak no bad pidgin agin me-fella.

By-m-by, plenty-big-swank passenger Yankee Boss Mister Zmansky, him-fella come sit in Crowsnest Bar belong Louis XIV Starlight Grill Room. Him-fella order him drink from Wine Boy and eat plenty cheese footballs. When by-m-by him drink come on silver salver balanced on Wine Boy him head, him-fella clap him hands and call out to me-fella: sir, would you step over here a moment?

Me-fella say: Yes sir, Mr Yankee Boss Zmansky, sir?

Him-fella point at drink on silver salver balanced on Wine Boy him head and say: Would you call that a very dry martini on the rocks with a twist of lemon?

Me-fella look at drink on silver salver on Wine Boy him head and say: No sir, Mr Yankee Boss Zmansky, sir. Him tube of lighter fuel.

Him-fella say: OK. Now will you tell me what I have to do to get a

"Good morning, madam. We are Jehovah's Witnesses, Double-Glazing division . . ."

dry martini around here?

Me-fella say: Sir, Mr Big-fella Belong Papa-him-on-top's Own Country must tell stupid Wine Boy, fetch plenty juniper berry juice with him dash of vermouth clink-clink and him twist of yellow fruit fall from tree pretty damn quick, shaken not stirred. Otherwise stupid Wine Boy fetch glass of pink paraffin with him olive.

Wine Boy hit me-fella on head with him silver salver and say: Me-fella not stupid. Him-fella Mr Big Yankee Boss Zmansky give me-fella plenty big tip so me-fella fetch him-fella Ronsonol from no-good serving boys them personal cellar.

Mr Yankee Boss Zmansky him say: Jesus!

Number One Boy Him Log. Day Two And One More Day

Me-fella bow-and-scrape to plenty-big-swank-passengers them come for first when-big-ball-in-sky-all-above sitting. Plenty-big-toff passenger Sir Ffitch-Ffrench, him bang him table with him spoon and tell me-fella to get across along-him-fella and him-fella woman with belong-what-name list of kai-kai.

Him-fella point at belong-what-name list under *Volaille* and say: Head Waiter, is this Coq au vin à la bourguignonne fresh or frozen?

Me-fella say: Sir Boss Mister Big-shot Ffitch-Ffrench, until soon before Number One Boy him get chop, all bird-from-sky on belong-what-name list come from freezer. Him bad man, Lord Boss Mister Ffitch-Ffrench sir. Him get drunk on Brasso and come too big for him boots.

Him-fella say: Never mind all that, Head Waiter. My wife merely wishes to know if the chicken is fresh?

Me-fella say: Sir Mrs Boss Ffitch-Ffrench him woman, all bird-from-sky on belong-what-name list him now so fresh that him not dead yet. Cookie come up along from down galley and cut bird-from-sky's throat at plenty-big-swank passengers them table, then him-fella pluck him bird-from-sky feathers while me-fella simmer mushrooms and baby onions in red jump-on-grape-water and bird-from-sky blood. Served with fried croutons and a selection of today's freshly-prepared vegetables from him trolley.

Mrs Sir Ffitch-Ffrench him woman say: How absolutely revolting. We shall have the Chateaubriand.

Me-fella say: Yes sir, madam, how you like him cook?

Him woman say: Rare.

Me-fella tell no-good serving boy go down below along galley and tell Cookie him cook Chateaubriand not plenty much for bigshot

"I hate to say this, but wouldn't it be wonderful if Paisley's mother had been on the Pill?"

passenger and him women chop-chop P.D.Q. By-m-by him-fella come back with big silver dish-belong-keep-hot.

Me-fella take off him lid and show Chateaubriand to Sir Boss Ffitch-Ffrench and him woman. Him woman say: Aaaarrrrrgggghhhh! It's a raw pig! Oh my God, I'm going to faint!

Me-fella say to no-good serving boy: You-fella bad no-good serving boy, you-fella been at him surgical spirit.

No-good serving boy him say: Me-fella sober as him-wear-wig-and-say-them-jury-have-rightly-found-you-fella-guilty. Cookie him run out of Chateaubriand, so him-fella think Sir Mighty Boss Ffitch-Ffrench and him woman them like Cochon de la Saint-Fortunat, done not plenty much chop-chop.

Me-fella say: Him-fella bad Cookie.

By-m-by him-fella Cookie come along up from down below into Louis XIV Starlight Grill Room and try to kill me-fella with him meat-axe.

Number One Boy Him Log. Day Two And Two More Day

All no-good serving boys drunk on plenty dry martinis with him twist of lemon. Me-fella serve all kai-kai to all plenty-big-swank passengers.

Me-fella run off him feet.

When him-fella eat him main course, by-m-by Mr Yankee Boss Zmansky clap him hands and tell me-fella what him-fella want for him pudding.

Something snap.

Me-fella pick up steak-knife from Table 43 and hold him at Yankee Boss Mister Zmansky him throat. Me-fella say: You bad man, Mr Boss sir! You-fella cannibal! You-fella eat d'agneau aux primeurs with all them trimmings and now you-fella want me-fella kill Lascar deckhand and boil him in pot. You cruel Mister Zmansky sir!

Him-fella shout: What's gotten into you? All I asked for was a goddam Baked Alaska! OK fella, him-fella continue, I've had enough of this, I'm going straight to the captain.

Number One Boy Him Log. No More Day

Big-fella-strong-with-scrambled-egg-on-cap, him give me-fella new job swab him deck. Big-fella-strong him plenty kind man, him-fella not make me-fella take him job. Him-fella say me-fella can take him or leave him.

"Would you be interested in a backhanded compliment?"

STANLEY REYNOLDS:

The Goose Steps West

"I SAY, you horrible little man, lend us a fiver. I don't seem to have any damned money on me and get your hands out of your pockets and don't slouch like that, you look like a damned yid, better make that two fivers." You can probably guess at the surge of pride that came over me at being addressed in such a close personal way by the great man. I was also very surprised because until then Sir Oswald Mosley had never said a word to me and seemed to be unaware of my existence. In years to come all that, of course, would be changed and the conversation above was to be repeated many times.

Those of us who knew Sir "Ossie" intimately are very sad because he is dead and unable to read his own obituaries. The obits have been marvellous. The *New Standard*'s Sam White, whom I always thought of as a wishy-washy liberal nigger lover and perhaps a Jewboy, writing from Paris where the great man died in self-imposed exile, called our Ossie "a kind of Mountbatten who went wrong" and said if things had been different Sir Oswald might have been a great success.

Personally I do not understand that remark about Mountbatten—was Lord Louis a sort of Oswald Mosley who went right?—but I do know what White meant about what a great success Ossie would have been if things had turned out differently.

Indeed in one of my most recent meetings with the grand old man I asked him where he thought he went wrong.

Pulling himself to his full height of six feet two he glared at me with his flashing black eyes and collared me with his vice-like grip (I once saw him arm wrestle "Papa" Hemingway at the Dôme for three days and three nights) and said, "You appalling little man, why are you so stupid? Are you sure you don't have some coon blood in that thick skull of yours? I went wrong when that old drunkard Churchill and that Yankee Jewboy Roosevelt with the negroid wife—you ever notice the thick lips on that shicksa?—invaded Europe and didn't get

tossed back into the sea but of course they had all the Jewboy money in the world plus Moscow gold behind them and what did my Fuehrer have? And speaking of that, give us a damned fiver. I seem to have come out without any money."

Always the aristocrat, the sixth baronet strongly denied that he would have got the lampshade and soap concession if Hitler had won the war. "Don't be ridiculous, you horrible little man," he said to me when I asked him about that. "Lampshades and soap, that's trade, and trade smacks of Jewboys and Paki greengrocers to me, it's your round whatever your damned name is."

As the *Daily Telegraph* pointed out in its long obituary (plus leader) the great man was a top flight sportsman and was one of the "six best fencers in Europe"—not fences as his Hebrew enemies would have. He was, I know, always a little embarrassed by what the *Telegraph* called "a rather hooked nose" but would sometimes joke about it saying, "Do you think there might have been a Jewboy in the woodpile?" We would all laugh and laugh until his Blackshirts stopped hitting us.

The story of his second marriage to Diana Mitford has never been properly cleared up. The wedding arrangements were kept secret and rumour had it that it was either at Hitler's headquarters with Hitler as best man or at Goebbels' office with Goebbels as best man. "The truth is, you appalling little man," Sir Oswald told me, "that it was both. Do you think I would stint a thing like a wedding just like some tight-fisted yid?" Ossie knew some great stories about Hitler and Goebbels and was quite convinced that if it were not for his club foot and rotten singing voice Goebbels could have been UFA's answer to Fred Astaire. Hitler, he said, could sing but was not much of a mover on the dance floor. It was true, he told me, about Hitler only having one, but the stories about Goebbels having none at all was something put out by the Kremlin and the Wall Street Jewboys.

And, of course, it was all nonsense about

Sir Oswald being anti-Semitic.

"Listen, you appalling little man, all that was got up in the press. When my Blackshirts used to go round the East End chanting 'Let's get the yids' they meant 'Let's get the yids to join the party' but the damned press kept reporting it wrong and when my boys sang the Horst Wessel song they only did it because they liked the tune, do you think a pack of ignorant yobs like them knew a word of German, they could hardly speak English most of them, God, did you see the low brows on most of them, they hardly looked human but don't mock the afflicted, that's what I always say."

Once I was present at his home in Paris when some sort of liberal Jewboy scum gutter journalist pressed Ossie about the alleged atrocities of the Nazis. With great patience, once he stopped foaming at the mouth and chewing the carpet, my Leader explained that that was all got up in the press and that what the Jews actually had was 'flu. "My Fuehrer knew that he would be misunderstood and he was sick as a parrot about that one," Sir Oswald said. "What a lot of you don't understand is that Hitler was ahead of his time. All that lampshade and soap business sounded bad at the time but that was before society got into, y'know, recycling and the whole ecology bit. Hitler, y'know, was over the moon about ecology and recycling. 'Ecology, Ossie,' he said to me, 'it's magic.' And all that medical experimentation they carried out in those what I like to call camps, if the truth were known they probably did a lot of good. Hitler told me the only thing he was worried about was would they work on people."

Actually, Sir Oswald was so calm and reasonable attempting to explain this to the journalist that I thought the man was convinced until the Mosley bovver boys broke his biro and his fingers and his legs and turfed him out.

A great kidder, Sir Oswald, and a great mover, just like his pal, Goebbels.

The last time I saw the great man he was still fuming about the uproar after *The Times* serialized his autobiography. Spitting bits of carpet as he spoke, Ossie said he was sick and tired of people writing to *The Times* saying he was some kind of Nazi when all he wanted to do was get the Jews and the coons. In later years, of course, he mellowed quite a bit and would not actually attack Jews when he saw them in the street but would merely puke his head off. At the same time it was always best not to do any Sammy Davis Junior impersonations when visiting Sir Oswald.

As I said he was every inch an aristocrat and a membership to the Establishment was his birthright, he would be most pleased at the kindly obits he has received, especially in *The Times*. When I last saw him his last words to me were: "Just who the hell are you, you dirty little man, you look like some sort of working class rubbish to me, just the sort of mob scum that let me down in the Thirties when I wanted to take over the world?" Those final words are engraved on my heart; better still, they're tattooed on my arm.

R. G. G. PRICE

You Ought to be in Pictures

"Tax evasion—for example, the surgeon's request that his fee for private treatment consist of a gift of paintings—is turning Britain into a nation of petty but persistent cheats."—*Observer.*

BRITISH MEDICAL JOURNAL

As a paediatrician, should I take my fee in Kate Greenaway and Ernest Shepard originals in order to show that I am sympathetic and a child at heart? Really I prefer cruel, fantastic painters like Wiertz.

If it is not too late, change over to geriatrics. Patients have had more time to accumulate and may be beyond the point at which they can take in news stories about sudden rises in the value of their wedding presents.

What fee should I ask for examining a patient and deciding that operative treatment is contraindicated?

This situation occurs so rarely that the market has never stabilised. Probably half a dozen pre-1850 silver spoons or a couple of late eighteenth-century naval prints would be about the right level.

What is the normal charge these days for doing an arthritic hip?

For cases from the Middle East, it can go as high as a Vermeer. For British patients, it lies somewhere between a Zoffany and a Sickert.

Is it worth accepting Frank Dicksees in hope of a rise?

There has been a steady growth in the auction prices of some once derided late Victorian and early twentieth-century painters. It cannot be assumed in all cases. Derision is not enough.

Does surgical treatment of severe spinal pain rate a most interesting view of Little Murphy by Boucher?

Send colour photograph fast.

During the course of a colostomy, I happened to leave a prosthetic toe in the abdominal cavity. My fee, a Graham Sutherland head of Tatum O'Neal, was paid at once. By the time that the patient's complaints of discomfort had induced her doctor to have her X-rayed, I had used the picture to pay my acupuncturist's bill and it was not available when her solicitors asked for its return.

I offered, instead, a portrait of the film star by a young painter who, in many

people's opinion, is a coming man. They spurned this opportunity of an exciting investment and demanded a Giorgione! I told them that this was nonsense. All the woman needed was for someone to open her up again and fish out the foreign body. Any junior could do it.

Can you suggest a reasonable compromise between one of the rarer Italian Old Masters and a portrait of Tatum by an inexperienced but promising beginner?

Do not give up the fight too easily: you are letting your colleagues down. The patient needed a colostomy and she had one. A routine theatre mishap should not deprive you of your just reward. A Beggarstaff Brothers poster or a Derwent Wood study for a war memorial should more than meet any reasonable claim.

Is it ever worth acquiring a painting simply for the frame?

Wait for a Victoria & Albert exhibition of frames and the book spin-off. Only if you have plenty of space is storing on the off-chance worthwhile. Never buy a frame containing Highland cattle crossing water by moonlight.

For removing a nasal obstruction from a High Court judge, I was offered a rather attractive picture of a young man and an angel by a painter new to me called Raffaello Sanzi. The fee seemed adequate, as the obstruction was quite small, only a sardine tin key. But was I, perhaps, rather letting the side down by accepting a painting simply because I happened to like it?

The artist is better known as Raphael. Foreigners often give unfamiliar names to painters and visits to some European galleries can be quite bewildering. The picture would be a handsome fee even for a heart transplant. Take it, but let an expert check for forgery.

I am a tough, out-going accident surgeon and Art is, frankly, not my cup of tea. But I can understand a good tax dodge as well as the next man. My grand-daughter, Lucinda, has been to the kind of school where any time not spent mucking out stables is devoted to concerts, art shows and even poetry recitals. She herself likes pictures where you can distinguish every leaf and twig and I must admit that I'm all for that. But her old Art mistress, whom she worships, likes pictures of parsons shut up in glass boxes and screaming their guts out.

There is one of these in an art dealer's near my consulting rooms. The price tag is about right for a comminuted fracture of the pelvis during a Saturday night; but I don't want the damn thing! Putting it on the waiting-room wall would reduce my patients to jellies, when I want to toughen them up: I am a great believer in sack races for fractured femurs. Is there any money in these alarmed ecclesiastics? That's what interests me.

Screaming popes may have slipped a bit; but their long term value should not be under-rated. There is no reason whatever to put pictures on your walls, just because you have them. Surely you have a cellar or an attic. Art is a commodity and commodities are frequently warehoused while their owners hold out for a better price.

Surely you are under-charging for week-end emergency work?

Is there any Finnish painter whose work provides a respectable reward for removing a brain tumour?

Probably. Why do you want to know?

BASIL BOOTHROYD:

BOOK OF BEASTS

MY animal book is held up again. The usual casting trouble. I was going to make it rabbits a year or two back, but was scooped by the fellow Adams, writing from a position of strength as a Department of the Environment rabbiteaucrat. Not, I may point out, that *he* felt he'd been scooped by Beatrix Potter, though it's true he broke away from the costumed animal tradition. You could scamper Watership Down from Nuthanger Farm to Sandleford Warren and not a rabbit in red plush knickers to be seen.

I then hit on moles. The next most strokeable characters. Foiled again. I haven't read *Duncton Wood*, and don't intend to. The fellow Horwood has taken the very moles out of my mouth.

Perhaps this isn't a bad thing. I wasn't fully sold on moles, to be quite honest. What with wearing their ears inside, and having eyesight that can just about tell night from day and that's it, they'd be a blundering lot to handle, let alone tough to present with any real appeal; they're short; how much grab has a four-inch hero? Besides, they have their pterygoid region inflated. I don't know what this means, without studying them in their natural habitat, itself no picnic. You'd have to ask Dr E. Perceval Wright, whose *Concise Natural History*, a thick work with its covers off which has somehow come down to me from an Ellen Timms, Sunday school prizewinner class of 1882, tells me things like this and worse, but it doesn't sound attractive.

You need attractiveness. Or that's the current thinking. How easy was that for Horwood? The reader glancing up from the page to see his lawn full of brown lumps can go off moles, except as reconstituted into gamekeepers' waistcoats. They live on worms, what's more. I could have had snags here with my big feast scene, the mandatory set-piece celebrating the famous mole victory over Mr Gobbler the goose and his henchgeese.

"'Another helping, Papa?' tempted Mother Mole, her strong flat forepaw, sharp-edged on its lower margin and with barely distinguishable fingers, poised over the dish of writhing delicacies."

"'Full up, dearest,' replied Father Mole, patting his inflated pterygoid region."

On the other paw, of course, they could be eating a crown roast, with knives and forks, napkins tucked under their chin glands. It's a question, how close to stick to nature. Are these moles, or four-inch people? The man Adams, I see, makes a foreword acknowledgement to Mr R. M. Lockley's "remarkable book", *The Private Life of the Rabbit*. This doesn't stop him from staging a dramatic river escape by punt, and readers trying to focus their mind's eye on a puntful of rabbits aren't sure whether they're seeing a rabbit-punt, measuring possibly a yard from stem to stern, or the larger craft of the Isis and Cam, easily accommodating four students and a guitar.

Relative sizes are tricky for animal writers. Or could be if they worried about it, which I often think they don't. Did Kenneth Grahame see Mr Toad's motorcar as a toad motorcar, a mere powered roller-skate handcrafted by God knows whom for a pretty narrow market? Or was it based on his glimpse of a ter-rific new 1908 Lanchester chugging past his window just then, seating two full-length dustcoats still feeling a mite insecure with no horse in front, whitewall bike tyres extra, ample floorspace 500 toads?

Writers have the shiftless habit of leaving dimensions to the illustrator. All Lewis Carroll revealed about the frog footman was that he was dressed in yellow and wore huge boots. Whether he only came up to the bottom stripe of Alice's stockings, or topped her by half a head, was Tenniel's problem. In the event he made girl and frog of more or less equal height: the same with the walrus and the carpenter, which was probably about right. He made the oysters a damned sight too big, though. Anyway for my gastronomic credibility. Still, he had to put feet and footwear on them somehow, the author having dropped him in it again. "O Oysters come and walk with us", went the invitation, so there was nothing for it but to leg and shoe them, a worse headache than settling on the inside leg measurement of a walrus's trousers, I shouldn't be surprised.

Animals wearing trousers were pretty new at that time. Judging from the endpapers of Dr E. Perceval Wright's book, advertising a wealth of works available to young Ellen Timm's generation, animals hadn't got into literature much. Or only as animals. *Field Friends and Forest Foes, The Four Cats of the Tippertons* and *The Ups and Downs of a Donkey's Life* carry no motoring or punting overtones. Copies of *Paws and Claws* or *Pussy Tip-Toes' Family* are probably rare now, but I think we should find, if we came across them, that they featured as few talking and clothes-wearing animals as other contemporaneous publications, mostly on offer at 1s.—*Chats for Small Chatterers, Sunday Readings for Little Folks, Wonderful Balloon Ascents*. I wouldn't be sure about *Notable Shipwrecks*, but any characters in there who weren't people, and swimming, would be rats only.

The cuddlesomeness of the rat isn't generally held to be high. He's been done anyway. In my quest for a strokeably furry cast I jib at taking a leaf, or rat, from Mr Grahame's book

Thinking of this, though, isn't it perhaps time that a wind of change blew through the literary willows? Even to be bluntly practical, it would be just my luck to be on the last chapter of an endearing stoat epic when some rat, or fellow, scoops me. Indeed, for all I know, the publishers' winter lists, already on the presses, are stuffed with stoat. Not to say weasel, ferret and mink. The only safe road, it seems to me, is to abandon fur altogether. Why not strike out with scales?

Dr E. Perceval Wright's remarkable book tempts me strongly with the Ringed

HOME HINTS

Statistical analysis of admissions to the Orthopaedic Traction, Frostbite and Glühwein Paralysis wards of the Hospice des Misérables at Garmisch-Toblerone indicates that most winter sporting accidents occur as a result of out-of-condition amateurs tackling such as a traversed Christiania stembogen somersault turn on the slalom without proper practice.

At least three weeks before departure, physically run-down skiers should begin programmed callisthenics in readiness for the slopes, getting out of bed in the Vorlage position with knees bent and body weight forward, taking off cleanly from the top step to go downstairs and coming back up again in a sideslip herringbone series of hops, 50 times.

Spend at least 30 minutes a day working Arlberg's ready-mixed muscle wax into ankles and the back of the knees and ask a friend to chop vigorously with the back of an old toggle clasp on any knotted cartilage. Work up to 200 press-ups per 5-minute session, keeping wrists supple with a tincture of elk fat and eat lots of pickle.

Caecilia, nicely drawn on p.399 and indistinguishable, if you put your thumb over its tapering head (where, as Dr Wright says, "the eyes are rudimentary and more or less hidden beneath the skin"), from a length of radiator hose. A tribe of these, given the necessary human joys and sorrows, hopes and fears, plus breathtaking escapes by punt, motorcar, etc, could give an entire new dimension to the animals-for-profit scene. Limbless, single-lunged and emitting a viscous slime when danger threatens, your average caecilia lives in tree

roots and likes to stay there. It hasn't been much popularised, unless in that old number possibly before your time, "Does your Mother know you're out, Caecilia", but I would see that as part of the challenge. If Grahame could do what he did for the rat, I don't see why I can't do the same for the caecilia. The limbless problem I naturally hand over to the artist. Is he going to be beaten by Tenniel's oysters? And if the young reader doesn't fancy stroking scales there's a lot to be said for dragging a stick along them and getting an interesting noise.

I'm not sure that all that stroking is healthy, in any case. Kraft-Ebbing, as any mole or rabbit must know, placed highly undesirable interpretations on the obsessive polishing of brown shoes—a thing that's always worried me a bit, actually: show me a brown shoe and I can't wait to get polishing—so it might be therapeutic, as well as novel, to team up my caecilias with other creatures repellent in aspect and short on fondling appeal, though surprisingly good-hearted, witty, courageous, resourceful, affectionate, and all things like that, once you grow to know and love them through my best-selling pages. I rate Dr Wright's Horrid Moloch (*Moloch horridus*) high on my short list for a completely unexploited hero. He's covered all over with more spikes than a running shoe, and if that isn't enough fun also possesses "curious skinny appendages which form flaps about the head and neck".

If I can launch him before David Attenborough has one peeping out of his shirt and having its chin-flaps tickled, I could be on to a winner. Moloch language might bother me at first. Horrid molochs seem to be largely Australians, and Australian dialect and vocabulary are lousy. Still, Adams showed what could be done in this predicament with the bird Kehaar, an

ally in the great punt escape who only spoke broken rabbit:

" 'Ya, ees goot,' said Kehaar. 'You go fine. But you do heem queek, ya?' "

This kraut gibberish gave no trouble to rabbits. My Australian ought to do the same for people. Even if it means buying a business lunch for Barry Humphries.

Failing that, Dr Wright's index alone remains a rich stimulus for big-money literary invention as yet untapped by the Adamses, Horwoods or the rest of the latter-day Beatrix Potter gang. I don't propose at this time to leak anything further on my latest project. If the publisher's promotion men want an advance snippet to give *The Bookseller*, they can say that I'm loosely thinking in the T's. The Turbot, Turnip Fly and Trapdoor Spider not to be ruled out.

But how much punting and motoring they get up to must for the moment remain my own little secret.

"Of course there's our ultra-economy package—you break your leg before you go."

"My wife doesn't! Understand me?"

Grief stricken, a woman telephoned the New York branch of the Good Samaritans. She felt, she said, like killing herself. "Great," the Good Samaritan said, "go throw yourself off the top of a building."

Daily Express

STANLEY REYNOLDS:

Weep and You Weep Alone

Dear Auntie Punch,
While the other girls have dates and go to the disco I have acne.

Have no fear. There is stuff to clear a spotty face. But is it simply acne that is keeping the boys away? You sound like a girl with fat legs to me. By the way, you sure that stuff is acne? Maybe it's congenital. Or leprosy. You'll know when your nose falls off.

Dear Auntie Punch,
What I always say is, "So long as you've got your health nothing else matters."

You sure are right, sir. I couldn't agree more. I often walk into the butcher, let him feel my biceps, take a look at my teeth, and see my suntan and he gives me 3 lbs of steak.

Dear Auntie Punch,
My girlfriend, Bobbie, is mad about horoscopes. She won't do anything without consulting them. I tell her it's all rubbish. But she don't believe me. Maybe she'll believe you, Auntie.

Sometimes I think it should be made against the law to print those horoscopes in newspapers and magazines where they are read by a lot of silly and impressionable young people. As the Bard said, "I do not pluck my judgement from the stars" and you know what a great "star" he was himself, retiring at only 44 when most of us have to toil along for many years after that unless they make you redundant.

Of course we are not influenced by the stars anymore than the sea—just to give a silly example—is by the Man in the Moon. Life is very mysterious. No one can tell what particular influences are working on you or your girlfriend, Bobbie. Personally I am influenced by invaders from outer space who get into my bath watrer and suck my vital juices.

Dear Auntie Punch,
My girlfriend, Mavis, has just thrown me over for a blackman. I feel kind of silly asking this, but is it...

Say no more. I wish I had a hot dinner for every letter I've had from men worried about that silly, little problem. The answer is: sure they do. Why do you think they're always lounging about laughing and joking?

Dear Auntie Punch,
My boyfriend, Edwin, my husband, and I were recently wed. Whilst we were not planning the patter of little feet I now find that I am pregnant. My Mum tells me I am being a silly goose, yet I still cannot help worrying that a baby will spoil the beautiful love my darling Edwin and I now know.

Use your head and don't listen to your Mum's old wives' tales. In spite of all the advantages of the permissive era, with all the information which is now available on hitherto taboo subjects, I still get too many letters from girls who wonder what a baby will do to their love life. Don't be silly. Of course it's going to ruin your love life. Some of those babies weigh as much as 10 lbs when they come out. You can imagine what that sort of stretching does to a girl. Of course actually having the baby is no worse than pushing a grand piano through a transom, but afterwards you can kiss fun sex goodbye.

Mother Nature, however, in her wisdom always compensates. After a woman has a baby she loses all her sex drive which is just as well because the husbands always start playing around after a baby is born.

Dear Auntie Punch,
Bernice, my wife, has become very extravagant, buying clothes, constantly nagging me to take her for expensive meals or on foreign holidays. I keep telling her we must save for our old age and in order to leave something for our three kiddiewinkies, Vera, Chuck, and Dave.

Wise as it is to save for that rainy day, your Bernice may have the right idea. Life is certainly for the living. Put it another way, have you taken a look at the news lately? Have you seen the scum roaming the streets? Smelled that stuff they keep putting in the air nowadays? You think this is going to last another 20 years? You think it will last ten, huh? Get out there and buy, eat, drink, spend! The great death cloud is coming if you don't get kicked to death in the streets first.

Dear Auntie Punch,
I often ask myself, What is money? Can money buy you happiness? Can money buy you the love of a good woman?

Yes, it can.

LET'S PARLER FRANGLAIS!

Le Catering de Noël

Maman: Chéri?
Papa: Mmm?
Maman: Il me faut £50.
Papa: Pourquoi? Tu es dans le grip d'un blackmaileur?
Maman: Non. Mais aujourd'hui je vais commencer le shopping pour le jour de Noël, et le dinner Noëlesque.
Papa: £50 pour un dinner? C'est extortion.
Maman: Non, mais réfléchis. Il faut acheter un turkey, sprouts de Bruxelles, pud de Noel, sauce de Cognac, dattes, nuttes, figges, tangérines, gâteau d'Xmas, ecstase Turquoise, des craqueurs, pies de mince, chocs aux liqueurs, stuffing de sauge et oignons . . .
Papa: Un moment, un moment! Est-il vraiment nécessaire, ce spread, ce blow-out? Pourquoi, toutes les années, un banquet Felliniesque, une orgie de Yule, une explosion Alka-Seltzérienne?
Maman: Tu as une suggestion alternative?
Papa: Oui. Un repast frugal. Un peu de céléri, un peu de fromage, un Perrier. C'est parfait.
Maman: *Perrier*? Le Noël? Perrier, c'est pour le Jour de Pugilisme.
Papa: Eh bien . . . quelques bouteilles de Beaujolais nouveau.
Maman: Oh, c'est très festif, je ne crois pas. Quel joli treat pour les enfants et les parents. Un peu de holly dans un Ryvita.
Papa: Personellement, je blâme Prince Albert. Il a inventé l'arbre de Noël (avec le pine-needle dropping problem), la carte de Noel (avec le greeting UNICEF en cinq languages), le carol-singing (via le medium de l'entryphone) et le heavy dinner d'Xmas. Moi, je dis—à bas les imports de Germany!
Maman: Tu préfères le spaghetti bethlehemais? Le tandoori turkey?
Papa: Pourquoi pas? C'est une change.
Maman: Tu es hopeless. Pense aux enfants! Noël, c'est une occasion pour les jeunes.
Papa: OK, j'appelle ton bluff. Enfants! Venez ici!
Emma, Lucy: Oui, papa?
Papa: Tu as une choix pour le dinner de Noël. Turkey avec tous les trimmings. Ou un light lunch, comme a eu le bébé Jesus. Un stableman's lunch, quoi.
Emma: Turkey est boring.
Lucy: Le light lunch est grotty.
Emma, Lucy: Nous voulons des doigts de poisson! Le Grand Mac! Le donner kebab! Le tray de relishes . . .
Maman: C'est ridiculeux. Vous aurez le turkey, comme normal, avec sauce de pain, sauce de currant rouge etc. £50, svp.

PAUL THEROUX:

Left Luggage

ANYONE who has barked his shins on a train from Clapham Junction to Victoria—and mine are still growling so badly from a crack I got only yesterday that I find myself seeking relief in Baskerville-sized cans of Pedigree Chum—anyone, as I say, who has bruised his elbows on the 10.41 "Gatwick Flyer", found himself cheek by jowl with a Barbie Doll in a mantilla ("Wouldn't it look super on the television, Reg?") and couldn't see the conductor for the sponge bags and the jugs of Parafino, is sorely familiar with the luggage habits of the English. Five days in Spain and they are as heavily-laden as Lord Amherst on his (1816) Embassy to China.

You might make the mistake of offering them a hand getting one of these bags out of the train, but I did it once and nearly dropped her—Crimplene suit and all—into the gap. The suitcases aren't any lighter than the people, but I've found that if you stoop and wince, muttering, "I've done me back," at the same time showing them a tube of Algipan, they wipe that imploring look off their sunburnt faces and heave-ho.

What is it with these people and their ten suitcases? The one-bag braggart is no better—his usually weighs a ton and is so thick with leather belts you suspect him of having taken night-classes in bondage. Most of the returnees have had a short holiday in a hot country, but with their skin the texture of puff pastry and their flesh raw from sunbathing they look like so many immigrant sausage-rolls with all their worldly goods in the aisle. What have they got in there, for God's sake? Boiler nuts?

Anthracite? Black and Deckers? Scaffolding? They are dressed like factory workers in Wuhan, so it's certainly not clothes. Is it souvenirs? The carcass of the last bull they saw jinking on to a matador's sword? Is it some shrunken-thighed Dago they're smuggling into Carshalton for a lifetime of indenture to Hoover their maisonette?

They are, of course, bringing what they think is required. It's interesting. The less people travel, the more they conceive, like the Chinese before them, the world to be filled with hairy-faced baboons who live in utter squalor, or worse, Uttar Pradesh. The first time I went to Africa, people with me—Americans, who boasted of having had a liberal education and who frowned at words such as "native", never mind "jigaboo"—brought crates of toilet paper, Kotex, Kleenex. The parting words of the father of a pal of mine at the airport in New York were, "Got enough flints?"

Flints? I told him that they had probably heard of matches in Nyasaland (for this was where we were headed), as they had recently burned down some civic buildings in their quest for *Ufulu* (Freedom) under the leadership of their *Ngwazi* (Conqueror) and *Cirombo* (Great Beast), a tedious midget named Hastings Banda. No, the kid said, the flints were for his lighter. He was going to be in Central Africa for two years and, a pipe-smoker, he had two years' supply of flints for his Zippo.

Luggage is the litmus test that identifies the true traveller from the timid bigot who, in his heart of hearts, doesn't hold with

"Do you realise that in the event of a nuclear war we've got just four minutes to withdraw into our shells?"

abroad. It is the Awayday Freak and the sunburnt yob on his Lunkenheimer Sunseeker Weekend who is the cart-horse—not the overlander who is headed, carrier bag in hand, for Baluchistan or the Upper Valley of Greater Zap.

We knowledgeable, trustful people travel light. Anything that does not fit under an airplane seat, I refuse to carry. The advantage of First Class—but it is the only advantage—is that you are allowed two bags. Indeed, virtually the only thing the flight staff do in First is serve as left-luggage attendants—but they do it with a smile. As a schlepper in Economy, I have a seat-sized bag, but even if it was bigger than it is, I could find a home for it somewhere among the life-jackets, which are little more than pathetic props for the pre-flight ("In the unlikely event . . .") lecture. Planes are becoming more and more like Friday night on the Glasgow Express—cupboards jerking open and spilling tennis rackets on to people's heads, coats and shoe boxes littering the floor, and a valise crammed into every corner.

Mine is under my seat. And my children are in possession of tiny Chinese knapsacks. They hold very little and such is the design of these back-packs that only a child of ten or twelve can get it over his shoulders. Why should I carry my children's junk? And realizing that the knapsack is small discourages any belief in their being able to hump Atom-Blasters or Microvision.

I have not checked a bag at an airport for six years. It struck me that by avoiding this headache I had an extra hour prior to travel, and two or more hours at the other end. Who is the first one through Immigration, first in line at Customs, first at the taxi-rank? Need you ask? And my children in Chinese knapsacks are hard at my heels. I see from my 1980 diary that I spent a total of 168 days

outside the United Kingdom last year—four trips to the States, one to Holland, and a month in China: no checking, no ticket-stubs, no watching the conveyor-belt for a burst suitcase that's too heavy to carry anyway, and even if I could, would be full of things I don't need. And when the people are still crowded around the—am I looking for the word carousel?—saying, "That looks like it . . . No, the brown one," I am barrel-assing down the freeway, already on vacation.

What's in the bag? For China, I took two pairs of trousers (I wore one), two sweaters, two shirts. I wore another shirt, and my jacket. Socks—three pairs; under-wear—four. That about wraps it up. Oh, yes, a razor and some blades; my toothbrush. No aspirin (they have headaches in Soochow too). When I think of it I bring Eno's Fruit Salts, but I didn't bring any to China. I wore my camera, my pen and notebook were in my pocket. I bought novels to read—they sell Keith Waterhouse in Canton—but gave them to Chinese hotel clerks when I was finished (what did that fellow make of *The Spoils of Poynton* or Zamyatin's *We*?).

The other people on my China tour were somewhat pitying when they saw my bag, but I had the last laugh when the weather changed and they were saddled with mink coats, steam irons and hair-curling kits that, such was their weight, would certainly have curled mine if I had to carry them from Chungking to Shanghai. Some of these people inquired rather circumspectly about how dirty I got, and what did I do with my dirty clothes? These folks humped laundry bags all over China; but China is a wonderful place for getting things washed. You hand the stuff over in the morning and have it back in the evening.

I did not meet Deng Hsiao Ping, but if

that had been on the cards, or if I had been scheduled to address the Central Committee or been asked to prosecute the Gang of Four, I would have brought a suit in a garment bag. No need to check it. You bring it on the plane and hang it on one of the many hooks provided.

I am luckier in my visits to the States, since I have a house—and a razor and fruit salts—there, and all the clothes I require. This is a mixed blessing. I still use my underseat bag, but I bring pipe tobacco in it (I have ten pipes in the States, and as I'm not allowed to smoke a pipe on the plane, what's the point of taking one?). Last summer, I brought five cans of Players Navy Cut and the facsimile—ten kilo—volume of Johnson's *Dictionary*. Going through Customs in Boston I was halted by a hag in a uniform.

"Is this all you have?"

The question is familiar: I've been through this routine before.

"That's it," I said. "That's about the size of it."

"Is *this* all you have?"

"I just answered that question," I barked.

"Don't get smart!"

Smart—this article must prove it?—is something I'm not. But she could not believe that I was spending two months in the United States with Johnson's *Dictionary*, five cans of tobacco and the clothes I was wearing. I tried to explain about the house, but she cut me off.

"Come over here," she said, and sat me in a cubicle. "I'd like to know a litle bit more about you." She opened the tobacco cans and leafed through the dictionary and gave me the third degree. I was out of the airport in under an hour—my record is ten minutes from touch-down to taxi-rank—but with a new resolve: next time, I thought, I'll bring a pair of socks.

"Would you care to see the English Quarter, señor?"

Jensen–television

THE SOUTH BANK SHOW
STEPHANE GRAPPELLI   YEHUDI MENUHIN

THE MARQUISE
RALPH MICHAEL
DIANA RIGG
RICHARD JOHNSON

POLICE SOCCER NEWS

The magazine for football fuzz!

EDITORIAL

Once again the actions of an unfortunate minority have brought the rest of the force into disrepute. No doubt Police Constable Jerkins felt that he was doing the right thing when he rushed on field in the second half of the Spurs v. Ipswich match and arrested all 22 players for "behaviour likely to cause a public disturbance." As he said afterwards, the conduct of the players seemed likely to cause a minor riot. Unfortunately, his own action caused a major riot. It was also unfortunate that P C Jerkins felt it necessary to question some of the suspects rather boisterously. No-one can condone the sight of a young constable knocking Senor Ardiles, though a foreigner, to the ground and beating a confession out of him, especially before TV cameras. Come on, lads! This sort of thing should be done in the privacy of your own station. We cannot have it said that football violence follows the example set by a few wilder members of the police.

By the way, this week's lucky arrest winner in Summons No. 9846372, at the Chelsea match. The prize is a white horse. Well done!

NOTTINGHAM COPPER SIGNS ON FOR FOREST!

"I am in an over-the-moon situation," says P C Garter

When plainclothes policeman Ted Garter set out for work on Saturday, it seemed just another ordinary day for an ordinary member of the Soccer Police, or "Football Fuzz". He had received reports of suspected offensive language, actual bodily harm and physical assault taking place at the ground, and had been ordered to mingle. This was mingling with a difference, though; his plain clothes on Saturday were shorts, Forest shirt and football boots.

"We were all over them," remembers Brian Clough. "I remember turning to Peter Taylor as we went 3–0 up and saying it seems as if we have twelve men on the park. I remember him turning back to me a bit after and saying, Bloody hell, we *have* got twelve men on the park."

"I was only doing my duty," says Garter. "The reports of bad language and assault I'd received

all concerned the visiting team, so I unobtrusively mingled on field in a left auxiliary sweeper situation until I was in a position to make an arrest."

What made the position slightly different was that two of those three goals had been scored by Garter. "The boy's a natural," enthused Clough. "He's big and strong and good with both feet. What lifts him above the average, though, is his uncanny ability to clear a path through a crowd without apparently resorting to overt violence. We signed him up at once. The signing-on fee of £3,000 to the Police Widows' Fund makes him the bargain of the season."

The game had to be restarted, of course, but a quick signing session ensured that Garter could take part in the second match, with Birtles being dropped. The game ended as a dream debut for goal-hungry Garter; not only did

he snatch a last minute winner, but he arrested the visiting goalkeeper at the whistle for his obscene reactions to it.

WEST MIDLAND POLICE THROUGH ON AWAY ARRESTS RULE

The Yorkshire Police, much fancied for this year's Crowd Control Cup, were generally reckoned to be home and dry after their first leg. West Midland could only notch up 23 arrests at the Birmingham v. Leeds match, a score which nobody could see as good enough to knock out the redoubtable Yorkshiremen on their home ground. And when at the return Leeds v. Brum fixture there were 47 arrests, things seemed to be cut and dried.

Then came the sensation. 12 of those arrests at Leeds had been made by West Midland police! That put the scores level at 35 each, and of course West Midland then went through on the away arrests rule.

"Our lads are as keen as mustard," said Inspector-Manager Grimble of the West Mids. "Many of them gave up their day off to travel to Leeds,

to notch up the necessary arrests. They waded in like demons. I'm proud of them. Especially of P C Bentwood, who scraped the late winning arrest on the train back to Brum. I think we're going to give the Met a shock in the next round."

POLICEMAN SUSPENDED FOR THREE MATCHES

P C Kent, a regular member of the Mercia first team, was said to have acted in an untypically hot-headed moment when he dashed into the crowd at last Saturday's United match and arrested colleague P C Root for causing an affray. "This is the sort of thing calculated to bring arrests into disrespect," said Inspector Marbles, after fining the lad £300 and suspending him. "But he's a good lad, with a record of many clean arrests, and this won't be held against him. Anyone can go mad for a moment and attack one of his own side. Trouble is, policing a football match these days is such a competitive business that the tension can get to you."

A troublemaker being removed from the Highbury pitch after arguing with a police offside decision. Later, a referee was detained.

NEWS IN BRIEF

"This is the result we came for," said Inspector Rougeole of the Sureté last night, after his men had fought a no-score draw with sections of the Ipswich crowd last night. "My garçons were magnificent. You could say that I am au-dessus de la lune. I am very confident about la deuxième jambe."

*

P C Swithin, who made a record 49 arrests at Second Division Shrewsbury last year, has been snapped up by the London Met and will turn out for them at the next Arsenal match. "It's sad leaving Shropshire," he said yesterday, "but I feel ready for the big time now."

City defender Ron Noble was arrested on the field for assault and battery—by opposing winger Stu Harris! "I was sick and tired of him having a go at me," says Harris, "so I made a civil arrest." A spokesman for the Police Associatioon said later that this was a worrying trend. While he was in favour of the public's vigilance, the actual apprehension of offenders was a job best left to the police or, if necessary, to the referee.

*

In Guatemala, Sunday, referee Antonio Perez drew a gun and shot a defender for repeated high tackling. He then sent off the wounded man for interfering with play.

SHOPTALK

ROY HATTERSLEY on Co-ops

FOR the Hattersley family, the Co-op was a constant source of political inspiration, groceries, milk, coal and half yearly dividend payments. My mother was not the woman to leave a single Bakelite token on the white-edged front step without being certain that she was getting the cheapest, freshest, earliest pint it was possible for contented cows to provide. So I suppose that the Brightside and Carbrook Co-op sold the longest burning Barnsley brights, the sweetest raisins and the freshest cheese in all Sheffield. But the Brightside and Carbrook was more than just a shop. It was a branch of our political party and its divi paid for our seven summer days at Bridlington or Skegness.

The dividend added an extra irritating dimension to every Co-operative errand. Traditionally, boys errant set out upon their quests with a half-crown wrapped in a piece of paper which bore a simple legend—"a pound of castor sugar", or "a tin of sardines". The transaction completed, the change is wrapped in the now illegible and crumpled note and the commercial traveller returns home to pretend that he is Len Hutton or Jackie Robinson, depending on the season of the year. Co-op shopping used to be more complicated.

It was essential to obtain and retain the "dividend check"—a flimsy piece of pink paper the size of a tram ticket on which the cost of the purchase and the dividend number of the purchaser were both recorded. There was never any difficulty in remembering the number. The problem was getting the gossamer billet-doux home. The slightest weakening of grip or concentration and the dividend check was whipped away

by the Pennine winds which always blew up Wadsley Lane and along Dykes Hall Road.

In vain did I argue that the divi would accumulate whether or not the kitchen drawer was littered with pink Co-operative confetti. The dividend coupons were both a proof and a promise. When the bottom of the drawer was covered we could book the boarding house. Our ideals had been vindicated. For those who marched behind the rainbow banner and stopped at the sign of the wheatsheaf, waiting for the millennium was made more endurable by an annual seaside holiday.

But it was at the B. & C. that I first began to suspect that morality and expediency do not always coincide. My errands were first run in the days before the CWS had an advertising logo, proclaimed the virtues of its products on television and hired the Scottish football team to popularise its tin of salmon and bottles of sauce. Indeed they were performed before logos were thought of, television invented or Joe Jordan born. So enthusiastic Co-op shop assistants attempted by word of mouth or sleight of hand to sell "own goods"—the Co-operative alternative to Pears soap, Tate and Lyle treacle and Bird's custard.

The difficult choice between idealism and monetarism was never left to me. My mother had calculated, to the final farthing and ultimate ounce, the alternative advantages of capitalist and Co-operative tinned peaches, sacred and profane sugar, ideologically acceptable and philosophically reprehensible split peas. My note always specified the nationality of the bacon I was to bring home and the bakery from which the biscuits must come. "A lb. of cream crackers—Crawfords *please*." I was never sure if the final felicity was underlined to emphasise our good manners or to reprove the man behind the bacon slicer for attempting to exploit gullible youth.

The tendency to cost-consciousness did nothing to dampen our political ardour. We lived in Hillsborough, the constituency of A. V. Alexander, First Lord of the Admiralty and Co-operative Member of Parliament. Our politics were invariably conducted on B. & C. premises. The Labour League of Youth met in the old cobblers' shop and listened to lectures on both Freedom for India and The Management of Dry Goods Departments. Our debates dealt with such recherché subjects as the desirability of branch managers being allowed to stand for election to the Board of Directors—a controversy that swept through and divided the Sheffield Co-operative Societies.

In the B. & C. we encouraged employees to run the society for which they worked. In the south of the city, Sheffield and Ecclesall did not. Rival Popes in Rome and Avignon could not have disputed theology more fiercely, pursued the apostate with greater zest or spoken more passionately for unity, whilst behaving in a way which made schism certain. We had no doubt that the founding fathers would have condemned the sect's heresy. And we had learned in the old cobblers' shop about men and women who had made out the first dividend cheque in Toad Lane, Rochdale, though, because of a perverse Yorkshire chauvinism, I believed it to be T'old Lane Store, the definite article being pronounced with an apostrophied "T" by uncouth Lancastrians.

The Rochdale Pioneers (amongst whom, in my infancy, I believed Gracie Fields to number) probably kept shop in a way that would have seemed familiar in the B. & C. of the Forties. Tea and sugar was sold "loose", weighed out on massive brass scales under the gaze of cautious customers. In dark recesses, far away from the front door, sides of bacon hung on hooks that ran along overhead rails and sacks of flour were heaped hessian upon hessian. In the yard at the back, steel gantries swung out from the walls to help with the manhandling of plywood tea-chests and barrels of vinegar.

Today the B. & C. is very different. The shops of my youth have closed and business is concentrated on self-service stores in busy suburbs. The last dividend was declared almost two decades ago and CWS "own brands" now confidently compete with products from the other giant manufacturers. People shop at the Co-op because of cost and convenience not conviction. Congratulations to the co-operative societies. But a cash-register's threnody for a generation that once believed that the New Jerusalem could be built (like summer holidays) on pink dividend slips.

"Professor Ziegler's working on a way to get our research grant renewed."

ARTFUL DODGERS

"The Rubens aren't reaching their
reserve price . . . pass it on . . ."

"We had better watch it—I think he's
getting suspicious."

"I couldn't stand her eyes
following me about the cell."

"Three Renoirs for a
packet of fags is a bit
steep, isn't it?"

Fake ceramics, supposedly by Bernard Leach and auctioned at Christie's, were in fact knocked up by prisoners at a Wolverhampton jail. Where, **MAHOOD** wonders, will it end?

"And how, may I ask, do you propose getting the Sistine Chapel to Sothebys?"

"What's all this, Larkin—a dirty cell protest or a Jackson Pollock?"

"Old habits die hard with Lefty. He's still giving them concrete boots."

"Nobby, dig another ruddy tunnel, we're running out of clay!"

Show Business

by BENNY GREEN

LAST month's television debate is about as relevant as yesterday's cold potatoes, and no more telling proof of this chastening proposition exists than my current plight. So long as the mad quadrille of industrial acrimony takes up my perishable prose and carries it over the sea to Skye or some comparably remote and backward outpost of civilisation, before bringing it back suitably disguised in the impersonality of cold print, it becomes impossible for me to maintain any pretence of topicality. However, nothing much ever changes in television, and it is because of that fortunate circumstance that it is a simple business to reminisce about the remote past in a way which might tempt the New Age to find analogies.

As always when confining the narrative to the bare factual truth, the great problem is to convince people you are not making it all up, the reason for this being a most revealing one. In my experience, executives generally tend to ape the mannerisms and attitudes picked up at a formative age from the mysterious melting pot of popular art. For example, many times in my boyhood I watched movies in which the swaggering,

fedora'd newspaper reporter, played by someone like Joel McRae or Dennis O'Keefe, came into work one day to find a man in white overalls scraping his name off the frosted glass of the office door. His role in life had made this whiteclad supernumary something of an empirical philosopher, who, when questioned as to the morality of his profession, would shrug and, without pausing in his scraping, say something like "I seen 'em come and I seen 'em go, but mostly I seen 'em go."

The hero would then make an attempt to confront his editor with this act of perfidy, only to find that the secretary who yesterday was all smiles, has suddenly turned into a cold fish. I usually found this sequence mildly amusing, but was inclined to dismiss its symbolism as a bit heavy-handed. It took a spell in television to show me that the sketch, so far from being symbolic, belonged to the school of stark social realism.

Back in the days of the franchise before the present one, when the affairs of the metropolis were being conducted by an organisation called Associated Rediffusion, I was asked to be the host of a talk show to go out three nights a week. As to the events leading up to this crass predicament, I will elucidate some other time, but the important thing is that I was new to the job and so was my producer, a lady armoured against her own unfortunate temperament with a habit of writing down everything you said and everything she said and everything anyone else said in a reporter's notebook, exactly in the style of the King of Hearts in *Alice in Wonderland* and with just about the same degree of intelligence. After about a week the notebook was full and she started on a second one, whether with the intention of one day selling the serial rights to a Sunday

ORSON WELLES   G.B.S.   A.J.P. TAYLOR

newspaper I never discovered; certainly the notes never appeared again in any deliberations about the shows themselves.

The High Executive who had decreed that my programme come into being was understandably nervous. It is not unusual for a performer to have no idea how he got there; nor is it unknown for the producer to be in a condition of jibbering imbecility. When BOTH of them are bumping into walls, then the prospects are not good. My first suspicion that the lunatics were running the asylum came when the High Executive, in an idiotic attempt to instil confidence, said I was a natural standup comic. As I regard that profession as being marginally lower on the scale of evolution than leading a press gang, the effect on my spirits can be imagined. What was worse was that the H.E., having decided that we needed close watching, resorted to espionage. He had a brother-in-law whose status of out-of-work actor qualified him perfectly for the post of chief researcher, in which position he could report back on everything we said or did. The nepotism was harmless enough, and I did not mind the spying, which was so inept as to put you in mind of the British Secret Service. What troubled me more was the implication that I was such a lamebrain that I wouldn't notice. And again, it seemed that our research would be neglected, especially as the chief assistant researcher had only accepted the post so as to have a desk at which to do his other job, the one he took seriously. The situation was, as the saying goes, interesting.

Soon after we started, we arranged a Shavian debate, with Orson Welles for Shaw and Professor Alan Taylor against. After about fifteen seconds Welles said that in his opinion Shaw was an even worse dramatist than Taylor said he was, which is rather like telling the audience at the start of the play that Hamlet's father isn't really dead at all. The next day I was told that the three shows a week were to be cut to one. When I arrived for work, it was to find a man in white overalls removing the name of the programme from the office door. We were subsequently allocated a smaller office, about three feet square, which made the spying easier and everything else harder. I then attempted to see the H.E.; but his secretary, who yesterday had been all smiles, had mysteriously turned into a cold fish.

Afterwards a man from Contracts tried to browbeat me into accepting one third of the weekly sum stipulated in my agreement. I told him I was perfectly willing to do this and save Associated Rediffusion from impending bankruptcy, except that the sum stipulated in my contract was so disgracefully microscopic that it would require a Senior Wrangler to divide it into three, and that under the circumstances, perhaps it might be for the best if they didn't try to chisel me. And that was that. After thirteen weeks I left the building never to return, and have never ceased to marvel since that of all those involved in the production of that stillborn series, there was not one, from the H.E. to the lowliest secretary, who possessed anything remotely approaching a morality.

VICTOR BORGE:

MORE LOST OPERAS

PELLEAS ET PELLEAS *by Spinanzo Wallawasta*

What is known about Wallawasta is very little, which is not surprising, as he was three feet tall. Wallawasta is known to have been unusually pale because of his diminutive size. The scientific reason is that the sun never reached him. By the time it reached all the way down to where he was; he had moved. In 1842 he met the future Mrs Wallawasta, and in 1843, when she bent over, she finally met him. Their life together, one may assume, was a series of ups and downs. Wallawasta wrote only one opera, as, after his first was performed, he was closed down by the Board of Health. In later life he found employment as a Monk. Monk Wallawasta he was called, and until the cops caught up with him, he and his mob made a bundle.

A tribute to the Me Generation of the 1860's, *Pelleas et Pelleas* is the touching story of a tortured, sensitive youth who falls in love with himself. Essentially, despite the tale's tragic undercurrent, this is a happy story, because Pelleas—in love with himself—discovers dates now only cost him half as much. The first solo, "O Solo Mio" ("Happiness is a reflection; Ecstasy is a three-way mirror"), has become a world anthem for narcissists, an anthem rarely heard, however, as they invariably sing it only to themselves. Wallawasta experimented with a new form here, but Mrs Wallawasta found out about it, and he had to give his new form $3,000 and a ticket to warmer climes, from which she never even sent him a postcard.

Due to the lack of proof that this is a happy story, the opera fizzles out toward the end of Act I, and the audience is being asked to accept an apology.

A STREETCAR NAMED TROLLEY *by Flubschmaut Schmetzaler*

Schmetzaler lived for his art (see Patrick Sneed's biography, "Schmetzaler: A Wasted Life"). His was a decidedly premature birth, as he arrived on earth at 8.10 a.m., April 18, 1879, four months

before he was conceived. From the beginning, he was a compulsive worker, composing 4,327 operas, 293 symphonies, 192 chorales and a cook book, in between sweeping the concert halls and picking up after the orchestra. Critical notices of the time often singled out his immaculate broom-work. Unfortunately, Schmetzaler lived in poverty all his life, and for this reason only one of his works survives, as the rest were lost when he moved. Schmetzaler, before he died, was in a quandary as to be buried or cremated. Finally, he compromised, requesting that he be buried, and his cemetery scattered at sea.

"A Streetcar Named Trolley" was written in three acts, but as Schmetzaler forgot to number the acts, no one knew how to present it, and it was never produced. However, intensive study of the score reveals signs of genius, as his friend Van Gogh often doodled on the parchment. Toward the end of his life Schmetzaler suddenly died before ever hearing his opera, and we should all be so lucky.

ROMEO AND THE OPTOMETRIST *by Hedwig Ludwig*

Ludwig was a child prodigy, performing before the crowned heads of Europe when he was three (they booed him roundly). At five he had written his first symphony, and at six-thirty his music-loving parents burned it. He was a prodigy in other areas as well, and before he was seven was carrying on an affair with Madame Marcelwave. Theirs was an ill-fated alliance, however, as he invariably fell asleep at bedtime. At nine all his creative talents seemed to be spent, and he became a composer of one hit rock and roll tune after another. However, with the onset of manhood, insomnia set in, and Ludwig regained his talents and displayed considerably more maturity (several of his scores from this period are virtually sex symbols). Tragedy seemed to stalk him wherever he went, but as it never caught up with him, he led a remarkably happy life.

"Romeo and The Optometrist" suffers from Ludwig's usual problem; a sweeping yet limited dramatic vision. In the opera, Romeo,

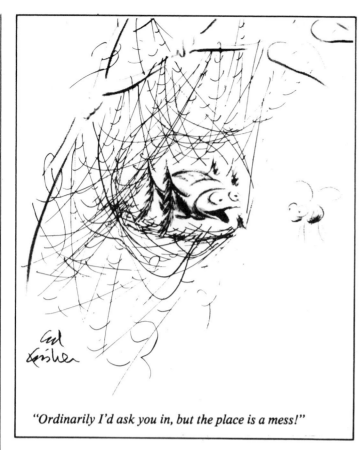

"Ordinarily I'd ask you in, but the place is a mess!"

mileage out of this than in his second opera, "Oedipus at Levittown". Romeo's first aria, "What? Me Date a 14-Year-Old? Do You Take Me for a Pervert?" is particularly thrilling, as it is not only short, but points out all the opera house's exit doors. So far as is known, no one has ever heard or read anything about the rest of the opera, a responsibility for which each succeeding generation has been exceedingly grateful.

ALL QUIET ON THE WESTERN OMELET *by Fredrik Sneebower*
Sneebower was enormously influenced in his adolescence by Jung (see his memoir of his first 19 years, "Jung and Foolish"), and later when he entered the field of opera it was his hope to create a work which would have as its subject the collective unconscious. Unfortunately, the collective unconscious was most fully realized by Sneebower's audiences, but there is no question he was onto something. (Generally it was the prettiest soprano in the chorus.) Sneebower was the first electronic composer, for example, in 1835 playing a one-man synthesized concert through an electric eel. Beforehand, Sneebower had fed in the notes, crusted lightly with brown sugar (unfortunately, prior to discovering the eel's predilection for sweets, the entire overture was lost, as Sneebower had marinated it in dill, and no matter how he tried, it would not go down). The first selection was an enormous success, particularly with lovers of seafood, but unfortunately the rest of the concert was cancelled, as, while Sneebower rested offstage between selections, a tone-deaf stagehand, finding the eel in distress, burped it, dislodging a cantata, a chorale, and 13 minnows. Sneebower had little more luck with his sole opera, "All Quiet on The Western Omelet". The central role was written for a contralto, but times were hard, and in its premiere it was sung by a whiny-voiced accountant with a deviated septum and a head cold. Luckily for Sneebower, the vogue for this style of singing was at its peak at this time, and six members of the audience sat through the whole first act before enlisting in the Prussian Army. "All Quiet" is remarkable for the musical tricks it played, mostly upon one's digestion. Its musical form is ABA CBA A$*. One passage does command riveted audience attention, although the fact that it was written to be played by a nude female cellist may have something to do with it. Sneebower has been venerated by musicologists for generations for, as more than one has put it, "getting out of the business".

a volatile lad from a leading Veronese family, becomes slightly chummy with an optometrist. His family mildly disapproves of this, and Romeo, rather than give up his acquaintanceship with the optometrist, in despair takes a short nap. The optometrist, mistakenly thinking Romeo has gone to sleep for the night, takes two sleeping pills, and dozes for twelve hours, to the mild disinterest of both families. All in all, however, Ludwig seems to get more dramatic

"I couldn't place the smell before but now I've got it. It's mothballs."

JILL TWEEDIE:

Passage through India

AT last it is in close-up, the dusky face of the railway clerk in Delhi, Holy Grail at the end of a two-hour queue.

"Where you going?" he says.

"Kishangahr," I say.

"Where?" he says.

"Kish-an-gahr," I say.

"Where?" he says.

"Kish. An. Gahr," I say.

"Where?" he says.

"Kishsh . . . annn . . . gahrr," I say.

This rivetting dialogue is repeated exactly twelve times. As a tiny blood vessel in my left eyeball explodes, the clerk's face lights up and he hands me a ticket.

"Ah, *Kshnghr*," he says and "Gesundheit," I say. Or rather, *Gsndht*.

The next evening I am catapulted from the tin innards of a motor scooter, low tech for rickshaw, into the hot black flickering inferno of Old Delhi Station. Immediately, a thousand men and boys attempt the abduction, assault and rape of my two Woolworth suitcases. Yelling like a banshee, I beat off the clutching hands, grab at the least terrifying brigand, deliver up my worldly goods to his turbanned head and attempt to keep them somewhere in sight as they bob, aloft, through the battlefield, over stacked sleeping bodies and between monstrously extended families tossing chapattis over countless fires.

And there is the train, quivering in the noisome gloom, hiccuping steam. How could I have imagined, in this Stygian chaos, that the vast bureaucratic bowels of India might possibly spew from their churning depths one label on one seat saying "Tweedie"? Tattered passenger lists hang like battle-scarred pennants from each carriage door. The train heaves and staggers, panic rises. No use, here, thinking you can hop on now and find your place later. The density of bodies in each box makes a tinned sardine seem lonely as a cloud and a reckless traveller, hurling himself within, would be frozen for twelve hours in the position he first thought of. But then the bearer strikes a match and, lo, there is my name. "Twdy." Another small Indian triumph wrenched from the jaws of unlikelihood. I scramble in, the train pulls out. It would be nice, now, to relax and have a quick nervous breakdown but, alas, there isn't room.

The fifth in a continuing series of anxiety attacks hits me. How will I survive the long night ahead, stuck in a rectangular wooden shed with four pallets to serve ten people?

Bars cover the glassless windows, on the ceiling three giant fans whip up the thick air. In one corner, behind swinging chest-high doors, lies Nemesis, the loo, use of which threatens a fate worse than death. To avert the threat, I take out my plastic water bottle and swig down two Lomotil pills, prescribed for diarrhoea but now required to institute a 48 hour intestinal go-slow. Within three minutes, all inner activity silts up and the new concretized me manages to smile faintly at the souls in the shadows around. A saried woman with a boy and girl. Two teenage girls with skinny plaits and decorous Moslem trousers. Two business men in Western suits. Two huge bearded and moustachioed Sikhs. The woman, the children and the girls fix their great dark eyes upon me and from then on manage, against all distractions and despite all other bodily movement, to keep them fixed, like bubbles in a shifting spirit level.

The men have better things to do. The business gents conduct an intimate discussion in telescoped English, full of vaguely familiar sounds like "cntrcts" and "mrgrs" and "tchnlgy", their heads gliding smoothly from one shoulder to the other in a mysterious Indian body language. The Sikhs, meanwhile, attend with slow solemnity to their toilette. Turbans are unwound and long pieces of netting produced, to be carefully bound over hair, under beards and across moustaches. Having thus out-Sharpled Ena, they pull down canvas hammocks from above, climb up, arrange themselves like two brass rubbings and lie perfectly still. Soon everyone has distributed themselves, the girls heads to feet on one pallet, the woman huddled on the end of hers with her daughter while the son stretches out in the lordly comfort due his masculinity, the businessmen share theirs in dignified yoga positions and, magically, I have one pallet all to myself. Already modestly shrouded in a long kaftan, I stretch out, too.

Outside, in the darkness, invisible India flashes by. I lie watching the fans in the ceiling. They are immensely old; each blade twists and groans in its endless circular journey. I know that the screws bolting them to the ceiling are at this very moment almost rusted through, at this very moment

"One night, son, all this will be yours!"

139

"You're lucky. Ten years ago we didn't have these anti-biotic dances."

edging off the last disintegrating thread. I know that as that thread gives, the fans will fly off their anchors, scythe their way through us at 100 r.p.m. and smear the remains against the wooden walls. But until that apocalypse I may as well sleep and I do, most refreshingly and thoroughly, until the morning and Kshngr.

So much for the Delhi Mail and its overnight journey to the plains of Rajasthan. Local trains are something else. The next week, I stand in the middle of nowhere beside a railroad track, waiting for a conveyance to Jaipur. I know I am at a station because there is a water pump, a tea stall and a knot of other human beings. Small children surround me and stand stock still, hoovering me into the black holes of their eyes. Their stare is so intense, so all-devouring and yet so peculiarly detached that I feel no more embarrassed than does a goldfish, gaped at in its bowl. I only wish that I had the wherewithal to be more entertaining, whisk a rabbit out of a top hat, draw coins from the air, saw myself in half.

A woman with a glossy brown kid, cute as Bambi, in her arms, comes to stand beside me. She makes a tunnel of her veil and giggles softly down it at me, flashing silver teeth. A dhotied man, skin as wrinkled as black hide, offers me water from the pump. I put my hands together in thanks and drink, thus imbibing the amoeba that will play havoc with my innards six weeks later in Kentish Town.

Eventually, when minutes have blurred into hours, a distant black worm in the golden landscape wriggles towards us and grows into a full-size train. This time the carriage has two benches facing one another and, if loo there is, it matters not where because I have relieved myself up to the last moment in the hygenic fields and am once

more bunged up with Lomotil. Of all fears in India—and waves of rational and irrational panic sweep constantly through the foreign system—none is as paralysing as the fear of excreting where no white man has excreted before, never mind woman. One resident woman friend still goes sallow at the memory of being caught short in a station loo. Oh that we could do as the Indians do and nip out, at stops, for a quick crouch by the railway lines, not given away by the moon-glow of our white bottoms. Men may cope reasonably well, by virtue of their more private plumbing. Women are forced to rely on the wonders of science.

This time, in my carriage, there are four other people, all shoeless and crosslegged upon the wooden slats. The young man opposite me has a crab foot; the huge joint of his big toe brackets out in a great claw. In England, most of us would prefer to fall head first out of a window than be forced to acknowledge the presence of such a foot. In India, on the other hand, or foot, it is an absorbing conversation piece.

The man who entered with me, his head swathed in a week's washing, cannot wait for the train to start before commencing his queries. The foot's owner is eager to answer, his eyes brighten, he rattles away. The foot is pushed forward for our better viewing, it is moved and turned and stretched for our edification. We are shown how the claw can be manipulated to pick up large objects, we are lectured on its manifold uses, its unique mobility. Its possessor gazes fondly upon it with ill-restrained pride, as upon an interesting invention or technological gadget well in advance of its time. At one point in his lecture, a commercial break is called, we feast on proferred sweetmeats and return, refreshed, to the foot, as to a beloved pet.

Nevertheless, even such an intrinsically

interesting subject as a deformed foot loses its magnetism in the face of time. Never, at any point, does this train go faster than I could run. The midday heat builds up and sets the flat landscape shimmering. Nothing moves out there. An occasional twisted thorn bush. An odd figure, standing motionless. Two creamy oxen, humped sentries. Now and again, almost without our noticing, the train slows down until it has stopped and figures appear, burdened with livestock. They climb in and others leave, setting off into the flatlands on a journey without milestones. Children run up and down the track, offering water, food, little gifts. They are as beautiful as the offspring of the Gods. I drink from my water bottle and it is like drinking liquid plastic, warm. The heat now muffles everything like a horsehair blanket, sweat trickles and sets the skin itching, sleep descends and lifts like fever. A lifetime passes, people are born and people die and we are still on our way, in a train, to Jaipur.

A woman alone, travelling by train in India, has little to fear because she is a woman, in spite of the fact that rape is endemic. Outside the swarming urban centres, the sheer jaw-slackening oddity of clothes, curling hair, white features and eccentric behaviour take huge precedence over sex. The pallid skin, in itself, casts a magic barrier around you that no one cares to cross. Rape, of course, has nothing to do with looks but, if it did, Englishwomen would be well protected too. There can be few human beings in the world so consistently and marvellously beautiful as Indian women, even unto the poorest and most hard-worked. They make us feel like Gulliver in Lilliput, clumping thick-boned giantesses, appallingly visible among the modest veils of village India, figures of fun and fascination denuded of desire. I, in my early forties, may anyway be beyond that particular pale but, in my travels, I met many pretty younger women who had trekked the width and breadth of the continent without mishap. One Australian girl, a rosy-cheeked and sturdy damsel glowing with the blonde health of her Icelandic forebears, informed me that the worst she had suffered was a gender-identity crisis, brought on by staying with a family of Indian daughters.

"They were so feminine," she cried in half-despair. "They found it hard to believe that I was a woman at all and so, in the end, did I. They were small and delicate, they prattled on in high little voices, my wrists were wider than their ankles and they couldn't lift my rucksack. Of course, they were horribly oppressed," she added and sighed, as she tramped off.

Of course they are. These beautiful creatures are bought and sold, raped and murdered, killed by endless childbirth, burned by greedy in-laws, burdened by the hardest of work or starved simply because they were not born men. Yet two out of three, imported to the West and given white skins in place of dark, would be feted into fame and prosperity, such is the curious perversity of man.

ANOTHER AMAZING HOLBEIN DISCOVERY!

LAST WEEK, this painting, attributed in the auctioneer's catalogue to *W. Disney*, was knocked down in Bond Street for £7.95, to include p + p. The buyer was a Mr James Eschweiler-Cooke-Fnelge. As he emerged from the auction rooms, he discovered that the painting was in fact a Holbein worth £17,000,000.

I asked him how he had learned this, and he said that he had popped into the nearest dealer's to enquire whether they could let him have a bit of string and an X-tel hook to hang it up, and the dealer had immediately identified the painting as a Holbein. The dealer's name was Mr Arthur Eschweiler-Cooke-Fnelge, of the Eschweiler-Cooke-Fnelge Galleries. Was he, I asked Mr James Eschweiler-Cooke-Fnelge, any relation?

"Hard to say," I was told. "There's a lot of us in the phone-book." When I produced the directory, Mr Eschweiler-Fnelge admitted that the other Mr Eschweiler-Cooke-Fnelge could have been his long-lost brother, snatched away at birth, but until that moment he had been under the impression that the gypsies still had him.

Since bidding for the painting had not been fierce (the only other bidder, Mrs James Eschweiler-Cooke-Fnelge, having dropped out when the price reached £7.90) even though the auction had been attended by many of the most famous art dealers in London, I asked a number of them why they had not been interested. At a somewhat noisy champagne reception afterwards at the Eschweiler-Cooke-Fnelge Gallery, Mr Greville Node, of Node Fine Arts, told me: "The picture was very dusty. It needed a bloody good wipe, in my opinion. I could see it was a Holbein, but we're a very busy gallery, and we can't spend all day with Jaycloths and Flash. Also, it was a very tatty frame."

Sir George Fulmyle, chairman of Fulmyle Pictures, agreed that they were Holbein experts, but said that he had never liked Holbeins where the people looked miserable. "My customers do not like to have these gloomy buggers hanging on their walls,"

he said. "I am keen to buy broad grins, and would even have been ready to bid for a wry smile, but there is no call for long bloody faces in this business."

This, however, was not what made Mr Ralph Pope-Cherry refrain from bidding. "I did not have my glasses with me this morning," he said, "and believed the figure to be someone from Securicor."

I asked one of the auctioneer's valuers how he had arrived at the catalogue attribution, and was informed that whenever a picture came in which he thought might be a Disney, he always contacted the Eschweiler-Cooke-Fnelge Gallery, who were the acknowledged experts in the field, and whom he had known and trusted ever since they had been at Eton together. "On this occasion, their considered opinion, originally, was that the picture was a still from *Bambi*."

NO CONSPIRACY

After Fiona Huggett of the Huggett Gallery told me that she had in fact subjected the painting to a detailed inspection during the view before the sale and found it to be too large to put in the boot of her car, I asked her whether there could be any truth in the rumour that a ring of dealers had deliberately refrained from bidding, in the hope that they would subsequently enjoy a share of the profits after the painting had been bought cheaply and sold later at its true value.

She told me that it sounded a jolly ingenious plan, but that anyone trying that sort of thing in so distinguished an area as the London art market could find himself in serious trouble. She herself had heard of a journalist who had done no more than ask a few innocent questions, and the next thing anybody knew, he was wearing his thumbs backwards.

FATHER'S DAY

HUNTER DAVIES
sums up two decades with
Mrs Hunter Davies

TO celebrate our twenty years of marriage, which I've been doing now for the last few weeks, I decided to make the supreme sacrifice. We've done something my way for the last twenty years so it seemed only fair that for the next twenty years we'll do it her way. Then we can decide which is best, I mean better. Caitlin's O-level English has obviously had a good effect on me.

Apparently I forced her, twenty years ago, to submit to my desires, though I can't remember it. It just seemed to happen. I can't even recall her struggling, putting up any fights or arguments, but she maintains on our honeymoon I ignored all her protestations and went straight ahead and had my selfish way. So, in the interests of equality and general selflessness, for the last few weeks we've been sleeping with the curtains open all night. I knew you'd be shocked.

I haven't got used to it. Probably never will. It's like sleeping in the open air with all those stars watching and goodness knows who or what else. And the mornings are hell. I'm awake at four, with these light summer mornings, and it's impossible to get to sleep again. I felt so secure, these last twenty years, hidden behind those deep delved curtains, snug in the dark, safe and protected, private as a plate. Now I'm sure the whole world is watching.

If I'm giving in on that, as yet another of my many touching anniversary presents, then let's change sides while we're at it. But she refused. I don't know how that happened either but we've always slept on the same sides, with me on the right and her—or should it be she—on the left. That's if you're standing at the foot of the bed, facing us, which you probably are doing these days, now those curtains are wide to the world. Even when we stay in hotels, we always end up taking the same matrimonial sides, like little clockwork men, programmed for ever.

I think this habit first started when the kids would barge into our bedroom in the middle of the night and demand their mother's attention, which I naturally didn't

object to. She had to be nearest the door to keep them off me which meant sleeping on the left side. I could do a drawing, just to get an extra mark.

She sees no sense in changing this pattern now, as our bodies have got used to it, and I couldn't think of any real reason, except it would be nice not to wake up with my right pyjama sleeve all damp where I've been dribbling in the night. I sleep on my right arm. Yet another twenty-year habit. So you would wake up instead with your left sleeve damp, she says. What's the difference. She's so practical.

Apart from my damp sleeve, and some lovely dark sleeps, there's not much else to report after twenty years of marriage. Three kids, a nice stamp album, a lot of old clothes. Just the usual ordinary things one accumulates. Yet if you read all these articles in the women's magazines and the women's pages, they're trying to make out I'm some sort of freak. They're all on to their third wives at least. And that's just the women.

Half the people getting married today have already been married before. Or is it half the people getting divorced have never been married. Any road up, the figures are everywhere. One paper makes a guess or thinks of a number, and it spreads like wildfire, with a veritable barrage of impressive divorce statistics tumbling out, just to make the uxorious feel kinky. Not just little articles. Whole series on whither marriage and why fifth husbands are sexier than fourth husbands and how you should get medals for looking at the same face over the same breakfast table for more than five years.

I've always looked forward to seeing her

"I like it, I like it."

over the breakfast table these last twenty years. After all, we've had a night in the dark. Perhaps the next twenty years in the light won't be so easy.

Yet when I look round our area, the world is full of married folks. I don't actually stare through the bedroom curtains, but they all seem pretty happy to me and set for a good long innings, though one doesn't go round talking about such things. We stick to safe things like stamps and old clothes.

We haven't of course *been* the same faces over the last twenty years. God, how I've changed. I think we'd been married one week before I asked her how she thought I'd changed. I've brought up the topic every other week since. It's my favourite subject, that and reminiscing about something that happened only yesterday, especially in the case of something that did happen only yesterday.

She's definitely mellowed. We used to have terrible fights and arguments, and then even worse rows over who started it. I don't think she's stormed out of the room slamming the door for, oh, it must be days. Having teenagers has helped. There's such a rush to storm out of the room that you've got to be really quick to get in first. It's not all that terribly impressive, if you slam out of a room which turns out to be empty, the rival slammers having gone first by another exit.

She now laughs at my little mannerisms that used to annoy her. Nothing serious, really. Eating food. Breathing. Walking. Those sort of humdrum things. Perhaps it's because I've mended my ways and learned to close my mouth when eating. Those correspondence courses were a good help. A famous publisher has conquered his noisy eating habits and he can teach YOU in thirteen easy lessons.

I've done the opposite of mellowing, so she says. I've become noisier, more frenetic and more hectic. She wishes I would slow down. What she wants, so she maintains, is less excitement in her life. She longs for monotony.

There are millions of ladies out there, just longing for a bit of our excitement, to be dragged on endless holidays, to other houses, to look at my latest stamps, at least that's what I maintain.

Ah yes, says she. They don't know how you *moan* about all the rushing around you do. You seem to enjoy being in a panic, otherwise you wouldn't continually wish it upon yourself.

I think we'll leave that subject now. How about the old body? Don't you think I'm *looking* better than I did twenty years ago? Tell the truth, now. Come on, I can take it. Forget the wrinkles. That's not fair. I mean the general overall condition. For a man of 44, you must admit. Don't be rotten. Look, I have let you open the curtains. Just tell me what you really think . . .

But she was gone. Didn't even slam the door. That's the secret of twenty years. Keep a few mysteries.

"*Congratulations, sir! Your luggage brings our total losses this year to exactly £100 million.*"

"*Actually, my twin brother is the bigger bore by about twenty minutes.*"

"They would put it that a little more maturity of judgment would obviously be required before we could be promoted."—A senior civil servant on how joining the strike might jeopardise his career prospects.

NO, MINISTER

A little more maturity of judgment,
The kind that one would normally display,
Is deemed to be essential
For achieving one's potential
And the steady elevation of one's pay.

Though frankly one regrets the present action,
Despite the ends that justify the means,
One can hardly call it cricket,
And it saddens one to picket
In a jacket used for gardening and jeans.

The loyalty one bears to one's employer
Is based upon one's conscience and belief,
But this odd idea of striking,
While not being to one's liking,
Would appear to be one's First Division brief.

A calculated risk to one's advancement
Is rarely seen among the higher grades,
And one has a shrewd suspicion
It would tend to breach tradition
If one ever had to mount the barricades.

Roger Woddis

FREAKY FABLES by HANDELSMAN

CRIME & PUNISHMENT & CRIME & PUNISHMENT & CRIME

Coming to the Trojan War, Aegisthus?

I'd love to, Agamemnon, but I feel I can do more on the home front. Yours.

'Bye, Daddy!

Insult to injury! You chopped up his father, too, wicked boy.

I was very young at the time, and anyway, his father had sautéed my brothers, just because *my* father...

AGAMEMNON HAD INSTRUCTED HIS COURT MINSTREL TO KEEP WATCH ON CLYTAEMNESTRA.

Oh, every night the slacker pokes the Queen, and I'll tell Agamemnon what I've seen...

Thanks for the timely warning!

There! Now sing about starving to death.

Well, it's corn and beans 'most every day, I'd as soon be eating prairie hay, come a ti yi yippee come a ti yi yay... me and my big mouth.

AGAMEMNON WAS SAID TO BE RETURNING FROM THE WAR WITH CASSANDRA.

Shall we murder him when he arrives?

Absolutely! I don't owe him a thing, the unfaithful rat!

Furthermore, he killed my former husband, just because...

Hello, everybody! We won the war! Meet Cassandra—she is into prophesying.

WELCOME HOME AGAMEMNON

Super to see you.

I have this premonition that we are about to be done in.

Murderous adulterers!

Shame on you, Electra! Go to your room!

I told you so.

True.

Dear Orestes,
I hope you are having a good time. When you grow up I want you to come back & kill Mommy & Aegisthus. They are adulterous <u>murderers</u> & also very mean. The weather is rotten too.
Your sister,
Electra
P.S. Mommy sends love.

YEARS LATER, ORESTES RETURNED.

Well, Clyt, we've done very well for ourselves, and—glork...

Orestes! That was very naughty!

Now do the other meanie.

Go to your roo—

Sorry, mother. The Delphic Oracle ordered me to do this.

I ordered you first.

ORESTES WAS THEN DRIVEN MAD BY THE FURIES.

Everybody loves a baby—
That's why I'm in love with you—
Pretty baby—boom—pretty baby—boom—

Have mercy! I'm an orphan! Also I come from a broken home...

MORAL: Revenge is sweet and sour.

Two Nights at the Opera

WHY don't they have a rehabilitation centre at Covent Garden? After two consecutive nights at the opera, I was much less than myself. Or, perhaps, much more.

It wasn't just the music. Though I must say you'd need to have a really untroubled mind to sit through the fidgety high spirits of Mozart's *Cosi Fan Tutti* on one night, and the rumbling angst of Verdi's *Un Ballo In Maschera* on the next.

And it certainly wasn't the stories that bludgeoned the senses. There is so little plot in *Cosi* that the opera is almost a straight musical concert. And the plot of *Un Ballo* is not merely simple, but simple-minded. I know Auden reminded us that people don't sing when they're feeling sensible, but this lot are ridiculous. I rather wished, after reading the programme notes, sponsored by Marks and Spencer and North Thames Gas, that Verdi had used more accurate information about King Gustavus III of Sweden, I mean, the bit about his father dying from over-eating could have been quite jolly. And as the real king was, in fact, a raving homosexual, we could have been spared the old boy's invented love affair, which clogs up Act Two so appallingly.

I've nothing against people having violent love scenes on the stage, but on this occasion the king's girl-friend was played by Montsarrat Caballe, who is a sizeable lady and not at all my idea of a desirable target for noisy adultery. My newspaper told me afterwards that at one point she staggered into the wings for a quick breather. If I didn't notice this at the time it was because I had reversed my opera glasses, turning the whole performance into a spectacle as tiny and remote as one of those prestige opera nights on television.

"Does it affect *you* like that?" said the woman next to me, who was sharing fifty pounds-worth of knee-cramping seats with her husband. "I know just how you feel. I can't bear to be so close to all that grief."

I didn't like to tell her that, for me, the reversed opera glasses were the next best thing to escaping from the opera house altogether. I *would* have tried to get away, but I met my colleague, Richard Baker, in one of the intervals, and somehow his absolutely square-to-the-world attitude, which is so comforting on news bulletins and elsewhere, made me feel ashamed.

We all know, incidentally, that one reason people go to the opera is to enjoy those long intervals. What other experience can compare with a slice of tired quiche and a glass of wine, as you sprawl elegantly on the grand staircase? Though this is, of course, a lady's privilege; probably because there is a special way of drinking on the stairs, with arms crossed, one hand on the opposite knee and the glass held meditatively beneath the further ear—a pose that would get you arrested if you were a man.

By the second interval I'd almost acquired, once again, a taste for opera. I say once again because in my late teens I accompanied an operatic soprano for two years. Sometimes to Boots the Chemist and sometimes to an ABC tea shop, but more often to a furtive rehearsal room. We *had* to be furtive because our contracts said that nobody must sing in Italian for the duration of the war, in case they were thought to be passing messages to the enemy. That was why we so often climbed the stairs at the back of a music shop, for a quick *Una Voce Poco Fa*, if you'll forgive the expression. Both off stage and on we used only the more popular fragments, but I emerged from all this feeling much more capable of sitting through a night at the opera without a feeling of disorientation.

So what has gone wrong? That is a good question, especially for somebody who has actually performed at the Royal Opera House. This appearance, I must say modestly, was merely during the war, when the place had been converted into a dance hall. But it was pretty thrilling for a sixteen-year-old to stand on that famous stage, facing tier upon tier of packed seats.

"What are you going to give us, Laddie?" said Al Bowlly.

"I'd like to play you a piano medley of tunes you all know and love," I said. I was speaking as one of Leonard Urry's Discoveries. "I shall begin," I said, "with *There Goes My Dream.*"

And there *did* go my dream, rather quickly. "Because we've got a lot of other acts to get through," said the late and great Mr Bowlly.

Anyway, you will understand that the other night I knew exactly how Pavarotti

"The Somme, Ypres, Passchendaele—I've misspelled them all."

"Well, what category do you want to start off with today: show tunes, football or great names in American painting?"

was feeling, up there beneath the spotlights. Except that nobody had bothered me with all that dying business when I was playing at Covent Garden. As I watched Pavarotti going through his routine of expiring on one elbow, I remembered somebody's definition of opera as "a musical play in which, if a man is stabbed to death, he promptly sings for forty minutes." And I was glad that at this point Verdi had altered the real-life story. In reality, my programme notes told me, the king was not stabbed, but shot with rusty nails which took a fortnight to finish him off. At last week's performance it only *seemed* like a fortnight.

As I sat through those two nights at the opera, wondering if I would ever see my house and family again, I suspected that I was becoming an addict—even though my mind was dripping pure thought into pools of limpid nothingness and playing tricks with tunes. At one moment my memory changed a Verdi phrase into *Oh Johnny!* and rushed me back to the last time I heard Florence Desmond singing that number in Derry and Tom's roof garden . . .

Suddenly everybody was standing up and shouting. Was the place on fire? Would all the faded theatre carpeting be torn to pieces in the rush? Would that cliche-ridden

striped wallpaper be destroyed? And would those dreadful chandeliers—symbols of a richer world—come crashing to the ground? As it turned out, it was not panic that had seized the audience, but a milder sort of fear. They were stamping and banging the seats to convince each other that they were really very lucky to have joined together in a combined expenditure of many thousands of pounds. They were, in fact, reassuring themselves—and trying to make enough noise to silence any small boy who might ask questions about the emperor's clothes.

Afterwards, the mildly wintry London was looking at its best. For me it is always the theatre outside that matters most; the views from Waterloo Bridge at night; the absurd fairy palace of an illuminated Harrods, or the hamburger-scented frivolity of the Kings Road. And all these things seemed lovelier because I had been trapped for several hours among what sounded like mad waiters ordering complicated Italian meals.

I said just now that I suspected I was becoming an opera addict. The fact is that even if I am never again invited to be a guest at Covent Garden I shall certainly fight my way in. I've been made to realise there are some experiences in life that are beyond reason and above criticism. Opera-going, I now see, can attract people partly *because* it is so hideously inappropriate to the present day; so financially unjustifiable, and so dangerously near to provoking hysterical fits in middle-aged boppers. There is something about opera that can reach where the other arts cannot reach, making you forget the odour of patronage from peddlars in chocolate, cigarettes, chemicals, beer and rubber. It is insidious and very nearly irresistible. In spite, as Mark Twain said, of all that singing.

"I have to admit, it certainly seems to have improved firing squad morale."

TERRORIST'S WHO'S WHO

MILES KINGTON's guide to this month's top splinter groups

Oct 3 Movement

The mystery group which has attacked Swiss property here and in Beirut, without apparent motive. They are in fact a desperate squad of disgruntled financiers, unable to acquire secret bank accounts in Switzerland, who have decided to spend the money on revenge instead. October 3, of course, is the date on which Swiss banks change the locks on all vaults.

Provisional COI

A high level British group which has set up itself as an alternative to the official Central Office of Information. They claim responsibility for every mistake made by the Treasury in excess of £5m in the last six years. Their methods are to feed false statistics and miscalculated budgets to the media and the public. Government ministers are privately very worried about this group, as they feel misinformation should be their monopoly, and they can do the job perfectly well without the Provisional COI.

The Airline Office Bombers

The AOB have bombed airline offices here and in Paris, New York and Rome. Their motive: they just do not like airline offices. "Their design and decor represent the worst in modern living," a spokesman says. "The average airline office is a cross between a dentist's surgery and a McDonald's. It's a disgrace. We stand up for the millions who have spent hours in these awful places, trying to change their Zurich flight for a stand-by to Frankfurt."

The Avenue of April 1 Army

In South America many streets are named after important dates in their country's history, but the inhabitants of the Avenida April 1st in Lima, Peru, feel aggrieved that they have been given a joke name. They would settle for any other date, a national hero or even an obscure poet, but the government ignores their request. In retaliation, they are blowing up the avenue bit by bit. "This show them we mean business," says a spokesman. "For an April 1st joke, this pretty damn good, no?"

Alimony International

A group of ex-husbands, embittered by the way they are financially crippled by Britain's divorce laws, have decided to embark on violent action to mark their protest. So far they have not decided what kind of violence would be best; a few are all for blowing up their ex-wives, but this might alienate public sympathy. Their most likely course of action at present is to blow up London statues of famous women. "We sent out a squad to do Edith Cavell, but when they got there they had a look and decided nobody would notice the difference. Meetings are a bit indecisive at the moment; in fact, we generally adjourn to the pub, have a sing-song and tell a few stories. Just like we did before we got divorced, I suppose."

The Abadan Seven

A tiny protest movement against the Ayatollah's fanaticism, who decided to start action last week by setting off a small bomb outside the Middle East Airline office in Abadan. They woke up the next day to find the whole of Abadan a smouldering ruin. Somewhat overawed by their own success, they have now disbanded.

The October 22 Movement

So-called because that is the date today. Tomorrow they will be the October 23 Movement. They pride themselves on being the only really good, modern free-lance protest group. Though without any axe to grind themselves, they will hire themselves out to any impassioned minority group which does not know how to make bombs or has not got an airline office in its vicinity. "We believe passionately in what we are doing," says managing director Sam Palmer. "We will not cease from direct action until we have heroically struggled to ensure that our clients get their money's worth."

The Gang of Nought

A minimalist art movement, which is incredibly concerned, involved and deeply disturbed about the way art should go, if any. So far, their main gesture has been to refuse to blow up Carl André's bricks in the Tate Gallery. By not damaging them, their argument goes, they have made the public aware of their irrelevance even more. These Bricks Are Not Worth Blowing Up, is the message. They really are very, very angry. They are also thinking seriously of not blowing up the ICA, but no decision has been reached on this one yet.

The New Year's Day Movement

An off-shoot of the Oct 22 Movement (see above). "Hello again," says managing director Sam Palmer. "We exist to advise splinter groups on a choice of name and image. With so many terrorist groups around, it's terribly important to get the right image and marketing approach to make sure that your just demands make the *Daily Telegraph*. the Armenian Secret Army is what I'd call a good name; ETA is what I'd call a bad name. Where's the message in that? The Basques have to drop twice as many bombs for the same publicity. We call ourselves the New Year's Day Movement because generally that's a very slack day among terrorists and we reckon no one else would want the name. Also, it's got kind of a nice feel to it."

The 1890 Dance Studios

Not a terrorist group at all, but a genuine dance studio, named after the year Nijinsky was born. Unfortunately, it sounds like a terrorist group, and their premises have been bombed by rival organisations three times (responsibility has variously been claimed by the Free Bolshoi Army, the Disco Seven and the October 3–10 Inclusive Movement). "We are faced with two choices," says head tutor Sam Palmer (no relation). "Either we retaliate and go into the terror bit ourselves, though I find that terribly pseudo-butch and macho. Or we change our name. I'd like to call the studio the Fokine Dance Place. Or is that a bit . . .?"

ON THE HOUSE

NOTED Tory "wet" MP Richard Needham of Chippenham tells me of an intriguing encounter in his constituency. Chippenham is famous for few things, but it is known throughout the world as the place where the celebrated rock 'n' roll singer Eddie Cochrane was killed in a car crash. He was travelling at the time from a gig in Bath and was accompanied by his girl friend and by that other noted rock 'n' roll singer Gene Vincent, who never quite recovered from his injuries.

There is some controversy in Chippenham about whether a memorial to the late Mr Cochrane should be put up in the town. Mr Needham, a great fan of the music of the period, is enthusiastic that this should be done, and agreed to appear in a programme filmed by the local ITV company.

With much excitement Needham and crew managed to track down the local chap who had been first on the scene of the crash. Yes, he said, he had been there. Yes, he had seen it all happen. Yes, he had administered what help he could and yes, he would tell everything on the programme. Lights and sound equipment were prepared, the gaffer placed on the appropriate chalk mark, directional mikes with wind baffles were arranged out of shot, and the old fellow began talking. "Yes, oy was there," he said. "Oy rushed out and saw them lying all over the road. Oy put moy coat on Eddie Cochrane. Oy never got it back."

Another well-known wet, not actually Needham, has come up with a marvellous time-saving plan which he plans to put shortly into action. He sits for a Northern constituency, one of the many which swung Mrs Thatcher's way in 1979, and which is, no doubt, regretting its folly as job after job disappears.

The MP says he is getting a printed form made for him on the usual "strike out where not applicable" lines. It will read roughly: Dear — — —, It was with great regret that I learned of the closure of your factory/mill/plant/offices with the consequent loss of 100/200/300/400/500/1,000 jobs. I will/will not be able to attend your protest rally/march/delegation to Downing Street. If there is anything further which I can do to help, please let me know. I am, yours sincerely, — — — MP. "This will save me hours a week," he chortled.

A third Tory wet tells me of an intriguing encounter in the "No" lobby with Mrs Thatcher. He was waiting to vote on some important matter, when Heather approached him and began chatting. I will not reveal the topic, since this might identify my informant.

He suddenly became aware that the most famous bosom in British politics—or at least half of it—was pressed firmly but accidentally against his hand, and remained so for quite some minutes as she talked happily away. It was, he tells me, encased in some durable supportive fabric.

"It was jolly interesting and I kept saying, 'gosh, lots of people would love to be in my position'," he tells me. "But I couldn't help feeling it ought to have done more for both of us than it did."

This column appears to be devoted almost exclusively to Tina and her doings, but they are the subject of quite endless fascination at Westminster. Recently the directors of the giant GEC company were making arrangements to receive her on an official visit. They rang Number Ten and pointed out that she might not care to call on one particular plant, since it would involve wearing protective clothing. Would she mind? "Not in the slightest," came the airy answer from Downing Street. "She just *loves* dressing up!"

I am sure that I am not the first to point out that the new Centre Party may be a hallucination. The initials of any alliance between the Liberals and the Social Democrats would be LSD.

Is there absolutely no limit to the self-esteem of Mr Bill Walker, the Tory MP for Perth, and the man whose support of the birch has earned him the soubriquet "Mr Whippy" from his colleagues? I ask the question following the latest extraordinary descriptions of his life in the Scottish prints, where we find recorded a top level conversation between Mr Walker and the President and Vice-President of the United States. After, we are supposed to presume, a tour d'horizon of Afghanistan, Poland and Iran, the obscure legislator discussed with Vice-President Bush the merits of the Famous Grouse whisky, which is made in his constituency. The general impression conveyed is that Mr Whippy is an intimate of Presidents, a confidante of the great.

Sadly the truth is a little more mundane, He crossed the Atlantic with members of the Conservative aviation group, and while in Washington, was invited with them to a fairly minor cocktail party in a large hotel. Mr Walker was in his full dress kilt. As they waited to be wafted upstairs towards the dry martinis, a flunky asked them to wait in the hotel lobby for a few minutes as "someone" was coming.

A limousine arrived at the door and out stepped Messrs Reagan and Bush, who were to address some women's convention, also being held at the hotel. A receiving line formed, and Mr Walker brazenly placed himself at the end. Of course the only thing he had in common with the real guests was the fact that he wasn't wearing trousers either.

The pair began pressing flesh, and as they zoomed past Mr Walker, the Vice-President essayed a brief remark about the Famous Grouse which was, quite possibly, the only thing about Scotland apart from the fact that some of the men there wear skirts. Mr Walker's moment of fame and glory was indeed merely a moment. I advise him to make less of these occasions in future, since they merely annoy his colleagues and inspire them to send accounts of his behaviour to magazines such as this.

SIMON HOGGART

"Nothing I can do, I'm afraid. It's an occupational hazard."

KATHARINE WHITEHORN
on
Military Outfitters

NO ONE who has seen the awesome gold-braided portraits adorning the Institute of Directors (till lately the United Services Club), or who watched the scene on TV recently where the officer had his kilt fitted ("Isn't it too long?" "No, that's right for an Argyll—it'd be an inch too short for Black Watch") can doubt that if there's one thing the military man fusses about, it's his uniform. A modern officer in his woolly pully may look so like his men nine-tenths of the time that he has nothing but his pips and his accent to distinguish him. He may have but one service dress and one mess kit (that's the one you commit suicide in when you've Mentioned a Lady's Name) but the rules for uniforms are as strict as ever.

Their military outfitters are keenly aware of their responsibilities. Go into the elegant Savile Row establishment of Gieves and Hawkes and you will find people who know the pips and tabs of every regiment by heart. Mr Ward, the doyen, was once accosted as he closed the shop by a woman crying, "Damn, I've driven forty miles for a pair of pips!" He calmly instructed a colleague with the exact details without even stopping to think. And their eye for an officer even in civilian dress is unerring: "Of course he's not in the Army, he's got a *green hat*."

They do consent to make uniforms for Omanis, Arab Emirates, even Belgians; but they are born for better things. Down in the cellar sleep in tin boxes the clothes worn by the Queen's Bodyguard. Before each State Opening of Parliament or State Visit, "These quite ordinary-looking chaps turn up and then they go out in *these*"—these being red jackets with gold braid, ceremonial swords, golden helmets with white, well, fairly white, plumes—all the accoutrements without which the Queen

would be as undefended as her poor daughter with her security guard and his dud gun.

Gieves, Alkit, Moss Bros—they, like Army regulations, apply to almost all services "except the Brigade of Guards"; these have their own special tailors (as do the Cavalry)": it can cost the nation £7,000 to turn out one of those bearskinned figures. Other regiments get a kit allowance of £400 to £600—(like absolutely everything else about the Army, it varies from regiment to regiment) swords, £300, are ceremonial and optional extras, and mostly supplied by doting parents or hired. The actual grotty stuff you wear to fight in is issued at places like Aldershot and may find its way eventually to such Meccas of the smart teenager as Lawrence Corner or Biggles; but officers get most of it for themselves. Pants and pyjamas, luckily, are left to a man's own discretion—one could hardly see the Army *issuing* the women's nylon tights which some smart regiments wear under their mess trousers.

The cost of all this is such that Moss Bros do a thriving trade on the second-hand side; in a room where cuttings about generals are shoved between the pages of the order book, a minion in brown overalls wanders in with a pair of immaculate boots, and details of regimental finery are pinned up haphazardly on the walls. Mr Ruddock has been at it for 60 years (though since he was first invalided out of the Army with "varicose veins on my tummy", he must have enlisted when he was about three); he recently ticked off a new Brigadier for fastening his Sam Browne the wrong way: "In my day you'd have been on a charge."

He says the higher up they get the less sensitive they are about things being second-hand, and there's a surprising amount of hiring, too: ex-officers going to weddings, ex-pilots celebrating the Battle of Britain, even fancy dress —though they always carefully put in a deliberate mistake on such occasions, lest anyone be accused of "personating". (And I met a mother who had bought a beautiful greatcoat in Crombie cloth for her long-haired son; as he put it on, some remaining insignia were

indignantly stripped from it by the trembling fingers of the salesman).

On the face of it, having every single officer's uniform individually made seems loony—and it's not even just the officers, the Sergeants' mess kits can be as fancy as any. And I simply don't believe the man at Gieves who said that any sort of ready-to-wear was impossible "because no two men have their waists in the same place"—if that were so, what about the second-hand? But one good argument was made for it by the Chairman of Alkit, possibly the biggest of the military outfitters, which has shops in garrison towns and regularly goes round the various messes laying out their wares for sale. If it were all done by the Government, standardized and centrally controlled with everything going through the Ministry's administrators, could it *possibly*, he asked be anything but four times as expensive? No.

The other argument's subtler. The dress of soldiers, all the idiotic little variations that mark the difference between one regiment and the next, are all part of that vital sense of identity which makes them feel as one with the Regiment; makes them willing to go out and do rash and revolting things rather than let down their brother warriors. Take that away, the argument goes, and they have to be brave and loyal for something far more remote and less acceptable, like a disliked Prime Minister or a home with the rain coming through the roof. Without the warrior's war-paint he isn't a warrior any more.

Only trouble is, all those intricate gold stripes and rosettes, all those tassels of a thousand knots are made by people like Miss Bignell of Gieves. And she is not only no younger than she used to be, but has started apprentice after apprentice without keeping one permanently: "I don't know *what* we'll do when she goes," moan her employers. And without her, and her like, what price the vital insignia?

It's an awesome thought that to bring the British Army leaderless to its knees, all the Russians really have to do is to shoot a few old women and muck up the pattern books. I just hope the thought hasn't occurred to them.

"I can't help wondering that there must be more to life than just wondering if there must be more to life."

BANX

MAKE IT SNAPPY

BILL TIDY grabs a bite of fast food

"*. . . and I've had four pizzas, ice cream and apple pie, coffee . . .*"

"*. . . it's cheap and you can bellow your order before you go in.*"

"*Poor tormented soul—it's fast alcohol he's looking for.*"

"*You've done it, Hoskins—the chair that no one can sit on for more than six minutes!*"

"If you don't stop saying 'One day my face'll be as famous as Colonel Sanders,' I'll belt you again!"

"Our Piccadilly outlet. Table 12. A man reading."

"Dad, Dad, Dad, can we take the jackets home?"

SPUDLAND 501 NEW POTATO FILLINGS

MISS KITTY WAITRESS SERVICE

"Damn, out on the pavement **again** before I could collect the Protection!"

ANTHONY BURGESS

Success

THE other day I picked up the latest edition of the *Pelican* survey of contemporary British fiction and found that I was still missing—along with, I think, John Fowles—from the index. I have never felt any particular chagrin about this neglect, but I would feel happier if the index indicated total neglect in the text itself (there's disgruntled dysphony for you). I mean, when you're totally ignored you know where you stand: you're too totally good for the ignorer. But in this survey my name turns up over and over again, not as a novelist but as a critic of novelists. "Mr Burgess (who has himself written the odd novel) says of Iris Murdoch . . ." That's how it goes, and I don't like it. Last spring I received, from the exquisite but powerful hands of Mrs Thatcher herself, an award as Critic of the Year. I had to take the award and smirk at the cameras, but I felt the wrong footing had led her and me and everybody to the wrong plateau, the one from which there is no descent. It was never my intention to be known as a critic. Criticism, or reviewing, is something done to pass the time or pay the gas bills. It's not really a vocation.

I regard my vocation, which I came to very late (at the same age as Conrad, but he had to learn English first), as that of novelist, and I have to consider now whether I have had any real success in it. The trouble with fiction is that there are two ways of looking at it—as a business and as an art. Just up the coast from me at Cannes, sitting glumly but royally on his yacht, is a man who has succeeded indubitably with the novel as a business. His name is Harold Robbins. He is, however, not satisfied with having sold a great number of copies of books about sex and violence: he wants to be regarded, on the strength of his evident popularity, as the greatest writer alive. Nobody will so consider him (he is not in any index of any survey that I know of) and this makes him somewhat sour. It does, of course, sometimes happen that the most popular novelist is also the best—Dickens, for instance; perhaps even Hemingway—but the one doesn't follow from the other. We expect great fiction to be too subtle or complex for popular acceptance. A good writer will often worry if his work goes into too many impressions: he will feel that he has not been subtle or complex enough. He will feel that he has been inattentive to his craft and turned out something like John Braine.

From the business angle I can point, though cautiously, to some small success. In twenty-five years of professional writing I have been able to make a living. Even if this means no more than being able to afford an egg for one's breakfast twice a week it is still a matter for pride: one has called no man *sir*, except perhaps a New York black cab-driver, and one has been able to telephone from one's bed at eleven in the forenoon and tell someone to go to hell. This living, however, has come from steady application to the craft, a determination to write at least one thousand words a day, and not at all from the kind of *réclame* that greets a *Catch-22* or a *Princess Daisy*. A lot of the money has come from journalism and from writing scripts for films that were never made. A fairly exiguous trickle has come from fiction. If there is any money in the bank it is there because I have gone on bullying a fairly small public into buying a Burgess book every year. I have had, in other words, to keep at it.

The trouble with me is that I provide evidence of affluence to the superficial reader of works of reference. I have three or four addresses, but that means only that I have had to leave one and move to another because of becoming *persona non grata* or discovering that the kidnappers are interested in my son, and certain governmental regulations (as in Malta) have forbidden my selling property. A colour supplement recently listed me with Ringo Starr and the tennis-player Borg as a typical tax-evader of Monaco. But low income is as good a reason as high for going to a taxless zone. If I could afford it, I would probably live in England. For every artist there is the fear that sooner or later he will be unable to produce art. He has no state pension and he has to look to a future without income. He must save what he can while he can, and the British tax system, which would be happier without self-employed artists, does not permit saving.

If I have a little money in various banks (I am not sure how little it is: this may well be a signal of affluence) I cannot point to a financial success commensurate with that of a Beatle or a Karajan or any other pop-musician. No millions, for God's sake. Success, then, must, if I *am* successful, lie elsewhere. If not in fiction as business, then in fiction as art? Who can say? Certainly not the fictional artist. I have produced about forty books, most of them novels or novellas, and I am not really satisfied with any of them. When critics express a like, or even greater, dissatisfaction, I can only nod glumly in agreement. The horrid truth, though, is that one cannot really make oneself any better. The results in one's work are less faults of artistic application than inbuilt and inextricable flaws in one's personal make-up. We would all write like Shakespeare or V. S. Naipaul if we could: not being Shakespeare or Naipaul rather hampers us.

THE glow of the sense of success comes, when it comes at all, if somebody has read one of my books (it is usually when that person is in a weakened state, typically in hospital), has found a fresh revelation of

the nature of life in that work, and is willing to express pleasure and admiration. Books, after all, are not written for critics but for people, especially when they are in a weakened state. That is real success, the feeling that the task of entertaining and enlightening at the same time has been adequately fulfilled. The kind of book that sells by the million rarely imparts to its readers the sense of epiphany: it has a different function and a good one—that of beguiling time and then inviting oblivion, a thing consumed with pips to spit out, no more. No matter how poor a writer is, if he has written a book which changes someone's life he has achieved the only sort of success worth having.

If a writer feels he is a success—he is known and read and even bought; American scholars write books about him; the reception clerk at the Algonquin knows his name—then he has a horrid sense that he is no longer travelling hopefully but has arrived. He has, in fact, reached one of those damned plateaux; he cannot climb any further and he certainly cannot go back to his old fearful and delectable struggles. I am thankful that I am not eligible for the Nobel Prize or the OM, the kind of success which says: "You've made it. We don't expect you to do any more. Now for heaven's sake leave it to the next generation." How can anybody—prize committee or critical synod—estimate what a writer is still capable of doing? Shakespeare got his critical accolade from Francis Meres when he was successful as a writer of sugared sonnets and romantic comedies; there he was, placed on the nation's Parnassus, finished, a success. How disappointed

Meres must have been when *Hamlet* and *King Lear* appeared. Success is a kind of death sentence.

The success of being known, which is success enough for many people, is not nowadays a thing to be honourably sought, since it is conferred instantaneously by a television appearance. Fame is neither here nor there. I have never yet been known to a British hotel receptionist or an airline agent. Giving my name to one of the latter, especially in America, I am usually genially asked: "Same as in Burgess Meredith?" or, in Britain, "Same as the chap who went over to the Russians?" Fame can be an aspect of success, but many of the most successful ventures of history have not brought fame. Milton accepted fame as the spur for writing well, but he meant fame for his books (and then only in the limited field of the learned and tasteful), never for himself. The great Murray, father of the Oxford English

Dictionary, repudiated fame with terrifying dignity.

Success, then, in the somewhat inflated sense which I'm imposing on it here, means a more than adequate reward for producing something that doesn't belong to the world of subsistence. A soufflé may be successful, but not in the way that a sonnet or a symphony is (both, as Oscar Wilde would say, equally useless). The man or woman who has produced successful work is himself or herself a success. The rewards, if financial, are not merely impertinent but injurious. Money means consumption, and consumption gets in the way of work. Shoals of letters of admiration have to be answered, and this means that there's less time for writing books. No wonder success brings depression.

To every artist who considers himself successful (as, with many reservations, I consider myself) there remains a prick of doubt about the road chosen. Perhaps the true sense of achievement was waiting in some other métier, the one that beckoned and was neglected. When I was young, before I decided that my métier was fiction, my ambition was to be a great composer of music. I worked moderately hard at the art and failed. Since becoming known as a writer I have been able to go back to my first love with some hope of having my work performed. But it is too late now to resume the old dreams of nine symphonies and five operas (although the next task I envisage for myself is a choral and orchestral setting of *The Wreck of the Deutschland*). I didn't work hard and long enough: if Polyhymnia (if that's the right muse) doesn't turn her back on me now, she grins rather than smiles at my music. But it is as a great British composer that I should like to have figured in the reference books, not as a critic who writes occasional novels, or as a novelist who helped to father a violent film, or (it happens occasionally) as someone who has achieved a moderate success with a large number of novels. What success has taught me is the extent of my failure.

ANTHONY BURGESS published his first book *Time for a Tiger* in 1956. Between that novel and his latest, *Earthly Powers*, he has produced some forty books, including several works of criticism and translations of French and Greek classics. He is a regular contributor to the book review pages of *The Observer* but is perhaps still most popularly known as the author of *A Clockwork Orange*. He lives in Monaco.

DAVID TAYLOR:

You Should Be So Lucky

MRS E. M. G. of Glos. writes: "I go to Bingo twice a week and have not failed to win something each time for nineteen weeks. I never could believe it is so lucky, as I never won anything before. Find enclosed 50p for another one."

What could have made it possible to knock down Mrs E. M. G. with a feather, according to the rest of this advertisement from Pixie Pens of St Austell, Cornwall, was a plastic ball-point pen, available in red, green, or blue, with a lucky Cornish pixie perched atop. Had she wanted a ball-point that writes black, the colour of Beelzebub, she'd have had to settle for a gold-plated lucky Irish leprechaun on the end. Either way, as Pixie Pens go on to point out: "Have you ever seen such value? Health, friends, wealth, love, happiness, success, use your lucky pixie pen for Bingo, football pools, love letters, exams, applications etc."

Just up the road in Swindon, Wilts., Mrs V. B. has stumbled on another snip and claims: "My husband could not believe it. I received my lucky cork on February 25th and on March 1st came up on Littlewoods pools, and on March 2nd went to Bingo and won £66.51!!" Swipe me if it isn't another winner from Messrs L. E. Fisher of Torquay, whose chunks of lucky Wishing Cork Tree have, recounts their ad, also amazed a mother from Boston, USA, who won a new Buick, stunned a lady from Bristol who lost her handbag containing £300 (sic) and other valuables *including a*

Piece of Lucky Cork and had the bag returned to her intact the same evening!! Well I'm blessed but—hang on—there's a housewife from Newark, it says here, who sent off for a monster slice of Lucky Cork and, stone the crows, three weeks later she won *two* football pools *and* her husband secured a very important post!!

All of which makes-you-think-doesn't-it testimonials I take from advertisements hard-selling the market for mail order hocus-pocus—suppliers to the superstitious and half-witted of everything from magical, hand-polished brass Joan the Wad charms, ancient gemstones of Occulus (as used by Pharaohs), herbal ointments for psoriasis, and a pyramid-shaped ring that's just the job for identifying the hidden forces emanating from people around you *and* "contains a SECRET COMPARTMENT which can be used to energise seeds or keep pills, diamonds and other small treasures" to offers for Fulbloom bust-enlarging cream, a paperback "amazing story of a man who purchased a new car with no money and the magic huna method by which he did it!!" and ". . . at last, the book that shows you in a no-nonsense, practical manner how to tap the vast power of your inner self to bring you all the money you need" just like the man who, says the ad, "worked as a waiter for low wages until he used Money Magnetism and now owns three restaurants of his own."

If there's a real mystery here, it's how such hokum gets past the Advertising Standards Authority which puts out posters urging all right-minded citizens to shop those people making claims that aren't honest, decent, truthful, accurate and so on. It may be thought that readers of such as *Old Moore's Almanack* are so far gone as to be untouched by sinister barminess, but listen to this loony library on offer to its readers from Finbarr Books of Folkestone, Kent: *The Miracle of Manaforce* promises "the startling revelation that you have THREE SELVES instead of one and can COMMAND them to bring you anything you want!" There's "The Mana Invisible Shield for protection from all danger and harm!" You can look forward to the day when you "gain unlimited power and control over people, animals, insects (sic) and plants through the Magic Energy Transference Ritual."

No? Well then, Gavin and Yvonne Frost, "leaders of over 12,000 witches", will part with "the secrets of MAGIC PSYCHIC POWERS" in their revelatory book, *Meta-Psychometry: Key to Power and Abundance*, and if and when you can put that down, you may care to turn to the *Modern Herbal Spellbook*, said to be the most complete compendium of "over 500 easy-to-do spells and rituals for gaining love, money, power over others, personal protection, etc., etc." and all for £2.75 post paid.

After that you may want to reach for an APAL—"a perfectly harmless imitation cigarette that you never light, just put it in your mouth when you have the urge to smoke and its soothing flavour will ease away the craving . . . *no morning coughs, no*

nerves, no tension AND you will be saving pounds and pounds . . . for that rainy day." The Health Culture Company of Bedford will send you "genuine unsolicited extracts of letters from grateful users" on request.

Send your name and birthday to Katrina in Hove and back will come "an Astroanalysis which will indicate your future prospects and quite likely offer a solution to at least one of your problems." Marie-Simone, of the Zodiac Lodge in Sutton, Surrey, offers you your very own lucky number *and* her "famous Tibetan TALLI Charm on a necklace, described by a famous writer as a MONEY MAGNET." Harry Benjamin, meanwhile, claims to have sold over 200,000 copies of *Better Sight Without Glasses*, available from A. Thomas & Co. of Wellingborough, Northants., along with such best-sellers as *Diets To Help Colitis* and *Lecithin: The Fat Fighter*, or *Increase Your Height* and *Self-Defence In The Home*.

"Is YOUR HAIR worth a postage stamp?" wonders Arthur J. Pye, founder of the "world-famous consulting hair specialists of Lytham Road, Blackpool, whose methods have apparently caused many friends of Mr J. A. L. of Gosport to comment on the fine condition of his scalp. Of course, he could have sent off to Cathay of Bournemouth and received *four separate flasks* of "Arboreal Hair and Scalp Course" with his Turtle Oil cream, Floral Arbour tablets for the relief of catarrh and New Life Laxative. If friends didn't remark on the startling effects, he could always send off to the Effective Speaking Programme in Edinburgh and post them the answer to Why Are You A Bore?, or, then again, to the British Institute of Practical Psychology in London N5 for a copy of *I CAN and I WILL*, said to sort out "blushing, stammering, feeling inferior and trembling."

Well, as Winchance of Darwen, Lancs., sums up: "Nothing is impossible", not when you clutch their Prosperity Pebble or The Chant of The Keys, "said to open the door to Wealth, Health and Happiness PLUS details of a winning treble chance method which is quite unlike any other."

You should be so lucky.

"Is there someone else, Gervaise, or do you really go to the Crusades every Thursday?"

The Diary of a Tulip

A field, February 20

Well, dear diary, today I and some of the others got born. Premature, as it turns out. They say it is all down to it being a mild winter but you could have fooled me. It is bloody freezing. You would think the town hall would do something. One minute we are as cosy as pigs in swill with our bulbs all wrapped in coconut fibre and peat, the next minute we are exposing our little shoots to the elements. It is totally unacceptable, this is. Why can't they put up a shed round us? It will not be the nurserymen's fault if the whole hectare of us don't go down with frostbite.

Still, thank goodness for small mercies, at least I was not born in a bowl. I have heard some terrible stories about being born in bowls. It is medieval, what goes on. Either you are stuck in a boot cupboard with bits of linoleum over your head and left to shrivel up, or you are deliberately left out on a windowsill where if it is not the birds pecking at you it is the cat peeing on you.

There is an old bulb lying about in this field which keeps saying that it has seen tulips come and it has seen tulips go, and according to this old bulb, even worse than getting born in a bowl in somebody's house is getting born in a jam-jar in an infants' school. That is when these sadistic teachers slice you in two to show the little perishers how you grow. I think vivisection should be banned.

February 28

Nothing much happened today except that a kid tiptoed through us. Waiting to flower is very boring, you would think they would lay on some amenities. There is nothing for a tulip to do except wave about, and you cannot do a lot of that when you are only a shoot. There should be some recreational facilities such as bingo or free music lessons.

The old bulb says that things will liven up soon enough, and then we will all wish they hadn't. Do not know what the silly old fool is rambling on about.

To pass the time, some of us had a discussion about what colour we would like to be when we come out. The one next to me on the right-hand side says it would like to be yellow, to go with its green stem. The one on the left-hand side says black, now that's an unusual colour. I think I have got born with a bunch of pansies. Speaking for myself, I would like to be red. A red tulip could hold meetings and get itself elected convener. I could then set about improving conditions for tulips. Perhaps this is my destiny.

March 7

We are all yellow. So much for that bit of excitement. As well as being very conventional, it is also very confusing. Fancy having ten thousand tulips in a field and all of them having to address each other as "Yellow one". It is not on.

The yellow one that wanted to be black reckons we should all have names, such as Petal or Blossom. This idea fair made the old bulb choke into its anti-mildew solution. If God had wanted us to be called Petal or Blossom, says the old bulb, He would have given us hooves.

Personally, I think we should have numbers. That is what we will do come the revolution, which I have decided to go ahead with even though technically I am not red. I shall be Numero Uno tulip.

March 11

I have been trying to rationalise the case for declaring war on the daffs in the next field. If the tulip collective could get its stems on that field, we could apply for planning permission for a combined leisure centre, old bulbs' luncheon club and branch library devoted to the works of Karl Marx and Percy Thrower.

Up to press, I have not been able to get the broad mass of tulips interested. They do not seem to give a monkey's how they are exploited. Bees can enter the collective bold as brass and guzzle pollen till it comes out of their nostrils, but do my fellow-tulips utter one peep in protest, let alone take appropriate action? I have seen lichen with more go in it.

Early this morning, though, something happened which may change the course of tulip history. As soon as the sun came out, Registered Tulip No. 1981/7,942/B6—that's the yellow one that wanted to be a black one—folds one of its leaves akimbo, puckers up its petals and starts poncing round and round on its stalk like Mother Nature's answer to Larry Grayson. Suddenly this zonking great gnarled hand reaches down out of nowhere and plucks it. Finito. Just like that.

Old Bulb No. 903 cracks on it was one of the nurserymen who had spotted an isolated case of tulip blight, but I know different. It was a totally unprovoked attack by those bloody daffodils in the next field. The nurserymen are merely their tools and lackeys. If I can get this message across, the tulips' long uphill struggle for recognition as a meaningful negotiating body will be away to the races.

Tragedy though it was, the premature departure of Tulip No. 1981/7,942/B6 for the great compost heap in the sky may prove to be a blessing in disguise.

March 27

Once again the daffodils have failed to respond in any manner, shape or form to our totally reasonable and justified demands. They will not even sit round the conference patch with us.

It is bloody intolerable. All we are asking them to do is to shove off out of it and grow in some woods or a ditch somewhere, thereby relinquishing territory which morally, historically and geographically belongs to the tulip collective. Unofficially, and at grassroots level, we have approached rank-and-file daffs offering them protection against slugs in their new environment, but

"Let's dispense with the formalities, shall we? We're all on first-name terms here!"

for all the feedback we are getting we might as well be talking to the big tractor thing that has suddenly appeared in the gateway of the tulip collective commune.

The lads are now behind me one hundred per cent, but we need the bargaining strength of DDT behind us. If I could get a crop spray and a few hundred gallons of unadulterated weedkiller into that daffodil field, it would be a different story.

Old Bulb No. 903 says that trouble will come soon enough without us going out looking for it. Such defeatist talk is unconstructive and not in the best interests of tulips. I am beginning to suspect that Old Bulb No. 903 is not a tulip bulb at all but an onion planted by the daffs to spread alarm and despondency.

March 28
It is terrible.

At dawn, there were 10,000 of us swaying proudly in the breeze, all hale and healthy except for a touch of white fly on our western flank. By 0900 hours the flower of English tulip-hood lay massacred. The big tractor thing, equipped with sharp blades like Boadicea's bloody chariot, simply mowed into us. Talk about Passchendaele: not a tulip is left standing.

Before getting cut up like a pickled beetroot, so-called Old Bulb No. 903 managed to gasp: "It is what I have been warning you all about. It is the Mother's Day Massacre. It happens every year. You are all going to be transported to Nine Elms and sold at inflated prices. The same thing will happen to the daffs on Easter Sunday, mark my words. It is fate."

Fate my back petals. It is the daffodils. Having got wind of our impending defence strategy that would have ploughed them into the ground like so much fertiliser, they persuaded the nurserymen to take reprisal action with the big tractor thing.

Their turn will come. If so-called Old Bulb No. 903 was not lying through its skins, the Easter Rising will make the daffodil field look like bloody Agincourt.
A vase, March 29
Of my terrible journey by farm-truck to Nine Elms, then by stinking closed van to a stall outside Fulham Broadway tube station, I will say nothing, except that I have raffia marks on my leaves that will stay with me for the rest of my life. I have finished up on a mantelpiece in a semi-detached house in Parsons Green. Working conditions are terrible. There is no sunlight to speak of and minimum care regulations are not adhered to. There is an azalea employed here that has not had a drink for three days. There is a rubber plant that has been allowed to get thick with dust. There is a mother-in-law's tongue that cries piteously for potting compost. To cap it all, the woman who owns the house is barmy. When there is no one in the room, she talks to us. She says, "All right, you lot—bloom! If you don't bloom, you're going in the dustbin." These threats are provocative, uncalled-for and unacceptable. Wait till we get some flower power organised around here.

A dustbin, April 3
Today the azalea, the mother-in-law's tongue and myself were cast aside like worn-out gloves, the mad-woman having stated to us, "All right, you have had your chance, you cannot say you have not been warned." According to some grass-clippings I have just spoken to, the bag of old tea-leaves on which we have been tossed is only a temporary billet, and we are destined to finish up on a corporation tip. This, apparently, is where cut flowers go to die. We will see about that. The time for moderation is over. We militants must now show our true colours—in my case, yellow, unfortunately. How I wish I had been born red.

(The tulip's diary ends at this point.)

"My one ambition is to evolve into something that's capable of making the occasional witty remark."

LET'S PARLER FRANGLAIS!

À la Kiosque de Fags et Mags

Kioskman: Oui, monsieur?
Monsieur: Oui. Une boîte d'allumettes, svp.
Kioskman: Bon. Nous avons les following categories:– i. Les bons matches d'Angleterre, dans une boîte avec un rotten joke à la flipside . . .
Monsieur: Non, merci.
Kioskman: ii. Les book-matches, fabriqués de wet cardboard, qui incinèrent votre thumbnail . . .
Monsieur: Non, merci, ditto . . .
Kioskman: iii. Une boîte de matches importés de Russie ou Finlande, contents avérages 14, qui sont un hazard de feu dans toutes les langues . . . .
Monsieur: Non, likewise.
Kioskman: Ou iv. Une grande boîte de 1,000 matches de kitchen, qui tombent sur le floor à chaque opening.
Monsieur: Pas likely. Donnez-moi un lighter français chuck-away.
Kioskman: Bon. Voilà.
Monsieur: Et un bar de choco.
Kioskman: Nous avons le Twister (choco de mint), le Hunky (choco de biscuit), le Honeymoon Special (Hunky avec fancy wrapping), et le Big-Bite (choco de macho).
Monsieur: Je désire le plain chocolat.
Kioskman: Ah, monsieur, nous n'avons pas le plain chocolat. C'est old-fashioned.
Monsieur: Alors, donnez-moi un bar de choco français chuck-away.
Kioskman: Bon. Quelque chose d'else?
Monsieur: Oui. Une plume de point de balle.
Kioskman: Français chuck-away?
Monsieur: Of course.
Kioskman: There vous allez.
Monsieur: Vous avez d'autres choses françaises et chuck-away?
Kioskman: Beuh . . . non. Ah, oui! Les Gitanes . . . les singles de Sacha Distel . . . les purple cachous avec flaveur d'after-shave . . . les miniatures de plonk . . . les remainders de Tin-Tin . . .
Monsieur: Je les prends tous!
Kioskman: Bon. Ça fait £14.60 . . . À propos, vous êtes un loony millionaire français ou quoi?
Monsieur: Non. Je fais la recherche pour la publication: *Lequel?* Vous êtes nominé comme un best buy.
Kioskman: Ah non, ah non! Si vous mettez ma kiosque dans *Lequel?* j'aurai une invasion de weekend-shoppeurs français.
Monsieur: C'est curieux. Toutes les kiosques disent ça.
Kioskman: C'est parce que les Français sont les shop-lifters les plus ingénieux de l'Europe.
Monsieur: C'est vrai?
Kioskman: Oui. Ils viennent over here et *(Censoré par le Board de Relations de Race).*

ARTS Counsel

MELVYN BRAGG
meets Martin the Movie Brat

A SMALL, let us emphasise small, let us not be rude but say we are referring to someone who, even at the age of 38, which he is, would be gently passed down to the front of a crowd to watch the procession go by; this well below average height man (and I point this up not to mock a feature but for the greater purpose of eventual irony) lopes into the room—shoulders not merely hunched but bent, head almost mowing the carpet—making himself look even *smaller!* He is wearing an outfit that would be a credit to a diminutive bookie's runner in a Damon Runyon yarn. His beard and moustache, though, come out of those proud Jacobean soldier portraits—full, fat, sleek black, with a cared-for look not too evident in the unhairy parts of the observable anatomy. He hoists up an arm, calls me "sir", smiles charmingly, collapses in a chair and treats himself for asthma.

This, ladies and gentlemen, is MR MARTIN SCORSESE, macho film director of the day, in whose hands and under whose influence Mr Robert de Niro, matchless macho of Manhattan, has bopped, slugged, stabbed, shot, slaughtered, battered and been battered, shot, stabbed, slugged and bopped: and almost slaughtered—several times as if to make up for not being quite finally done in. S'enough but no snuff. They're friends and business partners, after all. Just two lads out on the town.

All that's a bit unfair. Scorsese's a boy from Little Italy, downtown New York, below the street numbers, amazed to find himself making films instead of watching them or, later, studying them. His cinema literacy is so obsessive as to be comical: the afternoon I spent with him he literally could not have a cup of tea without remembering the scene where . . . and the shot . . . and did you notice? . . . and then there was . . . and she was wearing . . . and you know what *happened* to her? He's done a bag of movies—from exploitation movies for Corman to documentaries about his own family, to *New York New York* and *Alice*

Doesn't Live Here Anymore and then the shank of American-Italian street movies, *Mean Streets, Taxi Driver*; and now, in much the same vein, but black and white, *Raging Bull.*

There's a lot to say about Scorsese as one of the Movie Brats—the first generation of university film students to become Hollywood directors; all the homages and idealism; the resurrection of the Italian ideal of the family in such domestic dramas as *The Godfather* and *Mean Streets*; the interest in technology—*Star Wars, Close Encounters*: the Apocalyptic Budget—Gone with the Backing Syndrome; the ability—especially in Scorsese—to thread personal obsessions through commercial movies—that attempted mix between John Ford and Rossellini. But that's meat for another column.

There's much, too, to be said about Scorsese's current mission to save colour film for posterity. He had discovered that colour does not hold: to keep it fast needs thought and care, the two fairies furthest from film city. Then, there's his own sense of his films as the working-through of his Catholicism—"You have to redeem yourself on the streets," says the reverent Catholic hero in *Mean Streets*—it's a voice-over, though, spoken by Scorsese himself. Enter Graham Greene as a hero and pathfinder and it's an interesting maze—but no. Nor even; here, now, yet, the powerful but strange case of Mr de Niro. His potency in some parts is undeniable. Yet the way in which he prepares for the parts by *doing* it, provokes thought. For *Taxi Driver* he, well, drove a New York taxi for a while—OK? For *Raging Bull* he went into the gym for over twelve months and came out, boxing buffs say, with a real reputation. (STOP PRESS: The career of Mr Robert de Niro, the distinguished American Film Actor came to a dramatic end yesterday off the island of Oko Yono. He was following his usual practice of preparing himself scrupulously for the part in his new film—KAMIKAZE PILOT . . .)

Violence is the subject. If you were not fast enough to flick away your eyes in *Mean Streets*, you would have seen blood gushing from a nasty neck wound; in *Taxi Driver* you would have seen mayhem as de Niro with guns and bayonet savaged a clump of pimps; in *Raging Bull* you can see noses being knocked from one side of the face to another, bodies battered, insensibility exultantly induced.

Scorsese's first line of explanation is to refer to a remark by, I think, Sam Fuller (another cine-hero) to the effect that emotional violence is more distressing than physical violence. Yet the scene chosen by Scorsese to illustrate this point culminated in a man banging the head of another (senseless) man against the marble base of a statue. There's no ducking the fact of the act. A better line of explanation—and one which is hard to disagree with, however distasteful its consequences might be—is that which states the claim for greater "realism". Blood, so it goes, unspilt, and bullets unseen to penetrate, are immoral because unreal. Violence represented as

cardboard cut-out clouts and bloodless deaths from unlikely guns, is a cheat and, if the argument holds up, such a cheat can only encourage imitation. The *real* thing, the real nasty business of it all has to be seen to be avoided—well . . . And well again . . . Scorsese told me that the terrible slaughterhouse at the end of *Mean Streets* could have looked much worse. So there's further to go. I can see the claim of realism—both in itself (almost all great rebirths of art have used "greater realism" as their cry and their dynamic) and in its lack of falsity.

Yet the glamour-chic of violence cannot be sidestepped. We *know* that, realistic though it seems, no one is being hurt but us. La Motta might tell de Niro that he could be a good fighter but he doesn't step into the ring with a man determined to stop him. Yet we go to a cinema to meet a man determined to shock us. And in some of us, something in us wants it, some of the time. That, though, could be the justification for public hanging. It is the gap between the *faking* that is going on screen and the gut slap which is being served to us watching a screen which is somehow worrying. Would it be "better" if they really hurt each other? That's absurd. Yet they *do* set out to deliberately hurt us. Do they want to shift the balance of our finer feelings or the bowels of our baser motion? There's the centre of it. They'll claim the first—usually —and be sure that in many cases they will achieve the second.

So in two ways it leaves a nasty taste in the mouth. For if we are being played about with—then who do they think they are? It is far from being an easy one, though, and I would like to come back to it next week via the other face of contemporary America—Goodie to de Niro's Baddie —Robert Redford.

"Stop looking so smug!"

Radio 3

**121 5kHz/247 m
VHF: 90–92.5**

8.10* Stereo
The Likely Lads
Nothin' Ever Happens In Novgorod!
The wireless's wackiest duo are back in another season of Rimsky 'n' Korsakoff, starring **Rowan Atkinson** as Biff Rimsky and **Max Bygraves** as Brad Korsakoff, the likely lads from Novgorod. Why does Rimo keep writing letters telling all to César Cui? This makes Korsie jealous. Cui, Mouse Moussorgsky, Badger Borodin, Bags Balakireff and the rest of the gang at the Petrograd Free School of Music have an awakening desire to explore more deeply the mysteries of tonal art but suddenly Korsie wants to join the navy. "Cor blimey, Korsie," pleads Rimo, "one hit symphony and think of all that lovely lolly!" But the call of the sea seems to dull Korsie's interest in the rigorous and assiduous study of counterpoint, fugue and lovely lolly. "Nothin' ever happens in Novgorod," Korsie laments.
BBC Liverpool
(Repeated next Sunday, Monday, Tuesday, Wednesday, Thursday and Friday)

11.35 Stereo
The Salzburg Ruby
A Wolfgang Amadeus Mozart Mystery
Radio's fanciest dressed detective, along with his colourful, wisecracking sidekick, Frank Haydn, are off on another caper this week, investigating the theft of a valuable ruby from the boudoir of Princess Lichnowsky (Pamela Stephenson)

Whacky Frank Haydn joins Radio 3's ace composer-sleuth for another Wolfgang Amadeus Mozart Mystery—tonight's episode: The Salzburg Ruby.

when suddenly the composer-'tec is taken out by his old pal, Salieri, and given a little too much to drink. Was it Salieri who poisoned Wolfgang? What about Swieten? Or, for that matter, Süssmayer? All had equal reasons to be jealous of the way he could wash his hair squeaky clean and still have it manageable. Is the great detective, in fact, really dead or is he alive and well and supplying Muzack for Tesco's?
Black and white only
BBC Manchester
Mozart, One of The Best by Benny Green, see page 8.

VHF only

9.5 Stereo
The Right of Spring
by Howard Brenton, Nigel Williams. David Hare and Jim Allen
Rowan Atkinson, Penelope Keith, Pamela Stephenson
"The workers have a right, the right to strike but . . .
"This is the story of a workers' take-over that never had a chance, and the reason for that was simple."

Stravinsky, composer, social worker, and strike leader ..... Rowan Atkinson
Alexandra, a Tsarina ....
.... Penelope Keith
Rosa Luxembourgh, the worker's sweetheart .... Pamela Stephenson
Directed by Tony Garnett

"Cor blimey, I was filmin' a dole queue in Brum when I got to talkin' to this geezer an' he started tellin' me about this old time Russian geezer name of Igor Stravinsky, who was sort of the Stones and the late great much lamented John Lennon—that man was a saint, an absolutely bleedin' saint who only wanted peace

and so Reagan and Haig had him shot down and there are a lot of similarities between Vladimir Ilytch Lennin and John Winston Lennon and I think we bring that out in this play only I don't like calling it a play I mean what's 'play' about the workers' struggle? I see this more as a film without pictures, know what I mean? Anyway it was all there in this story this geezer was tellin' me in the dole queue in Brum, which incidentally is my hometown where they actually had the 11-plus when I was a kid, can you imagine that? How's that for Thatcherism? and anyway it was all there in this geezer Stravinsky's story of union bashing and lock-outs in Tsarist Russia. I mean it was just like neo-fascist neo-Thatcherite Britain today. Fantastic! I was over the moon. An' to think I never heard of this geezer Stravinsky before! I mean how's that for state school education in Britain today, keepin' the facts from the sons and persons of the workers! But I'm over the moon about this one."

See Page 8 Tony Garnett Over The Moon. Benny Green visits the director of The Right of Spring.

Ceefax sub-titles on page 170
Book (same title), £85.50, from bookshops

9.50 New Series
Bloody Mary and The Preacherman
"Ye are a sinful woman, a daughter of Jezebel and spawn of the Scarlet Woman of Babylon but I like you." So spoke John Knox, firebrand Protestant leader, when he first met Mary, Queen of Scots, who was *(Benny Green writes)* not only the hated Roman Catholic monarch but also a top notch musical composer of her day whose songs *Las! en mon doux Printemps* and the catchy, vital *Monsieur le Provost des Marchands* were popular standards of their day, played by all the big bands, and—it is perhaps a little known fact—were greatly influential on the work of such modern masters as George Gershwin and his lovely wife, Ira. Indeed the lilting counterpoint of Mary, the Q of S's tunes can be found echoed in *Summertime*, from the musical comedy *Showboat*, in which the lovely, haunting song, *He's Just My Bill An Ordinary Kind of Guy* was written by none other than P. G. ("Plum") Wodehouse, a great favourite of George Bernard Shaw, who was a friend of the great Gene Tunney. Shaw, you may be surprised to know, was at one time a serious contender for the amateur middleweight championship, although he never met George and Ira Gershwin. It was this unusual combination of being a queen of a

country—even a country like only Scotland—with a definite and very real talent for musical composition of a highly professional standard which led me to write this soap opera about the platonic love affair between Knox and the Queen of Scotland. Or have I got the wrong Queen of Scotland? Mary, a Scottish queen ....
.... Penelope Keith
Knox, a preacher .... Rowan Atkinson
BBC Wales

10.5 Stereo
A Night On Bare Mountain

MOUSSORGSKY

A sit-com with Country & Western flavour
(for details see Tuesday page 6)

Book (same title) by Desmond Wilcox, £35.95, from bookshops

10.15 Stereo
Allegro My Maestro
Episode 86 of Radio 3's continuing saga of the life, the loves, and the music of Ludwig van Beethoven. Last week the BBC Nine O'Clock News was interrupted with a news-flash that L.V. Beethoven had gone deaf. Who made L.V. deaf? Or did he merely plug his ears with wax himself in order to fool his hated enemy Steibelt, who had the nerve to challenge L.V. to a piano improvisation contest in Prague in 1798? What is Prince Lichnowsky up to? For that matter what is Prince Lobkowitz up to? And who are the counts, Razumowsky and Brunswick, and the Baron von Gleichestein? And what will L.V. do to revenge himself on Frau von Breuning who said, "That's kind of a gross fugue you've written"? Beethoven, a deaf pianist.................
.... Rowan Atkinson
Countess Waldstein, an haunty but loveable lady .... Penelope Keith
Modern Masters of the Musical Stage Who Have Lifted From Beethoven *(writes Benny Green)* see page 38.

See Op. 101, 106, 109, 110, 111, 115, 124, 127, 130, 131, and 135

JOHN WELLS:

Thatcher in the Rye

A Union Jack in snow white, blood red and vivid navy blue fills the screen, fluttering and snapping in a stiff breeze: then, to the distant strains of a Thirties-style German march and the insistent chanting of a hundred thousand voices "Thatch-er! Thatch-er! Thatch-er!" the Face of the Leader is superimposed on the flag, her upper lip lifted in a smile. Over this, the title in Daily Telegraph Bold Gothic—"THE TORY WAY PART XVI—EDUCATION".

A sudden roar of merriment, and the screen is filled with porous-nosed revellers in three-piece suits and upswept moustaches, swaying to and fro in a state of reckless inebriation. Some, shorter, balder, and more melancholy, seem unsteady on their feet, and liable at any moment to be borne under by the crush. Others, heavier and more energetic, haul themselves hand over hand across mountainous, garishly-painted Tory ladies of the night. A caption, "The El Piranha Rooms, Hendon". Tousled, slightly the worse for wear, but otherwise the perfect matinée idol, Education Minister Marsh Carlsberg de L'Isle fights his way towards the camera and treats us to a view of his bridgework.

Carlsberg: Society. Well, to be more precise, the North Hendon Used Car Dealers' Artistic Appreciation Society. (Beer cascades over his head, cries of "Sorry old chummy," etc.) But typical of the Tory Society we pledged ourselves at the last election (Inaudible witticisms and cheers) to protect and to foster. Because—make no mistake about

it—this society is a fragile and sophisticated one (Eighteen-stone barmaid passed over the heads of the crowd smiling at camera) that is constantly under threat. It is the purpose of this series of films to identify that threat, wheresoever it may come from. (Looks fiercely into camera, then consults small bald reveller who has appeared under his armpit) Was that all right? (Reveller collapses, but there are reassuring cries of "Bloody terrific, Minister, have another one!" from off-screen.)

We find ourselves at floor level, menaced by several hundred babies of various races, predominantly white, dribbling and puking their way towards us across the floor of a recently vandalised hospital. A caption: "THEM". Threatening chords, the film slowed down to emphasise the mood of horror. Carlsberg's voice is heard off.

Carlsberg (Off): Every day, the little creatures in this one room alone consume enough carbohydrates to supply the El Piranha Rooms, Hendon, with potato crisps for a full six minutes. Do not be deceived: these are not babies in the sense that we Tories know them—pink, self-reliant, responsible little citizens being carried past by the au pair girl at drinks time. These are clinging, work-shy layabouts, in many cases unable to stand on their own feet, a permanent drain on taxpayers' money that could be spent on lining up the gin-and-tonics on the bar at the El Piranha Rooms, Hendon, and creating more wealth in the private sector. What is worse, they

"But what if it should fall into the wrong hands?"

expect to be educated. And that is where I come in . . .

A door opens at the far end of the room. Carlsberg enters, wearing a gas-mask and protective rubber clothing, and wades purposefully towards us.

They are not prepared to contribute funds, pay for their round, except in terms of Income Tax which is vitally needed to pay for incentives to Big Earners. Which is why, as a Conservative, I have to put my foot down.

Puts foot down, strangled cries from the floor.

A fruit barrow, with bewhiskered spiv. Caption: "An Educationalist in the Market Place".

Rogue-Byceson: Ullo. My old china Marsh Carlsberg de L'Isle has set us a bit of a poser there. Only so many bites to be had at the old teacher's apple. Fair's fair, those bites must go to those who can afford them. (*Polishes Golden Delicious on sleeve, demolishes it with three gargantuan chomps, tosses apple-core over shoulder and chokes, remainder of speech incomprehensible.*)

We discover Carlsberg in front of a blackboard. Caption: "The Commercial Sector". Various public schoolboys loaf about in attitudes of nervous exhaustion, puffing at cigarettes and studying coloured brochures advertising the El Piranha Rooms, Hendon.

Carlsberg: Thank you, Rogue-Byceson. It is for this reason that we plan to introduce the idea of Student Loans. By borrowing the money to attend schools like this—in view of necessary cut-backs in the state sector, probably more like this: (*Caption sequence shows views of vandalised comprehensive recently gutted by fire*)—the student will no longer represent a drain at any stage—urchin, boot-boy or young hooligan—on the pockets of responsible members of our society.

A brief glimpse of the El Piranho Rooms, where revelry is on the increase and champagne is being opened. Then the outside of an Employment Exchange, where Rogue-Byceson stands muffled against the cold in front of shivering queue.

Rogue-Byceson: In the present somewhat bracing economic climate, you may be wondering, how is the student, on completion of his studies, going to pay us back if he cannot find the kind of cushy number in which to get up to the usual union high-jinks?

Exterior Wormwood Scrubs. Carlsberg pushes open studded wooden door.

Carlsberg: Conservatives have thought about that. Already dramatic reductions have been made in the prison population, much of which has been reabsorbed into our society—in most cases the North Hendon U.C.D.A.A.—in anticipation of the influx of young bankrupts. No Tory Government, however, is going to tolerate the burden of keeping these work-shy monkeys in luxury for the rest of their lives. They will be re-educated for useful work—probably behind the bar at the El Piranha Rooms, Hendon—securing yet another vital Tory economy. By the end of the century we hope to have wound up the whole education racket entirely.

We return to the El Piranha Rooms, Hendon, where various distinguished academics in broad arrows and manacles are seen serving shorts before the chandelier collapses under the weight of revelry. Caption: "The Tory Way—You Know It Makes Sense", patriotic music and slow fade to black.

THE "EMBASSY PLUS" COMPREHENSIVE COMPENSATION PLAN

CLAIM FOR JUST AND SUBSTANTIAL DAMAGES CONSEQUENTIAL UPON INDEFENSIBLE AGGRESSION AND RUINATION OF GOOD CARPETS BY AGENTS OF IMPERIALIST SUBVERSION TRAMPLING OVER DIPLOMATIC AND HOLY PREMISES AS THE RESULT OF ACCIDENTAL TERRORIST SIEGES

TO BE COMPLETED AND BROADCAST IN FULL—

1. Was damage to the embassy property caused by Fire, Flood, Riot, Civil Commotion, Explosion, Burst Pipes, Act of War, Smoke, Malicious Damage, Negligence, Falling Masonry, Armoured Boots, Unwarranted Incitement or Fomenting of Mindless Religious Fervour, Act of God, Para-military Bombardment, Rust, Beetle Infestation, Wanton Destruction or Vandalism by Fanatically Twisted Terrorists or Accidental Damage from Stun Grenades, including Consequential Spoilage from Blood, Choking Gases, Spilled Urine and Condensation from Sweat and Stumbling over Corpses? ANSWER YES OR NO...

2. Who started it?...

3. Is the embassy property used solely for accredited diplomatic dealings and NOT in any part used for the purposes of illicit or clandestine trading, including bulk handling of contraband, confiscated goods or laundered money, or for espionage, assassination squad training, storage of arms and narcotics or under-priced consumer durables, NEITHER for the incarceration of enemies of Islam, exchange of forged currencies, systematic torture of alleged relatives of usurped ruling faction, dissemination of propaganda or gnashing of teeth? IF YES AND NO, please attach further details ....
....
....

4. Is any part of the embassy structure or its surrounding compound in regular use as an assembly point for howling or rampaging mobs of demented, gun-toting, crazed so-called students? ....

5. Please itemise any specific damage to furnishings, fittings, personal effects, walls, ceilings, contents of freezer or safe, long-range transmitters, livestock, camping and sub-aqua equipment, sash-cords, binoculars, infra-red scanners, stop-cocks, Kalashnikov automatic rifles, equipment used for music or torture, skylights, loose slates, personal jewellery, franking machines or human limbs as a direct result of impact from boots worn on combat duty by members of the security forces ....
....

6. Estimate of gross costs of damage incurred as a result of blundering interference by busybody crews from *News at Ten*, other intermediaries, police psychologists, representatives of neutral governments, personnel from nearby pizza parlours, PO engineers, representatives of NOW! magazine etc..............
....

7. Are there any circumstances relating to your own or your colleagues' occupation, habits, health or bodily powers, stupidity, recklessness, inflammatory bent, tit-headed encouragements of hooligan revolutionary zeal, self-protective criminal double-thinking or any other material madness which might render you specially liable to accident, disablement, or having your silly head kicked in?..
....

8. Do the sums herein claimed represent the full replacement cost of diplomatic chattels and do you undertake to stop at that and to refrain from demanding further millions from the stashed away coffers of deposed former rulers, OR blood from stones, or still further humiliation of civilised governments already bending over backwards to save your face AND undertake to continue to supply as much oil as is reasonable at a price that makes some kind of sense? ANSWER YES OR NO AND ENDORSE IN BLOOD OF TWO OR MORE WITNESSES WHO MUST BE ALIVE AT THE TIME OF SIGNING:....................
....

SHOP TALK

**BARRY HUMPHRIES
on
Bookbinders**

EVERY Frenchman has a binder. They buy their books in unlovely paperback editions and only if a volume gives pleasure is it stiffened for storage. Although I have never visited France and see no reason to do so, I understand that every parade of shops there boasts a bookbindery. The average French housewife on a morning's shopping excursion will, between her visits to *patisserie* and *charcouterie*, pop into the local *Relieur* with her soft old Celines and Sartres and emerge with her stiffened Sagans and Simenons. The French, it seems, like to feel part of the publishing process and I belive even the humblest onion-stoled, loaf-toting Gallic cyclist spends as much time choosing the gilded leather raiment for a favourite author as his English counterpart spends at his turf accountant or Chinese take-away.

The traditional home of nudity displays a paradoxical coyness when it comes to exposing a bare book collection. English and Australian readers are less prudish and only a fastidious minority seems to care how its literature is clad. If you don't believe me, stop anyone in Regent Street and ask them to recommend a good binder. The chances are they will produce a hip flask of kaolin and sympathise with your condition or else direct you to some Soho specialist in restraining devices. I once asked an artful cab driver to direct me to the nearest West End binder. "You probably want Bond Street, mate," he replied sapiently.

Will it surprise my readers to learn that I regularly employ the services of several bookbinders in most hemispheres? There is no more delicious respite from a busy and fretful professional life than to visit the invariably recondite premises devoted to this esoteric craft. Presentation volumes to royalty, school prizes, and special commissions by noble libraries and learned institutions still provide Britain's diminishing band of fine binders with their bread and butter but a handful of discerning collectors such as myself still furnish them with the occasional smear of marmalade, if this viscous conserve may properly be evoked in connection with the conservation of the printed word. For the exquisitely attired volumes which issue from these fragrant old world ateliers should under no circumstances be fondled at the breakfast table.

My first visit to a bookbinder took place over twenty years ago in the South-East Asian city of Sydney. A cherished booklet of supernatural tales purchased from a sixpenny barrow had been inadvertently mauled by a marsupial and required immediate treatment. With the sorry little volume before me, its flimsy covers half devoured by a slavering rogue wombat, I frenziedly consulted the yellow pages of a softback telephone directory in search of the address of a reputable book restorer and hastened thither with my injured copy of *The Monk and the Hangman's Daughter*.

The rude Australian artisan who accepted this commission was a far cry indeed from the refined and dedicated persons who now caringly clothe my everyday reading matter. This man was obviously a binder of the "brutalist" school accustomed to ledgers and inventories, for when my gnawed rarity was restored to me it was crudely encased in chapped and hairy calfskin, reeking of knacker's yard and glue-pot, its fore-edges splashed and freckled with red ink and its fly leaves madly marbled in the manner of an old school exercise book. My mutilated masterpiece had been bandaged rather than bound and a task requiring the skills of a plastic surgeon had been performed by the veriest old sawbones.

Since that early experience I have selected my binders with the greatest care, assigning to a chosen few throughout the world the task of refurbishing my library. My books on travel go to a specialist in Bologna who reserves for me the finest of Levant goatskins; my poets are ensheathed by a Portuguese craftsman in Coimbra whose brother-in-law in a Lisbon backstreet elaborately tools their slender spines with gold leaf from Germany. As I write, the postman has delivered an enticing parcel gaudy with the philatelic emblems of Taiwan, which no doubt contains my latest consignment of *fin de siècle* Belgian erotica now discreetly, albeit sumptuously, bound in seasoned ape hide. A skilled old scoundrel in Vienna labours even now at his bench on folios devoted to the Black Arts which for

"I'm sorry, son, but it was kinder to put your lemming out of its misery."

absurdly superstitious reasons no other binder in Europe dares to handle. A firm in Bath have proved unequalled in envelluming my volumes of reasty curiosa whilst my extensive collection of books and pamphlets on the conservation of Australian wildlife is preserved in fine grained platypus skin culled by a clandestine Tasmanian operative. Run-of-the-mill novels and bedside browsing matter are handsomely refurbished by a famous old firm whose venerable premises occupy the garret of a crumbling Soho warehouse.

But in leaving a work to be bound here or indeed with any of my bookmen I must resign myself to its loss for a long while—sometimes even a decade—since the materials which are required for a "special job" are not always readily available. I have under glass a perverse work of the imagination published over eighty years ago and bound in human skin. In one of his notorious catalogues Leonard Smithers—Beardsley's printer—apologising for the enormous price of this volume states that "... owing to the severe restrictions of the medical schools, and the prejudices of Medical Men, it is extremely difficult to obtain any portion of dead humanity. Apart from the nature of the covering, the binding of the above item is an extremely fine specimen of execution."

So it is that when not searching in charnal house and private clinic for this gruesome tissue, bookbinders are ever on the lookout for new blood. Few young people are drawn to this exacting profession with its strange jargon of gathering and gauffering, deckles and doublures, dentelles and diapers, tools tubs, yapps and trindles and this rare race with its traditional skills is in very real danger of extinction.

It is true that a few idle Chelsea debutantes bored by their languid tasks at charity balls, weary of manning the phone in antique shops, of amateur picture restoration and attendance at Christie's Fine Arts Course, may be lured into a brief flirtation with the binder's art. However, this profession is now almost exclusively a geriatric preserve, rarely affording a youthful female apprentice opportunities for meeting a rich and attractive sexual partner unless, of course, her fleeting sojourn in the bindery should coincide with a visit by myself. I confess to at least one carnal encounter in the subfusc and hircine atmosphere of a binder's attic where a wanton trainee once tempted me to re-enact the improprieties of the printed page, earning me a rheumy wink from her ancient supervisor. Perceptive indeed would be the passenger aboard a Sloane Square bus or Tube who could accurately divine the origin of goatskin parings and gold leaf particles on the back of a shapely cashmere cardigan.

Sad to say, however, the tell-tale signs of a hard day at the bindery are rarely recognised by average members of the British public. Most people seem pitifully content that their books remain in the drab or gaudily vulgar wrappers they wore when they emerged from the factory. Shame on the book collector who in assembling a private library cares little or nothing for the physical appearance of its elements, and this neglect is all the more deplorable when one considers that in these days of inflation and high costs it is still possible to modestly apparel a book in fair quality gold-embossed leather for less than one hundred pounds. The prudent investment of a quarter of a million could absolutely transform your mousy shelves of Drabble, Bragg, Pym, Jong, Cartland and Weldon.

There must still be a few aristocratic beings in these islands who prefer to judge a book by its cover or why else would the colour supplements still carry Special Offers for all those sumptuously bound hand-tooled leather-look "Collected Works" which grandchildren are expected to cherish and Rickmansworth neighbours envy. Alas, some of the synthetics employed in the manufacture of these bogus "bindings" are not proof against the depredations of domestic animals and a mail order Super-Deluxe edition of Thackeray embossed by a whippet's teeth can prove more expensive in the long run than the unpalatable books which form my own collection.

I learnt my lesson the hard way twenty years ago and all my binders are now instructed to spray each book with a specially formulated toxin so that my library is now not only free of the fecund and insatiable bookworm or *Atropos Divinatoria genus Psocidae* but it has also never since been necessary for me to wrench a precious volume from the maw of a marauding marsupial.

"She built it up from nothing."

CAITLIN made us a lovely meal when we returned home last week from our summer wanderings. She was feeling very pleased with herself, having had her O-level results while we'd been away, though at the same time she was worried about having broken a window. You know what an ogre I am. Always being horrid to them. Sometimes I even answer back.

She usually manages to break at least one thing while we're away but this was the biggest ever, the largest pane in Flora's bedroom window. This is a happy homecoming, I said to myself. Hurrah for September once again. Let's not start the new season with a row. It was only when I was tucking into the baked potatoes that I began to wonder what on earth she'd been doing in Flora's bedroom. Why wasn't she sleeping in her own bedroom while we were away?

My sister Marion, social worker of this parish, was supposed to be in charge in our absence, but her social life is almost as hectic as Caitlin's. No, I won't start an inquisition now. This is a happy evening. Home again, home again, jiggety-jig. By the way, Caitlin, why is there no butter for the potatoes?

Bloody hell, I couldn't afford to buy butter on the measly housekeeping money you left me. Then what about your own money, my petal, from all your baby-sitting and other little jobs? I'm saving up, she said. I'm getting tatooed. I know a girl who's got a blue bird tatooed on her heel and it only cost her £5. Isn't that fantastic.

Here we go again. Another season, another running family saga. But that was only the beginning, the tip of the hamburg.

"Listen to this," she said, stuffing down the potatoes and reading from the *Evening Standard* classified. "A Triumph

FATHER'S DAY

HUNTER DAVIES

unpacks his bags

Convertible. Only £180. Now that really *is* fantastic . . ."

Caitlin is only sixteen so it's years before she can drive and she certainly won't be learning on my car, nor am I paying for lessons. I just ignored the motoring madness. Later, she announced that she and Fig were only thinking of *buying* a secondhand car now, while they're dirt cheap, then leaving it in the back lane till they're grown up and can drive.

We'll be going across America by car, just the two of us, oh, it'll be really great, the summer of 1982, after A-levels. We can't go

next year 'cos that's Morocco. First of course there's our half-term holiday this October in Paris. We've already booked up six days in a youth hostel while you've been away.

When I was your age I'd never been further South than Pen . . . but I didn't go on as I might have told her that before, perhaps around a hundred times. I scoffed a year ago when she said she was saving up to go to California on her own to stay with friends, but she went. Then it was Geneva with Fig and Sophe in a bloke's flat. Then this summer it was Portugal. It's best not to say anything. Just get on with your dry potatoes and be grateful that she's made us a lovely home coming meal.

She'd changed her style completely while we'd been away. The old men's raincoats and old women's smelly cardigans have gone and she's now into flowing silks and satins like an Eastern princess. Is prettiness on the way back. We said nothing. Natch. Although we both thought she looked terrific, for a change, we know better than to pay compliments. She'd be back into the old if she thought we approved of the new.

So, that's Caitlin for the new season, or at least the next half hour. After the sumptuous repast, thank you very much, triffic, I then fought my way back down the hall to look at the pile of rubbish waiting for me to open, hoping for some excitements, some new directions, but it was all VAT envelopes and heavily embossed cards from dodgy-sounding mini cab firms and emergency plumbers. The only interesting letter was from the Metropolitan police saying that my wife's handbag had been found in a taxi and would she come and collect it. She doesn't use a handbag and on the date when it was handed in, we were in Portugal. That's why it was interesting. I

"Typical of young people today—they've always got to be different."

dropped them a reply asking for details.

I then explored the house, breathing in the colours, admiring all the furniture, touching our possessions, but not the broken window as I didn't want my first return engagement to be at the Royal Free. One has to go away in order to see one's self. Absence makes the hair grow. There's a cliché there somewhere, struggling to get out.

My wife enjoys returning even more than I do. That's it, she says. No more travelling, no more holidays. Roll on winter and the dark nights, stuck in the house. I get upset when she says this, especially as she often says it while we're still on holiday. I take it as an insult to me, the Great Provider, worked my little fingers to the bone all year, haven't I, just to give the family lovely hols, and you now say you don't like holidays. I didn't say that. I *like* holidays, but I like being at home even better. Well, that will give us another topic for the new season ahead, round the cocoa and cheese, seasons of toast and mellow fruit loaf.

Next morning, I investigated the garden and hadn't Mother Nature been busy while we'd been away. My, look at those sunflowers. Almost as tall as the weeds. Hello, tortoise. I bet you'd like four weeks in the Lake District and two weeks in Portugal instead of hanging about this dreary little garden, eh, what. The jesting tortoise would not stay for an answer.

Next day we went shopping. Caitlin and her fellow window breakers had eaten everything in and out of sight. After two weeks in a Mediterranean climate it was such a pleasure to go to Sainsbury's and buy perfect Mediterranean fruit. The London peaches were not only vastly superior in size, neither rock hard and green nor brown and soggy, but were half the price of the fly-blown ones in the Algarve markets.

Sainsbury's even let you handle them now and weigh them yourself. Their lemons were equally superior to the ones in Portugal. There are lemon and peach trees all over the Algarve but you don't see many in North London. It's a shame Caitlin isn't doing Economics in the Sixth Form. She might have explained it all to me.

Jake, who now goes into the fourth year and has to wear a black blazer but don't make any remarks about it as he hates any personal comments, isn't doing Economics as one of his options, but he is going to do British Con. That could be something to do with Economics, I said. It might even explain fruit prices, but it turns out to stand for British Constitutional History.

Flora meanwhile flies up into the Junior School. Her days of glory as a Top Infant are now over, a fact which slowly began to dawn on her during the holidays as she realised she would be starting from the bottom again, amongst the youngest and smallest kids in the big playground. As a special dispensation for me, but only once and I must not think it will become a habit, I can walk up to school with her on Monday, her first day in the Juniors. But only for the first day. Just so she can find the right classroom. Thanks Flora, ever so good of you.

As for us, we people pretending to be grown-ups, September is a New Year for us as well. Families with school age children always live their year from September to September, but other adults rarely do. I always work up to a panic every June finishing one book or some such project. My working year begins anew every September when I get back to the typewriter, refreshed in mind and body, ready to moan to myself for another nine months.

My wife is starting a new novel and can't wait till they're all settled at school once more. She's drooling at the very idea of those blank pages just waiting for her lovely handwriting to race across them. At page 100 she'll doubtless begin to flag, as all these creative people do, but until then it will be tra la and such fun. You can't beat beginning. Happy New Year, everybody out there, good luck to both of you.

Oh, before I go first footing, three little things, just to clear the decks of last season's debris. I forgot to mention that Caitlin got three A's in her O-levels, plus five B's and 1 C, so that wasn't bad, considering. I haven't discovered how she came to break Flora's bedroom window yet but I don't believe her explanation that there was a fly buzzing in her bedroom and she couldn't sleep.

As for the mystery of the handbag, the Metropolitan lads have rung to say that it belongs to Ms Deirdre McSharry, Editor of *Cosmopolitan*. She'd left it in a taxi. Inside the bag, the police found a proof copy of my wife's latest novel. They immediately thought the bag must be hers. Perhaps I won't ask them to find out who broke Flora's window.

"Eamon here only needs to be run over by a 1978 Cortina for his complete set!"

HOME HINTS

If roof timbers crash through a ceiling or floors collapse, it may be a sign that woodwork is under attack from fungi or beetle infestation. Joists reduced to dust that smells of mushrooms or covered in fruity spores are an indication of Merulius Lacrymans or "dry rot" but if, when tapped, the wood knocks back, look for Xestobium Refuvillosum or "Death Watch Beetle".

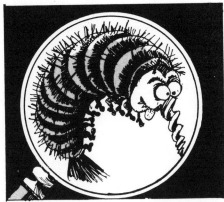

Where structural timbers resemble the inside of an "Aero" bar, Anobium Punctatum, the common furniture beetle or "woodworm", may be at work. There are approx 1,100 Anobiidae, such as Lasioderma Serricorne or the "cigarette beetle" which eats tobacco, mustard, chili peppers, cloves, raisins and some upholstery, but each is only 1–9mm in diameter. When disturbed, they pull their legs in and play dead.

Brace affected area with scaffolding, hack out badly rotted wood, then brush down, vacuum, and, protecting skin with a rubber suit and wearing breathing apparatus, treat with 2-3 applications of 10% Pentafin solution under pressure, stamping hard on any surface eggs. If you come across a teredo, a worm-like bivalve mollusc which destroyed Drake's *Golden Hind*, seek specialist advice.

Marque manquée

by CYRIL RAY

ONCE upon a time, it was a true-born Briton's proud boast that there was no such thing as bad beer—some beer was better than others, simply.

In Champagne, though, only the other day, I heard the head of one of the most eminent of *grande marque* houses say, not merely of his distinguished competitors but of the wines grown by peasant families in their own little vineyards, processed in co-operatives, and sold at the gate as eggs and strawberries are sold in Britain, that "there's no bad champagne—some's better than others, that's all".

There are thousands of *récoltants-manipulants*—grower-makers—in the region, their establishments ranging from a smallholding with farmhouse to sizeable buildings with imposing signboards, in scores of villages with names you have not come across until you see them displayed at one end of the main street and forget once you have seen them crossed out at the other.

Why there is no bad champagne is that the law leaves no room for it: champagne, to be allowed the name, may be made only from prescribed types of grape, trained and pruned to produce only so much juice, grown in a strictly delimited region and processed in a certain way.

Why some is better than others is—and I simplify drastically—that some vineyards, because of soil or drainage or exposure to sun, are better than others, their grapes more expensive. The great houses buy only from the best, and from many and various of them, so that their wines are well balanced in flavour and style. Also, they use only the juice from the first, and perhaps part of the second of the three pressings the law allows.

The roadside grower, so to speak, probably uses all three pressings, from his own grapes, which must be of the prescribed sort, from a permitted but most probably not a top-quality vineyard. His wine must be made by the *méthode champenoise*, but will be light and not suitable for ageing. It may well not have what a connoisseur would regard as a well-rounded, perfectly balanced style, but how many of us are connoisseurs of champagne, or can afford to be? It will be young and fresh, as it is sold as soon as it has undergone its required minimum maturing.

So, said my *grande marque* friend, the Parisian who undertakes the couple of hours drive to Champagne; has a slap-up meal at Fère-en-Tardenois or, near Epernay, at La Briqueterie or, lordliest of all, the three-starred La Chaumière at Reims, or simply picnics, as only the French know how, will take back in the boot of his car dozens of bottles labelled with obscure names that will provide graceful aperitif drinking until his next outing, at about half to two-thirds the price of the famous brands.

The great houses do not resent this. They cannot themselves provide all the champagne that France itself and the rest of the world need (some famous *marques* are now "on allocation" to their agents in this country); the roadside wines do not disgrace the noble name of champagne, and they would rather that those who like bubbly should drink champagne than other sparkling wines. They will always, then, turn to *grandes marques* for daughters getting married.

My advice then, to my fellow-countrymen taking their cars through north-eastern France this year, is to buy as much champagne by the roadside as they have checked can be brought back through customs. It is for drinking, not keeping; it will not have the breadth or the depth of a great champagne, or the elegance of one of the *de luxe* brands—of which more anon—but, unlike many bargains from foreign parts, it will not disappoint.

...try to remember exactly what He said...

GEORGE MELLY:

John Lennon

READING the newspapers, listening to the radio and television, you get the impression that everybody loved and has always loved John Lennon. Well they didn't. They loved Ringo and respected George and were seduced by Paul, but after the original honeymoon period with "The Fab Four", they recognised, quite correctly, that John couldn't be bought, wouldn't compromise, tried to change the world through a series of gestures which, because they were seriously intended but expressed symbolically, were bound to fail and could be dismissed with contemptuous laughter. Only a week or two ago the news that he never went out but baked bread every day and looked after his son, seemed good enough for a few schnide paragraphs. Lennon, the rich hippy with his six apartments and that ugly Japanese wife. Lennon, the cock-flasher, acorn-sender, bed-in-freak. Lennon, the Howard Hughes of rock.

Well, Lennon had just begun to go out again, was making a new album, and had renewed his love affair with New York as a city, "the safest on earth", and then a psychopath who identified with him pulled a gun and shot him dead. "I just shot John Lennon," he told the janitor. "Ungrammatical," said my friend Derek Taylor with angry despair. He believes a contempt for language shows a contempt for life. Lennon respected language.

Difficult to remember, ploughing through the eulogies in every newspaper, that Lennon was for a long time trapped in an enormous cage called the United States. If he left, they told him, he wouldn't be allowed back, so despite a great deal of pressure he wouldn't leave, and anyway he knew and they knew it wasn't the marihuana bust as they pretended. It was his opposition to the war that had enraged the Nixon administration.

Lennon was always the awkward one. There was the tremendous fuss when he said that at that moment the Beatles were more famous than Jesus Christ, which was in a sense true. He didn't say better or holier or eternally more famous, just more famous *then*; a statement of fact for which they burnt his records.

And yet I wouldn't exactly accuse the media of hypocrisy. They do, and I'm writing this only two days after his death, feel outrage because they sense that he was someone who was part of a whole generation's youth, someone who changed the sensibility of almost everybody, who proved, together with a few other key figures, that poetry was not an esoteric art but available for all. A newspaper today printed the famous photograph of Yoko and him showing their bare bottoms. At the time the response was outrage or ridicule. Now they look only vulnerable, only human.

The boy who killed him wanted attention. "Happiness," the Beatles once sung with satirical phallic intentions, "is a warm gun." The boy took it literally. The boy is happy. He is, for a moment, as famous as his victim. What Tom Wolfe called "The Me Decade" has found its pathetic spokesman.

I met Lennon several times and sometimes we got on and sometimes we didn't. I was one of the trad generation and he hated that because he felt that initially the jazz men had treated him with contempt, blocked his way and that of the music he believed in. When his first book, *In His Own Write*, was published I reviewed it favourably but at the publisher's party we nearly came to blows because I insisted, and would still insist, that the Black origins from which his very early songs derived were superior. He seemed to me arrogant. I suspect, with some reason, that he found me patronising. He was a hard man then, not at all the "happy little rocker" of the publicity handouts.

I didn't meet him again until after the Beatles had broken up when he and Yoko were on the same chat show. They were very quiet and benign and we had a friendly if rather disorientated conversation of some length. With his long hair and granny glasses, his gentle and affectionate manner, it was hard to recognise the tight-mouthed aggressive young man of five years earlier. We parted with much of that bear-hugging which was the fashion of the time. I had just published a book which was critical of what I felt were their rather *déjà vu* activities. I felt guilty about it. They seemed so at peace, and I thought Yoko was lovely.

Then they broke up and John had his hair cut and in the company of the singer, Harry Nilsson, that most seductive of ravers, hit the town again. They were known as "The Vampires" because they only came out at night. Rumours of shattered picture windows reached me. The old Lennon had surfaced with a vengeance.

I was in L.A. with Derek Taylor, formerly the Beatles P.R.O. and some time later a director of the ill-fated Apple. We were trying in vain to persuade Warner Brothers, for whom he was working, that there was a reason to invest some money in a middle-aged jazz-singer who had just gone back on the road. We were staying in a bungalow which was an annexe of the Chateau Marmont, that grotesquely beautiful example of Spanish Hollywood kitsch. I got up one morning and came out of the bedroom to confront Derek and John returning, with steam coming out of their ears, from a night on the tiles. It was a little tentative to start with. This was no longer the loving hippy but the old aggressive scouser full of drink and God knows what else; the rocker who had made it facing the trad-singer who'd tried to block his way. However, there was something we shared in common. We were both Liverpudlians and Liverpool is the most chauvinist place in the world. "Liverpool," wrote Alun Owen, who also wrote *A Hard Day's Night*, scars its children for life."

Somehow we got on to a scouse wrestler who spanned both our childhoods. His name was Jackie Pye and his speciality was throwing snot at the referee. With the palm trees of L.A. looming up through the smog outside, we recreated those nights in the smoky Liverpool stadium of twenty years before when Jackie Pye, to the delighted outrage of the crowd, performed his gimmick. It was an hysterical and unforgettable couple of hours.

He was less sympathetic in New York a few months later when I was singing there. Derek and I were staying in The Algonquin. Lennon and Nilsson showed up there "Baying for broken glass". John rang up my publicity agent at 2 a.m. and demanded carnal knowledge. She was not best pleased, and, perhaps to his surprise, made it clear.

His separation from Yoko didn't work out. They found they needed each other too much and the long rave-up was over. In their ever-growing complex of apartments Lennon became a recluse. He was only just ready to come out.

John Lennon offered an insoluble paradox. His huge fortune reduced the value of his gestures (he and Yoko once arrived in a white Rolls to fast on the steps of a church), and yet without his fame those same gestures would have passed unnoticed. He showed at all times great courage and indifference to mockery, but what he wanted—peace, goodwill, love—remain as elusive as ever. He was not ashamed to show that he had a penis and that he loved his wife, but his lasting value is in his music both before and after the Beatles broke up. Here he was both tough and tender, exact and universal, funny and tragic.

The sheer bulk of his obituaries is mysterious, beyond logic. Nothing he hoped for came about: wars rage, people hate, a young man buys a gun and waits outside the Dakota building; and yet everyone, it seems, feels diminished by his death.

BASIL BOOTHROYD:

GOOD NEWS!

WORRYING in the small hours about artificially pegged milk prices, the state of the Labour party, and not being able to remember the name of my dentist, I got this real shot in the ear from my bedside radio—my habit of dozing off with this on is another of my worries.

Said this Bush House fruit-voice, after the usual slug about here again are the main headlines, "Ecuador and Peru have agreed to a cease fire."

This changed everything. It may not have made a hell of an impact on the rest of Haywards Heath. They're worrying more about local chimney fires, and main headlines reading, "Furore as Pine Trees are Axed". But it lit up my bedroom like a Very light, pardon the outdated military reference to something the armies of Peru and Ecuador probably haven't caught up with yet.

The last nuclear scare, I said to a stranger on Burgess Hill recreation ground, "News not too good, eh?" And he agreed. He said we should have to wait and see how they got on in the replay. They're all Brighton supporters round here.

Not that I claim a worldwide acquaintance with events. I don't know what the Peruvians and Ecuadorians have been firing about—and if you do, my name's Michael Selby, whose removal from the governorship of Brixton, or its circumstances, has been worrying us all so much; if not as much, perhaps, as our concern over how many times the BBC will be showing us *Gone With the Wind* before the year's out.

The thing is that the firing is agreed to be ceased. All around places like Saraguro and Huancabamba, not to say along the Aguarico River and dotted about the inhospitable Andes, units are sloughing their unsoldierly uniforms and (after loosing off a few spares for luck) their drooping cartridge belts, and returning to civilian life.

Production will be resumed. For the Peruvians, grapes, coffee and zinc: the Ecuadorians, straw hats and xanthophyll, with a crate or two of vegetable ivory on the side. If you don't know what xanthophyll is, and thought ivory came from elephants, that's your problem; nothing, in any case, compared to the way your paper worked you up with Trevor Chappell's underarm cricket cheat, bringing official statements from New Zealand's leader and no less a recluse than Sir Donald Bradman. Group photographs of our new Council for Social Democracy noodles, bothersomely smirking, are nothing to what could have had you living in a cellar all this time, while the English shelling of Swansea brought retaliatory dive-bombing from the Welsh air force.

England and Wales have agreed to a cease fire. It isn't a main headline we could take at first hearing on the World Service. Curative though it might be for current anxieties in Barnsley over what Parkinson said about its Grammar School. Writers to the *Mid-Sussex Times* about refuse collection and the unreliability of paperboys might well check their pen, worried by bomb craters in the garden and the maddening reflection that people in Peru and Ecuador didn't even know we'd got a war on.

War is hell. But there's something to be said for it. If you wake up to find your roof gone, and Oxfam officials spooning out soup to refugees lined up in the shrubbery, it puts paid to your toothache, and for all you care the forgotten name of your dentist could be General Alfredo Luis Arcentales Burbano or Angela Rippon . . . whose imminent disappearance, linking arms with Miss Ford, is causing more comments in the average British bus-queue than any grenade lobbed into a machine-gun nest in the foot-hills of Mt. Pichupichu, should queuers have known that anything of the sort was going on.

Because we aren't only lucky on the national scale, not having been invaded since 1066 and even that didn't turn out too badly for anyone but Harold II, but our personal problems are agreeably diminished on hearing that firing has ceased in some foreign land where we hadn't even heard that it had started.

Well, I find this, myself. It happens that only last night, trying to replace an expired light on the landing, in the dark, and in seeking to recruit illumination from the bathroom gave its string in there a tug that pulled it out by the roots, I told myself that this was the end—and I hadn't even dropped the bulb then, which bounced down the stairs, made a left, and rolled into the dining room behind the sideboard. Let alone that in hooking it out with an umbrella I straightened up under the table and have an egg on my scalp to prove it. Was suicide the only way out, I asked, simultaneously worrying on behalf of EXIT, the self-destructor's friend, imminent of prosecution for giving helpful pushes into the dark, when only a day ago the Latin Americans were blowing each other up for gallantry awards?

So I feel better this morning.

How do you feel?

I mean, if you're still worried because you're constipated, or can't get a window-cleaner, or something's got lodged in the outside drain that makes the washing machine suds stand up against the wall like Cotopaxi above the snow line—and I'm not talking about the wider anxieties, about the disclosure that caning is still rife in Church schools, or, in other educational fields, teachers are getting £10,000 p.a. for staying at home—try counting your blessings. OK, I know it's none of my business. It's simply that I want to help you, like EXIT. At least meet me halfway.

Peruvian and Ecuadorian soldiers, counting the blessings of the cease fire, could get one of those bullets for luck up the bum before they'd counted to three. Deny it if you will, but you aren't stuck with worrying about that.

And if you think one cease fire doesn't brighten the whole world and personal landscape, owing to the fact that upwards of 45 other wars are still going, according to the latest information update by experts keeping track as best they can, you aren't in any of those either.

Not for you the unsporting bayonet in the rear midriff, the sergeants bawling you out for badly buffed buttons, the eternal waits for troop trains that have been sent off in other directions. Myself, I'm quite cheered, despite the appalling traffic conditions everywhere about which I might write to *The Times* any day if still publishing, by not having to pile my few sticks of furniture on to a hand-cart and trudge off starving into the unknown—an experience virtually unheard of in places like Esher, or even Barnsley.

No, it was good news, all right, stirring a forgotten content. Anyway in me. It's true I still can't remember the name of my dentist, but the pain's easing now. And, come to think, I at least remember where he hangs out. Given the need, what's wrong with just driving over to read his brass plate?

And not a mortar shell through the windscreen all the way?

THE PINEHURST CENTER FOR FOOLING AROUND, GOOFING OFF AND WASTING THE TAXPAYER'S MONEY

ON THE HOUSE

TO the Bedford Hotel, Brighton to attend the most boring political meeting ever held. It was organized by the Tory Unity Group as a fringe event at the Party Conference. The unity group is supposed to be full of Right-wing beasties who want to introduce capital punishment in primary schools and use selective torture as a means of ending strikes. To judge by last week's gathering, this lot couldn't organize a counter-revolution in a Brownie pack. It was as silent and somnolent as a grave-digger's siesta or a home game at West Ham.

It wasn't helped by the Chairman, Mr George Gardiner, the cadaverous MP for Reigate. Though he is just about the head beastie on the Tory Right, he has a boring voice, like a chain-saw winding down. This has a narcotic, comatose effect on his listeners. At the beginning of his speech he grated, "I do not wish to use this occasion to make a personal attack on Jim Prior."

"Why not?" asked somebody, reasonably enough. After that it was downhill all the way. Two men in front of me fell fast asleep and began snoring loudly. I saw Mr Robin Day's head start to nod gently and his eyes to close. As speaker after speaker droned on, the whole room seemed to sway in gentle sympathy, as if afflicted with Legionnaire's Disease. One man called on Mr Prior "to expose himself". But even this fluff, usually a trigger for any British audience to fall around in helpless laughter, went unnoticed and unremarked. I tottered out over the slumbering bodies in search of something more enlivening to do, such as staring at my fingernails for half-an-hour on the pier.

One star speaker at the conference proper was a young Oxford student called William Hague (no relation to the acid-bath murderer of the same name). Three years ago young William electrified the conference, shortly before he reached puberty, through a speech resonant with clichés and elderly saws. Afterwards, as the delegates rose to give him a standing ovation and Mrs Thatcher leaned forward to congratulate him, Lord Carrington whispered to his neighbour, Norman St John-Stevas, "If he's like that now, what on earth will he be like in 20 years time?" Norman answered, "Michael Heseltine?"

The Tory Party usually manages to organize its debates with superb efficiency. Dissent is stifled, amendments ignored, everything arranged to provide a seamless impression of calm moderation. The party managers miss no tiny detail, including the fact that the daily conference TV coverage is interrupted at 11 every morning for a children's programme. This means that hundreds of thousands of housewives are watching the box in the few minutes before the kiddy slot begins. Naturally it is vital that these people, many of them floating voters, see a dignified speech by a senior Tory leader, not some crazed loony from the constituencies who wants to bring back hanging, drawing and quartering.

To this end there is a woman whose job it is to pass a note to the Chairman at around 10.45, warning him that the key moment is imminent. A year or so back it was Keith Joseph who was on his feet, and the Chairman noticed that he was nearing the end of an extremely short speech. He passed him a note: "You must keep going until 11 o'clock." Joseph, never the sanest looking or sounding individual, suddenly slowed down to a crawl, slurring each word, leaving long pauses between syllables, altogether giving the appearance of a man totally demented. Thousands of housewives must have fled the party in terror.

Things are not one quarter as bad as at the Labour Conference. The week's saddest loss was the ferocious attack the rampaging Thespian Andrew Faulds, Labour MP for Warley East, was planning to mount on Tony Benn. Just as he was getting into his stride, the Chairman, Lena Jeger, cut off his microphone.

Among the pungent points Mr Faulds hoped to make was that Benn had briefly sent his children to private schools before they went to Holland Park Comprehensive, a fascinating fact few people know.

He was also going to say that, thanks to a bizarre technicality, Benn had, while Secretary of State for Energy, contrived to place the British Atomic Energy Authority in the private sector, so making him the only Labour Minister ever to engage in denationalization. I pass on these points as a service to Mr Faulds and to a wider public.

One man who has made a lot of money out of Jim Callaghan is Lord Wigg, the chap with the big ears who used to spy for Harold Wilson. He has been going round telling people that Jim will not give up the Labour leadership next month.

Lord Wigg told his chum Lord Home, that he had won a "pile" of money on the date of the last election, betting that Callaghan would not choose September 1978. He had got excellent odds. "I have known Jim a long time. He is a panicker who will not take any make-or-break decision if he can possibly fudge it," he confided to the spindly ex-Prime Minister.

A gruesome historic milestone has recently been passed. It has been pointed out by Mr James Prior, the Secretary of State for Employment and disgruntled, unwilling acolyte of Mrs Thatcher. He says that for the first time in anyone's memory the Treasury finds itself in agreement with radical Left-wing Cambridge economist Wynne Godley. Both of them agree that by the end of next year or by spring 1982, unemployment will reach three million.

SIMON HOGGART

"It's clear from reading your report, Anderson, that you have emerged unscathed from the information explosion."

GUN GO DIN

Every time someone in America is shot—which is every time—the cry for Gun Control is heard. A report is heard here from behind the bullet—proof drawing board of ARNOLD ROTH

REFORMERS CLAIM THERE ARE TOO MANY GUNS IN AMERICA AS THIS UNRETOUCHED PHOTOGRAPH SUGGESTS

HOW TO GET A GUN

BUY ONE

STEAL ONE

MAKE ONE

ASK THE GUN FAIRY

SOME NEED GUNS FOR DEFENDING OUR FREEDOM

SOME FOR HUNTING FOOD & TROPHIES

PERFORMERS WOULD HAVE ALL GUNS REGISTERED BY AUTHORITIES

THEN, WE COULD HAVE KNIFE REFORM . . . **. . . WHICH WOULD STAMP OUT CONVENIENCE CRIME . . .**

. . . . AND PUT IT WHERE IT BELONGS—IN THE HANDS OF PROFESSIONALS.

Occupational Hazards

"Not omelette again?"

"I may not be able to see you next week, Higgins. You're going to be a father again."

"Mother always said there'd be days like this."

"Hang on, didn't four of us carry him here?"

"What do you mean,
'Big Bang Theory'?"

HECTOR BREEZE

BANX

"It's not always easy being a medium."

"I was about to say, Mr (sputter, gasp) Capone—the trouble
is in the (gasp, gurgle) gearbox . . ."

173

Forget Them All My Days

FROZEN in a traffic jam up Fleet Street one day last week, I glanced idly at the face of a driver slipping downwards in his grey Rover. It was a sharp, thin, rich stockbroker's face—and the face of a man that I went to school with. I had not seen it for twenty years. As it accelerated away towards Ludgate Circus, I doubted whether I should see it again.

It will not be tremendously missed, for even *circa* 1962 it was not a very lovable or interesting face. But this was an unusual moment, for I seldom enter the old school time warp at all. The chief merit of my schooldays has been that since they ended, no peril or discomfort has ever seemed remotely as dreadful as those five years at Charterhouse. In Fleet Street or at Television Centre, there has not been much call for an Old Carthusian bingo night. Never having had the luck to work for *The Times*, I have been unable to nudge Mr Rees-Mogg in the elbow and mutter discreetly as one old Carthusian to another that he could do with a new foreign editor, and now I've missed that boat for ever. In a nutshell, since 1963 Charterhouse and I have left each other

strictly alone, and both of us have felt the better for it.

But I am fascinated by encounters with that other country where the ties of classroom and playing field remain pre-eminent for a lifetime. Who are the old men who give thousands, even hundreds of thousands from their personal fortunes to rebuild the old school gym? How strong is this gratitude for education that fills the backrooms of London clubs night after night with loyal little groups giving reunion dinners for their old housemasters? Even in these egalitarian times, there is still a sizeable chunk of England amongst whom the nostalgic mating call of schoolboy to schoolboy carries a magic across the passage of generations.

I had an early experience of this ten years ago in Belfast. I was cowering in a doorway watching a company of the Light Infantry fighting its way into the Ardoyne amidst desultory Provisional gunfire, when a helmeted and flak-jacketed captain suddenly broke from cover and scuttled across the street calling, "Max! Max! Don't you remember me? Roger De Coverley from Saundrites?"

The odd thing was that in our five years at school in different houses, I don't think that De Coverley Minor and I had ever exchanged more than a dozen mutually disinterested glances. But there it was—the joy of seeing somebody, anybody, from the dear, familiar old school amidst all those bloody Irishmen. He seemed enchanted.

Then there was Bury, even at fifteen a seedy figure, a year older than me in the same house. He persecuted me half-heartedly until we parted with mutual relief after he failed A-Levels. Around 1967, the telephone rang on my desk at the *Evening Standard*. A cheery voice announced jovially that it was Peter Bury, and how nice it was to talk to me after all this time. Would I believe it? He had opened a restaurant in Sussex. Wouldn't it be splendid if I came down for dinner as his guest. I might even think of writing a few lines about it for the

paper? I still feel shamed that I declined with such civility.

Beyond such relatively dramatic encounters, there have been a few ships-in-the-night brushes with slightly dim Tory parliamentary candidates, eager soldiers and faceless businessmen. Charterhouse always seemed dominated by the sons of city gents, a way-station between blameless childhood in Chobham and smooth entry to Lloyd's or Phillips & Drew. I always imagine that for hundreds of my old schoolfellows, the canteen queues in City stockbrokers provide a lifetime replay of Charterhouse lunches, fighting for a ham sandwich between Snotty Johnson of Bodeites and Peter Duckegg-Wilson of Gownboys. Is there never a *frisson* of embarrassment about the statistical probability of meeting the passionate sharer of one's fifteen-year-old cubicle twenty years later on the 5.11 from London Bridge?

It is the great beehives of commerce and industry that provide the most solid bulwarks of loyalty to The Old Place. In a restaurant in the City I was accosted some years ago by a middle-aged man in an Old Carthusian tie who inquired ferociously if I was "the little bounder"—the only occasion that I have heard the word used other than satirically—"who wrote a nasty article in some rag about the school?" For a moment, I thought I was to be threatened with horsewhipping. But it began to dawn on him that while he stood 5′ 4″ in his black brogues, I stretch to around 6′ 6″ fully extended. He gnashed his teeth and moved on.

A few years ago, I was introduced to the elderly father of a friend who came from a long line of Old Harrovians, and fanatical cricketers to boot. "Hastings, eh?" he muttered reflectively. "You were at Charterhouse? And how are the Old Carthusians faring this season?" I have seldom been so utterly nonplussed. Ignorance, sheer ignorance, was the only possible plea, from which my social standing in that quarter never recovered.

Like most schools, Charterhouse placed its highest premium upon conformity. It has been a pleasure to observe how unerringly one's schoolmasters picked as their captains and monitors boys destined for a lifetime of obscurity. At eighteen, they vanished into the great corporations of the land, still trailing their comets of schoolboy glory, and were never seen again. It is the freaks among one's schoolfellows who turn up today somewhere near the top of the pile. Jonathan King, a spindly and raffish figure as a teenager, is a vastly successful pop singer and record tycoon. Nicky Henson, who managed to seem pretty decadent even at seventeen, has become a well-known actor whom I see occasionally with some extraordinarily beautiful woman on each arm, and the sort of cockney accent that it takes ten thousand pounds-worth of education to acquire.

One boy who was considered chiefly notable for bulk and greed is a distinguished Fellow of All Souls. I have a shadowy memory of tramping along a route march behind the pack of a denim-clad cadet named Jonathan Dimbleby. Come to that, I

"This Job Opportunities scheme can be quite fun if you handle it the right way."

think I once played First Boy to his Addison or Steele (I forget which) in the school masque.

Schools are not very adept at deciding which of their old boys should be enshrined in the pantheon for the edification of future generations. In my day at Charterhouse Baden-Powell, the daddy of Boy Scouts, was still deeply revered. It is only recently that the dreadful cost of the wartime Chindit operations has become apparent, so I suppose that they can be forgiven for thinking so well of Orde Wingate. But there was a definite cloud surrounding the name of Robert Graves, and that of Simon Raven was mentioned only in very dark corners indeed. These writer fellows can never be thought much of until they have been dead as long as Thackeray and Max Beerbohm, whom they do like to celebrate. I always enjoyed possessing a letter from Beerbohm to my grandfather as editor of the old *Bystander*, declining to contribute an article about his schooldays at Charterhouse, because he feared that poison would inevitably creep into his pen.

My old headmaster was a man of exceptional moral conceit, and it would have cheered my middle years to think of him eking out a living coaching Iranian candidates for the Open University. Of course, life is not like that. He is now Director-General of the IBA, with a knighthood to boot. But it is encouraging to see that the present incumbent, Brian Rees, was questioned by police a few months ago on suspicion of being the Yorkshire Ripper. It is odd that everybody was unable to think how his name came before them. Very elementary, I fancy, my dear Rees. I imagine that the present generation of seventeen-year-old Carthusians, like my own, is encouraged to read Anthony

"*Old Charlie was a fine police officer.*"

Powell's *A Question Of Upbringing*. There is a notable incident in the book in which an Etonian anonymously denounces his housemaster to the police. Given schoolboys' *penchant* for derivative jokes, I suspect that Mr Rees need look no further than his own English Under Sixth for the author of that one.

Today, my only stabs of awareness of the old school strike when I see the pink and red stripes of an Old Carthusian tie. Is it my imagination, or is the wearing of old school neckwear in decline, even among those who like to appeal to its spirit? There is a shabby figure often to be found slumped in the corner of a club to which I belong whom I recognise (though by tacit consent we feign mutual ignorance) by his remarkably dirty O.C. tie as a contemporary at Charterhouse.

I saw a young Fleet Street reporter wearing a Carthusian tie the other day, but judging from what we have been hearing lately about the educational pretensions of a distinguished *Daily Mirror* journalist who sports an Old Etonian tie, he probably bought it in Moss Bros because he thought that it looked pretty.

But what passions these loyalties can generate! I am now reaching the moment of truth for all those who are hypocritically disagreeable about their old schools, when I have to consider where to send my own son. A friend who is a governor of Charterhouse keeps suggesting that I should put him down for the dear old place. He swears that it has all changed since my day. But then he would, wouldn't he? The past is not a country that I wish to visit, least of all through the eyes of my children. I remain puzzled by those who do.

"*I'm afraid he's becoming something of a cult.*"

FREAKY FABLES by HANDELSMAN

INK IN YOUR VEINS

SO you want to write your own life story but don't know where to begin? Well, I have published my life story 52 times in various fiction and non-fiction guises and it would seem that I am the chap to ask. Certainly, since my emergence as a public writer in residence, everybody asks me. My mail bag is full and Doris Black keeps coming in with an armful of her childhood in Islington. Starting is not her problem—finishing is her problem.

"Anna Ford has been offered £60,000 for her life story," is the current rumour. She is in rich company. Although depression, recession, even national and international bankruptcy is rumoured, publishers are waiting to pay fortunes for autobiographies (life stories). Not only to the famous like Ingrid Bergman and Dick Bogarde and David Niven and those who seem to crop up from all parts of the globe for Parky's show—but also to you. Your life story is as valid as anybody else's; nobody else can write it except you, it is your fingerprint, unique (the only one in existence).

"Why would anybody want to read the life story of Albert Woods or Jane Shatts?" you will ask (using your own name in the question). Well, the reason is that people are nosey. Better than the most exciting made-up fiction they like other people's lives. Vicars, wife-beaters, royalty and so on. Hence the existence of cheapo newspapers. It is gobbled up day after day—whereas fiction is not. This is because fiction is not true. Very often also you have got to puzzle your brains to know what it means, what it is about, what the author is "getting at". Very often there are hidden meanings in fiction which ruin the enjoyment. For this reason more and more books are being published that deal with ordinary everyday people and events (*Dallas*).

Do you want to go on or have I made it seem even more complicated (difficult)? Let us suppose that my words have excited you. You now desire and are mad keen to see your life story and the story of your friends and relations (strange happenings, illnesses, love-making even, perhaps a broken heart or inability to eat normal food) appear in print! Imagine your picture and your name or pseudonym (pen-name) on the cover!

"I wonder who wrote this risqué (naughty) story about Barnet?" people will say.

And it will be you (your own town of course, not Barnet always).

All right, then. Out with paper and pen or typewriter. Let me say at this stage that it would save you a lot of hard work if you had a secretary. This is what Barbara Cartland has. Barbara happens to be a personal acquaintance of mine and she will not mind me telling you about her most intimate writing system. She lies on a couch at Hatfield with her eyes closed. After all, she has published 2,567 novels! All about ordinary people doing ordinary workaday things. She has also published her own life story, *I Search For Rainbows*.

Let us suppose you have the writing materials to hand and are ready to start. Where to begin? This is the great "gob-stopper" of all time, isn't it? I am going to help you with a little anecdote of my own. It will show you how to tap your memory bank (and what savings!)

One day I happened to mention to my grown-up daughters, who were visiting on a wet Sunday afternoon, that I had got frog eyes. I don't know how the subject came up.

"What do you mean by that, Grandad?" asked one of my grandchildren, Leslie.

For a moment I was nonplussed (confused). It seemed to me that I have always known that I have frog eyes. But how? It is not the kind of thing one's parents would admit. Somewhere, sometime in my long life, somebody had called me Frog Eyes. Imagine my quandary (predicament—trouble), faced with such a personal question by my small, trusting grandson, not yet 18. And me, not only a writer myself, of some small (!) experience but also well accustomed to remembering even the tiniest fragment of my life and experiences, for this is my very living. And yet, and yet, and yet . . . "How do I know I have frog eyes?" I thought to meself.

For the present I passed the matter off. Fortunately, close friends of my own arrived to see me with a few bottles, not knowing I had family present. From being Dad and Grandad I was soon faceting (changing faces) like a diamond. This can be quite embarrassing of course. I heard one of my friends, himself a writer, telling my youngest daughter, not yet 42, how I had brought "another woman" into the house when she was a child. Of course, things like this are not uncommon and Jilly was not amazed or anything. But then I heard him telling her about the sleeping rota I got both parties to sign so as to avoid fighting over me. He had, of course, become confused with one of my fictionalised life stories. Then I accidentally said fuck—this you must avoid if you want your stuff to appear in W. H. Smiths.

Amid the fracas (set-to) I suddenly remembered who first called me Frog Eyes. don't know whether you know an actor on television called Dennis Waterman? Well, it

"Excuse me but I think you ought to know—you're being eaten."

"There's only one thing to know about being a dormouse. Everything eats a dormouse."

ffolkes

was not him. It was a chap who resembles the part that Dennis often plays of a kind of laid-back (relaxed) working class yobbo with a heart of gold. In other words I had got my "missing link".

"Cocker!" I suddenly said. Of course, everybody wanted to know the details once I had reminded them of what I had forgotten (so to speak). What I had forgotten in fact—and this will give you heart when it comes to rattling off your own magnum opus (big number)—was almost the whole of the 1950s. *My Lost Decade*! Yes, this is a famous piece of writing by F. Scott Fitzgerald, the American drunk. He also wrote, I believe, *The Lost Weekend*. Or was that Trevor Howard? Now here was me, not a drinker at all by writers' standards, forgetting a whole eight to ten year period in my life. What gold! I could hardly wait to get down to it, as we writers say.

Cocker was an important part of my 1950s. He was the doorman at the Studio Club in Piccadilly where we people from the arts gathered. Well, that was the intention of Augustus John (a painter) when he opened it, but by 1955 the membership covered a broader spectrum (area). For instance there was a hundred-year-old artist Monty Smythe, whom we used to conduct visitors round, and there was Daphne, a secretary at ITN, the famous television news company (yes, even then). Cocker was the life and soul of the party, as you can imagine. He it was who called me Frog Eyes.

"Here, give us your gun, old Frog Eyes!" he cried, one memorable night. You will be amazed to know that I carried a gun in those days. I am amazed. Everything comes flooding back now. What a treasure trove of writing material. You will find the same I am sure; locked away perhaps in an attic or some careless fragment of small talk. Charles Dickens is said to have got his idea for *Hard Times* from a square of newsprint hanging from a nail in a friend's lavatory.

My gun, you will be relieved to know, was made of plastic.

"Don't ma'er!" cried Cocker, who could not pronounce his t's or th's, being "of the people". "Fink wha' happens, Frog Eyes. You are driving up froo Hendon and meet the old Bill. Whass your car number, sir? You don't know. Search! Inside wiv him!"

That lost decade was a dangerous time for anybody fresh from Welwyn Garden City (where Flora Robson and Chris Barber came from, incidentally). Besides artists at the Studio Club there was a right "racy" crowd and one needed self-protection. We had three bankrupts! The "romantic encounters" that went on there in the Fifties were prodigious (many). For a time I was "on the run", so to speak, from a chap who used to go out with a young lady I was slightly friendly with. He was a brute and had made her pregnant and gone back to his sister. One night she had a miscarriage at the Odeon in Fulham Road, just in front of Pan Books. Afterwards I took her for coffee at the West London Air Terminal. She was a gorgeous blonde and very intelligent, having got a librarian's diploma. We had a lot in common.

"Your frog-eyed chick's not 'ere yet!" Cocker would cry, welcoming members in his warm personal way.

In brief then, before committing those "hallowed" memories to parchment, let me say this. Keep it clean. Everything doubtful in an autobiography must happen to somebody else. There are people like Cocker in most people's lives, full of earthy wisdom (by the way, he said frog eyes were due to the thyroid gland). Try to remember your own Cockers. You will not recall the ecstatic or traumatic events of the past by sitting down as that great drunk Ernest Hemingway used to do at the Café des Lilos I think it is. Remembering comes out of getting into a fracas and things like that.

Meanwhile, bonne chance (good luck)!

"Well, I still think having a second class mail was a mistake."

McLACHLAN

INTELLECTUAL PROPERTY FOR SALE AND WANTED

FOR SALE
DEEP CONVICTION

Presently owned by a Gentleman, this highly desirable intellectual property probably dates back to George II, with Victorian additions in keeping with the general style. Impossible to do full justice to this historic item in an advertisement, the property may briefly be described as a baroque construction based on the belief that black men have larger feet than other people.

Of particular interest to fascists, madmen, sociologists etc., this attractive item is available freehold.

FOR SALE OR RENT
$$E = mc \text{ something}$$

This interesting intellectual property, on which considerable time and effort have been lavished by the present owner, is ripe for development. Solid foundations are a prime feature of the property which awaits only the sympathetic hand of someone prepared to finish it to the highest specifications, after which it would be ready for almost any private or commercial use.

One excellent feature of the site is that it is connected to convenient nearby ideas by several well-trodden paths.

JUST IN THE MARKET!

SOCIALISM

This elderly Victorian property, although admittedly in a fairly dilapidated state at the moment largely due to neglect, is nevertheless ideal for conversion! An enormous complex of ideas of various shapes and sizes could be knocked together to form a most attractive modern property such as Social Democracy, Low Toryism, Militant Tendency and so on, or could simply be demolished to form a Vacant Lot, such as a government.

No reasonable offer refused, Access/Barclaycard/Diners welcome.

AMAZING VIEWS . . .

are just one exciting feature of the fascinating private property known locally as *MONETARISM*, a wonderfully inspired intellectual structure built on stilts out of thrilling new and experimental materials, many of them never before employed in any idea whatever, which give the whole feature the impression of floating above the ground, free and unfettered.

Naturally enough, since this is possibly the most expensive construction ever to have come onto the market, a substantial offer is invited. However, this is not as high as one might expect due to preposterous superstitions abroad in the neighbourhood that the structure is unsound, could collapse on its inhabitants at any time, and has a number of apprentices in its foundations who were inadvertently bricked up during the building and who can be heard, at times, shrieking to be let out (the so-called Howe Effect).

FOR DISPOSAL BY PUBLIC AUCTION SOMETIME IN 1983
(Unless previously vacated)

WANTED

We have a number of clients on our books who are looking for intellectual properties for speculative purposes. Top prices will be paid for all forms of **STRUCTURALISM, BIG BANG THEORIES, GAY DARWINISM, AGITPROP, TRANSCENDENTAL METAPHYSICS, ELITISM, ETHNOMODALITY,** and anything within easy reach of R. D. Laing for under a fiver.

A Dollarsnatcher Special from Gee-Whiz Travel & Rent-a-Royal Inc.

In the land of Christopher Columbus, Margaret Thatcher, Queen Elizabeth, David Frost and the Forsytes—

- MEET WITH REAL ROYAL ELEGANCE OVER A PEDIGREE ENGLISH "CUPPA" PLUS MERINGUES OPTION
- A ONCE-IN-A-LIFETIME OPPORTUNITY TO ONE-ON-ONE WITH TITLED GENTLEFOLK WITH THEIR WODEHOUSIAN STAFFERS, HAND-BUILT VINTAGE AUTOMOBILES AND REALLY CUTE DOGS
- A ROMANTIC JOURNEY INTO PRIVILEGE AND AGE-OLD LUXURY NO AMERICAN WILL EVER FORGET

To millions of adoring English yeomanry and their blush-cheeked virgin womenfolk, she's known simply as "Our Right Royal Step-Gran".

Wherever she parades on her fabled "Walkabouts"—to stately homes filled with antiques, to publishers where once Charles Dickens or Robert Morley may have trod, to ye olde English drug stores dispensing just gorgeous honey, mead or vitamin-rich potions once used at Stonehenge—the loyal crowds line her route, hoping for a magical glimpse of a tiara or maybe even a signed copy of *Love and Lovers* to cherish for all time.

But come high summer along the highways and byways leading to St Paul's—London's mediaeval masterpiece that soars to almost one third the height of the World Trade Center—the glory and excitement of her radiant world will reach unprecedented heights.

For who is able to resist the stirring sight of pageantry and

SEE FOR YOURSELF THE TIMELESS BEAUTY OF ONE OF BRITAIN'S BEST-LOVED ANCIENT MONUMENTS

tradition, romance and perfection, as golden carriages and liveried infantrymen lead a glittering procession that is outshined only by the coruscating loveliness of what millions of simple folk expect to be a riot of pink chiffon, sparkling gems and masterful millinery?

The networks will relay the spectacle coast-to-coast—but imagine the faces back home when you are able to advise friends, business associates and neighbours that you have personally said hi—and even lunched with her glamorous daughter and an actual English Earl!

Not since the Pharaohs built the Tower of London has England experienced such a profound outpouring of patriotic joy—and never before has there been such open eagerness to enrich the lives of American cousins—at under 2,000 dollars a head, including an autographed napkin, Wedgwood bust of the royal step-gran, and all the romantic novels you can carry.

★★★

A STUNNER OF A FAIRY-TALE VACATION

"Y'all folks are sure as hell welcome to come on over and share our patriotic joy," says this genuine English Earl as he looks forward to some fascinating conversation over luncheon in his antique English stately home. His lovely First Lady at Althorp is a direct descendant of the royal step-gran.

Top-selling souvenir in King Ethelred's Burgerie and All-Nite Drug Store at Althorp Hall is this Irish linen tea-towel depicting Sir Walter Raleigh on the deck of the *Golden Hind.* Mrs Reagan recently ordered two dozen to be made in finest cashmere in celebration of the royal betrothal.

The royal step-gran's enchanting stately home where Richard the Lionheart courted Beatrix Potter and where all major credit cards are accepted.

CONDITIONS OF BOOKING

Passengers must have a current certificate of competence to hold a knife and fork in the accepted fashion for lunching with English aristocracy and must sign an undertaking not to send footmen in search of cold beers. It is necessary to prove English or, in certain conditions, Irish ancestry not more than 7 generations prior to departure and to have staff advise their Lords and Ladyships of the main points *before* the No Smoking lights are illuminated and the conversation started up.

All prices quoted are based on single-occupancy Regency chairs at table and include canapés, one slice of King Arthur gâteau, tea in guaranteed bone china cup OR the set luncheon of cold cuts Rudyard Kipling, Queen of Hearts tart and a thimble of port but NOT burgers, bourbon, french fries or knickerbockers glorious. Transport to and from the souvenir complex is by chauffeur-driven limousine and in certain locations guests may rent unlimited-mileage landaux for touring the grounds or visiting Stratford-upon-Avon to see where England's most illustrious writer had the inspiration for *We Danced All Night.*

Discounts of up to 5 dollars are available for parties of 600 or more persons requiring only tea and a meringue EXCEPT on certain flights from Miami during the off-peak shoulder season when certain classes of Barbara's Heartland Supersavers will be charged as Earl of Spencer Bargain Brunch Bonanza fares.
NOTE: Secretarial services and stationery with crests and mottoes can be arranged if you plan to combine your glimpse of royal aristocracy with a business seminar or sales conference.

METROPOLIS

LIBBY PURVES's
London

T HE way they carried on, down West-
bourne Grove, you would have thought
that we were emigrating.

"Move to *Greenwich?* That's . . .
south of the *river*. Near . . . well, near
Lewisham and things. Practically *Kent*."

"It is no further from Oxford Circus," we
replied frostily, "than is Ealing Broadway.
Barely farther than Hampstead." But Ealing
they could accept; TV producers live in
Ealing. As for Hampstead, residence there
has long marked an intellectual rather than a
geographical distinction. It could be just
outside Birmingham and still be accepted
without derision. "Queen Elizabeth I was
born in Greenwich," I said defensively to a
Bayswaterian. "She," he replied, "did not
have to pack her nappies in a briefcase and
get onto the 0856 from Dartford every day
to be a Royal Infant. You must be mad."

And indeed our move was not without
misgivings. For five years I had made it an
article of faith not to live outside page 59 of
the London *A to Z*. Page 59 is a great
rectangle, encompassing the more canal-ly
bits of Maida Vale, the multicoloured
Harrow Road, grubby, cheerful Notting
Hill, seedy Bayswater and the knotted-
headscarf civilisation of Kensington. It just
excludes Chelsea, Shepherds Bush, Earls
Court and the wilder excesses of Sloane
country. On Page 59 you can buy food from

anywhere in the world, in shops where the
neon never sets: *dolmades* at dawn, curry for
elevenses, Kerrygold and Halvas and
taramasalata and water-chestnuts stacked
high behind the wired glass, forever. West
London is like a niffy old duffle-coat: pull its
hood over your head and live, cosily
blinkered, fed at the nipple of convenience.

At a price. You live there either at
monstrous cost, or in squalid insecurity or,
like us, in quarters so bijou as to necessitate
closing all the drawers and cupboards before
opening the door to the postman. One day,
Paul bought another sweater; and we had to
move. Of those places far enough out to buy
a house in, Greenwich was unquestionably
the nicest. Queen Elizabeth did well to be
born here. Round-the-clock hoummous
there may not be, but we can see the
topmasts of the Cutty Sark from our bedroom window, and the Naval College
reflects in baroque grandeur upon the
capital's river. We are not sorry we came.

Also, moving from the centre to the edges
of London has had a weird, and probably
overdue, effect on our behaviour. In the
raffish and anonymous streets of W2, we
were not above creeping out at dead of night
to hurl the odd sink, or roll of festering
underlay, into any handy skip. Probably
some rotten property developer, let him
empty his own rotten rubbish, and ours, we
would chortle, driving away at a screech
through the sinister squares.

In Greenwich, the neighbours have faces,
and we could perpetrate no such social
crime. Clocks tick in the corner shops; big
watchful cats sit in every window, keeping
the peace. My manners have improved. At
the check-out once in Safeways in Kensington, a woman—not ill-dressed—actually
tried to bite me when my trolley wheel
caught hers. The teenager at the desk
stared, rigid with ennui, at the opposite wall
as I dodged and weaved from the attacking
teeth. We were, all three, victims of Urban
Neurosis. You could write a pretty boring
book about us.

But here, we talk of cats and rainfall at the
checkouts; and when our brand new burglar
alarm goes off (sorry chaps, sorry, false
alarm both times, a man from Cape
Canaveral or somewhere is coming to
dismantle its ultrasonic brain on Monday)
the neighbours and police form a concerned
posse at the door in minutes. In return, we
slowly learn to be Good Neighbours, and
accept any crumb of advice on our bewildering new possessions—rafters, and damp-
courses and chimneys. Hell, we even have a
garden. Things keep coming up in it. As I
write, a purple thing has opened, and some
funny looking daisies. Perhaps they are
mutants, brought on by ultrasonic leakage

from the burglar alarm.

It is actually being gardened by telephone
from Spalding. My brother (a mutant
himself, having green fingers in our family)
came and looked over the terrain when it
was in twig. Now he telephones once a week
or so with instructions. "Are there any
yellow bits on the woody thing at the top
right hand corner? Good. Now, you know
the parsley . . . yes, like plastic parsley only
real—well . . ." Soon, pray God, he will
come back and tell us which are the weeds.
It all looks pretty good to us, poor pallid
evacuees learning to frisk amid the unaccustomed grass, barely five crow-miles
from Westminster.

T HE only problem is that to pay for this
blessed dilution of London life, outer-
Londoners have to put up with a daily
concentration of the evils they have left. The
dose is provided by London Transport. In
my page 59 days I contrived to go to work in
a BBC dawn taxi, in which I slept for seven
and a half minutes. I came back on foot, or
by bus (eleven and a half minutes' sleep).
Now again I travel on the Underground, and
have, to my horror, found myself reviving a
fearful game invented in the dark early days
of London life.

You travel up the escalator, eyes un-
willingly drawn to the posters as they march
in fatuous steps to a fatuous Paradise, and
you *classify* them. "Lust, lust . . .
gluttony, lust, avarice, gluttony, sloth,
envy, lust, lust . . ." I am actually so
practised at this frightful game that I can
keep it up for a whole stairway, without
pausing or walking backwards to decide

*"A glass of water? It's people like you
that make this route uneconomic."*

whether electric toasters are Gluttony ("delicious toast") or Sloth ("the only one with a plug already attached"). Lust is easy; Pride and Avarice are harder. To score all seven Deadly Sins in one journey, you have to change at Embankment and walk through the tunnel to catch Envy, Pride and Sloth all in the same insurance poster. A dreadful, neo-Muggeridgean diversion, and if you take it up you ought to be as ashamed of yourself as I am. The only cure is to read *Gone With The Wind*, nose to page all the way, and risk tripping over the flat bit at the top.

EXPOSED once more to this harsher London, I have at least renewed an old love-affair with the fabric, appearance, smell and taste and essence of that queenly building, Broadcasting House. When I first came here, and stood weak against the dark forces of landlords, bankers and footsteps following mine in side-streets, the battleship silhouette of Broadcasting House provided a symbolic and an actual refuge. The sour little flat over Gray's Inn Road (sharing with the severe Civil Servants who initialled every egg in the 1940s fridge), the Upper Room In Pimlico, the dank basement where the lesbian couple above raged and screamed with educational obscenity, were less home-like than the two BBC fortresses at Portland Place and at Bush House in the Strand.

In either, there was a far better chance of finding lights, companionship, warmth, and un-initialled food than ever there was at home. Breakfast at Bush after a night shift was invariably pleasanter than a lonely egg with LIB stencilled on it and a curt note on Min. of Ag. paper about Tea Leaves In The Sink-Tidy. Even now, after the journey through the subterranean sins, Broadcasting House is a grateful harbour. If they ever transplant us to some convenient Broadcasting Centre (probably Center, by then), they will have to build in a few gently curving, slightly musty corridors; a bottle-green carpet, a few Bakelite trimmings, a jug of ancient water on a scratched blue tray. And they had better bring Joyce, with her trolley of doughnuts and scones, too, or some of us might never truly happy raise the heart to go to work at all. Why, in Los Angeles, the only place I felt entirely secure in two whole weeks was aboard the Queen Mary at Long Beach. There is probably a whole generation—two or three generations—of broadcasters who are never truly happy away from Art Nouveau staircases.

AS I write, the Church Army will be mustering briskly for an assault on the streets. Behind them, timing their campaign for the 28th, the National Schizophrenia Fellowship; planning for May, the British Red Cross, King George's Fund for Sailors, and Christian Aid. They are all having Flag Days, to raise funds and consciousness simultaneously. Stock up on change, pin on a smile; although I shall not be appearing over the rim of a tin for any of the above, I solicit sympathy for those who will. My own annual outing is just over: it was Lifeboat Day last month. After several

"No, I don't think he looks too old, either."

years of Rattling For Kensington, I was not allowed to let a mere leap to the East excuse me. So I was on station, with a sou'wester, a plastic boat, and a tray of sticky flags, hoping to raise the odd tin of paint, or yard of lifeline, for the RNLI.

I have to report a less glorious year than usual. For a start, I failed to win the annual all-comers race to the plum position on Kensington High Street Station. The jammy beast who did, handed in a full box before nine, and is rumoured to have topped 50 quid. I found myself assigned to Outside Barkers. Psychology is all. Walking slowly along the pavement, you observe the flow of bodies: out of the Tube, along the pavement, slowing here to examine—ah!—perfect!—a display of navy reefer jackets behind the plate glass. Association of ideas: reefers, seafaring, Jack Hawkins, storms, lifeboatmen, brave souls, jolly good—10p in the box, clink, smile. You stand, as ordered by civil authorities, displaying permit, causing no obstruction nor soliciting actively—and rattle like hell. Rattle RATTLE rattle—clink—thank you—one for the little boy?—rattle rattle. A wearing way of earning £9.37 in two hours, but it all adds up, as we like to say, bashing our boxes down on the table at the Town Hall, watching their copper ballast flow onto the Formica.

And it has other compensations, in this most dazzlingly cosmopolitan city. A yellow-turbaned Sikh traffic warden put in 50 pence, murmuring, "the poor souls, to drown so." An old lady in black bombazine stuck her lifeboat bravely in her hat, amid the flowers; and once a stately Arab, with two veiled and giggling women bobbing astern, pushed in a lordly pound note in return for some street information.

("Please," he enquired with a gesture towards them, "please, where is the shop Motherscare?")

With enormous self-control (one is after all *in loco* lifeboatman) I refrained from directing him up the road to the Family Planning clinic as a suitable motherscare. Off he glided towards the buggies and Babygros; on each wife's black-draped bosom shone a nice blue sticky lifeboat.

"Mummy, when you say I mustn't speak to strange men, does that include Daddy?"

Mixed Blessing

by CLEMENT FREUD

THERE must be, must there not? (I mean, if there weren't, why would they go on holding them and sending me huge envelopes full of bumf) some purpose in National Gastro-Festivals.

Judging from the number of folders that land on my desk (folders are the hallmark of expensive PR firms) most London hotels have imported some egregious cook from a rich foreign country to fry things at us in the name of EEC friendship. There is also a team from the Seychelles boiling things in Park Lane; their aims are more obscure.

I attended two such occasions the other day: lunch for the greater glory of somewhere and dinner to make me feel better about somewhere else. The same gang of Fleet Street Freeloaders moved sluggishly from ante-meridian white Burgundy to early evening Ouzo. Different PR ladies introduced us to different chefs who had all been primed to say: "Have you been already to my country? Yes, I like it here, too. No, I have not been to the Connaught Hotel, thank you."

At the Swiss function, Swiss ladies in Swiss costumes poured Swiss wine and prepared Swiss Fondue to the music of an Alpenhorn blown by the Champion Yodeller of the Swiss Cantonese Games. Then we had Swiss *eaux de vie* and Emmenthaler cheese.

If you are the sort of person who would ask an American to Sunday lunch and precede the Roast Beef with Brown Windsor Soup, following it with Bread and Butter Pudding while the record player is switched on to military marches, then what I am about to write will be of no appeal. My message is that a little foreign food/culture/wine goes quite a long way and the worst method of persuading people to embrace the life-style of others is to force them to wallow in it.

Unlike some of my colleagues, I have never been outraged at the thought of serving spaghetti-and-chips or sweet and sour pork with pease pudding; though I can see the point of single courses being country-orientated, I do not accept that nationalism must last throughout the meal. While I like Chinese food I have no great love for Chinese puddings and cannot understand why they get upset if you ask for cheese after Peking Duck. If the Rumanians want to sell me something, I should be delighted to listen to their argument but draw the line at being overcome by three Rumanian courses plus local wine.

There are occasions when I feel like eating that most delicious of Japanese dishes, *Sukiyaki*, which is constructed by boiling thin strips of raw beef in a delicate broth of onion and beancurd, noodle and ginger, sweet peppers and celery.

There is no Japanese restaurant I know that will produce a treacle and ginger tart or a steamed marmalade pudding to settle this; none that would entertain an order of *Oeufs en Cocotte à la Crème* as a starter. As a result, I eat less *Sukiyaki* than I would like, which means that I drink less *Saki* (which I also like), all because I don't much go for glutinous rice, raw fish and *Tempura*, all of which I can manage without—but come as part of the package.

If you go to an Indian restaurant there is, because of the Raj and all that, a tendency to provide English alternatives to curries and Tandooris, soups made of pulse and honeyed, deep-fried puddings. But the alternatives are always English. Prawn Cocktails, Heinz Tomato Soup at the front end; ice cream or trifle at the other.

Why cannot one have *Tagliatelli Verde* before Madras Lamb, without going first to an Italian and then to an Indian establishment? They employ more than one chef—why not have them in charge of differing gastro-cultures instead of different courses? Come to think of it, "This is the Italian cook at the Bengali restaurant," is a very prestigious introduction.

To return to my peripatetic meal, restaurants do not mind people coming in for one course and a bottle of wine and leaving to go elsewhere for the next part of their dinner. In fact, they mind that far less than they mind customers eating very economically and spending an hour and a half over coffee. Regrettably, there are places that have a minimum charge, which can make the exercise uneconomic, but while it is now difficult to eat decently in London for under £30 for two, even a £5 minimum per head need not be a deterrent. Try *Chilli con Carne* with a bottle of red house wine in one place; a baked sea bass with black bean sauce and Sancerre 1979 in another, followed by American ice cream from a parlour; this is a very adequate way of making your companion feel ready for coffee and liqueurs at home.

There are all sorts of benefits, like appetite-inducing walks between courses and no preparation, hardly any washing up, at home.

On the debit side you just might get three parking tickets (or have your car towed away that many times) and if you wear a coat and check it in at cloakrooms, the exercise could spell financial disaster.

"Sorry, I'm a stranger here myself."

GETTING THE BOOT

LARRY'S cast-off soccer pros

LET'S PARLER FRANGLAIS!

Le Final de Cup

Maman: C'est fini?

Papa: C'est fini, quoi?

Maman: Le match. Le whatsit. La chose de Cup.

Fils: Oh, Mam! Il n'a pas *commencé*! Il commence à 3 pm.

Maman: Mais . . . maintenant il est 12.30. Pourquoi vous êtes là devant le box comme un gang de Muppetes?

Fils: C'est pour le build-up, Mam! Il y a les hautes-lumières du semi-final et du quart-final . . .

Papa: Le filme du policier sur le cheval blanc en 1926 . . .

Fils: Le final historique de Matthews . . .

Papa: Le chorus communal de "Abidez avec moi" . . .

Fils: La présentation à Lady Di . . .

Maman: Ah! Lady Di est là? Elle est mignonne, la petite. Mais je ne savais pas qu'elle jouait au football.

Fils: Oh, Mam! Elle ne *joue* pas. Elle donne un shake-hand aux 22 joueurs.

Maman: Pauvre petite. Ça commence, le heart-break de la routine royale.

Papa: Sssh! On interviewe Jacques Charlton.

Maman: Pourquoi?

Fils: Je ne sais pas. Toujours on interviewe Jacques Charlton. C'est une tradition perdue dans les mists du temps.

Maman: Incidentellement, qui est dans le Final?

Fils: Pardon?

Maman: Qui joue contre qui? Il y a deux teams, non?

Fils: Eeuh . . . je ne sais pas. C'est Ham de l'Ouest, n'est-ce pas, Papa?

Papa: C'est vrai? Je croyais la Forêt de Notts. Ou les Artilleurs.

Fils: Arsenal? Jamais sur votre nelly.

Papa: Anyway, c'est sans doute dans le Temps du Radio. Ah, voilà! Les bandes massées des Regiments des Gardes.

Maman: Je n'écoute rien. C'est complètement inaudible.

Fils: Oui. Les fans chantent toujours pour rendre inaudible les bandes massées. C'est une tradition perdue dans l'histoire.

Maman: Charmant.

Papa: Une bière, son?

Fils: Ta.

Maman: Donne-moi un shout quand Lady Di vient. Je vais faire mon knitting.

Fils: OK . . . Ah! C'est Kevin Keegan qui donne ses pre-match pensées! Cela signifie . . .

Papa: . . . que Southampton n'est pas dans le Final.

Fils: Correcte. Seulement 2 heures 20 minutes à aller . . .

MICHAEL PARKINSON
Success

IN fact, I never wanted to be successful. I simply wanted to be famous. The kind of fame I had in mind as a child was the kind given in Yorkshire to the one who wears the white rose on his cricket cap. More reverence than fame, I suppose. In my imaginings I didn't bother dreaming of making a century for Yorkshire, I concentrated on what it must be like to have people recognise you in the street and point at your house. Little did I know it but it was good training for the future.

Similarly as a junior reporter on a local newspaper in South Yorkshire my sole ambition was to have my name above the story. The story wasn't important, the recognition that I had written it was everything.

One day the editor called me into his office and briefed me on my first by-line story. It was, he explained, "the biggest society wedding the South Yorkshire coal-field has ever seen". This seemed to me at the time a contradiction in terms, but I didn't argue.

Reporting a wedding for a local paper is merely a matter of getting the names right and this time I made doubly sure, checking and re-checking the list. I sent my copy off to head office and waited up overnight for the result to be shoved through my letter-box. For the first time I was about to see my name above a story. Came the morning and I opened the paper with the nervousness of a playwright after a West End opening night. There, on the front page, was my masterpiece and above it, my name. I read the article with misty eyes and everything was as I had written it until I came to the last paragraph, which read: "At the end of the ceremony the happy couple exchanged presents. The bride presented the groom with a pair of cuff-links, the groom presented the bride with an electric cock."

No journalist to whom I tell this story believes it, but I can prove it because in the style-book of that South Yorkshire paper to this very day is the memo the editor sent round all the staff. It said: "In future clocks, electric or otherwise, will be referred to as 'timepieces'." Whenever I consider the past and contemplate my success, as I have been asked to do now, I bring myself down to earth with the observation that after 30 years as a journalist the only footprint I have left in the landscape of my craft is that I changed the vocabulary of one local paper.

If there is a key to being successful then it must be single-mindedness. The objectives can be very different: wealth, power, social standing, sexual conquest, fame or a combination of all of them. But the motive is the fuel and no one of my acquaintance became successful by chance. Nor, in my view, does luck have anything to do with success. The British love to take the view that success is a bedmate of happenstance. In truth—like the old definition of genius —it's a combination of inspiration and perspiration.

In my case the only inspirational thought I had was that in journalism, as in life, one thing leads to another but the chances of exciting exploration are considerably lessened by staying too long in any one place. Therefore, I decided at a very early stage in my career to take whatever work was offered without ever pondering my suitability for the job.

Thus, after a blissfully happy time on the *Manchester Guardian* where I reported everything from chip pan fires in Bolton to Labour Party conferences, I joined the *Daily Express* and became the worst foreign correspondent in the history of journalism when they sent me to the Congo. I slept in the bath to lessen the likelihood of death by a stray bullet and lived on a diet of United Nation's Press Cards which I ate whenever we were stopped at a road block.

This important self-discovery of fear and incompetence under fire would have convinced the normally sane young man that his future lay in the safer havens of journalism. Which does nothing to explain how, some time later, I came to be arrested as a spy in Zanzibar while working for *World in Action*, nor how I found myself surrounded by smouldering armour in the Six Day War trying to report the action for *24 Hours* while, at the same time, writing a column about the golden days of Barnsley Football Club for the *Sunday Times*. When I finally handed in my column to the Israeli censor I was once more nearly arrested for subversive activity on the grounds that "Ay up" and "Ee by Gum" were clearly code words defining important military installations.

The importance of all this madness was that it convinced me that I should explore my inadequacies further. Fame was still the spur and gradually I achieved that ambition to the point where nowadays I am rung up by newspapers wanting to know if I (a) sleep in the nude (b) believe in the male menopause (c) have anxiety dreams (d) would have a Corgi as a pet.

Moreover, I receive correspondence from people who are convinced that should I but place my hands on their brow they will be cured of migraine and others who tell me that every time they see me on television they want to throw up. I once had a series of letters from an old lady who said she saw her dead husband sitting next to me on every show and could I ask him to wave now and then, and another from a woman who became so friendly that she sent me a coloured photograph of a scar from her recent abdominal operation.

SUCH is fame, and the question is, has it all been worth it? Leaving aside the obvious financial rewards, which are high but not as astronomical as the Press would have you believe, the answer is yes and no. For me the great advantage of success and fame has been the way in which it has enabled me to indulge most of those fantasies we all nurture but rarely get the opportunity to fulfill. Thus, not only have I met and talked with Cagney, Astaire, Kelly, Richardson, Olivier, Gielgud, Fonda, Wilder, Lemmon, Matthau, Nureyev, Ali, Betjeman et al, I have also played cricket at Lord's, sat in the cockpit of a 747, sung a duet with Bing Crosby, boxed three rounds with Joe Frazier, played piano with Oscar Peterson and appeared in concert with a Symphony Orchestra.

This last fantasy filled me with the most dread. I was asked to narrate *Peter and the Wolf* at the Albert Hall. My fear was based on the fact that although I love music and had always dreamed of standing in front of a large orchestra, I cannot read a score. I met the conductor in a rehearsal room the day before my concert début.

"There is one problem, sir," I said to him.

"What is it?" he enquired.

"I don't read music," I blurted. He looked at me patiently.

"Don't worry. I do," he said.

The problem with success in Britain is that, on the whole, people don't admire you for it. The great curiosity towards it is not how it has been achieved but how it might be explained in terms of luck, birthright, education, double dealing or marrying the boss's daughter. This is not so much an egalitarian theory of life as a doctrine of the humdrum and it is one invented and briskly stirred by my fellow journalists.

No matter. I wouldn't swap my life for theirs. I know, because I've been there. And would I have had it differently? I doubt it. I might have written more but then, there is still time. The problem with an article like this is that it has a valedictory air about it, a feeling that what has been achieved is the summing up of ambition. Not a bit of it. The driving force which aids success might fade but never disappears.

My biggest success has been that never once in 30 years as a hack have I ever wanted to stay in bed unable to face the day ahead. Moreover, I believe I am much the same person I ever was in spite of the fact that my fellow hacks would have you believe that success and fame on television immediately transform you into some sort of monster.

In any case there is always someone who knows to give you advice when you are going off the rails. Just before he died I was talking to my father about this and that and he said, "You've done well, lad, and I'm proud of you." Then he paused. "But, it's not like playing cricket for Yorkshire, is it?" He knew the difference between fame and reverence, success and immortality.

MICHAEL PARKINSON, 46, was born in Cudworth, near Barnsley, the son of a miner. After school and the army, he joined the *Barnsley Chronicle*, moving on to the *Yorkshire Evening Post, Daily Express, Guardian* and *Sunday Times*. He made his TV début with Granada, then became instantly known to millions with his BBC chat-show. He lives beside the Thames at Bray with his wife, Mary, and their 3 sons, but will soon be moving to Australia to host a much-publicised programme and make strenuous efforts to improve his golf.

SUPPLEMENTARY BENEFITS

Now the Sunday Express has joined The Times, Telegraph and Observer with a colour magazine and the Mirror is coming soon, it's only a matter of time before the rest of Fleet Street catches up . . .

Incapability Brown

"As a matter of fact it's very practical—it's the vent to our fall-out shelter!"

"Sorry, but he wants the sand-dunes to face Mecca."

"I see you finally had a word with Jenkins about his untidy mowing."

"Don't look at me—you were the one who wanted a roof garden."

"Go easy on your admiration of the rockery—it **was** Gerald's dry-stone wall."

"In the drought of '76, we could actually see the chimney-tops of the old model village."

A New Year's Message from Dame Edna

THE International Year of the Possum starts on January 1st. Over the Chrissie period the UN nearly drove me crazy, phoning at all hours of the day and night on bended knee to pick my brains for an inspirational and humanitarian title for 1981.

The first idea that came into my head was the International Year of the Superstar and I must say the powers that be at the UN said they were "over the moon" about that one, but somehow it seemed a teeny bit too elitist and I suppose it would be cruel to expect all those Third World waifs to identify with a rich and talented Melbourne housewife 24 hours a day for a whole year—even if UNESCO choppers dropped them 12 months supply of Wisteria acrylic wigs and diamante butterfly specs. What a silly, self-centred wretch I'd be to let the world call a whole year after me anyway! Not even Woody Allen or the Muppets take themselves as seriously as that.

With my Chinese opposite number little Madame Mao in the news so much of late, I suppose I've been thinking along slightly oriental lines. They call their years after apes and foxes don't they, readers? So one of Australia's best-loved marsupials naturally sprang to my lips when I received that Mayday from the United Nations.

Incidentally, if there was a purge in my gorgeous Australian homeland I would probably be in Madame Mao's pinched little platform shoes right now, heaven forbid, and goodness only knows what would happen to my poor old invalid husband, Wheel-Chairman Norm.

I believe the Wildfowl Trust encourage people to adopt ducks and other types of scrumptious poultry and my sister conservationist, Brigitte Bardot, is heavily into seal adoption. What I'm hoping for like mad is that more folk on this side of the world, and I'm speaking now as a bi-hemispheric woman, will soon be inspired to adopt one of Dame Nature's most cuddlesome creations. I know there are some people in my home town of Melbourne who, if they heard me singing the praises of the possum, would say, "I'm afraid I can't follow you up that road, Dame Edna," and as a matter of fact there is a ghastly firm in my home town called Poss-off who come round at a moment's notice and brutally shoo darling old possums off suburban rooftops and TV aerials. Needless to say the cruel people who summon the Poss-off squad, don't deserve to have their tiles crawling with furry old fun-lovers in the first place.

But even if you don't happen to adore possums, you would be well advised to adopt one in preference to some of Australian's other marsupials, like the shark or the funnel-web spider, and I'll wager it'll be many moons before the UN names a year after any of these creepy-crawlies, though stranger things have happened haven't they, readers? I notice, for example, that the French have slapped a conservation order on their slimy old frogs and they can't be served up in restaurants any more. Quite frankly I doubt if this will be much of a loss to people like you and me with normal appetites; however, I am told the French are now going to import frogs from behind the Iron Curtain and it wouldn't surprise me in the least if half the Russian frog's legs are bugged or equipped with micro-chip surveillance devices. Mind you, let's face it, it's never been easy to tell which side the French were on at the best of times.

What, I can hear you asking, are the special qualities a possum's got that we should all try and emulate in '81? Luminous eyes, I admit, are not within everyone's reach, nor is a diet of eucalyptus leaves, so don't rush around to Harrods and defoliate their exotic shrub department! Yet you would be amazed at the number of people who ask me what a possum's breath smells like, panting up at you from close quarters. Since they nibble all that eucalyptus night and day they usually smell like a kiddie's chest after it's been given a good going-over with Vick's Vapour Rub. If ever I've got a touch of flu, I always welcome an opportunity to sniff a possum though, very often, this means climbing onto the roof at night where one can not only inadvertently upset the balance of nature, but fall foul of a posse of Poss-off personnel.

I suppose the most striking thing about my favourite marsupial is his pouch which he can never leave alone for five minutes. Possums are perfect symbols of the Eighties when you come to think of it, especially in England where people spend more time with hand in pocket than anywhere else on the planet. "Playing possum" is also a favourite UK sport, particularly if a little task rears its ugly head.

Incidentally, by now most *Punch* readers will have heard on the grapevine that I'm the Fourth Channel. All that I can now pray for in 1981 is that my bid for *The Times* is successful. Then my pouch of happiness will be filled to overflowing, Possums.

Dame Edna Everage is a division of the Barry Humphries Group.